# Shaping Communities

## PERSPECTIVES IN

## VERNACULAR ARCHITECTURE, VI

*Edited by*

*Carter L. Hudgins*

*and Elizabeth Collins Cromley*

THE UNIVERSITY OF TENNESSEE PRESS / KNOXVILLE

Shaping Communities

*To Joe Ernst, whose good cheer, wry sense of humor, appreciation for a well-reasoned argument, and delight in the built environment enlivened meetings of the Vernacular Architecture Forum for a decade.*

# Contents

# Illustrations

*Figures*

## Tables

# Preface

Like its predecessors, this sixth volume of the *Perspectives in Vernacular Architecture* series consists of expanded versions of the best papers delivered at annual meetings of the Vernacular Architecture Forum. Papers for this volume were selected from forty-three presentations at the meetings held at Portsmouth, New Hampshire, in 1992 and Natchez, Mississippi, in 1993. The eighteen essays that follow are contributions from the wide range of academic disciplines that for more than a decade have most actively shaped and contributed to the study of vernacular structures and places. In these essays scholars from the fields of American studies, history, folklore, architectural history, and architecture explore topics that are diverse in location, time, and meaning. They address places as distant from each other as rural Massachusetts and Hawai'i; they investigate building carried out by a half-dozen ethnic groups; and they study building forms as different as Native-American houses in Alaska and postmodern vacation cottages in the resort community of Seaside, Florida.

As a group, however, the essays are unified in their concern with community building and place-making. From eighteenth-century Newburyport to twentieth-century Seattle, the essays cover very similar analytical ground. Not too many years ago, as vernacular architecture first emerged as a topic of scholarly interest, most analyses focused on individual buildings or on building types, particularly those judged to reflect the character of a region or place. The essays in this volume reveal quite clearly that close analysis of individual structures will remain at the heart of vernacular architecture studies. It is, however, the role building plays in defining communities and how building shapes the discourse between individuals and the society and culture of which they are a part, and how building conveys a community's sense of itself, that has become the goal of many vernacular scholars.

## Vernacular Architecture and the Ideal

The ideas that shape communities take many forms. Whether consciously framed as designs or not, those ideals that shape the community inevitably manifest themselves in what people build. In California the community of Runnymede in East Palo Alto was founded in 1916 as a suburban utopia. Each family living there owned a place to live and enough land to make a livelihood from raising chickens. Industrialized methods maximized the number of chickens while reducing the amount of land required. Alan Mickelson and Katherine Solomonson trace the formation of this planned utopian community and then its unplanned successors—first Japanese floriculturists, and then African-American and other recent immigrant groups who also successively sought a suburban refuge in the landscape of a forgotten utopia.

Jeff Hardwick's analysis of Langston, Oklahoma, recovers the ideals that its founders, African-American homesteaders, brought with them to the prairie after they fled the South and its post-reconstruction strictures. The town they began to build in 1888 embodied ideals about community grounded in independence and self-sufficiency that shaped the town, relationships between neighbors, and interaction with surrounding communities more profoundly than did specific notions about architectural style. Following a first wave of "homestead" building, African-American householders in Langston selected bungalows, foursquares, and simple "progressive" house forms as appropriate, economical expressions of their independence.

Sometimes ideals in architecture clash, and that is the subject of Nora Pat Small's essay on late-eighteenth- and early-nineteenth-century houses in the southern Massachusetts town of Sutton. She draws on the literature produced by reformers who praised simple, small farmhouses as the most fitting housing for yeoman farmers of rural Massachusetts. They criticized big, two-story Georgian houses as pretentious and more fit for urban sites. The rural ideal espoused by reformers had a certain analytical appeal, but the honest yeomen of Sutton chose their own ideal: the big, two-story, Georgian blocks that best satisfied their needs.

Ideal architectural forms may have multiple sources, as Marlene Heck demonstrates in her study of "Palladian" forms in early-nineteenth-century Virginia. While a few wealthy planters in eighteenth-century Virginia found sources for their houses in English country houses and English and European publications, builders in later generations selected house forms from a vernacular repertoire that had absorbed and transformed Old World ideas. Spatial arrangements in Virginia's rural houses, especially the three- and five-part pavilion-and-wings houses that are the focus of Heck's essay, reflected New World solutions more than European taste.

A community's ideals are also reflected in its public architecture. Monique Bourque's study of the creation of almshouses in the Delaware Valley in the eighteenth and early nineteenth centuries discovers that siting and design revealed the care that citizens extended to the poor, the ill, and the insane. At the same time, these buildings were not too comfortable nor too appealing, lest the citizens for whom they provided temporary shelter prefer them to a life of labor. The architecture created to frame this institutional context also tells us about the period's attitudes toward racial and sexual segregation.

## Community Landscapes

Communities also shape shared spaces. Public landscapes are the result of street building, park construction, and community decisions that affect zoning and land-use regulation. Martha McNamara traces the evolution of a public landscape and the ideas that shaped it in her study of a portion of the town of Newburyport known as the "Frog Pond." Transformed from rustic eighteenth-century commons to genteel nineteenth-century park, the "Frog Pond" once held grazing cattle and was the location of a rope walk and other industrial activities, but these yielded to a new sensibility that reformulated the same space into a promenade with plantings, as well as the site for a new courthouse and a new jail.

A town's public spaces make its values legible to resident and visitor alike. Sometimes such public spaces are the result of a "master plan," and sometimes, as on Monument Avenue in Richmond, Virginia, they are the result of slow and fragmentary development. Kathy Edwards and Esmé Howard show how Monument Avenue grew out of decisions made between 1890 and 1930, resulting in a civic street that was the preferred venue for public rituals and celebrations as well as for construction of new houses for rising merchants.

Architecture and town planning can be used instrumentally to create a mood and instill an ideology. The designs for Seaside, Florida, a resort town on the Florida Gulf coast, are analyzed in Kathleen LaFrank's essay as an effort at cultural reinvigoration. By turning back in time to the architecture and town-planning forms from a simpler era, the developer and designers hoped to invoke a new version of earlier social relationships that they understood to be both harmonious and hierarchical.

Building materials give both substance and tone to a community's architecture, and these can also go through transformations. In Fredericksburg, Virginia, Gary Stanton's analysis reveals that a town built almost entirely of wood in the eighteenth century was transformed into brick and slate—a response to the fires that had periodically consumed the commercial and residential heart of the city. New materials were essential to secure buildings from fire if they were to be high and closely packed—the preferred form for early-nineteenth-century urbanity.

### Communities Shaped by Race And Ethnicity

In stressing the racial or ethnic character of builders and users, Thomas Ryan, John Vlach, Laurel Spencer Forsythe, and Alison Hoagland discuss

how architecture shapes identity. Modern scholars of regional architecture sometimes discover that older studies mask the contributions ethnic groups make to building traditions. Thomas Ryan takes apart a historical abstract, the "Dutch three-room house," in his study of Marbletown in the Hudson River Valley to reveal that older scholarship, eager to create a unified explanation of a regional building form, clouded the contributions that several European ethnic groups made to the evolution of the region's "typical" house. John Vlach explores the architecture that framed African Americans' experiences in southern cities before the Civil War. Vlach finds a set of living and working spaces that stretch from grand hierarchical house with out-buildings to hidden alleyways and shacks belonging to slaves living outside the domestic spaces occupied by their masters. Laurel Spencer Forsythe traces through her analysis of missionaries and native Hawaiians the reciprocities they engaged in to achieve comfortable houses. New England missionary families longed for New England frame houses but adapted Hawaiian materials and the local traditions of compounds or clusters of buildings to achieve their needs for domestic space. Meanwhile, native Hawaiians appropriated some Anglo-American house materials and furniture forms. Allison Hoagland's analysis of Alaskan native architecture and the efforts to save it demonstrates how complex ethnic questions can be. When Alaskan natives encountered Protestant missionaries at the beginning of the twentieth century, they enthusiastically embraced Christianity. Believing the missionaries' claim that their tribal architecture was pagan, they destroyed or abandoned numerous tribal houses and totem poles. U.S. government–sponsored preservation programs subsequently attempted to reconstruct tribal architecture, often teaching lost or fading crafts to local residents.

## Communities Shaped by Commerce

Commercial culture also shapes communities and generates new architectural types. One community-forming commercial structure was the market house, a building that important towns erected to contain and channel commerce and that also became an important anchor of civic life. Bryan Clark Green demonstrates in a study of market houses in eighteenth- and nineteenth-century Virginia that market buildings housed a town's commercial life—its bell, clock, scales, and official measures. But market houses, the locations of political meetings, social events such as balls and assemblies, and the headquarters for fire companies, were additionally the focus of civic activity, and the source of civic energy.

In the nineteenth century, the first downtown shops and photographic parlors gave genteel customers respectable and fascinating places to go. Lisa Tolbert's study of Tennessee towns of the mid-nineteenth century makes connections between a town's prosperity, measured in shops and goods, and the town's gentility, reflected in its female college. Both ladies and goods were products of a town's industry and mutually boosted its economy. Shirley Wajda argues that genteel nineteenth-century customers sought out photographers whose shops most resembled domestic parlors. There they met friends, admired decorative objects, and posed for the pictures they would exchange with friends and relatives. As in the contemporary house, all work-related spaces were concealed, masking commerce from "domestic" activities in the photo-parlor.

By adopting an entrepreneurial approach to the architectural forms espoused by the Arts and Crafts movement, Seattle, Washington, bungalow builder Jud Yoho shamelessly applied mass-production techniques to plans that sprang from handicraft thinking. Janet Ore's study reveals that in Seattle in the 1910s, Yoho adopted the forms and language of simple-life moralists and used their ar-

guments to mass-market bungalows whose designs he had copied from unknowing architects. Commercial architecture takes other forms, as Richard Longstreth's essay demonstrates. He considers department store strategy in siting and designing the first wave of non-downtown branch stores. In the automobile culture of the 1930s, department stores asserted their architectural presence in residential districts as they spread out from downtown centers. Neighborhoods' commercial districts were transformed by this new scale and by the parking structures that came with the branch stores, while some "lone-wolf" stores became the hub for new community developments.

The ways that communities defined themselves through vernacular building often raises a second theme—the tensions that accompany the intersection of cultures. John Michael Vlach's study of urban slave houses, Alison Hoagland's examination of the revitalization of totem pole and plank houses in Alaska, and Alan Michelson and Katherine Solomonson's analysis of Runnymede, for example, speak not only to how ethnic groups expressed their architectural preferences but how vernacular buildings, structures, and places are open invitations to the study of the processes of cultural accommodation. These essays offer clear glimpses of how architecture provides a material focus for the process through which disputed strands of culture are deployed in public where, after evaluation from all sides, they may reach resolution.

As a group, these essays speak also to the continued importance of field research, the intimate and intensive analysis of buildings, towns plans, and landscapes, and how these building blocks of community interact with and are affected by one another. Thomas Ryan, Nora Pat Small, and Laurel Spencer Forsythe make it particularly clear that vernacular buildings are often more complex than they appear. It is only from close analysis of the artifacts themselves that vernacular buildings and the communities of which they are a part can be revealed.

# Acknowledgments

This volume brings to a close our collaboration as co-editors of *Perspectives in Vernacular Architecture,* a task that has been a source of pleasure for us both. As we gathered this book from papers presented to finished essays, some of life's most wrenching changes have visited us, but through them and through the process of guiding this book to publication, our friends and colleagues in the Vernacular Architecture Forum have sustained us with kind words and welcome gestures. We are grateful for each one just as we say thanks to the many members of the Vernacular Architecture Forum who provided expert thoughts and comments on the essays contained in this volume. These comments played a central role in guiding the manuscripts and its essays from first drafts to finished essays. We also thank Catherine Bishir who, while she was VAF president, provided just the right kind of encouragement when we needed it. Of course, little in this volume or its predecessor would have been possible without the able guidance of our editor at the University of Tennessee Press, Meredith Morris-Babb. Her skills in calmly solving vexing problems amazed us both and earn from us our most sincere thanks. Historic Charleston Foundation provided a haven where much of this volume took its final form, and there Betty Guerrard and M. E. Van Dyke performed the kind of miracles with computer disks, fax machines, and overnight mail that ensure success.

# PART I

# COMMUNITIES

# SHAPED

# BY IDEALS

*Alan Michelson and Katherine Solomonson*

# Remnants of a Failed Utopia: Reconstructing Runnymede's Agricultural Landscape

Until World War II, the Santa Clara Valley south of San Francisco, California, was a rural landscape of small farming villages, truck gardens, and orchards. Since the war, spiraling populations and the growth of the high-tech industry have transformed Santa Clara Valley into Silicon Valley, a landscape dense in residential subdivisions, commercial strips, and industrial parks. Yet occasional hints of the area's agricultural past still remain, hemmed in by fast food restaurants and tract houses.

One of the area's greatest concentrations of agricultural remnants survives in East Palo Alto, a city adjacent to Palo Alto and minutes from Stanford University but separated from them by vast physical, cultural, and economic barriers. Today East Palo Alto is known to outsiders primarily for the gang violence and drug activity that is heavily, and sometimes sensationally, covered by the local media. But during the early 1910s and 1920s, East

Palo Alto was the site of Runnymede—also known as the Charles Weeks Poultry Colony after its founder—an agricultural utopia that drew over a thousand settlers from all over the United States.

Although Runnymede's small ranches became intertwined with later construction, the settlement's original structure continued to shape the area as it was transformed into a flower-growing center during the Depression, and then into the postwar suburban community of East Palo Alto. Woven into East Palo Alto's contemporary fabric are the distinctive architectural and spatial signs of the culturally and economically diverse groups that have made their homes in the area over the past century, each altering a landscape defined by a previous generation. In East Palo Alto today, the remnants of Runnymede—its street grid, spacious lots, and agricultural structures—have become a hotly contested issue in the multicultural community the city has become.

In this chapter, we will explore how East Palo Alto's landscape has been transformed, physically and conceptually, by successive generations with different and sometimes competing cultural values. Beginning with the conditions that gave rise to the distinctive configuration of Runnymede's landscape, we will consider the area's transformation in the context of dynamic cultural processes: how the landscape represents and shapes social relations even as it is reconfigured by them; how the template established early in the century at Runnymede has facilitated certain kinds of development while inhibiting others; how the landscape has functioned as a vehicle for the assertion of status and the construction of identity. Fundamental to these questions is the catalytic tension between rural and suburban values that has persisted in East Palo Alto throughout the course of the twentieth century. To explore these issues, we will couple a reading of the buildings and landscape with the consideration of promotional literature, archival materials, newspaper articles, and interviews.[1]

### Runnymede

Charles Weeks, an entrepreneur with a reformer's zeal, founded Runnymede in 1916.[2] At its peak, the colony's small farms, with their "garden homes," tankhouses, and chicken coops laid out on narrow one-acre lots, gave form to contemporary ideas about scientific farming, cooperative living, and individual enterprise. As one of a collection of similar settlements, most of which have all but vanished, Runnymede's residual landscape provides an important conduit to one aspect of the larger back-to-the-land movement that gathered momentum in the early twentieth century.

After experimenting on his own to develop an innovative method of chicken raising, Weeks dreamed of establishing an agricultural cooperative of independent, intensively cultivated one-acre poultry farms. His goal was to provide an alternative to the moral and physical unhealthiness of urban living and the monotony of assembly-line labor. In

a 1917 newspaper article he explained his views: "Man has wandered from his natural life to the artificial life of cities and has suffered therefrom. It takes only a little garden soil to make an abundant living with independence, health, and freedom. Why should men work long, weary hours in unhealthy places all the days of their lives for a mere subsistence when this fuller, more abundant way of living is so natural and practical?"[3]

As he formulated his ideas, Charles Weeks was inspired by William E. Smythe, an influential writer and social critic who had settled in San Diego in 1901.[4] Like many progressive reformers, Smythe feared the destabilizing effects of urbanization and industrialism on personal and family life. As an alternative, he advocated channeling urban populations into planned rural settlements of small family farms, each less than ten acres. These would be irrigated by a network of canals crisscrossing the arid western states to transform the desert into a series of oases of fertile soil and abundant produce. Families, each tilling their own small parcel of land, would work cooperatively with their neighbors to form both social and economic bonds. To boost yields and gain financial independence, they would also share information on the latest scientific methods and agricultural technologies.

Smythe, with Weeks soon following, rode the crest of a growing back-to-the-land movement that gained momentum even as increasing numbers of people were leaving farms and small towns for the city. Particularly well known was Bolton Hall, a Wall Street lawyer, whose book *A Little Land and a Living* (1908) paralleled Smythe's views on relocating people from the city onto small farms that would be intensively cultivated to achieve financial independence.[5] Advocates of the small farm favored it for several reasons. The breakup of large landholdings into smaller, more affordable slices was a strike for democracy, they said, for it made land ownership accessible to those of more limited means. On the new small farm, each family could till the land independently, employing no one, and being employed by no one.[6] And the small farm provided the ideal alternative for the city's overflowing population.

William Smythe's ideas soon formed the basis of what came to be known as the "Little Landers' movement," whose colonies dotted the West in the late nineteenth and early twentieth century, particularly in California.[7] He established his first settlements at New Plymouth, Idaho, in 1895 and San Ysidro, California, in 1908.[8] Each venture was planned to combine suburban comforts with rural independence and closeness to nature. To dispel the popular impression of farming as an isolated and backward pursuit, Smythe emphasized the collegial and cultivated social relations in Little Landers' colonies. His vision attracted widespread attention. The *Craftsman* advocated the Little Landers' concept as an answer to contemporary ills. When Smythe founded the magazine *Little Lands in America* to promote his views, Bay Area architect Bernard Maybeck published a series of "Maybeck Homes for Little Lands."[9] And President Wilson's secretary of the interior, Franklin Lane, consulted Smythe about his plan to resettle World War I veterans in soldier homestead colonies.

Drawn by Smythe's ideas, Charles Weeks visited the settlement at San Ysidro in the early 1910s and returned to the Bay Area to search for an appropriate place to start his own colony of small farms.[10] He realized that a successful small holding would require an abundant water supply, excellent soil, and proximity to urban markets. The site he selected for Runnymede stood on the shores of San Francisco Bay just two miles east of the gates of Stanford University, adjacent to the booming college town of Palo Alto, and only one hour by train to San Francisco. The area's rich, loamy soil could support a variety of crops, and its high water table made the drilling of wells for irrigation an easy task. In a region where there is a bewildering variety of microclimates, the site

enjoyed mild temperatures and a particular abundance of sunshine. Once Weeks had pinpointed the appropriate location, he teamed up with Peter Faber, a large landowner who subdivided his acreage into one-acre farms, and sold them off as new settlers arrived.[11] In effect, Weeks functioned as a cross between an entrepreneurial real estate developer and a social visionary.

Trumpeting the slogan "One Acre and Independence," Charles Weeks promoted his vision of self-sufficiency and personal initiative combined with economic cooperation and community spirit through a variety of books, pamphlets, and articles, and he ran ads in periodicals that reached people throughout the country.[12] He even set up a network of recruiters who acted as his agents. Locally, he circulated a float bearing a model one-acre farm. His advertising played upon the rural fantasies nourished by the myriad popular publications that glorified life in the country and suburb.[13] While many periodicals featured country life as only the wealthy could enjoy it, at Runnymede, according to Weeks, anyone of moderate means could find country happiness—and financial independence, too. There, Weeks said, a person could be the "creator of his own poetical paradise . . . surrounded by opulence and luxuries grown from the rich, well-watered soil." Runnymede's settlers would be "Contented People who realize that all that is worth while in life can be secured right in the home garden . . ." and who "get joy in the freedom out in the fresh air with the blue sky overhead" and a "little bit of heaven around their feet."[14]

Weeks's version of the California dream attracted a variety of people. In 1917 he reported: "Lawyers, doctors, ministers, professors, farmers, in fact people from every calling settle here, bent on one purpose—that of making a garden home. . . . This one purpose creates a bond of sympathy between all the neighbors until they are one large family."[15] Weeks delighted in telling of people who had given up the daily grind at their desks for a healthy life in the country, but the colony also attracted a variety of craftspeople who had always made a living by their hands. Many settlers were elderly couples who were persuaded by Weeks's promise of independence and leisure in a quiet rural setting paired with the cultural amenities of the city nearby.[16] In his promotional efforts, Weeks targeted World War I veterans, advocating an army to till the soil using technology for peace rather than war.[17] Poultry farming was also considered an appropriate endeavor for the independent woman,[18] and the names of many single women appear in the early ranks of property owners.[19]

Weeks's advertising made it clear that he wanted to populate Runnymede with prosperous middle-class people who had already been successful in their previous lives. The settlers, all of whom were of European ancestry, paid cash for the whole cost of their properties. Credit was unavailable. "This secures the settler absolutely," Weeks stated in 1917, "and attracts a prosperous class of people. The class of people at Runnymede is far above average, making social conditions enticing to all who visit the colony."[20] Weeks's vision of utopia was essentially bourgeois and exclusive. This would become problematic several decades later.

Within five years, Runnymede had attracted twelve hundred people drawn from all over the country, and it had become one of the largest poultry producers in the United States. When new colonists first arrived, they convened at Charles Weeks's own ranch to be trained in what Weeks modestly called the "Charles Weeks Poultry System." Central to his approach was a belief in the efficacy of new scientific methods and efficiency engineering in maximizing farm output. He also stressed the combination of community cooperation and individual enterprise. While each family had its own small farm, members of the colony purchased supplies, maintained shared warehouse and social facilities, marketed their produce as a group, and met on a monthly basis to vote on Runnymede's business matters.[21]

The structure of Runnymede's landscape gave form to Charles Weeks's dream of combining the best features of rural and suburban life to create a suburb of efficient small farms that facilitated both community and independence. Having come from a large midwestern farm, Weeks remembered how lonely farm life could be when families were separated by vast tracts of land. At Runnymede, he envisioned a farming community that put neighbors in close proximity to one another. Well-maintained streets were laid out in a grid lined with long, narrow one-acre lots, their short ends fronting the street. Runnymede's settlers then constructed small cottages or bungalows—"garden homes"—toward the front of their lots, leaving space for neat, unfenced front yards with sidewalks leading up to their front doors. Though the lots were extraordinarily deep, their frontages were similar to those found in other suburban areas with houses of comparable size. With this layout, Runnymede, when seen from the street, had the potential to resemble the neighborhoods of bungalows that had sprung up in the nearby suburbs of Palo Alto and Menlo Park.

Though the front yard was conceptualized as conventionally suburban, the rest of the lot was designed to support an efficient, independent agricultural enterprise (fig. 1.1). Adjacent to most houses stood a tankhouse that stored water from each farm's individual well, and along the sides of the back of each property stretched at least one long, narrow structure to house the chickens. The remaining space was devoted to gardens that were intensively cultivated to provide fruits and vegetables for the family and greens for the chickens. In an era when the efficient use of resources was highly touted, not an inch was wasted in the production of poultry and produce.

The small farm, merged with the bourgeois suburb, abetted social and cultural life as well as the use of cooperative facilities. Though many of the colonists settled on two to five acres of land rather than one—which meant that the houses

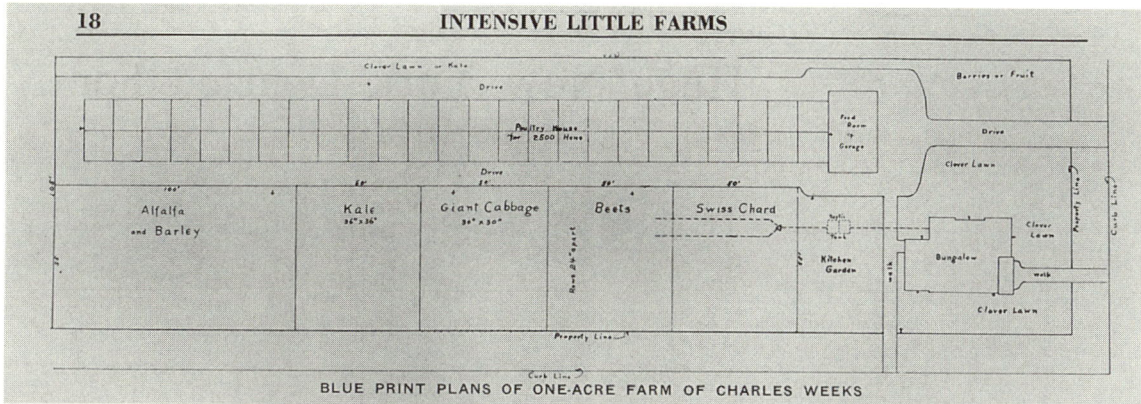

Fig. 1.1. A Model Acre. From Charles Weeks, "The Model Acre," *One Acre and Independence* (Oct. 1922): 9.

were more widely spaced than Weeks had first intended—Runnymede's families lived close enough to one another to exchange information and share a common delivery truck that could move easily from farm to farm, picking up produce to take it to market. All farmers also had ready access to the community warehouse, which was located on a railroad spur at the eastern edge of the colony.

Unlike many utopian or separatist colonies, however, Runnymede was laid out with no focal point—either architectural or spatial—to reify group consciousness. Point Loma, a Theosophist colony begun in 1897 near San Diego, featured a monumental domed temple around which the community's layout and activities orbited. The Socialist town Llano del Rio, begun near Los Angeles in 1914, had a community hotel. Runnymede, on the other hand, was first laid out as an uninterrupted grid with no predefined common spaces. If the community had a focal point, it was Charles Weeks's own ranch, a much larger enterprise separated from the colony proper by a meandering creek. Only after Runnymede was already established did Charles Weeks realize that the colonists needed their own area for social and cultural life, so he set aside some space for a small community center and a school.

The common architectural features of Runnymede's long, thin parcels, embodying the colo-

nists' shared acceptance of the Weeks poultry gospel, contributed to a sense of community identity and cohesiveness and distinguished theirs from other nearby farms. Tankhouses and poultry houses, familiar agricultural buildings adapted to Weeks's model of farming, were the key structures in the Weeks system of independent farms and the most salient landmarks in Runnymede's landscape (fig. 1.2).

The tankhouse that stood next to most of Runnymede's garden homes was the center of the small farm's irrigation system (fig. 1.3). Weeks believed that one of the most important keys to independence was an abundant, low-cost water supply. According to Weeks, "Independence as regards water is of the highest importance for the California farmer and the very essential of success."[22] Runnymede's tankhouses were sturdy two-story structures, rectilinear or slightly tapered in outline. Their heavy framing, enclosed and reinforced with a protective siding, supported an elevated water tank resting on a platform that was slightly arched to allow for rainwater run-off. The elevated reservoirs, most of which were left exposed, provided a gravity-induced pressure system for the farm family's needs. Similar tankhouses are still sprinkled throughout the Santa Clara Valley, stretching down to Gilroy, south of San José.[23]

Fig. 1.2. Bird's-Eye View of Runnymede. Courtesy of the Palo Alto Historical Association.

Fig. 1.3. Runnymede Tankhouse. Courtesy of the East Palo Alto Historical and Agricultural Society. Photograph by Trevor Burrowes.

The tankhouse formed the mechanical heart of the Little Lands farm. Arterial networks of electrical wires connected the tankhouse to surrounding buildings. Outside each tankhouse, a centrifugal pump run by a five horse-power electric motor pumped 250 to 400 gallons per minute, circulating water to the farmhouse, gardens, and poultry houses. Many of the mechanisms that made intensive farming on one acre feasible and comfortable were centered around the tankhouse. In addition to the pump, the pump's motor could also power other useful machinery such as feed cutters and washing machines. Electricity put new labor-saving devices as well as efficient farm machinery within the reach of the Runnymede rancher. For an agricultural community, this must have seemed a real step forward at a time when electricity was still an urban and suburban amenity unavailable in many rural areas.[24]

The tankhouse became a vivid symbol of the Little Landers' farms' factory-like efficiency, modernity, and independence. It represented the irrigation proponent's notion that in the West it could be possible for the individual to gain greater control of the land and enjoy higher yields and more consistency through irrigation than through the unpredictable rainfall on which farmers depended in the East.[25] In Runnymede's flat terrain, tankhouses also became landmarks, distinguishing one property from another. They varied in form and embellishment according to individual taste. Some farmers, such as Henry Bertram, painted their tankhouses to match the color schemes of their houses. One particularly well-to-do colonist, Arnold E. Martinelli, flanked his tankhouse with two garages, incorporating it into a symmetrical, formal complex to complement the large house he erected in front of it. Others distinguished their tankhouses by adding pyramidal roofs and railings around the tanks to form sheltered observation decks. From there, they could survey their land and the surrounding small farms stretching toward the Bay. When viewed from inside or out, tankhouses underscored the Runnymede landowner's independent status and command of territory.

While tankhouses became vertical markers for the individual farms, the long, narrow poultry houses stretched horizontally across the landscape, defining boundaries between properties (See fig. 1.2.). Weeks developed these unusual structures to maximize egg production and minimize land use and labor. All poultry farmers in Runnymede adopted Charles Weeks's method of poultry raising. Weeks shunned the traditional free range system, which required a large farmyard for a sizable flock. Instead, Weeks's poultry houses confined groups of twenty to twenty-five birds in coops measuring eight by eight feet. Though the enclosed method of chicken raising has come into question in recent years, early in the century it seemed a revolutionary step. Among the first to develop this concept was a man named Philo from Elmira, New York, who published a pamphlet that explained how to keep chickens in small pens. The pamphlet's sale made Philo a wealthy man, as thousands of people put chicken coops on the backs of city lots, in suburban backyards, and even on the roofs of tall buildings. With these rooftop roosts, Philo helped to bring rural pursuits to the city, while Weeks hoped to transfer city amenities to the country.[26]

The small coop's potential for combining intensive poultry raising with suburban life intrigued Charles Weeks, who maximized efficiency by lining up the pens in poultry houses that grew to be as much as 240 feet long. Their shape fit well on Runnymede's lots, which may have been structured to accommodate them, and their design made it possible for them to be tended by one family, or even one individual. The open front of each house was designed to maximize illumination by the sun. In the winter, electric lights supplemented sunlight to give the chickens "longer working hours." Water flowed automatically from well to coop, and shallow feeding troughs ran along the outside of each house, enabling the farmer, with no wasted motion, to walk along and fill the trough in one clean sweep. The linear course of the assembly line was thus incorporated into an agricultural setting imbued with Taylorized notions of efficiency.[27]

The length and number of poultry houses on a given property were also a tangible measure of a given farmer's prosperity. These "neat systematic poultry houses," as Weeks called them, could hold up to 1,000 chickens that could easily be tended by a single family or even an individual. Weeks estimated that the sale of the eggs yielded by 250 chickens would be enough to support one person, while 1,000 chickens could meet the basic needs of a family of four. Additional chickens yielded money in the bank. Weekly reports in the *Runnymede News* reinforced status distinctions by publicly indicating how many eggs each rancher in Runnymede had produced. Any Runnymede colonist could have calculated the number of chickens owned by neighbors by surveying the length and number of their coops. More chicken coops signified more eggs and more money and gave the family more voting shares and more power in the community. And Charles Weeks had the most of all.

Runnymede was set up as a cooperative, yet individualism, competition, and private enterprise formed its foundation and were expressed in its landscape. Runnymede's settlers fled the city, yet industrial values were incorporated into the management of the independent farm-factory. These values also permeated contemporary theories in home economics literature, which constructed the housewife as a businesswoman/domestic scientist engaged in the management of the home/laboratory. While in the traditional suburb the realms of home and factory had been sundered in the modern industrial world, in Runnymede they were expected to be conjoined. In Runnymede, the middle-class family labored together on a site of production with home at its center. The colony's promotional literature showed images of men and women working side by side, their neat "garden homes" hovering in the background. Alice Weeks, Charles Weeks's wife, wrote that "the small farm is so closely related to the 'center' of the home that you feel the atmosphere of the home life when you step your foot upon the soil of the small holding."[28] Even as industrial ideas infiltrated its agricultural environment, at Runnymede the work environment was also domesticated. Yet, as it sought to eradicate polarities between urban and rural, domestic and industrial, Runnymede espoused the values of the industrial world its colonists sought to escape but not to subvert.

Charles Weeks envisioned a future in which every city would have a suburb of little garden farms within commuting distance so that families could live a "wholesome life" close to nature. This was not to be. A variety of social, economic and spatial factors combined to break up the colony by the 1930s. In the early 1920s, Charles Weeks turned his attention to Owensmouth, a new colony he founded near Los Angeles. Runnymede lost its dynamic leader and its economic and ideological heart when Weeks vacated and sold his land, which contained the demonstration farm that showed new arrivals the stunning possibilities of the Weeks poultry method. There are hints that many of the original colonists found poultry raising, even according to the Weeks method, a more arduous task than they had imagined. Land changed hands rapidly. Fluctuating produce prices, tainted water, and finally the Depression made it increasingly difficult for the colonists to meet their needs on such small holdings. Once Weeks was gone and his poultry method was questioned, there was little to bind Runnymede's independent farms together. Runnymede's landscape as it appeared in the early 1920s did little to uphold Weeks's original vision of a unified suburban community. Because so many colonists actually settled on more than one acre, Runnymede's streets appeared too loosely strung to acquire the suburban density Weeks had desired. The gaps in the streetscape also detracted from the suburban atmosphere by revealing the spaces of production beside and behind the houses. This violated a fundamental tenet of suburbia—that spaces of production, if present at all, should be kept well hidden. At its demise, Runnymede's fragmented landscape was still fundamentally rural, with a patchy suburban veneer.[29]

## The Blossoming of Floriculture

The tension between rural and suburban values in Runnymede's landscape intensified as Runnymede's ranchers sold out or turned to new endeavors, new people moved in, and the area became known as East Palo Alto. By the late 1920s, new period revival houses had gone up on many of Runnymede's empty lots, while new and more densely developed subdivisions began to encroach upon the colony's boundaries. We are told that East Palo Alto residents considered these more classically suburban developments to be of higher status than Runnymede, which retained its bucolic atmosphere. Yet, even as development quickened during this period, East Palo Alto as a whole retained a predominantly rural character, especially compared with nearby suburbs such as Palo Alto and Menlo Park. In the early 1930s, East Palo Alto received a blow when the new Bayshore Highway plunged through its business district, cutting most of the community off from the other suburbs on the San Francisco Peninsula. This bifurcation crystallized the distinction between rural East Palo Alto, seen as something of a boondocks, and its more suburban neighbors on the other side of the highway.[30]

Compared with neighboring cities that were undergoing more rapid residential expansion, widespread agricultural activity continued in East Palo Alto well into the postwar era. Runnymede's grid of deep one-acre lots proved to be highly adaptable to new purposes.[31] Beginning in the 1930s, Italian and Japanese flower growers began to insert long greenhouses onto lots that once supported intensive chicken farming (fig. 1.4).[32] Compared with the low, enclosed wooden poultry houses nearby, most of the greenhouses were light, open skeletal structures of thin wooden (or, eventually, metal) posts with fixed translucent panels laid within simple sashwork. Roofs were gabled, often with vents along the ridge line and side walls.

Most of East Palo Alto's flower growers specialized in chrysanthemums, carnations, or lilies, which they shipped in refrigerated "flower trains"

Fig. 1.4. Runnymede Tankhouse with Later Greenhouses. Photo by Katherine Solomonson.

to eastern markets. The two largest Italian growers, Frank J. Siry and Frank "Lucky" Podesta, purchased extensive acreages in East Palo Alto in 1946 and hemmed in the Runnymede area with their long rows of greenhouses.[33] Before the war, due to discriminatory property laws, Japanese floriculturists, on the other hand, generally established themselves as tenant farmers.[34] Their businesses were abruptly disrupted when they were evacuated to the wartime internment camp at Heart Mountain, Wyoming, in May 1942.[35] Following the war, Asian-American families purchased land in East Palo Alto to establish truck farming, bonsai, or floriculture enterprises.

Floriculturists adapted well to the Runnymede landscape. The long, thin lots subdivided to accommodate the Weeks Poultry System were perfectly suited for the similarly proportioned glazed sheds. The greenhouses—around two hundred feet in length—stretched as long as the deteriorating poultry houses that stood next to many of them, but they were considerably wider.[36] Several greenhouses, many of them in rows behind Weeks-era bungalows, took up most of a one-acre property. This was agriculture every bit as intensive as in Charles Weeks's colony. Since setback laws prohibited the growers from erecting greenhouses in their front yards, as some would have wished, suburban values continued to inform the conception of the streetscape.

As in the Weeks colony, social, economic, and ethnic distinctions could be read in the agricultural structures erected after the war. Albert and Sally Nakai and Tsuruko and Don Nakanishi were particularly helpful in explaining these distinctions to us.[37] Like poultry houses, the size and number of greenhouses immediately communicated the grower's relative prosperity. So, too, did distinctions in materials. Prosperous growers of the 1940s could afford fully glazed two-hundred-foot houses, while less well-to-do farmers erected smaller sheds covered in cheaper, translucent polyethylene. The plastic was far less desirable, for it cracked easily and needed frequent replacement. In the 1950s, sheds composed of prefabricated metal skeletons replaced wood-framed structures. At first, these were within the reach of only the wealthiest growers with the means to switch systems.

East Palo Alto's greenhouses also marked ethnic distinctions. Japanese and Italian growers specialized in different kinds of flowers, and their greenhouses, as a consequence, looked markedly different. Japanese growers specialized in chrysanthemums, a royal and national symbol in Japan. To raise the delicate chrysanthemums, which could be damaged by overexposure to sunlight and wind, Japanese nurserymen clad large framed greenhouses, which lacked gables, in white cheesecloth. Each year East Palo Alto's Japanese growers would gather to help one another tack the cloth to the wooden posts, drawing together the Japanese community in cooperative labor for one family's benefit, an event reminiscent of a barn raising. The long cheesecloth houses, their walls flapping in the breeze, became a familiar, ghostly sight in East Palo Alto. Chrysanthemums blossom naturally during the autumn and winter. During the summer, Japanese growers draped a black, satiny material over the wooden frames to shield the chrysanthemums from the sun and to simulate the shorter days the flowers needed to bloom—a technique akin to, but opposite from, the use of electric lights to create "longer working hours" for the Weeks-era chickens. East Palo Alto's Italian growers were known for their lilies, which they timed to be ready for Easter. Their greenhouses could be distinguished by the thick coat of whitewash applied to the glass or plastic panes to protect the plants from the glaring sun.

These greenhouses, crowded into Runnymede's landscape, represented the significant social and economic changes that were occurring in the area. While Runnymede was visually unified by agricultural structures that represented a cooperative community and a shared approach to farming, the

greenhouses disrupted the formerly homogeneous landscape with a tangible sign of Runnymede's breakdown and the area's ethnic as well as agricultural diversification. Runnymede's lots were designed for kitchen and flower gardens, poultry houses, a goat, and even a beehive—complementary activities that were carefully proportioned to provide everything a family might need to eat, plus some surplus for cash. The flower growers, on the other hand, covered Runnymede's lots with assembly lines of floriculture designed for the efficient production of a single crop geared primarily for the marketplace rather than self-consumption. Runnymede's small farms were expected to be tended by one family, without outside help—something that was also true of the smaller growers—but the larger growers, with their long lines of serially replicated greenhouses, had an expanded enterprise that required hired laborers.[38] The value of efficient production obtained on both the Weeks-era farm and the flower growers' greenhouses, but the goals and the way they were expressed differed significantly.

In the meantime, Runnymede's tankhouses, once such strong symbols of individual self-sufficiency, began to lose their meaning along with their function. As subdivisions established centralized water systems and as well water grew less dependably pure, tankhouses lost their reservoirs or were removed as space was needed for other purposes. With the demolition of many of the vertical tankhouses, East Palo Alto became a predominantly horizontal landscape. As Albert Nakai pointed out, the rows of greenhouses, interconnected and extending for one hundred to two hundred feet in each direction, made the area resemble an industrial district of low warehouses. While Runnymede's farmers embellished their tankhouses to signify personal ownership and independence, later growers seemed less interested in individualization. Self-sufficient irrigation met its end along with agricultural independence.

## Postwar Developments

After World War II, developers constructed subdivisions of low-cost tract houses around Runnymede. Though densely suburban, one of the area's largest subdivisions, Palo Alto Gardens, was laid out along meandering streets to evoke the agrarian landscape suggested by its name. (In contrast, Runnymede, founded on agrarian ideals, had been developed on a grid.) The new subdivisions had wide streets, designed for the automobile, that were finished with sidewalks, curbs, and gutters. As in Runnymede, front yards were open and unfenced, but the much smaller backyards were conceived as private spaces for leisure rather than production. In the meantime, Bayshore Highway was transformed into a freeway that literally and figuratively widened the gulf between East Palo Alto and its suburban neighbors.

Not long after the new neighborhoods were settled, local realtors assaulted East Palo Alto, the most isolated area on the San Francisco Peninsula, with a variety of block-busting techniques. They distributed pamphlets threatening the collapse of real estate values; they drove busloads of African Americans through the area; and they goaded existing residents to sell their houses and buy new ones in the new subdivisions farther south. As European-American residents struggled to maintain the status quo, East Palo Alto became one of the most explosive sites of desegregation in the San Francisco Bay Area. By the late 1960s the majority of the population had become African American. During the 1980s, the arrival of Latinos and Pacific Islanders transformed East Palo Alto into the multicultural community it is today. As Silicon Valley's fortunes skyrocketed, East Palo Alto's declined proportionately. The community has become the peninsula's chief source of drugs, and violent crime has soared. A local newspaper recently superimposed a "gangland map" over the area still structured by Runnymede's agricultural landscape.[39]

During Runnymede's peak, the area had been a wide-open landscape demarcated by poultry coops and punctuated by tankhouses. Recent events have turned East Palo Alto into a fortified suburb where various types of boundaries have been drawn and redrawn. Many of the deteriorating remnants of Runnymede stand behind high fences of wood, chain link, and razor wire. Elaborate wrought-iron grillwork fills the windows of some of Runnymede's "garden homes" and defines the edges of extended-family compounds. Waist-high chain-link fences mark the boundaries of front yards, both in Runnymede and the postwar subdivisions. East Palo Alto's greatest barricade is Highway 101, with its high sound walls and swiftly moving traffic, which cuts most of the city off from the more prosperous communities on the other side.

Today much of Runnymede's original configuration remains, defined by the distinctive long, thin lots and undeveloped backyards where some raise vegetables and even a few chickens. Pressure to develop available land on the San Francisco Peninsula intensified during the 1970s and 1980s as the computer industry burgeoned in Silicon Valley. Hoping to profit during the real-estate boom, developers began to eye the undeveloped space in the Runnymede area. While Runnymede's tight grid and deep lots proved highly adaptable to floriculture, they have lent themselves less easily to conventional higher-density suburban development, especially because much of the undeveloped space happens to be the deep backyards behind existing houses. The most common strategies have been to construct housing with no street frontage at the back of the lots or to bundle together several lots, which are then thrust through with a cul-de-sac. For example, Lonnie Bogan, the African-American developer of Mandela Estates and a resident of East Palo Alto, fit fourteen houses clustered around a cul-de-sac onto two and one-half acres (fig. 1.5). A high steel fence with a locked gate barricades the compound from the rest of the city. The two-story dwellings take up almost all of each tiny lot, leaving little or no yard space for either recreation or cultivation. Bogan, whose goal was to establish a new model for East Palo Alto development, geared the tract to prosperous East Palo Altans who desired a protected enclave with the curbs, gutters, sidewalks, and street lights characteristic of many postwar suburban developments. Connection to the landscape, either economic or recreational, is minimized in favor of personal security and increased interior space. The development stands in marked contrast to the more rural atmosphere that persists in the Runnymede neighborhood. In an area that was once unified by common agricultural features, Mandela Estates' large houses, high fence, and manicured cul-de-sac become a shared, inward-turning symbol of success.[40]

While developers have been carving Runnymede's lots into new configurations, others have found new uses for the area's surviving agricultural structures. Today East Palo Alto has one of the greatest concentrations of tankhouses remaining in northern California. With their sturdy frames and small footprints, tankhouses have proven to

be highly adaptable. Tankhouses in tourist destinations such as Mendocino and Sonoma Counties have been converted into shops or bed-and-breakfast rooms; one provides the focal point of a shopping mall. On the densely developed San Francisco Peninsula, tankhouses have become romantic reminders of the agricultural landscape that was devoured by Silicon Valley. In the city of Los Altos, for example, a tankhouse slated to be torn down for new development was removed to the civic center for restoration and display.[41] In East Palo Alto, on the other hand, tankhouses are generally valued more for their usefulness than their nostalgic appeal. Their owners have converted them into storage sheds or residences through a variety of additions and changes: porches and balconies, new rooms, vivid turquoise and pink paint (fig. 1.6). Runnymede's poultry houses are mostly gone, but a few survive as storage sheds or as components of the fences marking boundaries between lots. Near the deteriorating poultry houses are the skeletons of greenhouses, tangible signs of the flower industry's decline in the 1970s.[42] Most of East Palo Alto's small growers died off or were forced out of business when imports from Colombia began to drive California growers out of the market.

Today, East Palo Altans are contending with different visions of the city's future development.

Fig. 1.5. Mandela Estates. Photo by Katherine Solomonson.

Fig. 1.6. Runnymede Tankhouse Transformed into a House. Photo by Katherine Solomonson.

With its diverse community, the remnants of the city's agricultural past have become highly charged symbols. One faction sees East Palo Alto's suburbanization and economic development as a sign of progress. To augment the city's tax base, they lobby hard for the demolition of Runnymede's older buildings to make way for revenue-producing commercial developments and subdivisions. They hold up as a model the postwar Palo Alto Gardens subdivision, with its newer tract houses, wide streets, curbs, and sidewalks—as opposed to Runnymede, with its older bungalows and cottages, narrow rutted streets, and deteriorating reminders of the agricultural past.[43] From this perspective, new developments such as Mandela Estates represent the level of comfort and security enjoyed by the inhabitants of the more prosperous suburbs nearby.

African-American critics of this type of dense infill development, however, have dryly characterized Mandela Estates as an ill-conceived effort to get out of the fields and into the plantation house. They belong to another faction, led primarily by African Americans, that wants to see East Palo Alto develop an identity distinct from the suburbs on the other side of the freeway. One group in particular, the East Palo Alto Historical and Agricultural Society, known as EPA HAS, has embraced the historic landscape and cooperative agrarian philosophy of Runnymede. One of EPA HAS's goals is to maintain and renovate Runnymede's remnants and to preserve the openness of the landscape for agricultural purposes. Inspired by the urban garden movement, EPA HAS espouses Weeks's ideas about intensive, independent farming on a small scale and his notions of cooperative marketing. Its goal is to seek the city's economic revitalization through agriculture. With the aid of EPA HAS and other groups, some of Runnymede's remaining one-acre lots have been transformed into private, community, and cooperative gardens that supply jobs and food for local consumption. Greenhouses are being reused for new agricultural collectives or individual produce businesses. Kitchen gardens, tended by African-American families, provide produce for the table, continuing agricultural traditions brought from the South.[44] Recently arrived Samoans have established taro gardens in their front yards, violating suburban conventions that relegate food crops to the back of the lot.

East Palo Alto's garden movement and the utopian vision that serves as its historical anchor have generated an increasing amount of publicity, providing a positive antidote to the emphasis on crime in the local news.[45] But this vision is not without its inherent tensions. Debates have erupted over a number of issues, including the Runnymede area's narrow streets, devoid of curbs and sidewalks. The nearby city of Atherton, one of San Francisco's wealthiest suburbs, has similar streets (but in better repair), which its residents enjoy as an evocation of country life. Yet, as Solomon Tucker pointed out at an EPA HAS meeting, a feature that means one thing in Atherton can mean something quite different in East Palo Alto. Many of East Palo Alto's African-American and Latino residents came from rural areas in the southern United States or Mexico. Some were attracted to the area because of its familiar semi-rural atmosphere, but for others the remnants of Runnymede's agricultural past, including its "unfinished" streets, are a reminder of an aspect of their own past that they prefer to leave behind.[46]

The idea of reviving the wide-open, expansive quality of Runnymede's early years also presents some difficulties (see fig. 1.2). The fences that segment East Palo Alto's landscape, especially those that bound front yards, detract from the image of suburbia that Weeks, as well as some contemporary East Palo Altans, find desirable. High fences of chain link, redwood, and wrought iron demarcate inward-looking compounds. They supplant the open, grassy suburban front yard—the individual home owner's contribution to the shared vision of the subdivision-as-park—with an assertion of individual identity as well as protection.

The lower fences surrounding many front yards may foster connection as well as separation; as James T. Rojas has observed in East Los Angeles that for Mexicans and Mexican Americans, fences often create individualized, semiprivate transitional spaces that recall the walled or fenced yards and courtyards associated with traditional Mexican houses, a recent memory for many East Palo Altans. In the "enacted environment," says Rojas, the fence may function as a social catalyst, defining a succession of spaces for interaction, even as it provides security.[47] Because of this, the proposal to remove fences in the Runnymede area in order to return to Weeks's original vision could work against a feature that contributes to social life in today's more diverse community.

The diversity of contemporary East Palo Alto versus the homogeneity of Weeks's conception of Runnymede is another important issue. According to EPA HAS, some have countered the group's proposals by pointing out that Runnymede's history and remnants are not directly related to the ethnic heritages of most of the people who now live in East Palo Alto. Since Runnymede was essentially bourgeois and exclusive and its colonists primarily white and of European descent, they suggest that the Runnymede plan may be inappropriate both as a planning model and as a vehicle for the construction of a new identity for East Palo Alto. The unified vision of Runnymede, based in an Anglo-American concept of suburbia combined with a new vision of agricultural life, belies the cultural divides that exist in East Palo Alto today.

EPA HAS, on the other hand, focuses on Runnymede's ideology and economic system rather than on ethnicity to discover values that may draw the community together. Trevor Burrowes, EPA HAS's

president, suggests that the rural past that so many of the city's residents share—a past that cuts across ethnic boundaries—also connects them with East Palo Alto's historic landscape. Runnymede's landscape, and the cooperative ideals that informed it, could be revived to provide training, jobs, and sustenance for the city's residents, with the possibility of eventually transforming East Palo Alto into the produce capital of the Bay Area.[48] Agricultural metaphors are even beginning to inform discussions of East Palo Alto's future. Ruben Barrales, country supervisor for East Palo Alto's district, likened the need for planning decisions that acknowledge strength in variety to companionate gardening—the purposeful mix of different kinds of plants for healthy growth.[49]

The successive transformations of East Palo Alto's landscape raises the question of how recent arrivals to a given area may shape, enact, and be shaped by a landscape they have inherited but not created. In many cases, East Palo Alto's residents have responded to and adapted the landscape with little or no conscious engagement with the previous forces that shaped it. Members of EPA HAS, on the other hand, are making a conscious effort to develop a new connection with Runnymede's historic landscape. Despite contested meanings, members of EPA HAS and those who share their vision have embraced the water tower, the poultry house, and the one-acre lot as symbols of the agrarian, communitarian ideals they wish to revive, ideals which, they hope, will transcend class, ethnic, and economic boundaries to unite a factionalized community and forge a new sense of place. How the remnants of Runnymede can best be adapted to rekindle an earlier vision of unity while acknowledging current diversity remains to be seen.

## Notes

1. Our research on Runnymede began with a historic resources inventory of East Palo Alto, California. This was initiated by the East Palo Alto Historical and Agricultural Society and sponsored by the San Mateo County Historical Association, which provided the funding. We would like to thank the San Mateo County Historical Association, especially its executive director, Mitchell Postel, for supporting our work, and the East Palo Alto Historical and Agricultural Society, especially its director, Trevor Burrowes, for their invaluable insights and assistance. Thanks also to Warren Bruland for his help with the figures. Our work contributes to the growing literature on the transformation of landscapes, the dynamic processes involved in shaping, reshaping, and imbuing them with new meaning. See, for example, Catherine W. Bishir, "Yuppies, Bubbas, and the Politics of Culture," in *Perspectives in Vernacular Architecture, III,* ed. Thomas Carter and Bernard L. Herman (Columbia: Univ. of Missouri Press, 1989), 8–15; Elizabeth Collins Cromley, "Modernizing—Or, 'You Never See a Screen Door on Affluent Homes,'" *Journal of American Culture 5* (Summer 1982): 71–79; Howard Wight Marshall, "A Good Gridiron: The Vernacular Design of a Western Cow Town," in *Perspectives in Vernacular Architecture, II,* ed. Camille Wells, (Columbia: Univ. of Missouri Press, 1986), 81–88; Margaret Purser, "All Roads Lead to Winnemucca: Local Road Systems and Community Material Culture in Nineteenth-century Nevada," in *Perspectives in Vernacular Architecture, III,* 120–34, emphasizes that material culture should be seen as an active factor in shaping human actions and their meanings rather than as a passive reflection.

2. Very little work has been done on the history of Runnymede or the configuration of its landscape. For a brief discussion, see Robert Hine, *California's Utopian Colonies* (San Marino, 1966). For a more fully developed view of Runnymede in the context of East Palo Alto's built environment from the nineteenth century into the 1980s, see Trevor Burrowes, "East Palo Alto: The Dark Horse, A Study of the Built Environment of East Palo Alto," an unpublished paper sponsored by the East Palo Alto Historical and Agricultural Society.

3. *Palo Alto Times,* Nov. 14, 1917, 4–5.

4. On William Smythe, see *The National Cyclopaedia of American Biography* (New York: James T. White Co., 1927), 17: 443–44. Smythe outlined his

ideas in a number of influential journals and treatises that included a journal he founded called *The Irrigation Age*; "Real Utopias in the Arid West," *Atlantic Monthly* 79 (1897): 605–9; *The Conquest of Arid America* (1899; reprint, Seattle, 1969); *Constructive Democracy* (New York, 1905); *City Homes on Country Lanes* (New York: Macmillan, 1922).

5. Bolton Hall, *A Little Land and a Living* (New York: Arcadia Press, 1908), and *Three Acres and Liberty* (New York: Macmillan, 1907). On Bolton Hall, see Lee, 28, and Peter J. Schmitt, *Back to Nature: The Arcadian Myth in Urban America* (New York: Oxford Univ. Press, 1969), xvii n. 4. Schmitt draws a distinction between the coinciding back-to-the-land and back-to-nature movements, the latter of which was motivated by a quest for Arcadia rather than a means to make a living.

6. In the irrigated West in particular, some forwarded strong arguments against holdings so large that a family needed to hire outside labor because they believed that irrigation apparatus needed the skill and close attention that only the landowner could maintain. See Donald Worster, *Rivers of Empire: Water, Aridity, and the Growth of the American West* (New York: Pantheon Books, 1985), 117–18.

7. On William Smythe and the Little Landers' movement, see Henry S. Anderson, "The Little Landers' Land Colonies: A Unique Agricultural Experiment in California," *Agricultural History* 5 (Oct. 1931): 139–50; Lawrence B. Lee, "The Little Landers Colony of San Ysidro," *Journal of San Diego History* 21 (Winter 1975): 26–51; Worster, *Rivers of Empire,* 118–25; Bruce Kamerling, "The Arts and Crafts Movement in San Diego," in *The Arts and Crafts Movement in California: Living the Good Life,* ed. Kenneth R. Trapp (New York and Oakland: Abbeville Press and the Oakland Museum, 1993), 212–14. Although some work has been done on the Little Landers' movement, no one has previously undertaken a close analysis of how the Little Landers' landscape represented and reinforced social relations.

8. Other Little Landers' colonies included those in Tehama County and Lassen, both founded in California before 1901; Los Terrenitos, founded in about 1912 and located in the Monta Vista Valley about seventeen miles from Los Angeles; Hayward Heath, established by 1916 near the town of Hayward in the San Francisco Bay Area; and Walden, near San Francisco.

9. See Kamerling, "Arts and Crafts Movement," 212 and fig. 166.

10. Smythe encouraged Weeks to form a colony based on his poultry-raising techniques, and when Weeks began his efforts to attract settlers, he gave talks illustrated with stereopticon slides to support the venture. Charles Weeks, "William E. Smythe Passes Away," *One Acre and Independence* 4 (Nov. 1922): 12; and Lee, "Little Landers Colony," 44.

11. Though Smythe helped them promote Runnymede, Weeks and Faber never went into partnership with him to make their settlement an official addition to the string of Little Landers' colonies with which Smythe had been directly involved. This may have been because Little Landers' colonies were currently under investigation for their viability and Runnymede's founders found it preferable to distance their venture somewhat from the Little Landers' movement. See Lee, "Little Landers Colony," 44.

12. Weeks outlined his ideas most thoroughly in a book entitled *Egg Farming in California* (San Francisco, n.d.) that features his head, inscribed in an egg, hovering over long rows of poultry houses. His monthly magazine, *One Acre and Independence,* discussed Runnymede's progress and reported on Weeks's subsequent venture, Owensmouth, which he founded in the early 1920s near Los Angeles. Both of these publications served to spread the word as well as to preach to the converted. *The Runnymede News,* which was aimed primarily at Runnymede's settlers, detailed the colony's activities. A variety of other promotional materials may be found in the Palo Alto Historical Association files at the Palo Alto Public Library.

13. Among these were *Country Life, Countryside, Suburban Life, Indoors and Out,* and *House Beautiful,* for example, as well as articles such as "From the Horrors of City Life: The Experience of a Dweller in Flats, in Boarding Houses, in Nineteen Feet of Baked Mud, and in Suburban Homes Who (the Illusion of City Life Gone) at Last Found Happiness in a Country Home." This article, by Thomas Dixon, a popular novelist, appeared in *World's Work* 4 (Oct. 1902): 2603–11. See Schmitt, *Back to Nature,* 27–32, on this and other publications that fostered back-to-nature enthusiasm.

14. *Egg Farming in California,* 113.

15. *Palo Alto Times,* Nov. 14, 1917, 4.

16. To show that he would not exploit the elderly, Peter Faber announced that he would "not permit any

dear old lady with $500 or $600 to settle upon a stone pile at Runnymede and try to make a living upon it." *Palo Alto Times,* July 24, 1916, cited by Lee, "Little Landers Colony," 44. There had been some discouragement at San Ysidro, where some of the settlers found themselves trying to till inferior soil.

17. *Egg Farming in California*; Nettie K. Gravett, "The Disabled Veterans and the Garden Home," *One Acre and Independence* (Nov. 1922): 19.

18. *Santa Clara Valley* (Palo Alto, Times Publishing Company, 1911), 32, a promotional publication issued by the Palo Alto Woman's Club, gave a lengthy affirmative to the question, "Can women make a success of ranching in this valley?" Independent women had tilled small irrigated farms of as much as forty acres since the late nineteenth century. As early as 1878 Minnie Austin and three other women, all former schoolteachers, bought an irrigated farm near Fresno. Their neighbor was a Danish woman who raised raisins on her five-acre holding. See Worster, *Rivers of Empire,* 100–101. *Overland Monthly* 9 (1887): 624, reported: "The work of irrigation is so light that women who bought their twenty or forty acre tracts . . . enjoy guiding the small streams from furrow to furrow" (quoted in Worster, *Rivers of Empire,* 101). The role of independent women in the irrigated farming movement deserves further attention.

19. Some of these women were joined by their husbands after World War I was over. Others were widows, and others were single women who embarked upon chicken ranching on their own. Information about Runnymede's settlers has been gleaned from *One Acre and Independence,* maps dating from 1922 and 1925 that inscribe the names of the owners on each plot, and city directories. Copies of these maps are in the collection of the East Palo Alto Historical and Agricultural Society, East Palo Alto, California.

20. "Runnymede is a Successful Colony," *Palo Alto Times,* Nov. 14, 1917, 4.

21. The cooperative aspects of Runnymede's organization reflected the influence of the contemporary formation of large citrus and walnut cooperatives in California.

22. *Palo Alto Times,* Nov. 14, 1917, 4.

23. For a typology of tankhouses, see Leon S. Pitman, "Domestic Tankhouses of Rural California," *Pioneer America* 8 (2) (1976): 84–97; and Allen G. Noble, *Wood, Brick, and Stone* (Amherst: Univ. of Massachu-

setts Press, 1984), 83–84. Also see Brian F. Terhorst, "The Changing Forms of Sonoma County Tankhouses," unpublished graduate seminar paper, Sonoma State Univ., Fall 1989. According to Terhorst, enclosed tankhouses—as opposed to water towers which have their structural elements left exposed—began to appear in the San Francisco Bay Area as early as the 1860s.

24. On rural electrification and labor-saving appliances, see Ann McCleary, "Domesticity and the Farm Woman: A Case Study of Women in Augusta County, Virginia 1850–1940," in *Perspectives in Vernacular Architecture, I,* ed. Camille Wells (Columbia: Univ. of Missouri Press, 1987), 25–30; and Roger Miller, "Selling Mrs. Consumer: Advertising and the Creation of Suburban Socio-Spatial Relations, 1910–1930," *Antipode* 23 (July 1991): 263–301.

25. On the irrigation movement in California, see Worster, 99–118.

26. Weeks, *Egg Farming in California,* 43.

27. On Charles Weeks's poultry house design, see Weeks's own descriptions in *Egg Farming in California;* "The Model Acre," *One Acre and Independence* (Oct. 1922): 9; "Scientific and Artistic Poultry House for Intensive Egg Farming," *One Acre and Independence* (Nov. 1922): 1; and Thomas Stewart, "The Charles Weeks Poultry House," *One Acre and Independence* (Sept. 1922): 5–6, and (Nov. 1922): 5–6.

28. Alice J. Weeks, "The Place of the Woman in the 'Little Farm' Home," *One Acre and Independence* (Sept. 1922): 7.

29. According to David C. Streatfield, in the layout of early-twentieth-century bungalow gardens in California, the vegetable garden was consistently hidden at the back of the lot near the garage, screened by vines and shrubs. See "The Arts and Crafts Garden in California," in *The Arts and Crafts Movement in California,* 50. For an excellent study of the way architectural style and space diluted and in some ways contradicted the ideology underlying another agricultural colony, and may even have contributed to its failure, see Annmarie Adams, "Charterville and the Landscape of Social Reform," *Perspectives in Vernacular Architecture, IV,* ed. Thomas Carter and Bernard L. Herman (Columbia: Univ. of Missouri Press, 1991), 138–45.

30. Insight into the suburban vs. rural images of East Palo Alto and its districts was provided by numerous interviews and newspaper articles. A Sept. 13, 1992, interview with Marjorie Wiley Jones, who lived in the Runnymede area during the 1930s, and a Sept. 4, 1993, interview with Mary Vitale MacLachlan, a former resident of Palo Alto Park, a 1920s East Palo Alto subdivision, were particularly helpful.

31. As Howard Wight Marshall has observed, though the grid may appear to be rigid, it is actually flexible, allowing for considerable variation. See "A Good Gridiron," 86–87.

32. During the first half of the twentieth century, flower growing was San Mateo County's largest industry. See Michael Svanenik, "When Flowers Were a Blooming Business," *San Mateo Times,* Mar. 24, 1989. On the cultivation of asters, see *Palo Alto Times,* Aug. 20, 1937.

33. On Podesta's arrival in East Palo Alto, see "Local Flower Industry at Easter Peak," *Palo Alto Times,* Apr. 7, 1950.

34. California's lawmakers passed alien land laws in 1913 and 1920 specifically to prohibit Japanese-born immigrants from owning property. See Timothy Lukes and Gary Y. Okahiro, *Japanese Legacy: Farming and Community Life in California's Santa Clara Valley* (Cupertino, Calif.: California History Center, 1985), 57–59. We have found that scattered Japanese families rented land and cash-farmed small holdings in the Runnymede area during the 1920s. In the early 1930s there were only one or two Chinese families in the East Palo Alto area. According to Henry Mock, a member of one of these families, his parents felt grateful that someone was willing to rent land to a Chinese farmer. Interview with Henry Mock, Aug. 27, 1992.

35. "144 Japanese Say Good-bye to Homes Here," *Palo Alto Times,* May 26, 1942.

36. Burrowes, "East Palo Alto," 10, has noted the formal similarity between the rows of poultry houses and the rows of greenhouses.

37. Detailed information about Japanese floriculture was given to us in the following interviews: Albert Nakai, June 11, 1993, July 9, 1993, and July 21, 1993; Sally Nakai, July 19, 1993; Tsuruko and Don Nakanishi, Aug. 24, 1993.

38. It should be noted that the smaller growers, who occupied only one acre in the Runnymede area, crammed as many greenhouses as they could onto their lots, but one family generally tended them all and also maintained a kitchen garden.

39. David Bank, "Nation's Homicide Capital: City of Courage, Fear, Hope," *San Jose Mercury News,* Jan. 31, 1993.

40. On Mandela Estates, see Shelby Grad, "Handsome Homes Arise in East P A," *San Jose Mercury News,* July 28, 1991; and Karen Liberatore, "Developer's Dream Inspired by Mandela," *San Francisco Chronicle,* Aug. 5, 1992.

41. See "Rescuing Old Water Tower: Los Altos' Agricultural Past to Go on View at Civic Center," *San Jose Mercury News, Peninsula Extra,* May 19, 1993.

42. According to Burrowes, "East Palo Alto," 12, the survival of a few nurseries in East Palo Alto is due primarily to the Williamson Preserve Act, which specifies that some agricultural land must be maintained in urban areas under certain conditions. Burrowes cites *East Palo Alto Community Plan EIR* (San Mateo County, Calif.: Department of Environmental Management, Planning and Development Division, 1981).

43. Burrowes, "East Palo Alto," 18.

44. Leroy Musgrave, presentation at East Palo Alto Planning Workshop, Mar. 27, 1993; interview with Mrs. Travis, May 3, 1993; conversations with Trevor Burrowes, director of the East Palo Alto Historical and Agricultural Society, during 1992 and 1993.

45. See, for example, Sibella Kraus, "East Palo Alto Begins to Reclaim Garden Heritage," *San Francisco Chronicle,* July 15, 1992.

46. Solomon Tucker, discussion at EPA HAS meeting, Aug. 26, 1992. Tucker was reflecting on feedback he had gotten from some of his neighbors.

47. James T. Rojas's discussion of Mexican and Mexican-American use of space in East Los Angeles concurs with our observations in East Palo Alto. See "The Enacted Environment of East Los Angeles," *Places* 8 (Spring 1993): 42–53.

48. The viability of these ideas has been suggested in an economic analysis sponsored by Urban Ecology.

49. Barrales's comments were delivered at the East Palo Alto Planning Workshop.

M. *Jeff Hardwick*

# Homesteads and Bungalows: African-American Architecture in Langston, Oklahoma

As the sun rose on April 22, 1889, American settlers moved into the nearly two million acres of the "Unassigned Lands" in the center of Indian Territory. As part of this mass movement into Oklahoma, African Americans saw the land rush as an unparalleled opportunity and founded over thirty all-black towns in central Oklahoma. Edward P. McCabe and William L. Eagleson founded Langston, Oklahoma, in 1890 and proclaimed it to be "the only distinctively Negro City in America" (fig. 2.1). This pair hoped to establish a black majority in the Unassigned Lands and thus secure black political and economic control of the area. Langston, Oklahoma, founded by and for blacks, was one of the more successful attempts at founding an all-black city and offers a fascinating place in which to consider African-American cultural productions.[1]

Through the *Langston City Herald,* the town's founders actively promoted Langston City and encouraged African Americans living in the South to

move: "FREEDOM! Peace, Happiness and Prosperity. Do you Want all These? Then Cast Your Lot With Us & Make Your Home in Langston City. . . . Remember, it is not a picnic we are inviting you, but to join hands with us in an active and earnest effort to better our conditions and open to the race new avenues through which they may obtain more of the good things of life." In an 1890 letter to the American Colonization Society, A. G. Belton, a southern African American, described the dire situation in the South and the hopes African Americans had for Oklahoma: "We as a people are oppressed and disenfranchised we are still working hard and our rights are taken from us times are hard and getting harder every year we as a people believe that Africa is the place but to get from under bondage we are thinking Oklahoma as this is our nearest place of safety." In 1888 the *Topeka Citizen* of Kansas proclaimed: "Let every colored man who wants 160 acres of

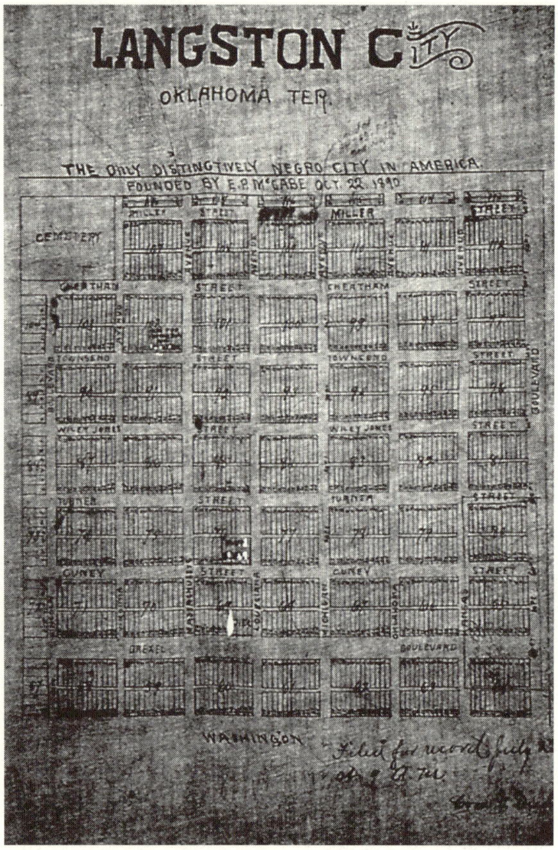

Fig. 2.1. Langston City Plat.

land, get ready to occupy some of the best lands in 'Oklahoma', and should it be opened up, there is no reason why at least 100,000 colored men and women should not settle on 160 acres of land each." When Langston residents recall their families' move to Oklahoma, they often speak about the sense of possibility that Oklahoma represented.[2]

Mildred Robertson, an eighty-seven-year-old Langston resident, described her family's situation in Mississippi and what Oklahoma meant to them: "My people lived down at the bottom of Mississippi [Centerville] close to Louisiana. . . . Well, they had a little more freedom in Oklahoma. They didn't have nothing, but they had a little more freedom, 'cause those people [in Mississippi] worked the year round and bought their groceries at the store and when they gathered their cotton crop and paid this man off; they didn't have nothing much to live on." Mrs. Robertson emphasized the potential that Oklahoma land signified for southern blacks: they wanted to leave the stifling atmosphere of sharecropping that in many instances differed little from slavery. Waymon Snellgro, a resident of Langston since 1900, also remembered his family moving because "[y]ou still had plantations and all that stuff down there [in Alabama]. [Settlers] [s]aw a better life in Oklahoma."[3] If the Unassigned Lands promised "a little more freedom" for Mrs. Robertson's family, then the houses—roof, walls, and floors—made that expectation more than a dream.

A critical awareness of the mythic quality of one "American experience" inspires an exploration of variety within the nation's history and architecture. By detailing unique contributions and characteristics of German-American or African-American architecture, scholars hope to expand accepted notions of history. The result often demythologizes one national history by describing the multiplicity inherent to that history and then erects separate monolithic, circumscribed understandings of one group's experiences of architecture. This portrayal creates historical narratives emphasizing separation, exclusion, and isolation from popular cultural forms. Following this thinking, "African-American architecture" is discussed as if such a reductionist and essentialist past actually existed.

An approach that acknowledges the full range of historical experiences within an ethnic group or race, as suggested by sociologist Paul Gilroy, has the potential to "celebrate complex representations of a black particularity that is *internally* divided: by class, sexuality, gender, age, ethnicity, economics, and political consciousness." Delineating the variety of domestic architecture in Langston through residents' recollections and the houses themselves reveals how this community of African Americans conceived of and used houses. When asked about the kinds of houses in Langston, older residents name three classes of architecture: homesteads, bungalows, and Langston Housing Authority houses. This essay will look at homesteads and bungalows. Descriptions provided by residents of Langston proved to be invaluable in documenting these houses and, more significantly, in reconstructing the more intangible aspects of people's daily lives within them.[4]

To lay claim to land in Indian Territory, settlers had to show physical improvements on their tract. In 1891 the *Langston City Herald* detailed "How to Take a Homestead": "As evidence that you do claim it [the land], you must make some visible improvements. Drive a stake with your name on it; cut timber to lay the foundation of a house; do a little plowing or some other act that will show to others that you have occupied that particular piece of land." When settlers arrived in Langston, they constructed a house greatly dependent on their economic circumstances. The most costly was frame, next was log, and the least expensive was a dugout. People in Langston group dugouts, log houses, and frame houses together under the name "homesteads." The word homestead designates not a single form of house, but the three kinds of houses of earliest African-American settlement. Any of these homestead structures accomplished the purpose of visible improvements and provided a legal right to 160 acres.[5]

The least costly homestead for a settler to build was the dugout, or cellar. Residents used both terms interchangeably. By digging a hole and using the earth and trees on their land, settlers could quickly and cheaply construct a house. Trees, taken from bottomland cleared for agriculture, shored up the sides and roof of the house. The floor was red clay that with increased use became, according to resident Jim Jones, "like cement." Typically, the cellar had one eight-by-ten-foot room. Residents entered the cellar by descending wooden or earthen stairs placed before a ground-level door. An 1890s photograph entitled "Mansion in Oklahoma," taken near Langston, shows

Fig. 2.2. 1890s Photograph Entitled "Mansion in Oklahoma." From the Swearengen Collection, courtesy of the Lloyd Lentz Company, Guthrie, Oklahoma.

an African-American family by its log-fronted dugout (fig. 2.2). Vertical logs served as the house's gable-end and held a front door frame. Other logs supported the dirt roof, and a stove pipe appears toward the rear of the roof. This house illustrates the kinds of materials readily available and easy to use from the settler's land.[6]

One Langston dugout survives through residents' recollections. Constructed before 1900, the house was carved out of a hill by Amanda and Robert Dirks in a narrow ravine too rough for agriculture on the west side of town. Mildred Robertson, their neighbor, remembered the Dirks's dugout: "Oh, well some of them people who lived over there in a dugout, the Dirks." The house had two rooms, "one for cooking and sitting the other for sleeping." A substantial rock chimney served the house's fireplace, where Amanda Dirks would "cook in that fireplace." The Dirks family's housing choice was constrained by their economic resources. In the 1905 personal tax, they were assessed four dollars, the second-lowest amount in Langston. In August of 1908 Robert Dirks advertised himself as "The Wood Man" in Langston's newspaper, *The Western Age,* saying he was "prepared to furnish nice seasoned wood ready to burn." Mildred Robertson and other residents remembered that Amanda and Robert Dirks still lived in their cellar in the 1940s, which suggests that for the poorest of Langston's residents dug-outs were permanent, long-term houses.[7]

The most common homestead for settlers in Langston was the one-room log house. The Langston Town Meeting Book suggests the availability and relative low price of logs. On March 8, 1892, "Lawyer A.L. Ayers presented a bill [$4.00] from King for hauling logs to build the City Prison."[8] Settlers with time, energy, and trees could construct a log house, larger and more substantial than a dugout.

Queen and Frank Jones's log cabin, built in 1892, is the only remaining homestead of this once ubiquitous material (fig. 2.3). The one-room house measures twenty by sixteen feet with four frame additions, all built after 1940. Upon arriving in Oklahoma, the Joneses lived in a dugout and then a year later constructed themselves a log house where the family continued living until the 1970s. The house had a stove on the northern end, a loft, a door to the west, and two board windows. The Joneses located their house in the northeast corner of their 160 acres near three other neighbors and a crossroads store and thus formed a small social cluster on the open, gridded plain.

Jim Jones referred to his grandparents' log house as a "sitting room, bedroom, living room, room, or log cabin. People used all those names depending on what you were doing there." Explicit in

Fig. 2.3. Queen and Frank Jones's One-Room Log House. Built in 1892 with four frame additions after 1940.

Mr. Jones's designations and interpretation is the *changing* character of the space. The room is a bedroom when people are sleeping, a sitting room when people gather, or a log cabin because of materials. The definition of the space hinges "on what you were doing there," the actions performed in the area. This multiplicity of naming suggests a flexible way of imagining and living in the space. People's actions provide the log house with its ever-changing designations; an architectural name is not something inherent to the structure itself, but rather is socially and individually selected. Residents also made the one room more flexible by dividing the space into temporary "rooms" by hanging curtains.[9] Women made these curtains of unfinished quilt tops, quilts, muslin sheets tie-dyed with Warner tree leaves, or cotton sacks stitched together. Langstonians hung curtains to transform the interior spaces of the one-room house into separate spaces. Amanda Gross, when asked about any partitions within her one-room log house, said that she would "sheet it off" with two curtains made of quilt tops. They extended eight feet into the room, and she would "push them back to the wall" when they were not needed. The number of curtains were hung "according on how many people [were] in your house." She explained, "This [sheet] would cut this [bed] off from this [area] over here. . . . That's the way you divide yourselves." Jim Jones said, "You hung curtains to divide rooms. Didn't have no partitions, 'cause you didn't have money to do the work." As Michael Ann Williams's work in rural North Carolina among whites has suggested, sheeting off beds created smaller rooms and private spaces within one seemingly undifferentiated space. These cloth walls or ephemeral partitions are the types of structures within domestic spaces that are often hidden from architectural historians without people's descriptions; moreover, these descriptions suggest the ephemeral yet significant actions that occurred within these one-room spaces.[10]

While utilitarian, the patterns and colors in the quilts or tie-dyed sheets also were aesthetic expressions. As Viola Jones recalled, "You couldn't help but see them, 'cause they stood out when they were up." Amanda Gross described dyeing flour sacks "to keep them from being white" because she wanted some "kind of off-color streaks." Fashioned by women, the cloth walls materially communicated an ability to create works, both functional and beautiful, for family members and guests to admire and use. Likewise, women brought out "fancy quilts" on Sundays to transform iron or wooden bedsteads into a colorful display and a testimony to their skills.[11]

In addition to one-room dugouts and log houses, a few homesteaders built more costly frame homes, doubling the living space of the other homesteads. Three frame homesteads built by the Amos, Lounds, and Clement families survive in the Langston area. All of these frame homesteads were constructed on a masonry foundation with balloon framing covered by clapboard. The Clement homestead is fourteen feet, two inches by thirty-two feet, four inches (fig. 2.4), and the Amos house measures fourteen feet, six inches by thirty feet, six inches. Both have two nearly square rooms side by side that utilized a central chimney for stoves in both rooms. The Lounds house is identical to these two houses in construction, but has a unique floorplan. Measuring twenty-four feet by twenty-four feet, the house has four square rooms, each twelve feet by twelve feet. Even though in plan the Lounds house's four rooms make it significantly different from all other homesteads, locals still refer to it as a homestead. This designation suggests that Langston residents order housing types more by the roles dwellings play in people's lives rather than by the form of the house's exterior or interior. The Lounds house is considered a homestead because it is located on their homestead acreage and because it sheltered the first Lounds family to live in Oklahoma.[12]

Langston homesteaders purchased lumber for

Fig. 2.4. Clement Homestead.

these houses from one of two local sources. Twenty-two lumber companies in Guthrie, ten miles up the road, or merchants in the nearby town of Coyle both had access to the Santa Fe railroad and out-of-state, milled lumber. Langston's town meeting book reveals another source for wood and cement, the Arkansas Lumber Company. On March 26, 1918, the town records read, "we would pay the Arkansas Lumber Co. $33.00 for cement." Mizura Clement Allen recalled that her father purchased framing from the Arkansas Lumber Company. Whether residents purchased framing from the Arkansas company, a Coyle merchant, or a Guthrie lumber yard, the expense of materials, transportation costs, and construction time kept frame houses beyond most families' means. Jim Jones commented that time and money prohibited his father from adding a frame kitchen to their log house until the early 1940s.[13]

Whether a dugout, one-room log house, or two-room frame house, a homestead signified a legal claim upon a parcel of land. The settling of the Unassigned Lands gave some African Americans the occasion to own land for the first time in their lives. Ironically, African Americans' access to Oklahoma land was prefaced by the removal of Native Americans, highlighting the degree to which groups marginalized by dominant culture are placed in direct competition with one another for limited resources. For African Americans, this land connected them to other blacks living in a town built for and by African Americans and to a new way of life largely independent of whites. Homesteads embodied expectations of a future life built on social and economic independence. While this architecture embodied aspirations for the first generation that constructed it, the houses continued to be inhabited, and they were imbued with new meanings by future generations. At the same time, other Langston residents began constructing a new kind of house.

Houses built after 1900 marked the arrival of a new housing type in Langston. People in Langston refer to these houses as bungalows. At the turn of the century, Sears, lumber companies, and numerous housing companies sold plans and materials for the construction of bungalows.[14] As compared to homesteads, this new Langston housing was more standardized in plan and materials. Yet, even with the building of these bungalows, not all other houses were abandoned or rendered obsolete; people like the Joneses or the Dirks continued living in their homesteads. In this way, then, the addition of bungalows actually increased the variety of domestic architecture in Langston. Like the word homestead, "bungalow" comprises several kinds of structures. Langston residents divide bungalows into two groups: around 1900, people built what are now referred to as old style bungalows, and then in 1914 people began constructing new bungalows.

Only three old style bungalows survive in Langston. Like the Lounds homestead, these houses have four perfectly square rooms (that are twelve feet by twelve feet) entered by front and rear doors, topped with a hipped roof and a central chimney stack that served at least two stoves in these houses. In attempting to grasp how these square houses fit into the history of Langston's architecture, I asked Amanda Gross, "Now, what would you call the square ones?" She responded, "You see that one [Jacobs house], that you were talking about, it was the old bungalow. And as

the people grew and know better then they went to fixing the bungalows, like this [Franklin's house]." After building the old bungalow people built "a longer house," David Petty explained.[15]

More of the new bungalows or longer houses survive and comprise nearly 50 percent (150/231) of all Langston's extant houses. The first new bungalow, Jeff Franklin's house (fig. 2.5), was constructed in 1914, and Jake Watson built the last one in 1973. Although separated by sixty years, the materials and form changed little between these two houses. The new bungalows are constructed of frame walling supported by a concrete-block foundation around the perimeter with piers underneath the joists. They are one story and have a rectangular plan with four to six rooms, measuring twenty-four by forty-five feet. Entering by the front door, people step directly into a front room followed by a dining room and then the kitchen in the rear; two bedrooms are arranged in a parallel row with a small hall and bathroom in the middle.

Mildred Robertson defined a bungalow as having one roof or a saddle roof. Mrs. Robertson's identification of a unique roof parallels the popular conception that overhanging eaves characterized a bungalow. The 1920 *Book of Bungalows* emphasized that "[n]othing can be more pleasant than a bungalow with a low-pitched roof spread-

Fig. 2.5. Jeff Franklin's 1914 Bungalow on the Corner of Washington and Meridian.

ing well out from the wall face." Queen Esther Williams Vic echoed Mildred Robertson's definition of a bungalow when she pointed to Jeff Franklin's house and said that the way the roof hangs over the entire house made the house a bungalow. Franklin's house manifests other emphatic and popular bungalow elements, such as squat and square columns, a front porch, built-in bookcases, and a bay window in the dining room.[16]

However, not everyone defined a bungalow solely by the style of the roof. When asked what defined a bungalow, Jim Jones pointed to his own house and compared it to his parents' log house.[17] He said that the bungalow was a new kind of house built after homesteads. In Mrs. Robertson's definition, the houses possess a formal quality defined by the roof line; aesthetic form and fashion embody the idea of a bungalow. In Mr. Jones's definition, bungalows represent a total change in the town's architecture, a historical occurrence. While they are different, both of these definitions recognize the bungalow for its common characteristic of being *new* to Langston.

Conversation with Langston residents suggests the breadth of the bungalow designation. In trying to determine how four-square houses related to the rectangular bungalows, I asked Mrs. Gross. She replied that "[p]eople build houses like they know to build them at that time. . . . From time to time when people got where they could do better, 'cause you see there wasn't anybody rich out here. Just like they doing clothes as they could do better they changed patterns. But they let it have the same name, but it's a different pattern." Mrs. Gross's comment suggests that even though the pattern or template for a house changed, people still conceived of the new houses as bungalows. Langston residents group houses according to a historical occurrence of change within the building tradition, and not solely on floor plans. The name applied to these houses was "bungalow," even though the pattern changed from square houses to rectangular houses.[18]

Mrs. Gross's description should make historians of material culture question how they generate and rely on typologies based primarily on formal characteristics. This is similar to Juan Pablo Bonta's counsel that architecture is better referred to by classes than by types. As he asserts: "Buildings achieve meaning . . . only through their belonging to certain classes. The notion of class is broader than that of type; classes can be typological (functional or formal), or historical."[19] Bonta's notion of class is appealing because of its flexibility and breadth. Buildings that may be quite different in formal qualities—such as four-square houses in one group and rectangular bungalows in another group—can be assembled and understood as components of one class of structures. This inclusive aspect allows the grouping together of houses with extremely different formal qualities to reflect how people within a community categorize houses in their own architectural history.

Five larger houses emphasize this broad conception of bungalows in Langston. Three of these five houses are the only two-story houses surviving in Langston and are located on two blocks of Melvin B. Tolson Boulevard. Materials and size formally differentiate these five houses from all other bungalows. Today people refer to these houses by the original owner's name. As David Petty said, "Well, they could be included with bungalows, cause they kind of look like them, but they are bigger."[20] This comment implies the underlying feeling about these houses; they may be bungalows, but they are more prodigious than the majority of bungalows.

The 1929 red rock Tay-Lo-Rest house (a pun on Take-a-little-rest and the owner's name, Professor Taylor) presents a good example of these larger bungalows. One of the most substantial houses in Langston, the Tay-Lo-Rest house was constructed with locally quarried stone, with a stone fireplace flanked by built-in bookcases, an elevated front porch, a matching stone garage, and a pediment over the front door (fig. 2.6). Through these physical displays Professor Taylor underscored his own prominence by employing architectural expressions. While substantial in size and finish, this house did not separate itself completely from the surrounding community. In fact, its floorplan (with entrance into a front room, followed by a dining room then kitchen with parallel bedrooms and bathroom all on the first floor) duplicated the smaller bungalow floor plans. While the outside of the house may be stylish and conspicuous, the inside was spatially familiar to other residents of Langston.

Two houses built by Howard and Ada Wiggins Clement in 1927 further illustrate the relationship between larger and smaller bungalows. The Clements built a tenant house (twenty-nine feet, three inches by thirty-eight feet, three inches) identical in plan and material to other bungalows with a front room, kitchen, three bedrooms, and bathroom all on the first floor. The house the Clements built for themselves differed significantly from other bungalows with its five-foot-high foundation, large, covered front porch on brick supports, hipped roof, central dormer window, and built-in corner cupboard next to a bay window. Equally unique, the floorplan had a first-floor sitting room, study, separate dining room, and second-story bedrooms.

Fig. 2.6. Facade of the Tay-Lo-Rest House of 1931 on Tolson Street.

In 1927 when the Clements hired a builder to construct these houses, they were extremely prosperous. The year before they had struck oil. They moved out of their frame homestead, two miles from town, and into a brand new Langston bungalow, so that their four daughters could attend high school and Langston University. The houses testify to the Clements' wealth within Langston and the delineation of economic classes within the town through architecture. Ada and Howard Clement attempted to inscribe their place within Langston through an imposing house and by not constructing their own dwelling like their tenant house or other bungalows. The Clement house symbolized the original dream of Langston's settlers coming to fruition; the Clements had 160 acres of land, 3 houses, economic security, and educational opportunities.[21]

Not everyone enjoyed such good economic fortune. For instance, upon their marriage in 1952, Jim and Viola Jones moved in with his parents into their one-room log house. Soon they added a frame bedroom and kitchen, transforming the one-room log house into the spatial equivalent of a new bungalow.

Although many people continued to live in homesteads while their neighbors raised bungalows, homesteads were not built after 1900. Homesteads gave the first generation of Langston settlers a stake in the land; second-generation settlers built bungalows. In part the difference between the two kinds of houses was their location. Homesteads were located in the countryside surrounding Langston, and bungalows were built in town.

Sometimes, as was the case with Allen and Arvenia Collier, the move to a bungalow signified a difference between generations. Adam Collier grew up four miles north of Langston in "a log cabin like everyone else's out that way." Arvenia Trice had spent her childhood three miles to the east in Pleasant Valley in a two-room frame homestead. When they married in 1940, Arvenia Collier, a successful midwife, had already constructed a new bungalow with a front room, dining room, two bedrooms, a bathroom, and a kitchen on Monument Street. By building a bungalow, Arvenia Collier broke from her parents' generation and their frame homestead. She defined herself in contrast to the first generation of settlers by erecting a house unlike theirs in materials, plan, appearance, and location.[22]

It would be too simple to understand bungalows as always representing a break between generations. In Arvenia Collier's circumstance the bungalow represented a major shift from a rural farm to the main commercial street of Langston, from a two-room homestead to a six-room bungalow. In 1940 Thelma Cumby hired Mr. Allen to build a house for her. She chose the location and number of rooms. Thelma Cumby and Mr. Allen built the four-room bungalow diagonally across Turner Street from her parents' house and down the street from two of her sisters' houses. Ms. Cumby's bungalow differed externally and internally from her parents' house, yet the proximity of the new house to the older house continued to link her to her family's economic and social circles.[23]

Bungalows in Langston illustrate the use of a nationally popular form of housing within an African-American community. Appropriation and participation in popular culture by African Americans presents a troublesome topic for scholars searching for "authentic" forms of African-American cultural production. However, portraying African-American culture as an unchanging, static form that did not negotiate with, create, or employ popular culture confines and restricts historical understanding. For, as historian Robin Kelley observed about zoot suits in 1940s Los Angeles, African Americans "appropriated, transformed, and reinscribed coded oppositional meanings onto styles derived from the dominant culture."[24] African Americans in Langston utilized and re-accented the vocabulary of popular housing forms for expressions within a local context.

In 1900 when Langstonians began building

new houses, their visions lay with innovative styles of popular architecture. The 1920 Langston University president's house demonstrates this choice. In its original site, the large, brick edifice sat at the end of a long row of oak trees. The trees graced either side of the original lane into the university from the road to Guthrie. At any other university, the president's house might be expected to be a large, classically inspired building complete with columns, pediments, and Palladian windows. In Langston, however, the style chosen was a very modern, boxy Art Deco building. Looking more like a new radio than an ancient Greek temple, the house embraced the present and looked toward the future. Likewise, residents did not employ the demotic style of Colonial Revival architecture anywhere in Langston. Choosing not to erect buildings with Colonial Revival flourishes implies a strong decision by Langston residents. The Colonial Revival style may have defined and communicated a romanticized past—a past that most of Langston's ancestors had experienced in slavery and not in freedom—while bungalows communicated ideas that looked more to the future than the past. The White House, as the university president's home is called, and the other bungalows of Langston are radical physical statements of optimism, of hope, and of tangible, physical progress for the second generation of residents.

Langston's houses express the physical embodiments of people's lives, dreams, and realities. Langston's history is not recorded by museums or statues, but by individuals. One object, however, pieces together a picture of land, people, and history: a quilt Amanda Gross made for a recent family reunion. This enormous quilt features her family tree. Her parents, who originally settled the Langston area, make up the trunk; her brothers and sisters form the limbs; and the four siblings that died at birth are the upper branches. Her parents' grandchildren are the leaves on the limbs, and Mrs. Gross's own grandchildren form more leaves under the tree. Quilts, as we have seen, were used in the log houses as architectural partitions and are an expressive tradition within Langston. Amanda Gross's description of the quilt also offers a compelling metaphor for the interpretation of houses. For instance, when I asked Mrs. Gross about the vines composing the border, she told me how she conceived of them:

> I brought leaves from Arizona, and got leaves off the campus, and got leaves from out there in my yard. . . . I don't know which leaves I chose. And my cousin I told her I wanted a vine all the way around it. When I was little Grandma and them used to go fishing on the creek down yonder where we were talking about at. And I would fish and then I would go and sit in with my feets in the water and then I'd bury my feets in the sand and I'd lay back and there was a elm tree and it had vines all up in it. Looked so pretty. And that's the way I wanted it. The vine all the way around the quilt, that's the reason the vines around it. So my cousin take a paper sack and draw the patterns of the vine. And Gracie Mae [her daughter] cut out these leaves for me.[25]

Amanda Gross's explanation of the vines portrays a combination of history, personal memory, family, and the ability to express an artistic vision. Untangling meanings in houses is equally complex.

The metaphor of Amanda Gross's quilt is not meant to suggest that analysis of houses should move to a purely biographical realm. However, by paying attention to the details of personal narratives, architectural historians can avoid making sweeping characterizations about a group's architecture. Likewise, people's words have the potential to redirect a historian's interests and interpretations to new questions and new information. As Langston residents' descriptions of Langston's houses emphasize, meanings are not inherent in the form of the house but are continually re-created by users within a specific context. When used in conjunction with artifacts, oral history not only explains questions about architecture but also extends the understanding of architecture by underscoring the intangible actions that provide architecture with its day-to-day significance.[26]

Most important, searching for "authentic" forms of African-American architectural experience disregards variation within African-American communities and African-Americans' negotiation or reinscription of popular culture. This narrow approach essentializes African-American cultural productions by selecting and recognizing a few of the many. The variety of architectural experiences within Langston illustrates the flaws in conceptualizing African-American architecture as a singular, static idiom or as one monolithic phenomenon. Beginning to recognize the human and artifactual complexity within African-American communities should compel architectural historians to consider the underlying syncretic form of cultural production within all communities.

## Notes

I am indebted to Bernard L. Herman, Tom Ryan, Gabriel Lanier, Nancy Van Dolsen, Allison Elterich, Adrienne Birney, Hilary Anderson, Marina Moskowitz, and Elaine Rice for all of their insights and support. This chapter benefited greatly from the time and knowledge of Amanda Gross, Mildred Robertson, Mayor Viola Jones, Jim Jones, Waymon Snellgro, and David Petty.

1. Quote from Langston City Plat, Mar. 3, 1889, Guthrie County Courthouse. The land had been taken by the United States Government from the Creek Nation in 1874 for the settlement of displaced Native American tribes. Because no tribes had been allotted the area, it became known as the Unassigned Lands. The lands to the east of the Unassigned Lands were leased to the Iowa, Sac and Fox, Kickapoo, Pottawatomie and Shawnee, and Seminoles. These eastern lands, as well as the rest of Oklahoma, eventually suffered the same fate as the Unassigned Lands and were

opened to land runs. For general histories, see Ray Allen Billington, *Westward Expansion: A History of the American Frontier,* 4th ed. (New York: Macmillan, 1974), 626–29; John Morris and Edwin McReynolds, *Historical Atlas of Oklahoma* (Norman: Univ. of Oklahoma Press, 1965); and Howard F. Stein and Robert F. Hill, eds., *The Culture of Oklahoma* (Norman: Univ. of Oklahoma Press, 1993). For more information on African-American towns in Oklahoma, see Kenneth Marvin Hamilton, *Black Towns and Profit* (Urbana and Chicago: Univ. of Illinois Press, 1991), 99–137; Jere Roberson, "Edward P. McCabe and the Langston Experiment," *The Chronicles of Oklahoma* 51 (Fall 1973): 343–55; George O. Carney, "Historic Resources of Oklahoma's All-Black Towns: A Preservation Profile," *The Chronicles of Oklahoma* 69 (Summer 1991): 116–33; and William Loren Katz, *The Black West* (New York: Doubleday, 1971), 245–64. The Oklahoma Historical Society has a paper entitled "Oklahoma Negro Settlements" in its packet of articles on Boley, Oklahoma, that lists the African-American towns: Arkansas Colored, Bailey, Boley, Bookertee, Canadian Colored, Chase, Ferguson, Foreman, Gibson Station, Langston, Lewisville, Liberty, Lima, Lincoln City, Lincoln (later Clearview), Marshalltown, Norfolk Colored, Overton, Redbird, Rentiesville, Summit, Taft, Tatums, Tullahassee, Vernon, Wellston Colony, Wildcat (later Grayson), Wybark. Residents of Langston added the towns of Boyington, Green Pastures, Hargrove, Haskell, and New Lima to the list of African-American towns in Oklahoma.

2. "FREEDOM!" *Langston City Herald,* Mar. 18, 1892. A. G. Belton to William Coppinger, Aug. 13 1890, American Colonization Society Papers, Manuscript Division, Library of Congress, Washington, D.C., as cited in Edwin Redkey, *Black Exodus: Black Nationalist and Back-to-Africa Movements, 1890–1910* (New Haven: Yale Univ. Press, 1969), 9; and Katz, *The Black West,* 250. *Topeka American Citizen,* Mar. 1, 1888, as cited in Hamilton, *Black Towns,* 99–100.

3. Taped interview with Mildred Robertson, Dec. 16, 1992. Taped interview with Waymon Snellgro, Aug. 10, 1992. For a telling view of the dire circumstances of African Americans in the post-Reconstruction South of the 1890s, see Ida Wells-Barnett, *On Lynching* (1894; reprint, New York: Arno/The New York Times, 1969); see also Redkey, *Black Exodus,* 5–7.

4. Paul Gilroy, *The Black Atlantic* (Cambridge: Harvard Univ. Press, 1993), 32. See also Werner Sollers, "Of Mules and Mares in a Land of Difference; or Quadrupeds All?" *American Quarterly* 42 (2) (June 1990): 169; Sollers, *Beyond Ethnicity: Consent and Descent in American Culture* (New York: Oxford Univ. Press, 1986).

5. "Home Sweet Home," *Langston City Herald,* Dec. 26, 1891.

6. See Loyd Lentz III, *Guthrie: A History of the Capital City 1889–1910* (Guthrie, Okla.: Logan County Historical Society, 1990), 19. Lentz states that the photograph was taken near Guthrie, which is ten miles southwest of Langston; Katz, *The Black West,* 249. Taped interview with Jim Jones, Aug. 8, 1992. See also George McDaniel, *Hearth and Home: Preserving a People's Culture* (Philadelphia: Temple Univ. Press, 1982), 68–72. Thanks to Gabriel Lanier for pointing out McDaniel's identical quote on earthen floors from African Americans in Maryland. McDaniel considers earthen floors to be a surviving tradition of a West African practice. See also Michael Roark, "Storm Cellars: Imprint of Fear on the Landscape," *Material Culture* 24 (2) (1992): 46–47.

7. Taped interview with Mildred Robertson, Aug. 12, 1992. Personal Tax Records, 1905, Logan County Courthouse, Guthrie, Oklahoma. *The Western Age,* Aug. 7, 1908.

8. Langston Town Meeting Book, Langston City Hall, Mar. 8, 1892.

9. Taped interview with Jim Jones, Aug. 5, 1992.

10. Taped interview with Amanda Gross, Aug. 21, 1992. Taped interview with Jim Jones, Aug. 16, 1992. See also Michael Ann Williams, *Homeplace: The Social Use and Meaning of the Folk Dwelling in Southwestern North Carolina* (Athens: Univ. of Georgia Press, 1991), 61. She describes curtains being used in a similar way in rural white households of North Carolina.

11. Viola Jones, personal communication, Aug. 8, 1992. Taped interview with Amanda Gross, Aug. 21, 1992.

12. The Clement house is located two miles east and one mile south of Langston in what was Iowa Indian lands. This area was opened for settlement in 1890. The Amos house is located two miles south of Langston in the Unassigned Lands that were opened in 1889. The Lounds house is located in Payne County along the Cimarron River.

13. Langston Town Records, Langston City Hall, Mar. 26, 1918, unnumbered page. Personal communication, Mizura Clement Allen, Aug. 20, 1992. Jim Jones, personal communication, Aug. 14, 1992.

14. See Alan Gowans, *The Comfortable House* (Cambridge: MIT Press, 1986); Cheryl Robertson, "Male and Female Agendas for Domestic Reform: The Middle Class Bungalow in Gendered Perspective," *Winterthur Portfolio* 26 (2/3) (Summer/Autumn 1991): 123–41; Gwendolyn Wright, *Building the Dream: A Social History of Housing in America* (New York: Pantheon, 1981), 166–68; Katherine Cole Stevenson and H. Ward Jandl, *A Guide to Houses from Sears, Roebuck and Company* (Washington, D.C.: Preservation Press, 1986); and Susan Mulcahey Chase, "Rural Adaptation of Suburban Bungalows, Sussex County, Delaware," in *Gender, Class, and Shelter: Perspectives in Vernacular Architecture, V,* ed. Elizabeth Collins Cromley and Carter L. Hudgins (Knoxville: Univ. of Tennessee Press, 1995).

15. Taped interview with Amanda Gross, Dec. 12, 1992. Taped interview with David Petty, Dec. 12, 1992. The three old bungalows are the Jacobs, Jones, and Carter houses. Architectural historians refer to these types of structures as foursquares. See Gowans, *The Comfortable House,* 90–93.

16. Mildred Robertson, personal communication, Aug. 15, 1992. R. Randall Phillips, *The Book of the Bungalow* (London: Offices of *Country Life,* 1920, and New York: Charles Scribner's Sons, 1920), 11. Queen Esther Williams Vic, personal communication, July 10, 1992.

17. Jim Jones, personal communication, Aug. 5, 1992.

18. Taped interview with Amanda Gross, Dec. 12, 1992.

19. Juan Pablo Bonta, *Architecture and Its Interpretation* (New York: Rizzoli, 1979), 128–29. The literature on architectural, not to mention archaeological, typologies is vast, varied, and often contentious. For a brief sampling, see Bernard L. Herman, *The Stolen House* (Charlottesville: Univ. Press of Virginia, 1992), 3–14; Fred W. Peterson, *Homes in the Heartland: Balloon Frame Farmhouses of the Upper Midwest, 1850–1920* (Lawrence: Univ. Press of Kansas, 1992), 25–39; Henry Glassie, *Folk Housing in Middle Virginia: A Structural Analysis of Historic Artifacts* (Knoxville: Univ. of Tennessee Press, 1975), 13–18, 41–65, and 114–22; and James Deetz, *In Small Things Forgotten: The Archaeology of Early American Life* (Garden City, N.Y.: Anchor Press/Doubleday, 1977).

20. Taped interview with David Petty, Dec. 18, 1992.

21. Mizura Clement Allen, personal communication, July 19, 1992.

22. Taped interview with Adam Collier, July 26, 1992.

23. Thelma Cumby, personal communications, Aug. 14–16, 1992.

24. Robin D. G. Kelley, "The Riddle of the Zoot: Malcolm Little and Black Cultural Politics During World War II," in *Malcolm X: In Our Own Image,* ed. Joe Wood (New York: St. Martin's Press, 1992), 162. See also Williams, *Homeplace,* 90–92. Williams discusses a similar change in housing in Kentucky and suggests continuities in use between older "folk" houses and the "non-folk" bungalows. The floor plans of the rural bungalows she describes are similar to Langston's houses. This similarity suggests the need for a broad study, especially concerned with experiential aspects of popular architectural forms, of rural bungalows across the South.

25. Taped interview with Amanda Gross, Dec. 12, 1992.

26. Some of the more fascinating architectural studies that use oral history to illuminate the complexity of space are Gerald Pocius, *A Place to Belong: Community Order and Everyday Space in Calvert, Newfoundland* (Athens: Univ. of Georgia Press, 1991); Williams, *Homeplace*; McDaniel, *Hearth and Home*; Charles Martin, *Hollybush: Folk Building and Social Change in an Appalachian Community* (Knoxville: Univ. of Tennessee Press, 1984); Henry Glassie, *Passing the Time in Ballymenone: Culture and History of an Ulster Community* (Philadelphia: Univ. of Pennsylvania Press, 1982); and Annmarie Adams, "The Eichler Home: Intention and Experience in Postwar Suburbia," in *Gender, Class, and Shelter.*

*Nora Pat Small*

# New England Farmhouses
# in the Early Republic:
# Rhetoric and Reality

An examination of the early-nineteenth-century speeches and writings of New England's rural reformers, a group composed almost solely of urban-based gentlemen, reveals an uproar over proper rural building form.[1] From the 1810s to the 1830s individuals and institutions dedicated to agricultural improvement and rural reform disparaged the growing number of large farmhouses they observed in the hinterlands. For the rural reformers beauty and convenience translated into small, one-story cottages; for the prosperous farmers it translated into two-story, symmetrical dwellings with ells. The divergence of rhetoric from reality provides the observer of vernacular landscapes with a window onto a countryside in transition. This chapter offers a brief synopsis of the reform rhetoric devoted to rural building practices and a lengthier analysis of the buildings themselves. The reform literature serves here as a reminder that buildings are viewed and experienced from multiple perspectives.

In his 1819 address to the Massachusetts Society for the Promotion of Agriculture (MSPA) Josiah Quincy, politician, gentleman farmer, and advocate for rural reform, exhorted Massachusetts farmers to pay heed to neatness, comfort, and order and not to let "the sound, practical good sense of the country be misled, by the false taste and false pride of the city." A farmer so misled "will throw up a building thirty, or forty, feet square, two, or two and a half, stories high, four rooms on a floor, with an immeasurable length of outbuilding behind."[2] Although he exaggerated its typical size considerably, Quincy here condemned the two-story-with-ell house being built by prosperous farmers and rural artisans throughout southern New England.

Farm-journal articles and agricultural fair orators echoed Quincy's denunciations for the next two decades. Rural reformers and agricultural improvers, drawn from that rank of genteel society that did not rely on farming to earn a living, repeatedly cast the countryside as the seat and source of the nation's strength and morality. Anything suggestive of dissoluteness, such as extravagance in building or reaching beyond one's station, they decried as a threat to the moral fabric of the nation. The *New England Farmer* editor pursued the theme of preserving rural areas from the corrupting influences of urban profligacy and unnecessary displays of wealth. In 1823 the journal merely cautioned farmers against building a large house unless they had a good deal of capital and advised against the increasingly popular practice of building farm structures adjacent to the house.[3] By 1825 articles in the *Farmer* and other agricultural journals wholeheartedly condemned the practice of building large houses, which, they noted, impoverished the farmer and was "at variance with correct taste." The *New England Farmer* elaborated, offering an alternative to the distasteful tendencies of rural builders: "There is nothing connected with a farm, considered either as an object of taste or economy, that is more pleasing or delightful than a small house. . . . The wish to be thought of more importance than we really are, and the notion that this importance will be estimated from the spacious mansions in which we may reside, is too prevalent among every class of society; but in no one is the consequence more prejudicial, or its influence more deeply felt, than in the agricultural community."[4] The writer commented bleakly on the waste inherent in two-story rural dwellings, most of which contained at least two rooms that were used only for infrequent formal occasions. He concluded that had the farmer built a smaller house he would have been "encircled by many sincere friends, with a competency of this world's goods to make life comfortable, imparting joy and content to a virtuous and happy family."[5]

Through the early 1830s, farm journals and rural reformers declined to offer specific instructions on how a farmhouse should be arranged. They maintained that common farmers should express their taste and demonstrate their economy in a small dwelling, a house suitable to their station and adequate to their needs. The two-story-with-ell house was an inappropriate habitation for the yeomanry. Generally the journalists and reformers agreed that the house should be neat and uniform so as to impart a sense of comfort and happiness, but they went no further.[6]

While the orators and essayists fumed, farmers of middling and upper rank built two-story houses with tripartite, bilaterally symmetrical facades and one- or one-and-a-half-story ells; they rearranged facades of older buildings and added ells to the main blocks. The general characteristics of tasteful building—beauty, cleanliness, order, and economy or convenience—seem to have been universally agreed upon, but the outcry of reformers against a widespread and popular building form reveals that definitions of those characteristics were open for debate.

I discovered the difference in definitions between the self-styled reformers and those who were actually transforming the rural landscape in the course of conducting fieldwork in Sutton, Massachusetts. Sutton, a mixed agricultural and manufacturing community in the south-central part of the state, was a place of prime political and economic importance in Worcester County throughout the eighteenth century and into the 1820s.[7] Overshadowed by 1830 by Worcester as an industrial and transportation hub, the town nevertheless thrived; its inhabitants continued to combine farming and manufacturing into the twentieth century. The field investigation encompassed thirty pre-1840 dwellings and barns. Deed and probate records, local and federal tax lists, censuses, genealogies, vital records, memberships, and town officer lists provided most of the archival documentation on the buildings and their owners. This sample permitted the construction of an architectural chronology as well as a profile of those who built or remodeled the houses and outbuildings.[8]

## Eighteenth-Century Antecedents

Advocates of rural reform feared that country folk had abandoned their commonsensical, traditional ways and had adopted urban mannerisms. In truth, the disparaged two-story houses combined long-standing practice and modern building requirements. To discern the innovations as well as the continuities in rural building practice in early-nineteenth-century New England, the customary practices that preceded the new two-story houses must be examined. Gable-roofed, single-story dwellings presided over the majority of eighteenth-century Worcester County farmers' homelots, although two-story houses were common in some communities, such as Sutton (fig. 3.1).[9] The single-story form of the center-chimney, hall/parlor, lobby-entry house had been established by the first decade of the seventeenth century in parts of southeastern England. At the end of the eighteenth century, the form dominated all but the oldest and wealthiest communities of Massachusetts.[10] The 1798 Federal Direct Tax Census reveals that most Worcester County dwellings stood one story tall and possessed one of two typical floor areas—six hundred or one thousand square feet. These outnumbered two-story dwellings by two to one.[11]

Nearly one-quarter of all dwellings in the county measured less than six hundred square feet on plan. At 600 square feet on plan, a house typically consisted of two main rooms divided by a chimney bay and a lean-to running the length of the rear of the building. A two-room-deep, two-room-wide plan with central chimney encompassed approximately one thousand square feet, as did the rarer double-pile, center-hall dwelling.[12] The approximately 25 percent of dwellings that measured less than 600 square feet on plan were not necessarily hovels. A one-story, interior end–chimney house that survives in Sutton from around 1788 measures just over 550 square feet in plan (fig. 3.2). Only two structural bays wide,

the ground floor of the house contained three rooms and an entry lobby. The staircase in the entry provided access to the cellar and to the garret, both usable spaces.

The detailed schedules of the 1798 Federal Direct Tax that indicate numbers and sizes of houses do not survive for Sutton, but comparisons with other towns can help establish a profile of the town's late-eighteenth-century building stock.[13] Throughout the 1700s Sutton and Brookfield, which lies about twenty miles northwest of Sutton,

Fig. 3.1. Davenport House, South Sutton, c. 1767. The side ell is undoubtedly a nineteenth-century addition. From Benedict and Tracy, *History of the Town of Sutton,* 361.

Fig. 3.2. Two-Bay House, c. 1788, Manchaug Village, Sutton. The original chimney was located in the right bay of the house. The current chimney and enclosed porch are modern additions.

were two of the four largest towns in the county. Like Sutton, Brookfield was an affluent farming community. In that town somewhat less than half of the houses stood two-stories tall in 1798. In Mendon and Uxbridge, just to the east and south of Sutton, two-story dwellings accounted for about one-third of the housing stock. Neither town was as wealthy as Sutton, but both ranked among the wealthiest 40 percent of Worcester County towns.[14] If the local patterns hold, one-third to one-half of Sutton's dwellings had two full floors at the end of the century. Thus, two-story houses were already a common, if not predominant, rural house form in the post-Revolution years. Although rural reformers like Quincy complained about height, it was a combination of building practices rather than one feature that irked them.

Quincy alluded to one such practice in his Massachusetts Society for the Promotion of Agriculture speech when he noted farmers' tendencies to "throw up" overly large houses. In other words reformers were concerned with the rapidity with which these large houses, complete with four rooms on a floor and attached outbuildings, were built. This manner of building contrasted sharply with the previously common practice of building by accretion. Throughout the seventeenth and eighteenth centuries in Massachusetts home owners added to their dwellings in stages.[15] Since the first century of settlement in the Massachusetts Bay Colony, houses had grown from plans of one room with chimney and often a lean-to, to two rooms or more with a center chimney. All phases existed simultaneously in the colony, but individual houses often began as portions of the single- or double-pile center-chimney, hall-and-parlor form. Fieldwork revealed that this seventeenth-century custom of expansion also held true for eighteenth-century Sutton, as it did throughout the region.[16]

Although probably outnumbered by single-story dwellings at the end of the eighteenth century, Sutton's two-story, pre-Revolution houses have survived in greater numbers than smaller houses. These houses contain the evidence of the customary practice of building by accretion. Two stories did not necessarily imply a hall-and-parlor plan. These single-cell (i.e., having a living area one structural bay wide), two-story structures, common in the seventeenth century, remained popular well into the eighteenth century, as extant Sutton houses testify. Five of the ten two-story pre-Revolution dwellings investigated for this study began as single-cell structures with gable-end chimneys.[17] By around 1780 all five had been enlarged to center-chimney plans with the addition of a second major room on the opposite side of the chimney. By 1800 three of the five were deepened to double-pile plans, while the other two remained one room deep.

An exception to customary building practices—phased construction, center-chimney plans—is the Malachi Marble house, an unusual mid-eighteenth-century, story-and-a-half, center-passage dwelling (fig. 3.3).[18] When many of his contemporaries were building or adding to two-story, center-chimney dwellings, Malachi chose to build a story-and-a-half, central-passage house with interior-end chimneys. By constructing a dwelling of just over one thousand square feet Malachi remained well within the common experience of his neighbors and of Worcester County inhabitants in general. He set himself off, however, with his choice of a center-passage plan. Malachi's use of the passage may have been a statement of stature and taste made within the bounds of local propriety.[19] Whatever the case, the center-passage plan remained a rarity in Sutton for another forty years.

### New Construction

Georgian external bilateral symmetry became the standard for facade arrangement in the late eighteenth century as builders abandoned such old-fashioned characteristics as asymmetry or long, sloped roofs over lean-tos. So pervasive was the aesthetic that of forty eighteenth-century houses still standing in Sutton, none survived into the

Fig. 3.3. Elevation of Marble House, c. 1763–70. The original chimney stacks are gone. Their former locations can be discerned from cut-outs in the roof ridge pole.

twentieth century with an unbalanced three-bay facade. Structural investigations of three such dwellings have revealed that all three were built with an uncentered single window on either side of the middle bay. They were all altered to five-bay facades by around 1800. Vernacular dwellings of the early Republic frequently employed the matched chimneys and hipped roofs that had characterized Georgian building as well; in modified form, these features became characteristic of the more delicate post-Revolution classicism known to architectural historians as the Federal style.

Generally speaking, local builders adopted popular aesthetics that called for symmetry and slenderly proportioned classical detail but retained traditional plans in whole or in part. New 1810s and 1820s houses were distinguished from one another, as their earlier counterparts had been, by the manner in which the central core or structural bay was used.

In the extensive rebuilding that followed the Revolution in southern New England, rural builders did not abandon the by-then ancient center-chimney, hall-and-parlor plan.[20] Rather, in this house type the lobby entry and hall and parlor remained constant, but the chimney location did not. The chimney might be found in its traditional central-core location or as paired stacks in the rear or end walls. When the builder removed the chimney stack from the central core, he retained the lobby-entry stair and added living or storage space behind it.

The single-pile, lobby-entry plans with end- or rear-wall chimneys appeared in Sutton by c. 1806 and remained in use into the 1870s.[21] Enoch Stockwell's house is the earliest documented example (fig. 3.4). Stockwell, a successful farmer referred to as "gentleman" in an 1806 property transaction, bought or had built a two-story, lobby-entry, hall-and-parlor house (fig. 3.5). Constructed adjacent to the farm's mid-eighteenth-century center-chimney, gambrel-roofed house, the new dwelling exhibited all of the characteristics of the modern building mode—a slim profile, bilateral symmetry, and paired end chimneys. On the interior, the location of chimney stacks in end walls allowed for a small room, about seven feet by eight feet, behind the dog-leg stair with access to both the hall and the parlor.

Fig. 3.4. Elevation of Phelps/Stockwell House, c. 1806. The protruding entryway is a twentieth-century addition. Otherwise, the elevation is little changed from its original construction. The "little house," the original eighteenth-century dwelling, retains its gambrel roof on the back side. The front slope appears to have been raised in the nineteenth century.

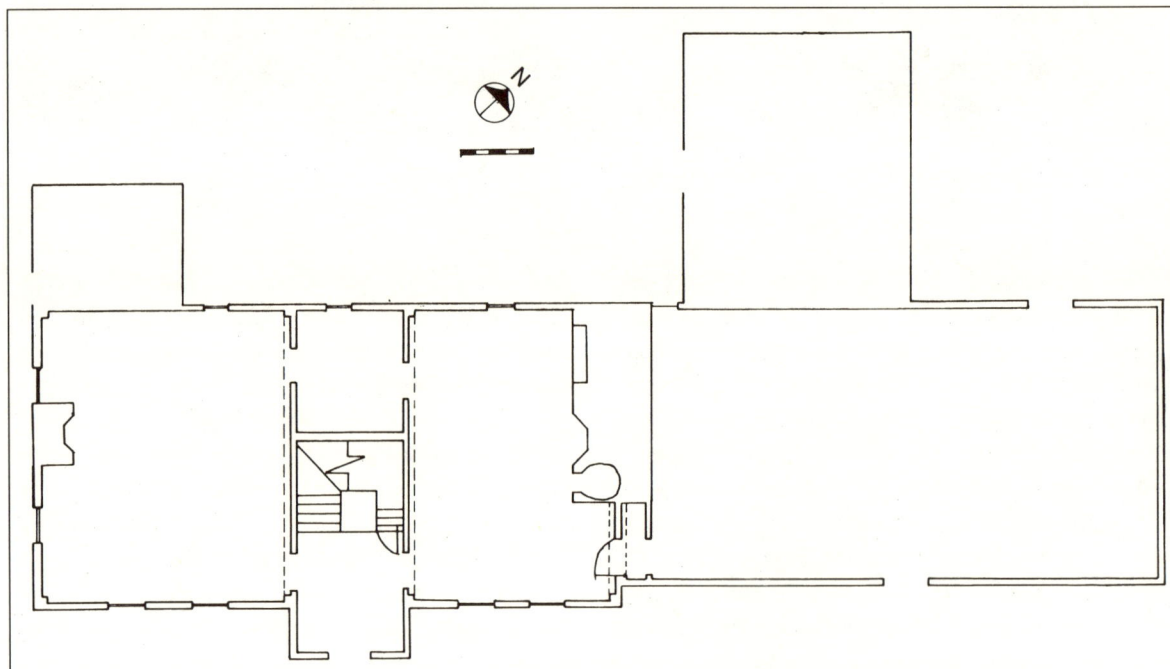

Fig. 3.5. Plan of Phelps/Stockwell House. With the placement of the chimney stacks in the end walls, a small room or large pantry replaces the center chimney in this variation on the hall-and-parlor plan.

At least four other examples of similar lobby-entry, hall-and-parlor dwellings dating from the 1810s and 1820s are extant in Sutton. While that arrangement appears to have been popular, variations on the lobby-entry plan abounded. In one house, built c. 1818, the "chimney bay" was reduced to the width of an enclosed straight-run stair. In another, dating from 1835–38, the chimney stack that emerges from the center of the roof is actually two stacks that merge in the attic. The twin stacks served stoves in the front rooms on the first and second floors as well as a bake oven and a small fireplace. The vacated chimney core contained a walk-in pantry with built-in shelves.

The Georgian center-passage form that gained popularity among the eastern seaboard's urban gentry in the second quarter of the eighteenth century served as the basis for the second major plan type found in this sample. Builders varied this plan by constructing single- and double-pile versions, one or two stories tall, with the passage sometimes running the full depth of the two-room-deep versions, sometimes only half the depth.

The center-passage plan, formerly a rarity in rural New England, became a popular choice in early-nineteenth-century Sutton.[22] Two of Sutton's thriving farmers who chose to build two-story, center-hall farmhouses were Salmon Burdon and Timothy Burnap Jr. Burdon and Burnap were contemporaries, born in 1779 and 1786 respectively. Both served for three years on the board of selectmen, as well as simultaneously on the school committee in 1835. Both possessed landholdings that surpassed the local average. Burdon's 1813 farmhouse was substantial and stylish but not extravagant. The two-story main block of the house was a single room deep. The central passage, which led to the rear ell, divided the two rooms of the main house (fig 3.6). The hipped roof and paired windows on the end wall, characteristic of full double-pile Georgian structures, belie the abbreviated form of this dwelling. Burnap's 1815 farmhouse was also a two-story, central-passage house with rear ell, but he built his dwelling two rooms deep and with a gable roof.

While the main blocks of Sutton's Federal-era dwellings were far from revolutionary in plan, they were also far from predictable or static.[23] Numerous variations on the lobby entry and central passage survive. The willingness of Sutton's builders to create variations on a theme or to experimentally depart from tried-and-true methods can also be seen in their innovative structural systems. By the second half of the eighteenth century, principal-rafter/common-purlin roof systems with diamond-shaped ridge poles were common all over Sutton. The diamond ridge poles were superseded in the late eighteenth century and early nineteenth century by five-sided ridge poles, but the principal rafters and common purlins persisted for a short time.[24]

The plan of the main dwelling block and the structural system are only part of the story of the innovative rebuilding that swept through much of rural southern New England. No matter what the plan, elevation, or framing, virtually all new rural dwellings were built with an ell, and older buildings acquired one. The ell, referred to by contemporaries as an outbuilding, a "small house," or a "little house," was an independently roofed addition to the side or rear of a house. It seems to have fulfilled the early-nineteenth-century demand for convenience in architecture, which was viewed as a necessary component of beauty.[25]

The sample of houses investigated for this study included thirteen that had been built between 1794 and 1838. All were constructed with ells. Fifteen out of seventeen pre-1790 houses had ells added after c. 1790. Houses acquired ells in a number of ways and in a variety of locations. The construction of the c. 1806 Stockwell dwelling, mentioned above, relegated the single-story eighteenth-century house to a gable-end ell. In other cases, small outbuildings dragged to the new house site served as ells or

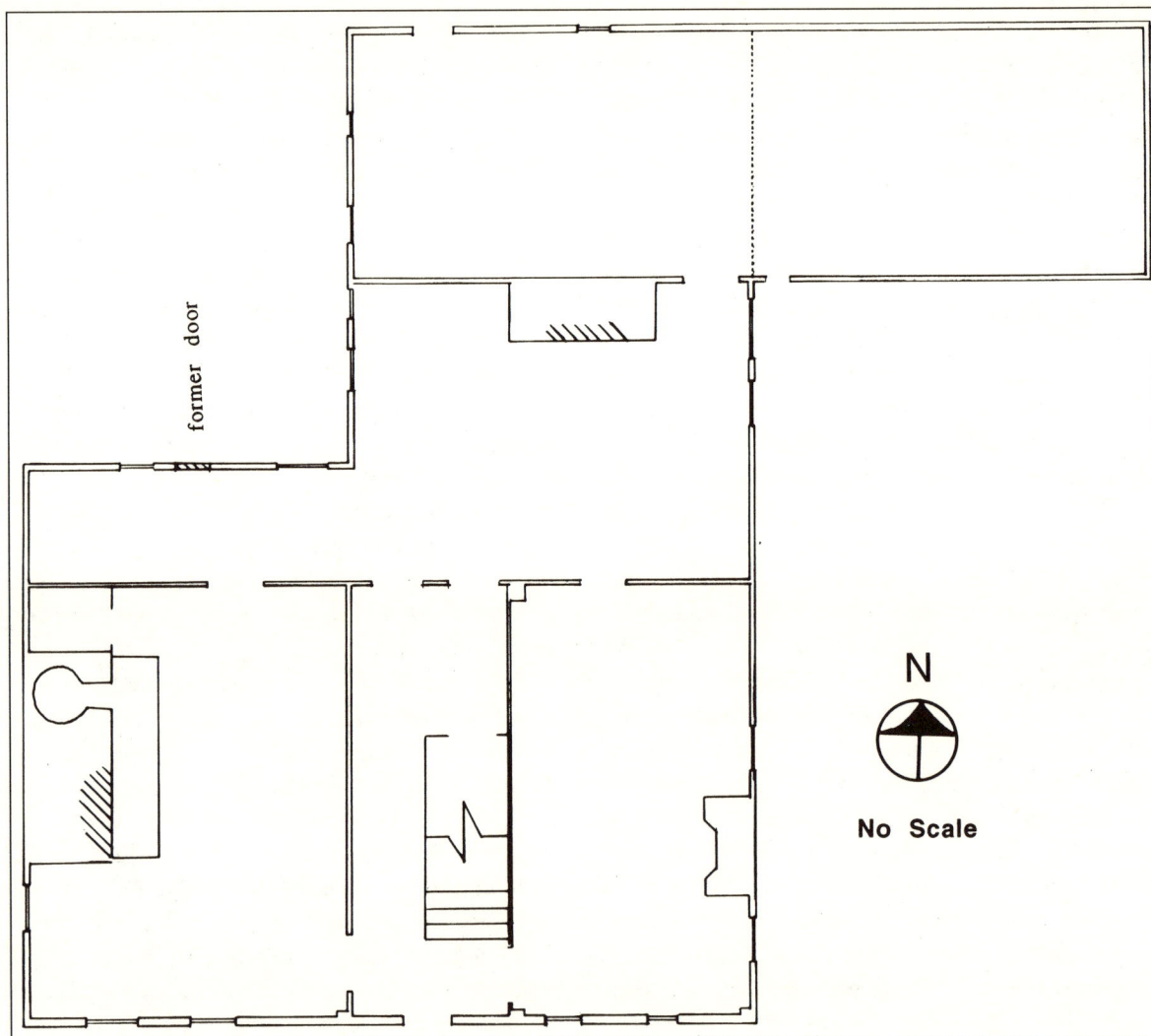

Fig. 3.6. Plan of Salmon Burdon House, 1813. The integral rear ell offered additional work space. Note the presence of a hearth and bake oven in the main block of the house.

ell extensions. Daniel Putnam, a house carpenter, abutted an older workshop to the rear of his c. 1810 two-story dwelling. Peter Sibley, a farmer, built his c. 1811 house—a two-story, double-pile, center-passage dwelling—with an integral rear ell and attached an older shed to the gable-end of the new ell.

The almost universal abandonment of lean-tos for ells should not be surprising. By the late eighteenth century, Georgian massing and elevations were standard. A lean-to, whether to the rear or side of a building, would have destroyed the symmetry of roofline and profile crucial to Georgian aesthetics. The independent roofing system and separate entrance gave the ell the appearance of a little house. Indeed, a line from a nineteenth-century rhyme, "Big house, little house, back house, barn," indicates that this was the general perception of the appendage. Larger ells, with their own chimney stacks, appeared to function as independent service wings.

In central Massachusetts, however, the physical distinction between house and ell did not translate into functional separation. Archival and physical evidence from Sutton bear out the interdependence of house and ell and the multipurpose nature of ells. Bartholomew Hutchinson and Moses and Nathaniel Putnam added side ells to their early-eighteenth-century houses in the first decade of the nineteenth century. The histories of these wings reinforce the conclusion that the new ells, like the spaces within the main body of the house, could and did serve multiple functions.

When Bartholomew Hutchinson sold an undivided half of all his property to his newly married son, Simon, in 1806 they had to decide how to accommodate the new family. The common practice at the time, when two families occupied the same dwelling, was to expand the old house. Eighteenth-century expansion strategies of two-story houses included raising the roof of single-story rear lean-tos to the height of the front of the house. The Hutchinsons, however, retained their rear lean-to and expanded their house in the modern way—by adding a side ell.[26] The scale of the new ell indicates that it could have housed either the new family or activities of the main house that would have been displaced in order to properly accommodate two separate households.

While we are forced to speculate on the precise function of the Hutchinsons' new ell, their neighbor Moses Putnam left us more concrete evidence. At the death of his father in 1812, Moses submitted to the estate administrators an account of his running of the farm, which he had begun in 1779.[27] This document indicated that in 1806 Nathaniel Putnam requested that Moses build an addition to their shared house consisting of a "small house, wood house, milk room." In Thomas Hubka's work on connected farm buildings, he finds that the "little house," the section of the ell closest to the house, contained a kitchen, and the "back house," frequently distinguished from the little house on the exterior by a slightly lower roofline, contained work rooms such as dairy or

laundry rooms, storage space, and privy.[28] The function of the Putnams' small house is unknown, but it is clear that the new structure accommodated dairying activities and served as a storage area for the wood needed to operate the hearths, bake ovens, and set kettle—essentially a built-in boiler for such chores as laundry or cooking livestock feed—in the main house.[29] The Putnams used their new space to expand domestic work areas, not to supersede older work areas.

A very clear example of the manner in which ell functions were linked to those of the main house is seen in the 1835–37 Zadok Woodbury house. Woodbury built his two-story, double-pile house with a gable-end ell (fig. 3.7). On the east-end wall of the ell, the Woodburys built a chimney stack that housed a small fireplace, a bake oven, and a set kettle. They located a well on the north side of the ell chimney stack, within two feet of the set kettle, which required plenty of water. The front ell room was spacious enough to accommodate day-to-day food preparation as well as dairying activities. The four windows on the east and south walls provided ample natural light and ventilation. The rear room of the ell apparently served as a woodshed, as its interior remained unfinished until recent years. Large quantities of wood could be stored here, under cover and within close proximity to the fireplace.

In short, the ground level of this ell was a highly efficient service space. It had direct access to the main-house hall with its bake oven, stove, and pantry, as well as to the cellar beneath the main house where the dairy room was located.[30] The Woodburys' ell thoroughly exemplifies the notion of convenience so sought after by thriving and busy rural New Englanders.

## Divergent Perspectives

To the genteel advocates of rural reform, the tendency of increasing numbers of the rural middling sort to build larger dwellings represented a precipitous decline in moral and economic discipline.

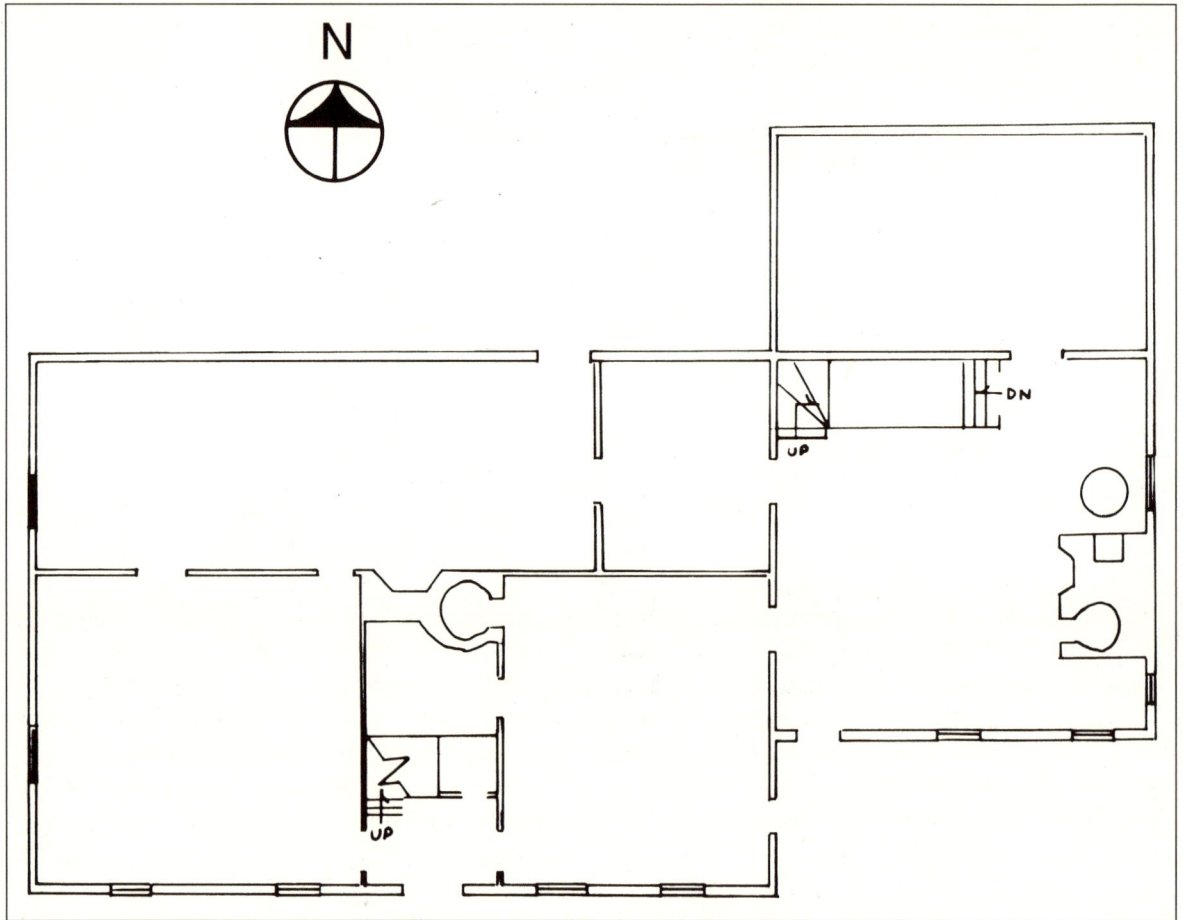

Fig. 3.7. Plan of Woodbury House, c. 1835. The family retained the use of one of the front rooms in the main house as a hall or kitchen.

They leveled much of their criticism at farmers, whose virtue and economy were directly tied to the success of the new republic. They spoke of wasted space and wasted money, not recognizing the tremendous economic and occupational shifts that required or enabled farmers and artisans to rearrange their living and working spaces. The rural reformers of the first four decades of the nineteenth-century saw only departure from old and revered ways; they missed the fact that modern practices were embedded in tradition and built upon it.

Early-nineteenth-century builders modified familiar building forms to meet new design expectations and practical needs. The proliferation of taller houses and attached ells in rural New England in the early nineteenth century, in spite of reformers' protests, did not signify a wholesale rejection of traditional building patterns nor of customary utilization of space. The new massing of a main block with ell and end-wall or rear-wall location of chimneys were variations on either the old hall-and-parlor plan or popularized versions of the Georgian central-passage plan. As it had in the eighteenth century, the farmhouse continued to function as a center of production where rooms served multiple uses, and the entire dwelling often housed more than one nuclear family.

Not only did local builders modify familiar building forms to meet modern living and working standards, but they also altered the building process itself. When Sutton's builders constructed new dwellings they raised the frame for the entire house rather than building in stages as many of their ancestors had. They experimented with different types of framing systems, modifying and even abandoning purlins and principal rafters. Ells, virtually unknown in eighteenth-century rural New England, became ubiquitous. The preference for central-chimney plans disappeared as Georgian-inspired center-passage and modified traditional entry lobby plans became equally popular.

The two-story-with-ell rural dwellings signaled their occupants' modern attitude toward the organization of space and work, an organization driven by new market demands and strategies, but shaped by then-current standards of beauty and convenience. Resembling in detail and massing the homes of the gentry, these houses diverged from their genteel counterparts most obviously in terms of scale but most importantly in terms of function. Serving the multiple occupations of rural families, and frequently multiple households, these houses were not built for a strict adherence to the separation of public and private and work and social spaces that marked the dwellings of the most wealthy. Rural reformers' fears that farmers were behaving in a profligate manner were misplaced. Instead, farmers and other rural residents were arranging their domestic and work spaces in a manner most conducive to conducting their day-to-day tasks and to promoting their economic security.

## Notes

1. For an analysis of the social standing of the reform-minded gentry who constituted the membership of the Massachusetts Society for the Promotion of Agriculture, see Tamara Thornton, *Cultivating Gentlemen: The Meaning of Country Life Among the Boston Elite: 1785–1860* (New Haven: Yale Univ. Press, 1989).

2. Josiah Quincy, "An Address Delivered before the Massachusetts Agricultural Society, at the Brighton Cattle Show, Oct. 12, 1819," *Massachusetts Agricultural Repository and Journal* 6 (Jan. 1820): 10.

3. *New England Farmer* 1 (45) (June 7, 1823): 353.

4. Reprinted from the *National Aegis* in the *New England Farmer* 4 (6) (Sept. 2, 1825).

5. Ibid.

6. This changed by the late 1830s when farm journals and progressive agriculturists began to offer specific suggestions and even house plans and elevations. See Sally McMurry, *Families and Farmhouses in Nineteenth-Century America: Vernacular Design and Social Change* (New York: Oxford Univ. Press, 1988).

7. For Sutton's role as a central place in Worcester County, see John Brooke, *The Heart of the Commonwealth: Society and Political Culture in Worcester County, Massachusetts, 1713–1861* (Cambridge: Cambridge Univ. Press, 1989), especially 27, 30, 102, 169.

8. A detailed analysis of the buildings and their owners appears in Nora Pat Small, "Beauty and Convenience: The Architectural Reordering of Sutton, Massachusetts, 1790–1840," (Ph.D. diss., Boston Univ., 1994), 125–32, 187–222.

9. Gambrel roofs were far rarer than gable roofs. Only three eighteenth-century gambrel roofs survive in Sutton. They appear to date to the first half of that century. One was used on a two-story house, the other two on single-story dwellings. On the use of gambrel roofs as a mark of distinction, see Kevin Sweeney, "Mansion People: Kinship, Class, and Architecture in Western Massachusetts in the Mid-Eighteenth Century," *Winterthur Portfolio* 19 (4) (Winter 1984): 235–36, 241.

10. Abbot Lowell Cummings, *The Framed Houses of Massachusetts Bay, 1625–1725* (Cambridge, Mass.: Belknap Press of Harvard Univ. Press, 1979), 16–17, and figure 21.

11. According to Michael Steinitz's analysis of the 1798 direct tax schedules for Worcester County, single-story dwellings of six to seven hundred square feet and one thousand square feet dominated the landscape. See his analysis of the 1798 Direct Tax Census in "Rethinking Geographical Approaches to the Common House: The Evidence from Eighteenth-Century Massachusetts,"

*Perspectives in Vernacular Architecture, III,* ed. Thomas Carter and Bernard Herman (Columbia: Univ. of Missouri Press, 1989), 16–26.

12. Based on measurements of extant dwellings in Sutton.

13. Schedules from the 1798 Direct Tax that do survive for Sutton indicate value of dwellings and number and value of acres held.

14. Steinitz, "Rethinking," 20.

15. See Cummings, *Framed Houses*, 23–24.

16. For seventeenth- and early-eighteenth-century examples, see Cummings, *Framed Houses*; and J. Frederick Kelly, *Early Domestic Architecture of Connecticut* (New York: Dover, 1963), 5–20.

17. By "single cell" I mean that the footprint consisted of two structural bays, one of which contained the chimney stack, the other of which was living space. These houses never extended beyond the chimney bay more than one room or perhaps one room and gable-end lean-to. That single cell of living space was often divided into discrete spaces with nonstructural partitions.

18. J. Frederick Kelly dates the widespread use of the double-pile, central-hall form in Connecticut to the third quarter of the eighteenth century, but also illustrates late-seventeenth- and early-eighteenth-century examples in *Early Domestic Architecture of Connecticut,* 16–20. Fiske Kimball dates the initial arrival of the central hall plan in the colonies to the late seventeenth century when it appeared in such houses as the c. 1680 Peter Tufts house in Medford, Massachusetts, the c. 1676 Sergeant house in Boston, and the 1686 Foster Hutchinson house in Boston. The 1716 McPhedris-Warner house in Portsmouth, New Hampshire, also had a central-hall plan. Kimball suggests that seventeenth-century examples were rare and that the form increased in popularity among the gentry in the second quarter of the eighteenth century. See his *Domestic Architecture of the American Colonies and of the Early Republic* (Charles Scribner's Sons, 1922; reprint, New York: Dover, 1966), 44–46, 62, 70, 267. For early examples in Rhode Island, see Antoinette F. Downing and Vincent Scully Jr., *The Architectural Heritage of Newport, Rhode Island, 1640–1915* (New York: American Legacy Press, 1967), including Whitehall, 1729, plate 85; and the Jonathan Nichols house, c. 1748, plates 88–91.

19. On the gentry's use of architecture as a means of setting themselves off physically and socially from commoners, see Fraser D. Neiman, "Domestic Archi-

tecture at the Clifts Plantation: The Social Context of Early Virginia Building," in *Common Places: Readings in American Vernacular Architecture,* ed. Dell Upton and John Michael Vlach (Athens: Univ. of Georgia Press, 1986), 292–312, particularly 311–12; and Kevin Sweeney, "Mansion People," 231–55.

20. On the persistence of central chimney hall/parlor plans in Worcester County, Massachusetts, see unpublished survey data on Barre Four Corners neighborhood, Nora Pat Small and Myron Stachiw, surveyors, Old Sturbridge Village, Research department files, Sturbridge, Mass. Three of the fourteen Sutton houses in this sample that were built between 1790 and 1840 had central-chimney plans. They dated from c. 1792, 1812, and 1835.

21. Richard Candee has dated the appearance of this house type in Portsmouth, New Hampshire, to 1798. See his *An Old Town by the Sea: Urban Landscapes and Vernacular Building in Portsmouth, New Hampshire, A Field Guide to Portsmouth and the Piscataqua,* produced for the 1992 Vernacular Architecture Forum conference, 10–11.

22. On the use of central-hall plans by the Connecticut River Valley "River Gods," and its relative rarity throughout rural New England in the eighteenth century, see Sweeney, "Mansion People," 238–39.

23. For more on the diversity of house plans in the early nineteenth century, see Myron Stachiw and Nora Pat Small, "Tradition and Transformation: Rural Society and Architectural Change in Nineteenth-Century Central Massachusetts," in *Perspectives in Vernacular Architecture, III,* 135–48.

24. One example of the retention of a traditional plan with innovative framework was the c. 1812 Thomas Harback house. The builder of this double-pile, center-chimney, hall-parlor structure used a five-sided ridge and common rafters braced with a single purlin that ran on the bottom of the rafters near floor level. The purlin, in turn, was supported by a brace that ran on a diagonal between the floor and the purlin. Another brace ran from the center of the diagonal member to the purlin.

25. For discussions of convenience as a necessary aspect of proper building, see Robert Morris, *Select Architecture,* 2d ed. (London: Robert Sayer, 1757), introduction, n.p.; Enos Hitchcock, *The Farmer's Friend; or the History of Mr. Charles Worthy* (Boston: I Thomas and E. T. Andrews, 1793), 49; Asher Benjamin and Daniel Raynard, *The American Builder's Companion:*

*or a New System of Architecture: Particularly Adapted to the Present Style of Building in the United States of America* (Boston: Etheridge and Bliss, 1806), 67; Stephen W. Johnson, *Rural Economy* (New Brunswick, New York: William Elliot for I. Riley and Co., 1806), 92; Hannah Barnard, *Dialogues on Domestic and Rural Economy* (Dated Pamphlets, American Antiquarian Society, Worcester, Mass., 1820), 13.

26. This description is based on a c. 1878 engraving in Benedict and Tracy, *History of the Town of Sutton, 1704–1876* (Worcester, Mass.: Sanford and Co., 1878), 232.

27. Worcester County Courthouse, Worcester County Probate, Nathaniel Putnam Estate, Series A, Case 48425.

28. Thomas Hubka, *Big House, Little House, Back House, Barn: The Connected Farm Buildings of New England* (Hanover, N.H.: Univ. of New England Press, 1984), 44–52.

29. Moses recorded the purchase of the ten pound, four ounce set kettle in 1807. Set kettles were placed into a brick housing beneath which fires were built. They were used for boiling large quantities of water for such things as laundry and for cooking livestock feed.

30. The dairy room was partitioned off from the rest of the cellar by plastered brick walls, its floor paved with flagstones. Additional storage space was provided between the piers of the main chimney stack foundation, which was fitted with shelving.

CHAPTER

# 4

*Marlene Elizabeth Heck*

# Building Status:
# Pavilioned Dwellings in Virginia

Joseph Carrington Cabell deliberated for months from his snug Williamsburg lodgings before purchasing a small house in January 1808. Hesitant to commit himself to life near "the miserable little village," as he described the James River settlement of Warminster, Virginia, Cabell waffled on his decision. He traded several letters on the matter with his confidant, Isaac Coles, and closed one exchange by observing, "I am determined to be in no hurry, to examine the ground well, and to decide cautiously." The prolonged equivocation prompted a stern response from Coles, who clearly had tired of Cabell's ambivalence. "I would sooner see you fixed any where than remain another year in the midst of so much perplexity, uncertainty and doubt," Coles admonished, explaining, "I am so anxious that you should immediately commence some fixed plan of life. . . . Not only your friends but the world expect this of you—you have been a wanderer long enough." Coles's New Year's Eve

message continued by warning Cabell that he would have no social or political future until he acted decisively: "It is now fit that you should have a home and that you should be the master of it—not a mere Guest among your friends and a stranger in your native state. Until you do this you can have no real weight or influence in society." Such reproof from his closest friend likely stung the politically ambitious Cabell. Coles's reproach succeeded. Joseph Cabell purchased the modest structure, which he renamed Edgewood, and over the next six months he expanded it into an imposing five-part dwelling (fig. 4.1).[1]

Joseph Cabell's construction efforts draw attention to a broader regional pattern of domestic building, one largely overlooked by historians of Virginia's vernacular traditions. A few miles away, Joseph's cousin, the politician Samuel Jordan Cabell, had just completed a similarly extensive remodeling. Samuel, who a few years before had unwillingly

Fig. 4.1. Edgewood, Nelson County, Virginia, in the 1930s. Photo by Frances Benjamin Johnston, courtesy of the Library of Congress.

relinquished his U.S. Senate seat, hired a locally renowned workman to transform his three-room dwelling, Soldier's Joy, into another striking five-part house, enhanced by Venetian doors in the hyphens and an upper-story center bay. As work on the other two structures neared completion, Joseph's physician brother, Dr. George Cabell Jr., took up construction on Bon Aire, his three-part house.[2]

Moreover, the Cabells were not unique in their appropriation of the three- and five-part house form. Just miles from their James River plantations in Virginia's Piedmont region, several houses nearly identical to the Cabells' appeared in the years just before and after their construction campaigns. Benjamin Harris, an Albemarle County planter, erected his tripartite Mountain Grove around 1803. Sometime between 1805 and 1810, Thomas Goodwin radically transformed River Bluff, the one-room, side-passage house he had purchased some sixteen years before, by adding two flanking wings to the original dwelling and moving the entry into the gable end. Wintergreen, located a short distance from River Bluff, was enlarged by Hawes Coleman, probably around 1815. Coleman attached two wings to an existing I-house, creating an awkward

three-part adaptation of the architectural ideas of his neighbors. And, around 1822, Charlottesville merchant and politician Nimrod Bramham built Oak Lawn, a brick dwelling related in form and proportions to Bon Aire and Mountain Grove. In the Virginia counties beyond the Piedmont stand dozens more examples of three- and five-part houses.[3]

Such a concentration of similar houses within a limited area suggests that their builders shared domestic needs, aesthetic ambitions, and a knowledge of regional building practices. Factor in the expensive and cumbersome remodeling some undertook to achieve the distinctive form, and evidence mounts that the multipart form had a sharply defined value to those who constructed it. This essay seeks to explain why a number of early-nineteenth-century Virginians selected this particular dwelling type. Specifically, it addresses the broader architectural tradition of which these houses are part and suggests a new way of assessing them and their builders' intentions. This chapter argues that these builders selected a building type, now known popularly as "Palladian," and adapted it to their building needs. What resulted from this reworking was a regionally created, locally understood building form that students of vernacular practices recognize as pavilion-with-wings or center-block-with-wings house types.

At the study's center stand the three Cabell cousins of Nelson County and their houses. The Cabells' story can be told in detail because they left a collection of winged pavilion houses and an archive of personal papers that documents their lives around the time Edgewood, Soldier's Joy, and Bon Aire were under construction. The evidence left by this group of young Virginians demonstrates the manner in which builders reworked existing architectural models, deliberately simplifying and transforming them to conform to their particular circumstances and domestic demands. By erecting new center-block-with-wings houses or in radically altering existing structures to achieve the multipart configuration, the three

cousins built large dwellings capable of demonstrating their elite status.[4]

## *The Cabells' James River Houses*

Samuel Cabell, the senior member of the trio,
committed the house he had occupied for
twenty-one years to a grand transformation,
making his the first winged-pavilion dwelling in
the family. The newly married Colonel Samuel
Cabell had moved into the original Soldier's Joy
with his wife, Sally Symes Cabell, in the fall of
1785. Samuel's father, Colonel William Cabell
Sr., built Soldier's Joy for the young couple, and
rare construction documents, prepared for a local builder who often worked for the senior
Colonel Cabell, disclose the father's role in the
design of Soldier's Joy. A complete floor plan and
detailed specifications show that Colonel Cabell
Sr. commissioned the construction of a three-
room house (fig. 4.2). As has been shown by Dell
Upton, this house type, which consisted of the
public realm of a hall and dining room (often
separated by a passage) and the private domain

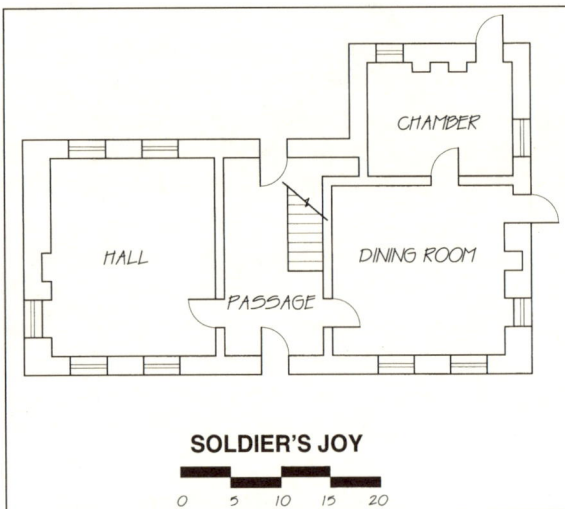

Fig. 4.2. Original Plan of Soldier's Joy. Redrawn by
Susan Halla from contract between Col. William
Cabell Sr. and James Robards, 1784.

of the chamber, was widely built in the region.[5]

By 1806 Samuel and Sally Cabell had out-
grown life in a three-room house. An affable
host, Cabell seemed motivated to remodel, in
part, by the need for additional entertainment
space. His expanded dwelling included a handsomely detailed room, known through family
history as a ballroom, that served as a terminus
for a suite of other highly decorated and finely
furnished public rooms. Perhaps on the recom-
mendation of Thomas Jefferson, his Piedmont
neighbor and political colleague, Cabell hired
Jefferson's workman, James Oldham, to enlarge
and remodel the dwelling. According to
Oldham's correspondence with his famous em-
ployer, he came to the job after Cabell's "many
pressing invitations." Oldham explained to
Jefferson, "I considered it would be as well to
waite [*sic*] on him; he has for a considerable time
expressed a desire for me to build some additions
to his present dwelling." Cabell's eagerness to secure Oldham's services is easily understood. He
had been trained by Jefferson, the country's most
acclaimed amateur architect, and, together with
James Dinsmore and John Neilson, Oldham
formed the triumvirate of master builders who
executed Monticello's great turn-of-the-century
remodeling. Comfortable with such large-scale
renovations, the skilled carpenter added hyphens
and wings to Soldier's Joy, and transformed the
traditionally designed structure into a symmetri-
cally composed, five-part dwelling (fig. 4.3).[6]

Samuel's cousin Joseph was the next to
take up a remodeling project on his newly
purchased property. Abandoned by its original
builder in 1803, Edgewood stood empty a few
miles down the James River from Soldier's Joy.
With the acquisition of Edgewood, Joseph
finally secured the permanent residence that
would be his political base for the next forty-
eight years. Perhaps the long deliberative process had permitted Joseph to think in detail

Fig. 4.3. Soldier's Joy, Nelson County, Virginia. Early-twentieth-century view from a print in collection of current owners. Courtesy of the Virginia Department of Historic Resources, Richmond, Virginia.

about the kind of house he wanted, for after the 1808 purchase, he immediately set out to craft the structure into one more to his liking. Limited finances appear to have dictated the decision to improve an existing house. Restraints on spending also forced Joseph to forgo hiring an experienced workman such as Oldham. Instead, he organized a team of local workmen, masons, and his own slave laborers to expand Edgewood into a five-part dwelling. Cabell wrote modestly of turning the property into a "comfortable box," but the unavoidable problems of working in a remote area with an untrained work force proved constantly aggravating to the impatient builder. Joseph and his wife, Polly Carter Cabell, finally took up residence at the house in the summer of 1808, while the construction continued around them (fig. 4.1).[7]

Just as Joseph settled into Edgewood, a third Cabell began his pavilion-with-wings building campaign. Dr. George Cabell Jr. started construc-

tion on his house, Bon Aire, about 1809 on an adjacent tract west of Joseph's land. Unlike his cousin Samuel or his brother Joseph, who were forced by circumstances to remodel existing structures, George Cabell built an entirely new dwelling. He selected the highest site on his property, a hilltop overlooking the James River, for his three-part dwelling, and directed that its most visible walls be laid in a decorative Flemish bond. George Cabell's few surviving papers do not reveal the name of any workman or builder affiliated with the project, but similarities between Bon Aire and Point of Honor, a nearly identical dwelling constructed in Lynchburg for his relation Dr. George Cabell Sr. suggest the hand of the same workman. George relocated his medical practice from Warminster into one of the two brick dependencies that flanked the house and supplemented his income through the continued cultivation of cash crops on the Bon Air tract (figs. 4.4 and 4.5).[8]

Fig. 4.4. Bon Aire, Nelson County, Virginia, in the 1930s. Photo by Frances Benjamin Johnston, courtesy of the Library of Congress.

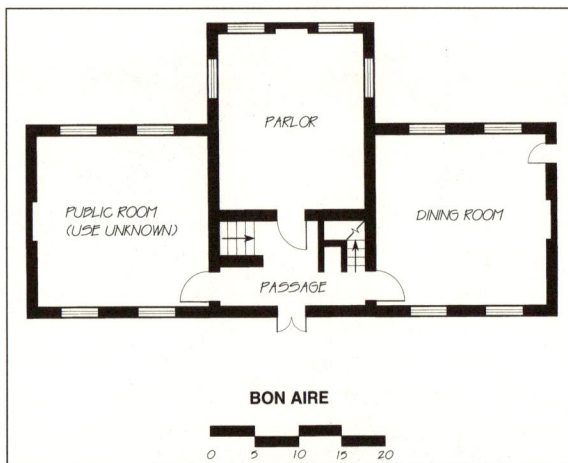

Fig. 4.5. Bon Aire, First-Floor Plan. Drawn by Susan Halla.

In brief, then, these separate building campaigns produced three winged pavilion houses that achieved their final near-identical form through quite different, often painstaking means. When we consider that elite Virginians such as the Cabells had several building types or construction options available to them, it seems curious that all three would have settled on the same form—especially when two of them began with existing structures that represent two distinct building types and the third built new, out of whole cloth. And if mere expansion had been Joseph and Samuel's principal goal, they could have enlarged their dwellings in any number of ways, some far easier and less expensive than the solution they selected. In light of these factors, their decisions appear a deliberate rejection of alternative building types such as the traditional three-room, side-passage, and I-houses—that is, the houses of their neighbors. Indeed, the Cabells' architectural solutions reveal a desire to distinguish themselves from their immediate community and affiliate with other builders of the central-pavilion-and-wings house type.

Certainly the multipart form had a long history of use in the state by the time it was picked up by the Cabells and others. A number of Virginia's eighteenth-century elites had used center-block-with-wings houses as one more marker of their upper-class position and its associated powers and privileges. Some of these builders, like John Tayloe of Mount Airy and George Washington of Mount Vernon, are as well-known to architectural historians as they are to political historians. Others, including John Bannister of Battersea, go unrecognized beyond the state's borders. But all would have been familiar figures to the Cabells, who moved in Virginia's elite social and political circles. The three cousins would have known, as well, the association of these distinguished dwellings with the financial independence and material affluence, political prestige, and leadership status of their owners. Because of their particular social and political circumstances, it seems reasonable to assume the Cabells were drawn to this form, in part, because it had functioned in Virginia for nearly seventy-five years as an architectural shorthand for wealth, political influence, and status. The right type of house, they hoped, would help them attain their own social and political goals.

## The Problem with "Palladian"

For the Cabells and their fellow builders, the "right type of house" meant a winged pavilion dwelling. Without exception, each of the houses under consideration shared this basic configuration. A three-part composition was the minimal acceptable version, and as spatial needs dictated and finances permitted, paired hyphens and terminal wings expanded this basic model into five- and seven-part houses. The center block or pavilion of these houses dominated through its size and elaboration of detail, as it had throughout the whole history of multipart building. Most center pavilions rose a full two stories, but rare one-story versions exist with their preeminence announced by broader dimensions or projecting facades.[9]

Surprisingly, those who wish to study these early-nineteenth-century three- and five-part houses have little relevant scholarship to draw upon. To date, only art and architectural historians have paid much attention to this house type, which they characterize as "Palladian." For them, the adjective identifies an influential domestic building type crafted by the sixteenth-century architect, Andrea Palladio. Published prints of Palladio's villas popularized the distinctive multipart form and aided in its transplantation from the rich agricultural lands surrounding Venice to the European countryside. British builders enthusiastically adopted the form for their country house designs and made Palladianism the ruling style in England during the second quarter of the eighteenth century. Palladian designs crossed the Atlantic in the mid-eighteenth century via various English pattern books, and these printed models informed Virginia's earliest and best-documented Palladian building campaigns, including Mount Airy, Mount Vernon, and Battersea. The form found substantial favor among the state's pre-Revolutionary elite, and, once introduced, the multipart building type entered the Virginia builder's repertoire until its highly ordered configuration fell from favor during the Victorian era.[10]

Early-twentieth-century architect and historian Thomas T. Waterman drew the form's temporal and stylistic boundaries and established the "Palladian" canon in his important 1946 *Mansions of Virginia*. A review of the literature on Virginia ar-

chitecture written after the publication of *Mansions of Virginia* reveals subsequent histories borrowed uncritically from Waterman's work, perpetuating his imprecision and unsubstantiated theories, including an attribution to Thomas Jefferson of several multipart designs. Waterman's chronicle, once set down, became the architectural gospel, unassailed by later revision.[11]

The search by Waterman and his followers for celebrity designers, pattern book authors, and matching decorative elements impeded other explanations for the organization of these houses and their broad reception in the state. Never mind that the built versions, and especially their floor plans, strayed far from the published image; such issues stood beyond their determination to fix the probable design source. Nor did they pause to contemplate *why* Virginians—typically status-conscious Virginians—repeatedly returned to the winged pavilion model. What did this form signify for these builders? Could there have been some symbolic, spatial, or organizational appeal to the three- and five-part house? The appearance of the building type once more in the early nineteenth century, again freshly transformed, raises these questions once more.[12]

To be sure, none of the Cabells ever used the term *Palladian* to describe their building efforts, and their combined substantial libraries lack even a single volume of any eighteenth-century pattern book. If, as three of the region's best-educated and well-traveled builders, they claimed no direct knowledge of Palladio and his published offspring, most likely the same was true of builders of more limited means such as their neighbors, Hawes Coleman and Thomas Goodwin. Clearly, these builders picked up the use of a building type whose remote history they did not know. But they were vastly aware of its *recent and local* history, and they decided it satisfied their complex building needs better than their existing houses or other building options. It is the winged pavilion building type's persistence into the nineteenth century, and its clear independence from Palladio, Jefferson, English pattern book authors, or other notables that suggests its meanings should be found outside of the explanatory models of traditional architectural history.

## The Social Purposes of Pavilioned Dwellings

In the search for architectural sources that informed these early-nineteenth-century houses, the inquiry should begin with the earlier three- and five-part dwellings distributed across the Virginia landscape. The Cabells, Hawes Coleman, and Thomas Goodwin were among the builders who found their models in existing elite buildings, especially those completed in the years just before the Revolution—the ones grandly (and misleadingly) described by Waterman as "Palladio's Roman Country House Style." Over decades of uninterrupted use, these three- and five-part compositions had become familiar features of the Virginia landscape. Those who constructed such houses as Soldier's Joy, Edgewood, Bon Aire, and River Bluff ably and deliberately extracted from the earlier examples those features that suited their social and domestic purposes.

Certainly the construction of these houses signaled, in part, the post-Revolutionary economic recovery experienced by gentry-class Virginians. Renewed trade with Europe, an increase in crop prices, and the resources of inherited wealth funded a building boom at the turn of the nineteenth century. But just as essential to the construction of these dwellings was the desire for an established architectural vocabulary that conveyed one's status. Many Virginians who built three- and five-part dwellings in the early nineteenth century were attempting to communicate their political and social standing—either those on the make like Thomas Goodwin of River Bluff or those, like the Cabells, who sensed a threat to their formerly secure political and social rank. At the time, Virginians could assert authority and confirm ruling class position

in several ways, including marriage into the state's family dynasties. Joseph Cabell's marriage to Polly Carter, stepdaughter of the Williamsburg jurist St. George Tucker and heiress to important Carter family property, was just such a move. Possession of powerful state and federal political offices also indicated status. Accordingly, Samuel Cabell ran for the United States Senate, and Joseph won a seat in the Virginia legislature. The increased prestige of professional life in post-Enlightenment America influenced George Cabell to elect a medical career. And, as it had for scores of Virginians before them, the act of building a substantial dwelling, especially where it stood out in its landscape as exceptional, was an aggressive mark of authority.[13]

For the Cabells the act of house building complemented the distinction they sought in the political and social realms. Samuel, Joseph, and George Cabell, eager to acquire or retain "real weight or influence in society," deliberately constructed or remodeled their houses in the most emphatically elite way they could. By appending various combinations of wings and hyphens to their original structures the Cabells visually and symbolically severed themselves from those Virginians whose resources and architectural knowledge limited them to more customary vernacular dwelling types. Untethered from their local architectural world, the Cabells found themselves among the ranks of other upper-class Virginians who lived in vernacular three- and five-part villas. Possession of such a house seems to have carried such weight, in fact, that Joseph and George Cabell invested their limited funds to this end; Samuel Cabell deliberately sought out a skilled workman well trained in this specific architectural vocabulary. Their domestic building decisions vividly illustrate the pavilion-and-wing form's enduring power in Virginia as a potent cultural sign.[14]

But these builders were *selective* and adopted only certain formal components of the established building type. The modifications, omissions, and additions they made were not the results of imperfect transcriptions, but conscious efforts to create a house type that accommodated their domestic needs, while retaining the features necessary to identify the buildings as part of an elite lineage. Early-nineteenth-century dwellings such as Soldier's Joy, Edgewood, and Bon Aire do not demonstrate an inability to translate fine designs under remote and limited conditions, but were *calculated* further transformations of the previous generation of multipart buildings. We see in Soldier's Joy, Edgewood, and Bon Aire—and in the dozens of other same period three- and five-part houses—a dynamic selection and appropriation, whereby features of the model that fit their requirements and pockets were retained deliberately, and other unnecessary elements were cast off or altered.[15]

The multipart composition was so strongly realized as the most essential feature of the house type that other architectural qualities were sacrificed to achieve it. When Thomas Goodwin transformed his side-passage house, River Bluff, into a three-part dwelling in the early nineteenth century, the original southern gable end became the principal facade. Goodwin cut a door into this elevation to permit entry, but left an upper window— now a very noticeable asymmetrical feature on the facade—unaltered. Far more than notions of order or symmetry, Goodwin sought the all-important form of a central pavilion flanked by lateral wings. All builders who ambitiously aimed to create a high-status improvement, whether they were elites such as the Cabells or would-be elites like Thomas Goodwin, singled out the balanced, dominant center pavilion framed by subordinate wings and hyphens as *the* requisite feature. While compressed, simplified, and reduced in scale from their eighteenth-century antecedents, the hierarchical three- and five-part organization of Soldier's Joy, Edgewood, Bon Aire, and their contemporaries marks them as architectural descendants of Mount Airy and Battersea. But, more instructive, the final form of these dwellings demonstrates a *local* invention or manipulation of a long-established building tradition.

Only this compositional integrity remained consistent from building to building. For every other physical feature, Virginia's early-nineteenth-century multipart house builders showed a willingness to vary, modify, diminish, or omit. Building materials might be the finest of Flemish-bond bricks, as at Bon Aire, or unexceptional weatherboards, as at Wintergreen. Venetian openings at Soldier's Joy amplified the stylish, power-seeking message of Samuel Cabell's five-part dwelling, but most other houses did not exhibit such self-conscious or self-referential markers. Interior ornament ran the range from the extraordinary carvings at Soldier's Joy to the extraordinarily plain surrounds at Hobson's Choice. James Oldham's contribution may be the sole example where architectural publications were consulted to guide in the carving of an order or other detail. A significant number of these houses, perhaps even the majority, share the same floor plan. As most are three-part examples, the center pavilion holds a lateral passage with a parlor placed at its rear. Single rooms dedicated to public use flank the pavilion. But Samuel Cabell kept his original three-room house, and Hawes Coleman retained his I-house plan. In scale and dimensions, variations abound. And while three-part houses were most common, many erected sprawling five-part vernacular villas.

## The Domestic Organization of Pavilioned Dwellings

Certainly the three- and five-part form's symbolic power accounts in large measure for its great appeal, but alteration of existing houses such as Soldier's Joy, Edgewood, and River Bluff highlights two other features that ensured the pavilion-with-wings house type's continued use: its flexibility as an architectural model and its suitability to the routines of domestic life. The multipart form's simple arrangement of a dominant element flanked by secondary elements was architecturally flexible enough to transform several traditional house types, including three-room, side-passage, and I-house plans, into symmetrical winged pavilion dwellings. Soldier's Joy and River Bluff illustrate the conversion of a three-room and side-passage house into the core of the composition, while Joseph Cabell turned the unknown plan of the original Edgewood into the nucleus of his remodeled dwelling. One other attribute recommended the use of the three- and five-part model in these projects: the winged pavilion dwelling also honored existing spatial relationships between private and public domains that had been resolved in houses great and modest during the eighteenth century. Such flexibility and spatial coherence were essential because at the same time that they erected these tradition-inflected declarations of their authority, the Cabells adapted the center-block-with-wings house type to the practical considerations of early-nineteenth-century plantation life.[16]

The three cousins created their houses as they began to withdraw from a world that no longer bestowed the deference and respect they thought rightfully theirs. In the language of the nineteenth century, their houses became "asylums," places of retreat and repair from a public realm perceived as increasingly disordered and indifferent to social rules and rank. But houses could become protective domains only if two conditions were met. First, they had to permit customary activities to continue without disruption. By the third quarter of the eighteenth century Virginia's elite builders had distilled their domestic routines into four rooms—passage, dining room, hall, and chamber. Early-nineteenth-century Virginians like the Cabells inherited these ideas about the naming, use, and specialization of rooms from the state's previous generations of builders. Like their parents and grandparents before them, Virginia's early-nineteenth-century gentry required specific rooms for dining, for entertaining family and close friends, and for private conversations and intimate exchanges. In their newly fashioned dwellings, these were the essential domains of the Cabells' houses, and any

architectural solution they elected had to incorporate, at minimum, these four specific rooms.[17]

Yet, by the early nineteenth century, Samuel and Joseph Cabell's material possessions increased beyond what could be contained in smaller quarters and their social lives grew more complex, requiring an attendant change in their domestic sphere. Probate inventories and tax records disclose the accumulation of substantial libraries, mahogany furnishings, musical instruments, collections of plate, china, and crystal, while family correspondence details the constant stream of visitors that demanded their hospitality and drew down their pantries. Such great material assembly and expanded social responsibilities strained the dimensions and use of their original quarters. The two builders needed a house type that filled a second condition by providing new rooms for storage and display, polite entertainment and musical performance, and guest lodgings. Samuel and Joseph Cabell found such domestic needs could be folded into the hyphens and wings that they attached to each end of their existing homeplaces.[18]

And what of the Cabells' wariness about the world beyond their houses and their desire to create a secure haven closed to everyone but the invited? These concerns translated into architectural decisions that guaranteed the desired separation from all but family and select society. Most builders are reluctant to alter the *interior organization* of their dwellings, as such changes transform a social landscape that has been carefully contrived, usually over a long period. For the Cabell cousins, this meant the demarcation of house interiors into public and private zones, so carefully worked out by Virginians during the eighteenth century, had to remain intact. While the Cabells' social needs now demanded new and additional quarters, they still required a system of segregation that distinguished between open and restricted domains. Samuel and Joseph Cabell would have rejected any architectural solution that disrupted spatial patterns that maintained social command and the boundaries of public and private spheres. The Cabells elected the winged pavilion model because it allowed them to preserve social and spatial relationships even as they reconfigured familiar spaces and added new rooms.[19]

Virginia builders had long favored a center passage as an effective means of controlling admittance and orchestrating domestic activity. For example, Bon Aire's lateral passage served to mediate movement between rooms or to block one's entry altogether, a function analogous to that performed by the center passages at Soldier's Joy and Edgewood. From the lateral passage at Bon Aire, one had direct access only to other public rooms, a circulation pattern similar to those at Soldier's Joy and Edgewood. Such spatial arrangements facilitated the requisite separation of public and private spheres. At Bon Aire, a smaller, three-part dwelling, public rooms occupy the entire ground level, while chambers are found in the upper story of the center block and in the half story over the wings.[20]

At Soldier's Joy (and likely also at Edgewood), a five-part dwelling, the center passage essentially separated the public sphere of parlor and ballroom, and the semi-private/private domain of dining room and chambers (figs. 4.2 and 4.6). The original floor plan, historic photographs, and standing structure that document the remodeling and enlargement of Soldier's Joy also demonstrate how the pavilion-with-wings configuration easily accommodated the elaboration of both public and private space without disrupting previous arrangements. A hierarchy of decorative features confirms this first-floor division into two separate domains. The parlor, the hyphen room, and the ballroom were handsomely appointed with carved cornices, molded chair rails, and stylish Federal mantels. Ornament declines in degree and quality at the passage and into the dining room; architectural features are noticeably absent from the more sparsely detailed private quarters beyond the dining room. The simple lateral expansion extended the two axes of activity. Rooms for assembly and entertaining were now distributed along the public axis, while additional family quarters opened on the other side of the passage, in the private domain.[21]

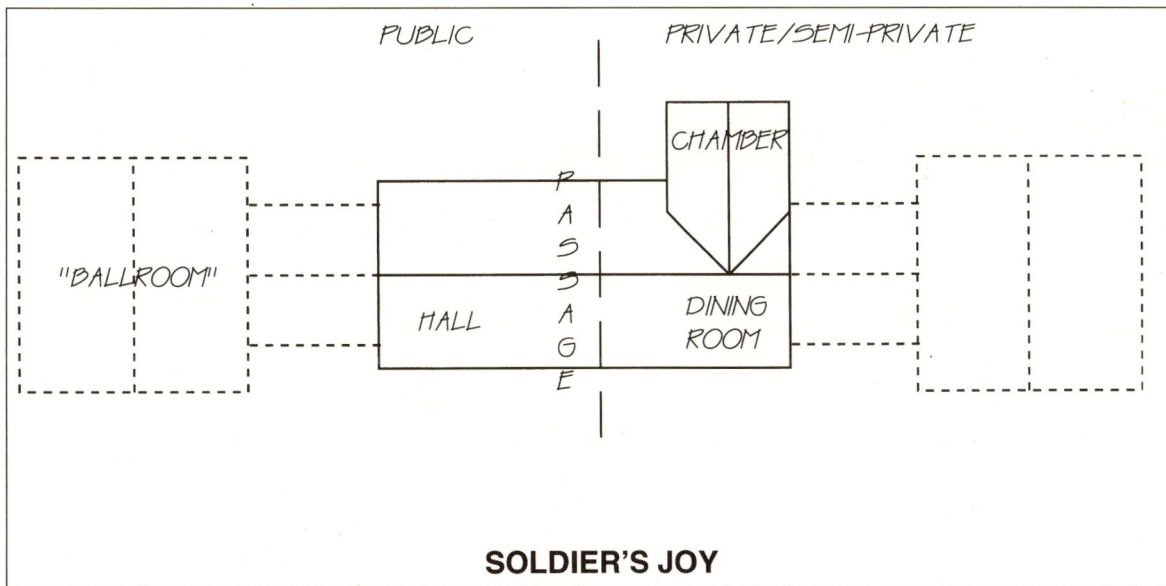

Fig. 4.6. Soldier's Joy, Plan of First Floor. This plan shows the division of public and private spheres. Drawn by Susan Halla.

## *Implications*

The Cabell houses demonstrate that Virginia's winged pavilion tradition continued well into the nineteenth century. This dwelling type endured because it had become a powerful social marker and a flexible domestic model. Its distinctive appearance amplified and clarified social rank to a local culture in need of such defining emblems. Most provocatively, the model was easily adapted to honor existing domestic relationships and sufficiently flexible to accommodate additional spatial demands. The simple exteriors and expanded interiors of these houses are telling statements of the ways in which builders such as the Cabells resolved changes in both their public and private lives.

The Virginia story has implications, too, for the study of nineteenth-century three- and five-part houses constructed elsewhere. Builders left the state, taking the distinctive building type far from the site of its eighteenth- and nineteenth-century transformations in the state's Tidewater and Piedmont regions. Today one may follow a trail that leads out of the Virginia Piedmont, around the area of the Cabell houses, into North Carolina. Once across the North Carolina border, the architectural path splits in two and continues southward. By the 1820s, winged pavilion dwellings could be found from Georgia to Mississippi. In 1843 Hervey George built his tripartite dwelling at Chimney Rock Farm in Tazewell County, in far southwestern Virginia. George's handsome brick house marks the last of the Virginia examples. By this date the form had left the state on a course toward newly settled western lands. While this westward spread of three- and five-part houses has not yet been chronicled, in time the form turned up in Ohio, Indiana, Kentucky, and at least as far as Missouri.[22]

The winged pavilion form appealed not only to vernacular builders, but also to the country's first architects who earned their living from professional practice. Famed architect Benjamin Henry Latrobe found the spare, pared-down three- and five-part forms ideal for his Neoclassical tastes when he provided multipart proposals for the 1798 Harvie-Gamble House and the 1807 Benjamin James Harris House, both in Richmond, the 1801 Edward Shippen Burd House in Philadelphia, and the 1813 expansion of Ashland, Henry Clay's Lexington dwelling. While best known for his Gothic Revival country houses, Andrew Jackson Davis supplied his clients with a varied collection of designs, including inventive Egyptian Revival public buildings and more sedate three-part houses. The uninterrupted use of these designs into the mid-nineteenth century can be explained, in part, by the expansion of the architectural press. Widely published pattern book authors such as Minard Lefever kept the winged pavilion form before the designing public during the Greek Revival period. But the continued construction of three- and five-part dwellings suggests that the form proved adaptable to both domestic needs and stylish ideals, as center pavilions became temple fronts and flanking wings recessed to emphasize the grandeur of the pedimented and columned principal facade.[23]

Historians of America's pavilion-with-wings tradition can now move beyond concern for a building's pedigree, the presence or absence of identifiable architects, or the degree to which a dwelling adheres to fashionable published models. Soldier's Joy, Edgewood, and Bon Aire enable us to better understand the reasons American builders repeatedly selected and transformed the three- and five-part forms some half century after their first memorable appearance in the Virginia Tidewater. They are but three of the many winged pavilion dwellings that show the active role of architectural form in the mediation of social change.

## Notes

I wish to thank Elizabeth Cromley, Carter Hudgins, and anonymous readers for their instructive comments on earlier versions of this chapter. Karen Endicott, as always, proved ever generous and wonderfully perceptive. Susan Halla's graphic skills are gratefully acknowledged. Special thanks are given to Kevin Reinhart for patient late-night editing and bountiful trans-Atlantic support.

1. Isaac Coles to Joseph C. Cabell, Dec. 31, 1807, Cabell Family Papers. The correspondence between Joseph C. Cabell and Isaac Coles is found in the Cabell Family Papers, Alderman Library, Univ. of Virginia (hereafter referred to as Cabell Family Papers, UVa).

2. Samuel Cabell's political loss to Thomas Mann Randolph, Thomas Jefferson's son-in-law, is discussed in Dumas Malone, *Jefferson the President: First Term, 1801–1803* (Boston: Little, Brown, 1970), 408–9.

3. Information on the houses discussed in this essay is contained in the survey files of the Virginia Department of Historic Resources, Richmond.

4. Public records and family papers reveal the Cabells' constant engagement with architectural projects. Between 1750 and 1815 family members built or remodeled as many as eleven significant dwellings, in addition to their more routine involvement with the construction of plantation outbuildings and important local public buildings. Information on the Cabell family houses is distributed among family papers at Alderman Library, Univ. of Virginia, Swem Library at the College of William and Mary, the Virginia Historical Society, and the Library of Virginia. The most complete record of the family's history is found in Alexander Brown, *The Cabells and Their Kin* (Richmond, Va.: Garrett and Masie, 1939).

5. British forces captured Samuel Cabell in South Carolina, and he spent eighteen months as a prisoner of war near Charleston. The name he gave his dwelling, also the title of a popular Revolutionary War ballad, no doubt refers to its owner's pleasure at resuming life at his new James River plantation. Dell Upton, "Vernacular Domestic Architecture in Eighteenth-Century Virginia," *Winterthur Portfolio* 17 (2/3) (Summer–Autumn 1982): 95–119.

6. James Oldham to Thomas Jefferson, Mar. 9, 1806, Massachusetts Historical Society Papers (microfilm), Alderman Library, Univ. of Virginia. Because the wings and west hyphen at Soldier's Joy were demolished in the 1920s, a floor plan of the expanded dwelling is unavailable. For an extensive chronicle of Jefferson's workmen, including James Oldham, see Richard Charles Cote, "The Architectural Workmen of Thomas Jefferson in Virginia," 2 vols. (Ph.D. diss., Boston Univ., 1986). A brief sketch of Jefferson's many workmen is provided in K. Edward Lay, "Charlottesville's Architectural Legacy," *Magazine of Albemarle County History* 46 (May 1988): 28–95.

7. National Register of Historic Places nomination for Edgewood (Nelson County), files of the Virginia Division of Historic Landmarks, Richmond; Cabell Family Papers, UVa. Edgewood burned in the 1950s before its floor plan could be documented. The house's general form and dimensions were recovered from fire insurance policies.

8. National Register of Historic Places nomination for Bon Aire (Nelson County), files of the Virginia Division of Historic Landmarks, Richmond; Cabell Family Papers, UVa. Dr. George Cabell Jr. studied medicine with the senior Dr. George Cabell in Lynchburg during the period Point of Honor was under construction.

9. For an example of the uncommon single-story winged pavilion house type, see the National Register of Historic Places nomination for Hobson's Choice (Brunswick County), files of the Virginia Division of Historic Landmarks, Richmond.

10. James Ackerman, *The Villa: Form and Ideology of Country Houses* (Princeton: Princeton Univ. Press, 1990), especially chaps. 4, 6, and 8. For a recently published discussion of the movement of the Palladian villa type from the Veneto to Europe and the American colonies, see Robert Tavernor, *Palladio and Palladianism* (New York: Thames and Hudson, 1991).

11. Thomas T. Waterman, *Mansions of Virginia, 1706–1776* (Chapel Hill: Univ. of North Carolina Press, 1946). Waterman principally was concerned with identifying associated architects, tracing details and forms through English pattern books, and describing stylistic details. The Center for Palladian Studies has sponsored a sustained examination of Palladianism, including many Virginia examples, in its trio of conference publications, *Building By the Book 1* (Charlottesville: Univ. Press of Virginia, 1984), *Building By the Book 2* (Charlottesville: Univ. Press of Virginia, 1986), and *Building By the Book 3* (Charlottesville: Univ. Press of Virginia, 1990). For examples of this, see Calder Loth, "Palladio in Southside Virginia: Brandon and Battersea," and William M. S. Rasmussen, "Palladio in Tidewater

Virginia: Mount Airy and Blandfield," both in *Building By the Book 1*. Mills Lane briefly discusses a few examples of winged pavilion houses in his *The Architecture of the Old South: Virginia* (Savannah: Beehive Press, 1989), 132–37, but his text is descriptive rather than analytical and follows Waterman's example in its concern for identifying pertinent pattern books and affiliated designers. See also Frederick Doveton Nichols, "Palladio in America" in *Palladio in America* (Milan: Electra Editrice, 1976), 101–16; and Charles E. Brownell, "Laying the Groundwork: The Classical Tradition and Virginia Architecture, 1770–1870," in *Making of Virginia Architecture* (Richmond: Virginia Museum of Fine Arts, 1992), 36–56.

12. See Loth, *Building By the Book 1,* 19: "Credit for popularizing the Morris versions of Palladian schemes in Virginia, and making them a design source for houses spread from tidewater to the mountains, and from the piedmont down into North Carolina and even Georgia, belongs, it would seem, largely to Thomas Jefferson." The discussion of Virginia's Palladian tradition in Tavernor's *Palladio and Palladianism* offers no fresh or original observations. Rather, Tavernor's explanation depends on the familiar references to Jefferson-dominated Palladianism. He writes, "Parallel to the pressing demands of state office, he [Jefferson] succeeded in planting the seeds of Roman classicism in America which went beyond the simple empiricism of pattern-book Palladianism" (*Palladio and Palladianism,* 189). Architectural historian Edward Chappell observed, "The western progress of Palladianism from Vicenza to Richmond County has received its full share of textbook pages, leaving us with a few mildly convincing examples and a not very useful view of society." Edward Chappell, "Looking at Buildings," *Fresh Advices* (Williamsburg, Va.: Colonial Williamsburg, 1984), i. Also see Dell Upton's observations on Palladianism as a "limiting stereotype" in most accounts of Virginia's architectural past in "New Views of the Virginia Landscape," *Virginia Magazine of History and Biography* 96 (4) (Oct. 1988): 426–27.

13. A more detailed discussion of these contributing factors can be found in Marlene Elizabeth Heck, "Palladian Architecture and Social Change in Post-Revolutionary Virginia," (Ph.D. diss., Univ. of Pennsylvania, 1988), 157–216; 261–99.

14. Virginia's "Palladian" tradition and its association with the state's elites are summarized in ibid., 236–83.

15. Discussion of a similar phase of winged pavilion house building in Alabama described the three-part dwelling Belle Mont (c. 1828) as a "'primitive' Alabama interpretation of Villa Cornaro," a not uncommon analysis of these modest vernacular dwellings. Louise Joyner, "Palladio in Alabama: An Architectural Legacy," *Preservation Report* (Sept./Oct. 1991): 4.

16. Upton discusses the evolution of spatial relationships in "Vernacular Domestic Architecture in Eighteenth-Century Virginia."

17. Cary Carson and Lorena Walsh, "The Material Life of the Early American Housewife," paper presented at the Philadelphia Center for Early American Studies, Dec. 1981; Upton, "Vernacular Domestic Architecture in Eighteenth-Century Virginia"; Mark R. Wenger, "The Central Passage in Virginia: Evolution of an Eighteenth-Century Living Space," in *Perspectives in Vernacular Architecture, II,* ed. Camille Wells (Columbia: Univ. of Missouri Press, 1986), 137–49; and Mark R. Wenger, "The Dining Room in Early Virginia," in *Perspectives in Vernacular Architecture, III,* ed. Thomas Carter and Bernard L. Herman (Columbia: Univ. of Missouri Press, 1989), 149–59.

18. A fifteen-page probate inventory made in 1819 records Samuel Cabell's impressive collection of personal possessions. See inventory for Samuel Cabell of Soldier's Joy, Nelson County Will Book C, Library of Virginia. The countywide assessment of personal property taken in 1815 revealed Cabell family members owned the largest and most valuable houses in the county, as well as the greatest number, widest variety, and highest quality of furnishings. See Nelson County Personal Property Tax Records, 1815, Library of Virginia. The range of fashionable goods found at Soldier's Joy, Edgewood, and Bon Aire and their social use is discussed in Marlene Elizabeth Heck, "Appearance and Effect Is Everything: The James River Houses of Samuel, Joseph and George Cabell," *The American Home: Material Culture, Domestic Space and Family Life* (New York: W. W. Norton, forthcoming). Joseph Cabell frequently mentioned visits of family and friends in his correspondence. See the Cabell Family Papers, UVa.

19. See, for example, Henry Glassie, "Eighteenth-Century Cultural Process in Delaware Valley Folk Building," *Winterthur Portfolio* 7 (1972): 43. For a thoughtful example of public/private divisions, see Orlando Ridout V's instructive analysis of the division of John Tayloe's country and city residences into public

and private "zones of activity" in his *Building the Octagon* (Washington, D.C.: American Institute of Architects Press, 1989).

20. The development and use of passages has been charted by Fraser D. Neiman, "Domestic Architecture at the Clifts Plantation: The Social Context of Early Virginia Building," *Northern Neck of Virginia Historical Magazine* 28 (Dec. 1978): 3096–3128; Upton, "Vernacular Domestic Architecture in Eighteenth-Century Virginia," 98–107; and Wenger, "The Central Passage in Virginia," 137–49.

21. A discussion of interior finish as a key to room use and hierarchy can be found in Chappell, "Looking at Buildings," and Ridout, *Building the Octagon.*

22. Catherine W. Bishir documents these early-nineteenth-century houses in her exemplary study, *North Carolina Architecture* (Chapel Hill: Univ. of North Carolina Press, 1990). For examples of winged pavilion houses in the southern states see Mills Lane, *Architecture of the Old South: North Carolina* (New York: Abbeville Press, 1985); Mills Lane, *Architecture of the Old South: Georgia* (New York: Abbeville Press, 1986); Mills Lane, *Architecture of the Old South: Mississippi and Alabama* (New York: Abbeville Press, 1989); Mills Lane, *Architecture of the Old South: South Carolina* (New York: Abbeville Press, 1990); Mills Lane, *Architecture of the Old South: Louisiana* (New York: Abbeville Press, 1990); and Joyner, "Palladio in Alabama." For discussion of Chimney Rock Farm, see the National Register of Historic Places nomination for Chimney Rock Farm/The Willows (Tazewell County), files of the Virginia Division of Historic Resources, Richmond. Examples of winged pavilion houses in Ohio, Indiana, and Kentucky are found in Walter C. Kidney, *Historic Buildings of Ohio* (Pittsburgh, Pa.: Ober Park Associates, 1972); Richard N. Campen, *Architecture of the Western Reserve, 1800–1900* (Cleveland: Press of Case Western Reserve Univ., 1971); Thomas M. Slade, *Historic American Buildings Survey in Indiana* (Bloomington: Indiana Univ. Press, 1983; Rexford Newcomb, *Architecture in Old Kentucky* (Urbana: Univ. of Illinois Press, 1953); Clay Lancaster, *Antebellum Architecture of Kentucky* (Lexington: Univ. Press of Kentucky, 1991). Isaac Meason provides an example of a Virginian who transported the pavilion-with-wings form when he moved westward. Meason left Virginia for southwestern Pennsylvania, where he lived a prosperous life as an ironmaster. In 1802 he built a large five-part "Palladian" house.

23. Benjamin Henry Latrobe's domestic projects are discussed and described in George Tatum, *Penn's Great Town: 250 Years of Philadelphia Architecture Illustrated in Prints and Drawings* (Philadelphia: Univ. of Pennsylvania Press, 1961); Talbot Hamlin, *Benjamin Henry Latrobe* (New York: Oxford Univ. Press, 1955); Brownell, et al., *Making of Virginia Architecture*; and Lancaster, *Antebellum Architecture of Kentucky.* For Davis, see Amelia Peck, ed., *Andrew Jackson Davis, American Architect 1803–1892* (New York: Rizzoli, 1992). For examples of winged pavilion house designs published by Minard Lefever, see his *Modern Builder's Guide* (New York, 1833), frontispiece, "Design for a Country Villa" or his *Modern Practice of Staircase and Hand-Rail Construction* (New York, 1838), plate 3, "Perspective View of a Design for a Country Residence."

Monique Bourque

# "The Peculiar Characteristic of Christian Communities": The County Almshouses of the Delaware Valley, 1790–1860

The almshouses of Philadelphia's satellite counties were illustrations of their creators' ambivalence about industrial and commercial progress, about the proper form of a self-sufficient American society, and about the poor themselves.[1] This was the central issue at the heart of the planning and construction of all nineteenth-century institutions: planners and administrators struggled to erect buildings that would provide adequate housing for their inmates in a reasonably economical fashion, while doing justice to themselves and to their charitable intentions. Why were the county almshouses so different from one another in layout when enabling legislation, rules and regulations for operation, and administrative attitudes toward the poor were so similar throughout the region? Variation in physical appearance and arrangement of functions within these institutions reflect individual communities influenced by available funds and the personalities of those involved in planning and construction.[2]

Historians have disagreed about whether the construction of poorhouses was the result of a shift in attitudes toward the poor as communities changed in the wake of economic development in the early republic. The adoption of institutional solutions for social problems has been presented as a decision to adopt punitive measures in the care of the poor, a new set of controls over the movements of individual paupers, and an increasingly rigid set of ideas about who was entitled to relief.[3] David Rothman has associated the construction of numbers of American almshouses with the benevolent movements of the 1830s and has attributed public enthusiasm for institutions as part of a larger commitment to social reform; by the mid-1840s, this commitment had become caretaking, as administrators recognized their powerlessness in the face of profound social change.[4] In the Delaware Valley, the first "boom" in almshouse building occurred sooner, between 1790 and 1820, and may more properly be associated with the emphasis of a young republic on self-sufficiency and Christian duty.[5]

Closer attention also suggests that administrators may not have seen their institutions as failures. Members of a committee of the Board of Trustees of the Poor for Gloucester County, New Jersey, congratulated the county almshouse in 1830, saying:

> Your Committee after viewing the house, and observing the apparent contentment of its Inhabitants; as well as the several apartments; and conveniences, so well adapted to the situation of the family, are induced to state that it is the peculiar characteristic of Christian communities; denoting an extensive advancement in the refinement of Civilization, when such Asylums are established in order to meliorate the Condition of the Poor and afflicted; where every necessary care and attention are readily administered to them: where the sick and diseased, either in body or mind, meet with Christian Sympathy, and suitable medical attendance.[6]

In addition to providing for all of the physical needs of the institution's "family" of inmates, the almshouse provided an uplifting moral environment in the form of "Christian Sympathy."[7] When visitors toured the region's almshouses to see the "wretched humanity collected there . . . all humanely cared for,"[8] they recognized these and other public institutions as "so many schools in which the man of flint is taught to pity, to feel; the moralist to reflect; the proud humility; the wicked repentance. All may receive lessons of instruction on the vicissitudes, frailties, sufferings, degeneracies & abasements to which humanity is subject and from which we have patents of exemption."[9]

The buildings' exteriors provided the same encouragement for the viewer to regard the institution as a moral example. When Sarah Holsworth embroidered the recently constructed Lancaster County Almshouse on her sampler in 1799, the

text asked for the intervention of the Savior so that she and her schoolmates "May Love thee great and small" (fig. 5.1). Public buildings, such as poorhouses and penitentiaries, appeared on the physical landscape as attempts to respond to social problems more effectively and on a larger scale; they appeared on samplers and dessert plates because they helped communities to define themselves as compassionate in the face of economic and social change.[10] Whether or not the inmates emerged from their institution as productive members of society, the institution itself stood as a monument to the generosity of the community and to "an extensive advancement in the refinement of civilization."[11]

The almshouses of the Delaware Valley were an important part of both the social and the physical landscape in the county seats where they were located. They were large structures housing anywhere

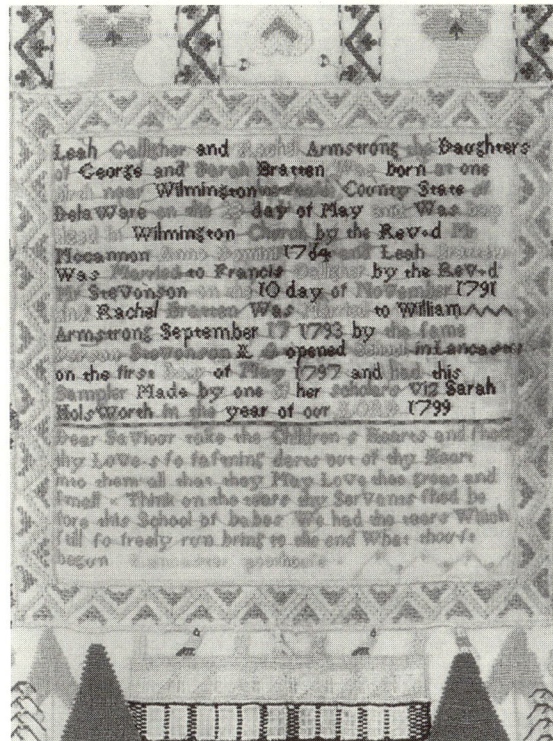

Fig. 5.1 Sampler by Sarah Holsworth, 1799. Courtesy, Winterthur Museum.

from 50 to 250 inmates, surrounded by extensive fields and outbuildings. In addition to serving as places of refuge for the unfortunate in an unstable local economy, they were an important source of contracts for local business. As employers of many local artisans and unskilled laborers, local Overseers of the Poor also helped to determine which of the working poor could avoid entering the institution.

Floor plans and other representations of almshouse structures, and surviving documents from their planning and design, suggest that for early-nineteenth-century almshouses the process of design and construction differed little from that of other public buildings of the period. These records indicate that the contractors most directly responsible for planning and construction gave first priority to providing for the physical functions that took place within the buildings and, second, to what the exterior would say to the community about those functions.

The physical appearance of institutions thus figured largely in ongoing discussions of the administration of relief and in evaluation of the community's responsibility to provide for its poor. Almshouse exteriors provided the public with solid evidence of the efficacy of their good intentions.[12] The simplicity of their exteriors both reassured the community that its money was not frivolously spent and spoke to emerging tastes in antebellum American architecture (fig. 5.2). A clean and plain physical environment and a regular regimen of work were the two most important components of administrators' programs for shaping not merely the behavior but also the character of the poor: together, these primary features of institutional life would both discourage the shiftless from taking up permanent residence in the almshouse and inculcate the poor with the principles of republican conduct: the most important of these principles was the conviction that work was a means to self-improvement and to economic and social advancement.

Boards of guardians and committees in charge of coordinating almshouse design and construction vacillated between trying to keep costs down and adding essentially decorative features, such as cupolas, which were common to other public buildings. The often imposing exteriors enclosed plain—and occasionally cramped and unhealthy—living quarters. Intended to impress the paupers with the gravity of their situation, the interiors in particular played an important part in administrators' attempts to shape the behavior of the poor.[13] Interiors were sparsely furnished, and paupers were seldom allowed to bring personal belongings into the institution. Administrators specified high-quality materials for new construction and described inmates as a "family," even as they cautioned that the paupers' diet should not be so good as to "operate as an inducement for others to envy the condition of a pauper"[14] and noted that the "family" was "composed of persons indiscriminately brought together from the lower classes of society where former habits have not been much given to cleanliness."[15]

The persistent metaphor of the inmates as a family and the essential character of the almshouse as domestic, and therefore fundamentally different from other sorts of public institutions, took physical shape in the works of folk painters like Charles Hofmann and Lewis Miller. While Hofmann's paintings of Pennsylvania almshouses are well known for their representations of these institutions as sun-drenched, busy, and bucolic in tone, Miller's painting of the "new" York County, Pennsylvania, jail and the almshouse, c. 1854, makes an explicit contrast between almshouses and other public buildings.[16] The stark, fortresslike facade of the jail contrasts sharply with the front of the almshouse, which features three entrances from a piazza ornamented with columns, numerous windows, and a number of people (including children) going about their daily business around the building, while a train steams past in the center background (fig. 5.3).[17]

Fig. 5.2. Chester County Home, c. 1800. Artist unknown. Courtesy of the Chester County Historical Society.

Fig. 5.3. York County Jail and Almshouse, c. 1854. Drawn by Lewis Miller. Courtesy of the Historical Society of York County, Pennsylvania.

The balance between economy and generosity was neatly expressed by architect Robert Mills in the letter accompanying his plan for the Baltimore almshouse. He emphasized the importance of adequate air and light in the workrooms and of "endeavoring to do away with the idea of exhibiting this institution in the gloom of a prison" and insisted that "cheerfulness and an air of freedom should be strongly marked on the face of this building." At the same time he reassured the Trustees of the Poor that "simplicity and economy" had been vital considerations in his design, as "beauty is founded upon order . . . and Convenience and utility constituent parts."[18] An 1854 observer echoed Mills's sentiments in his commentary on the recently constructed second Chester County almshouse, noting that it was a "plain, substantial, and commodious building, imposing from its size and the fine position it will occupy, but without unnecessary ornament."[19]

The importance of utility as a component of good looks had become, by the mid-nineteenth century, a policy statement for the construction of public institutions in general in the Delaware Valley and was advocated in some quarters as a proper guide for the construction of private residences as well. In public institutions, excessive decoration was seen as a waste of taxpayers' money just as surely as overfeeding the inmates would be. "Expend not one dollar on tasteful architectural decoration," Dorothea Dix advised Pennsylvania legislators, "Let nothing be for ornament, but every thing for use. Choose your location where the most good can be accomplished effectually, at the least cost. Let economy only not degenerate into meanness. Every dollar indiscreetly applied, is a robbery of the poor and needy, and adds a darker shade to the vice of extravagance in misappropriation of the public funds."[20]

Defending the directors of the poorhouse against rumors of planned extravagance in the construction of a second Delaware County almshouse, a correspondent detailed both the sepa-

ration of the sexes in the new structure and its plainness of appearance, indicating that the structure was well-planned and not wasteful of public funds. The buildings would be "plain pointed stone work," and the house would be "furnished as plain as possible, as economically as will answer; as for the ornamenting with FOREIGN TREES and shrubbery, that has not been mentioned or thought of by the Directors."[21]

Distinction between areas of the buildings in regard to finishing details was not simply a matter of contrasting interior and exterior spaces. Construction records also indicate a clear distinction between public and private spaces. In the specifications for Gloucester County's second almshouse, finishing details were more ornate in areas intended to be viewed by visitors: in the wings, the doors on the first floor were to be "moulded both sides," those on the second floor "moulded inside," and those on the third floor (the most likely location for sleeping chambers) were to be plain. While the main stairs were "to be neatly and substantially put up, $1\frac{1}{4}$ yellow pine nooseing and cove step, 1 inch risers, 6 in. newell, 4 in. moulded rail, 2 in. moulded baluster, all of best quality of ash," and the stairs to the observatory would have a door, the specifications dictated that "all of the other stairs plain, yellow pine steps and 1 inch risers, step mearly rounded on front edge." "White enamelled registers" would conduct heat in the center building, where most administrative functions were housed, while "all others" would be "Japan."[22] The contrast between plainer and more ornate spaces was, of course, a matter of who would use these spaces. The rooms for inmates were plainer in construction and presumably barer of ornament than the steward's private apartments or the meeting rooms for the overseers.[23] Dorothea Dix described the interiors of the almshouses she visited in Pennsylvania and New Jersey as whitewashed and sparsely furnished. She noted approvingly in her 1845 survey that comfortable furnishings, "especially with beds and bed clothing," were a "creditable distinction of nearly every poorhouse in Pennsylvania, including also general cleanliness."[24]

In the Delaware Valley, communities had turned to county-funded institutions beginning in the 1790s. All of the county almshouses in the Delaware Valley expanded between 1820 and 1860, with additions or rebuilding of main structures. Earlier almshouses resembled private residences, because they were pre-existing houses that had been taken over and sometimes added onto for the purpose of housing additional paupers. When New Castle County moved to a county system, the county Overseers of the Poor purchased a residence already used as an almshouse for the poor of Christiana Hundred, and planned an addition for the extra paupers they expected to receive into the house. Communities constructed new buildings when the relief system changed to one based on counties rather than townships or hundreds, when a building burned, or when shifting county boundaries or the creation of a new county left another without an almshouse.[25] When overseers rebuilt or extensively remodeled the region's almshouses, the new structures were not merely larger; they were also equipped with improved machinery and equipment for heating, cooking, and sanitation. When new buildings were especially constructed for the purpose of housing the poor, they invariably were planned and constructed as large-scale public buildings.[26]

The county almshouses of the Delaware Valley were most often located on the outskirts of towns or even, as was the case with the Burlington county almshouse, several miles from the nearest village of any size.[27] While the almshouses in the larger market towns, such as Lancaster, or small cities, such as Wilmington, were originally constructed on the outskirts of these towns at the end of the eighteenth century, they were surrounded by the urban areas as the cities grew.[28] In some communities anti-almshouse sentiment almost certainly played a role in the decision as to the institution's location. The bucolic setting for these institutions was primarily a result of decisions to operate farms in conjunction with almshouses. Administrators assumed that an agrarian environment would exercise a benevolent effect on the health, and perhaps the habits, of poorhouse inmates by removing them to an environment relatively free of urban temptations such as taverns. The counties maintained almshouse farms of anywhere from less than a hundred acres, as in Lancaster, to more than three hundred acres, as in the case of Burlington County, New Jersey, and in some poorhouses the inmates raised much of their own food.[29]

Architects became increasingly prominent in the business of construction in antebellum America, particularly in urban areas, such as Philadelphia, and with regard to the construction of public buildings. Public building projects, including almshouse construction, helped to promote antebellum changes in building practice, particularly an increasing split between professional contractors, who specialized in planning and coordinating construction, and professional architects, who were most concerned with designing buildings.[30] At the same time, the planning and construction of individual institutions reflected the fluidity that still existed in notions of architectural expertise and professional authority.

Almshouse planners were often not architects but contractors, like "carpenter and master builder" Robert Smith, who designed Carpenter's Hall and the second Philadelphia almshouse, known as the "Bettering House." The involvement of men such as Robert Smith, Dutton Otley, and architect S. D. Button in numerous construction projects suggests that there was a pool of contractors who concentrated on public buildings in general. Unlike the architects of many of the early- and mid-nineteenth-century British workhouses, American almshouse architects did not work from recommended plans published by a central relief authority; nor did any American architects make a career of designing almshouses exclusively, as did several British architects.[31] Institution planners varied in adherence to similar administrative principles in the internal layout of structures, but there was a clearly understood common "vocabulary" of features from which architects and contractors drew specific exterior arrangements. The alms–houses of the Delaware Valley resembled one another rather than English workhouses or alms–houses from elsewhere in the country, though examples were available for emulation in Boston, Baltimore, New York, and other eastern cities beginning in the eighteenth century.[32] Some architects were known for their employment of particular features or materials or for characteristic placement of specific elements, such as staircases.[33]

Planners arrived at designs for most of the counties' first institutions in a relatively informal manner; designs included contributions from a particular county's overseers of the poor, from the contractor (who also oversaw construction), or from both the contractor and the overseers. But most of the counties' second institutions, constructed after 1830, were built by contractors according to the plans of someone described as an architect. Committees appointed by the boards of overseers continued to exercise a strong influence on the process, in that they selected both contractors and architects. The primary contractor continued to select the workmen to whom to subcontract the finishing of the building (windows, brickwork, plumbing).

A committee-based method of soliciting plans and of deciding upon building design before approaching contractors was common to most public building projects in the Philadelphia region in the first half of the nineteenth century. Some committees hired an architect or builder to provide the plans and then began to search for a contractor.[34] Other committees settled on an idea for an almshouse, generally based on several visits to other institutions, then asked potential contractors to provide plans as well as bids for the construction. In these situations the community ex-

ercised a more direct influence on the final shape of the institution. A committee appointed by the Trustees of the Poor for Chester County visited the New Castle County almshouse and provided dimensions taken from it to "a number of Artificers or Mechanics" who had expressed interest in taking on the project of construction.[35] The committee for Bucks County's almshouse viewed the poorhouses of Lancaster, Chester, and Delaware Counties before modeling their building after that of Delaware County.[36]

Committees charged with planning improvements as well as new buildings visited other buildings for inspiration throughout the antebellum period. When Chester County's Trustees of the Poor decided in 1802 to build a new stone barn, "that now on the poor House farm being insufficient," they viewed the just-completed barn of a local farmer and adopted the same plan on a larger scale.[37] An 1840 committee of the Gloucester County Board of Chosen Freeholders visited the Pennsylvania Hospital, the Schuylkill County Almshouse, and the Pennsylvania State Prison to examine their heating, cooking, and plumbing facilities and equipment.[38] These same committees evaluated the completed construction before making the final payments to contractors.

Whether the new almshouses were combinations of old and new structures or entirely new constructions, the design and erection of these institutions were shaped by the contributions of community members, by contractors charged with executing the plans and specifications, and by the committee members who were formally charged with responsibility for the appearance of the new (or updated) institution. New Castle County's construction committee, charged with an addition to the center block of the three-story stone house they had purchased from the Overseers of the Poor for Christiana Hundred, reviewed the Philadelphia almshouse for plan ideas.[39] Plans for the addition were submitted by a group of "some Workmen and other Members of the Community."[40] Interaction between members of the community and the Board of Trustees of the Poor continued throughout the construction, as citizens proposed the construction of an extra story on the middle section of the building and the addition of a cupola containing a bell intended for use in regulating paupers' activities.[41] Interested citizens were so committed to the project that a subscription was taken up to meet the costs of the additional construction.[42]

Like other sorts of public buildings, the newly constructed almshouses were generally built from brick or local stone. Exteriors tended to have a dormitory-like appearance, not unlike that of other large residential buildings such as seminaries and colleges. The main residential buildings were usually composed of a two- or three-story center block, with two-story wings on each side, and housed the main administrative functions of the institution in addition to sleeping rooms on the top floor and dining and meeting rooms on the ground floor (fig. 5.4). Kitchens, when contained in the main building, were on the ground floor (when there were two kitchens, one was in the basement).[43] The Chester and Lancaster County almshouses both had piazzas. Outbuildings were usually constructed of brick or stone and included barns, spring and milk houses, smokehouses, dyehouses, weaver and carpenter shops, and at least one "factory." The property of the Chester County Almshouse initially included a tanyard, which was rented out for some years before it was sold.

Arrangements for heating the house, cooking the meals, and cleaning the paupers and their clothes were of considerable concern in planning or evaluating institutions. The heating, cooking, and sanitation facilities were where pragmatism met larger social and moral concerns. Cleaning the inmates and encouraging them to eat appropriately were important parts of their reform and helped to convince visitors that tax money was being spent appropriately. Newspaper accounts of new buildings therefore spent considerable

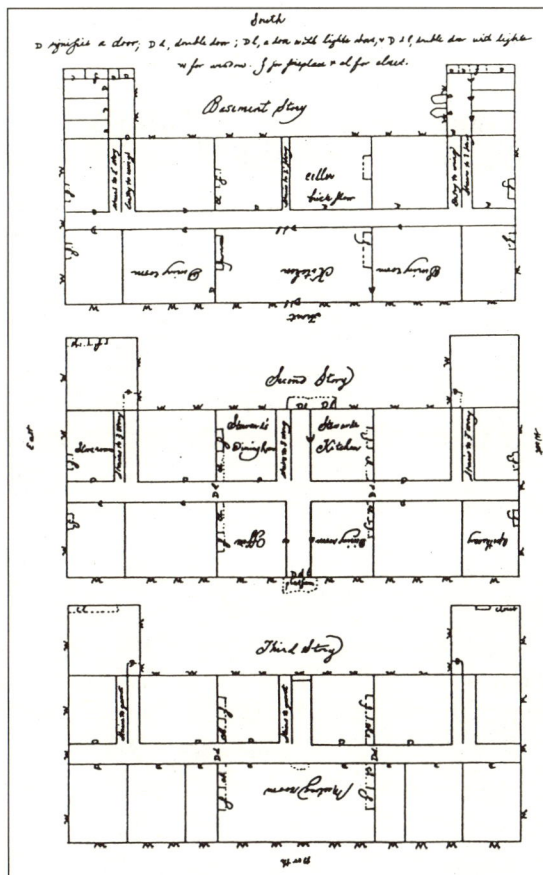

Fig. 5.4. Floor Plan, Lebanon County Almshouse, 1835. Records of the Franklin Fire Insurance Company. Courtesy of the Historical Society of Pennsylvania.

space describing kitchens, arrangements for providing water to the various areas, and specific equipment. Delaware County's second almshouse was praised for its "Julius Fink's patent ranges with water back and circulating boiler attached," its "Mott's Patent Portable Boilers, with a water supply to each," the bathtub and "shower bath" in the paupers' bathroom, and the washhouse for cleaning the inmates' clothes. The same commentator also applauded the building for "the style of architecture in which it was designed, and the manner in which it was erected," which "presents an imposing appearance to the passer."[44]

Poorhouses resembled other sorts of large residential buildings such as jails and colleges in arrangement of interior space, because the architects of such buildings shared similar concerns: the control of the movements of inmates, the efficient handling of the basic needs of physical existence, and the avoidance of conflicts between town residents and denizens of the institution.[45] The *Delaware County Republican* clearly indicated both the flexibility of interior spaces and the essential similarities of public buildings in offering the grounds and buildings of the first Delaware County almshouse for sale in 1854, when the newspaper noted that "this building, with little expense, may be converted into a commodious mansion, suitable for a boarding house, or a house for some public purpose."[46]

Classification of the inmates—their separation by age, sex, and moral character—was an issue of great concern in nineteenth-century discussions of poor relief. In common with British relief administrators, American commentators generally believed that classification of inmates was the key to efficient relief, in that the establishment of a classification system would more readily allow the control or expulsion of the unworthy or morally suspect. Whether or not individual commentators agreed that the receipt of regular relief inevitably degraded the recipient, they were unanimous in their belief that forced association with the lazy or degenerate would corrupt inmates of good character, "impairing the order of the institution, and the comfort of its feeble inmates."[47] Worse still, the proximity of male and female inmates might encourage the production of illegitimate children, and the almshouse might become "a very monster which altho its members are daily diminishing in number by death—possesses the power of procreating and reanimating itself."[48]

American poorhouse planners hoped to construct buildings such that the structures themselves would perform much of the work of separation by making physical interaction among different categories of paupers difficult or impossible. In practice, however, the interior arrangement of buildings did not generally allow for separation of the inmates as recommended in policy literature. Administrators felt other issues of internal management were more important. The smaller almshouses, such as those of Hunterdon County, New Jersey, crowded paupers into buildings that had originally been private residences and afforded little or no privacy to the inmates. Later construction for the smaller institutions took the form of additional outbuildings for the sick or the insane; these buildings provided only for the separation of inmates by gender. The additional construction necessary to allow for separation of inmates by character would have been prohibitively expensive. Within the main residential structures, the arrangement of accommodations for the inmates could vary considerably. Stewards and overseers shifted both work spaces and "lodging rooms" to other rooms or buildings as required by the changing needs of inmate populations and by changing expectations with regard to the amount of work extracted from the able-bodied; the boardrooms seem to have been the only rooms which were not used for more than one purpose.[49]

In individual institutions, larger decisions about policy were complicated by issues such as whether to separate married couples and mothers and their older children (groups that presumably wished to stay together) or blacks from whites (groups that presumably wished to remain apart).[50] Administrators' efforts at classification of inmates were most often focused on separating the sexes in order to discourage pregnancies; when structures were criticized for poor planning, failure to effectively separate men and women was the most frequently given reason. The second Chester County almshouse was criticized for its double stairway, which was situated in the center of the building and made it possible for male and female inmates to pass one another on the stairs on their way up to separate quarters upstairs.[51]

Like separation of the sexes, racial segregation was only partially realized; Delaware County allotted separate sitting rooms to its black and white inmates, but does not appear to have segregated the sleeping quarters.[52] Uniformity in materials throughout the rooms probably intended for sleeping, as indicated in insurance surveys and construction specifications, suggests that, in counties where blacks were not segregated in separate buildings, the quality of accommodations did not differ greatly between blacks and whites. When institutions did house black inmates separately, such housing was generally inferior in quality and often consisted of sheds or smaller outbuildings located at some distance from the main building (fig. 5.5). Separation of the races in county relief institutions was not dictated by whether or not the state was a slave state. Blacks were segregated in New Castle County in Delaware and in Baltimore, but they were also given separate quarters in the almshouses of Pennsylvania's Chester and Delaware Counties. African Americans were not necessarily housed in the county institutions elsewhere in the South.[53]

Facilities for medical care for blacks and whites in the outlying counties also varied widely, but this was not simply the result of racism. While it is clear that the quality of medical care for blacks in Montgomery County's almshouse was inferior to that offered white inmates, whose hospital was larger (and insured, which the institution's "colored hospital" was not), African-American inmates do not appear to have fared worse than the insane inmates.[54] Indeed, housing for black inmates was frequently adjacent to that of the insane, or even in the same structures. The Kent County, Delaware, almshouse maintained its deranged inmates and "poor Negroes" in a single building until at least 1853, as did Chester County, Pennsylvania.[55]

The proximity or combination of quarters for blacks and the insane suggests that in many institutions care for the insane was considered primarily an administrative issue rather than a medical one until well into the nineteenth century. The violently insane were generally confined to small unfurnished and often unheated cells, sometimes equipped with chains for restraint, which were

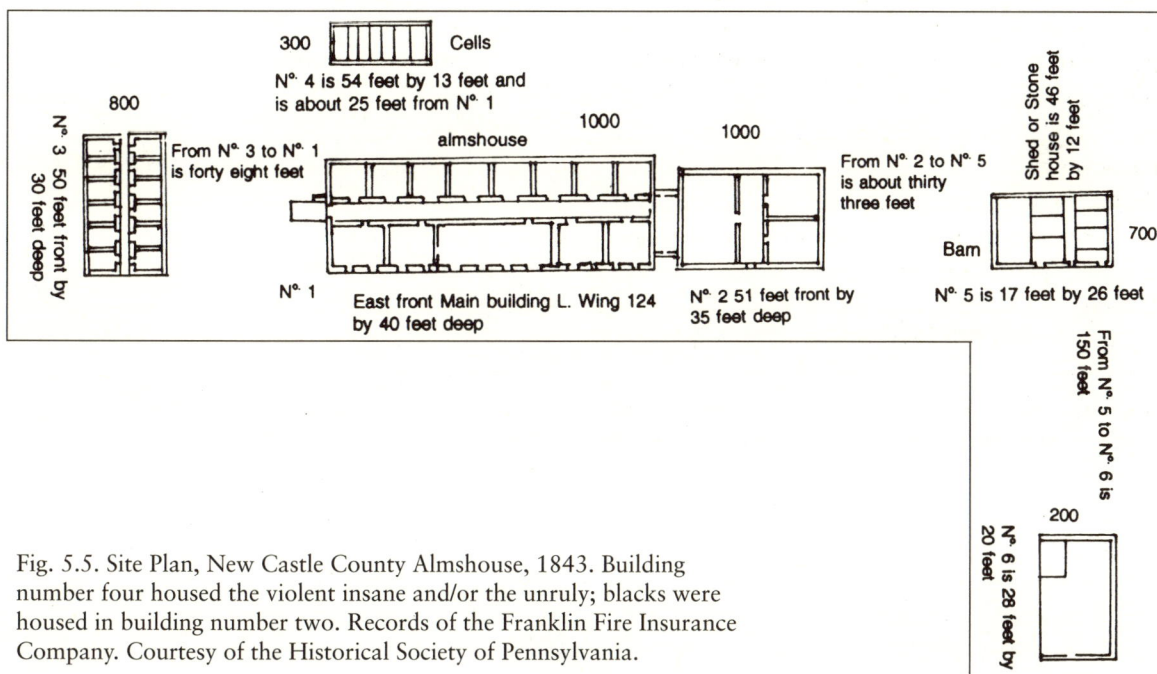

Fig. 5.5. Site Plan, New Castle County Almshouse, 1843. Building number four housed the violent insane and/or the unruly; blacks were housed in building number two. Records of the Franklin Fire Insurance Company. Courtesy of the Historical Society of Pennsylvania.

located either in the basement of the main building or in separate structures, just as the sane but unruly inmates were (fig. 5.5). The merely "feeble" or "silly" were generally not given special quarters.[56] In most almshouses these residents mingled with other inmates for at least the first quarter of the century; in the Lancaster County almshouse, for example, the mentally afflicted were found in both the hospital and the main residential building.[57]

The increasing importance of the institution in late-eighteenth- and early-nineteenth-century poor

relief is indicative of a commitment to a different sort of solution to the administrative problems of poor relief. These new structures, with their simple, regular exteriors and the corresponding routinized quality of the lives of their inmates, underscore a growing conviction on the part of administrators that regularity was the key to reform and that the most effective discipline was self-discipline. The almshouses of Philadelphia's satellite counties are physical demonstrations of both Christian charity and community self-definition.

## Notes

1. This essay is excerpted from the author's Ph.D. dissertation, "Virtue, Industry, and Independence: Inmates and Labor in the Almshouses of the Philadelphia Region, 1791–1860," (Univ. of Delaware, 1995). The study includes New Castle County, Delaware; Berks, Bucks, Chester, Delaware, Lancaster, Lebanon, Montgomery, and Schuylkill Counties in Pennsylvania; and Burlington, Gloucester, Hunterdon, Mercer, and Salem Counties in New Jersey. The author wishes to thank Thomas Valente, Brian Greenberg, Anne Boylan, Lynn Brocklebank, and Bernie Herman for reading early drafts of this essay.

2. It should be noted that amounts appropriated for poor taxes do not necessarily represent available funds; counties often had trouble getting that money from individual tax collectors, presumably because the tax collectors were unwilling to collect it in the first place.

3. In examining the planning of the Bucks County Almshouse in the first decade of the nineteenth century, historian Thane Bryant has argued that the decision to create this institution was a decision to adopt coercion as a method for controlling the poor. See Thane Bryant, "Economy and Humanity Happily United: The Almshouse in Bucks County, Pennsylvania, 1790–1822," unpublished ms., 1989.

4. David J. Rothman, *The Discovery of the Asylum: Social Order and Disorder in the New Republic* (Boston and Toronto: Little, Brown, and Company, 1971).

5. See, for example Gary B. Nash, "Poverty and Poor Relief in Pre-Revolutionary Philadelphia," *William and Mary Quarterly,* 3d Series, 33 (1) (1976); Douglas Lamar Jones, "The Strolling Poor: Transiency in Eighteenth-Century Massachusetts," *William and Mary*

*Quarterly,* 3d Series, 32 (2) (1975); Elizabeth Howell Goggin, "Public Welfare in Delaware, 1638–1930," in *Delaware: A History of the First State*, ed. H. Clay Reed (New York: Lewis Historical Publishing Co., 1947), vol. 2.

6. Report, Committee of the Board of Trustees of the Poor, Gloucester County, New Jersey, May 28, 1830. Gloucester County Historical Society (hereafter referred to as GCHS).

7. Ibid.

8. Sidney George Fisher, *A Philadelphia Perspective: The Diary of Sidney George Fisher Covering the Years 1834–1871* (Philadelphia: Historical Society of Pennsylvania, 1967). See Ellen Dwyer, *Homes for the Mad: Life Inside Two Nineteenth-Century Asylums* (New Brunswick and London: Rutgers Univ. Press, 1987), chap. 1, for discussion of these casual visitors as an administrative problem for insane asylums. Administrators reacted to the problem by limiting public visitors to certain days and times.

9. Eliza Cope Harrison, ed., *Philadelphia Merchant: The Diary of Thomas P. Cope, 1800–1851* (South Bend, Ind.: Gateway Editions, 1978), 90–91. Entry for Oct. 3, 1801.

10. For an example of an image of a public building (the Eastern State Penitentiary) on a dessert service, see Norman Johnston, with Kenneth Finkel and Jeffrey A. Cohen, *Eastern State Penitentiary: Crucible of Good Intentions* (Philadelphia: Philadelphia Museum of Art, 1994), 69.

11. Report, Committee of the Board of Trustees of the Poor, Gloucester County, New Jersey, May 28, 1830, GCHS.

12. This architectural vocabulary has been applied to the study of other institutions as well. Nancy Tomes has argued that the exterior of the Pennsylvania Hospital for the Insane made a "powerful architectural statement" to patients and their families about the efficacy of the new "moral Treatment" for insanity. See her *The Art of Asylum-Keeping: Thomas Story Kirkbride and the Origins of American Psychiatry*, 2d ed. (Philadelphia: Univ. of Pennsylvania Press, 1994).

13. There is little direct evidence in the form of explicit statements for the planning of interiors as a way of shaping the behavior of the poor; most of the discussion centers on the bad effect that living too comfortably in an institutional setting would have on the habits and moral health of the indigent. Historians have begun to explore this question, but available secondary literature has focused on British workhouses and charitable institutions. See, for example, Anne Digby, *Pauper Palaces* (Boston and London: Routledge and Kegan Paul, 1978); Deborah E. B. Weiner, *Architecture and Social Reform in Late-Victorian London* (Manchester and New York: Manchester Univ. Press, 1994).

14. Minutes, Directors of the Poor and House of Employment, Lancaster County, Apr. 9, 1811, Lancaster County Historical Society (hereafter referred to as LCHS).

15. Report, Committee of the Board of Trustees of the Poor, Gloucester County, New Jersey, Sept. 5, 1840, GCHS.

16. Tom Armstrong makes this observation of Hofmann's paintings in "God Bless the Home of the Poor," *Historical Review of Berks County* 35 (1970).

17. For discussion of Miller's life and work, which centered in and around York, see Lewis Miller, *Sketches and Chronicles: The Reflections of a Nineteenth Century Pennsylvania German Folk Artist* (York, Pa.: Historical Society of York County, 1976). For Pennsylvania folk art in general and other representations of Pennsylvania almshouses, see Jean Lipman and Tom Armstrong, eds., *American Folk Painters of Three Centuries* (New York: Hudson Hills Press, 1980); Tom Armstrong, "Pennsylvania Almshouse Painters" (Exhibit Catalog of paintings in the Abby Aldrich Rockefeller Folk Art Collection, 1968).

18. Mills quoted in John M. Bryan, ed., *Robert Mills, Architect* (Washington, D.C.: American Institute of Architects Press, 1989), 63, 67.

19. *American Republican*, Jan. 31, 1854.

20. Dix, "Memorial Soliciting a State Hospital for the Insane Submitted to the Legislature of Pennsylvania," in *The Almshouse Experience: Collected Reports*, ed. David Rothman (New York: Arno Press, 1971), 53–54.

21. *Delaware County Republican*, Sept. 28, 1855.

22. Specifications, Gloucester County Almshouse, 1860, New Jersey State Archives.

23. Little documentation is available for what sorts of decoration or objects were in the steward's quarters in any of these institutions. It is tempting to suggest that any ornamentation in terms of moldings or additional closet space would have been partially intended to provide inmates with an object lesson in the rewards of hard work (a steady job and comfortable quarters); however, such ornamentation would likely have little utility as object lessons, as few inmates would have seen these interiors.

24. Dix, "Memorial to the State of Pennsylvania," in *The Almshouse Experience*, 35. Her views on the quarters for the insane were almost invariably negative in the extreme, regardless of how well she believed the sane inmates were housed.

25. I refer here to the construction or adaptation of the main residential structures or hospitals only; the construction of new outbuildings, even large, potentially expensive structures such as barns, was a much simpler process.

26. The first residential building of the Lancaster County Almshouse and Hospital, constructed in 1799–1800, presented the same dormitory-like exterior appearance that the later-constructed county buildings did, and in general dimensions was similar to the second Gloucester County almshouse constructed in 1860.

27. See, for example, Judith M. Olson, *Pemberton Township: a History* (Pemberton, N.J.: Friends of the Pemberton Community Library, 1976), 71, and Scott's *Atlas of Burlington County* (1876).

28. James H. Mast, "John Pearson's Description of Lancaster and Columbia in 1801," *Journal of the Lancaster County Historical Society* 61 (2) (1957): 54. The New Castle County almshouse was relocated outside Wilmington in 1884–85.

29. The purchase of such large acreage may also have indicated a recognition on the part of overseers that extra acreage could be sold in years of difficulty or profitably rented to a tenant who would improve the land. The location of almshouses in relation to local businesses such as mills was most often a consideration because these businesses might expect to have regular dealings with the institution.

30. Catherine Bishir and Donna Rilling have discussed the widespread participation of artisans, particularly carpenters, in the boom in speculation in land and buildings in the early years of the nineteenth century. See Catherine W. Bishir, et al., *Architects and Builders in North Carolina: A History of the Practice of Building* (Chapel Hill and London: Univ. of North Carolina Press, 1990), and Donna Rilling, "Artisans, Entrepreneurs, and Speculators in the Philadelphia Building Trades, 1790–1840," paper delivered at the Philadelphia Center for Early American Studies, 1992.

31. Norman Longmate, *The Workhouse* (New York: St. Martin's, 1974), 286–91.

32. Architects and contractors were both aware of and willing to use European models that they thought appropriate: the Lancaster County almshouse (built 1799–1801) and the Chester County Prison (built 1836) featured kitchen ovens and chimneys modeled after the designs of diplomat Count Rumford. Rumford had designed Houses of Industry in Munich and other cities as an official at the Bavarian Court in the late eighteenth century. Mast, "John Pearson's Description of Lancaster and Columbia," 54. Margaret B. Schiffer, *Survey of Chester County, Pennsylvania, Architecture: 17th, 18th, and 19th Centuries* (Exton, Pa.: Schiffer Publishing, Ltd., 1976), 340. The primary models for the prison were other prisons, specifically the Eastern Penitentiary (built 1828), and the Moyamensing Prison in Philadelphia (built 1835). Thomas U. Walter designed both the Chester County Prison and the Moyamensing Prison. Walter's specialty was institutional structures; he also designed the 1858 West Chester Young Ladies' Seminary, the Chester County Courthouse, the Bank of Chester County, two churches, Horticultural Hall, and another school, in addition to residences and institutional structures elsewhere in and outside the state. For Rumford's views on workhouse management and institutional architecture, see Sanford C. Brown, *Collected Works of Count Rumford* (Cambridge, Mass.: Harvard Univ. Press, 1970), vol. 5, *Public Institutions.*

33. Robert Mills, for example, was widely known for his use of brick in his jails and curving staircases in his other buildings. See George J. Giger, *A Model Jail of the Olden Time* (New York: Russell Sage Foundation, 1928), and Bryan, *Robert Mills.*

34. This method of planning public buildings was not new to the nineteenth century. The Board of the Pennsylvania Hospital, the construction of which was funded by subscription, solicited plans from Samuel Rhoads and Joseph Fox before decisions were made about contractors. See William H. Williams, "The Pennsylvania Hospital, 1751–1801: An Internal Examination of Anglo-America's First Hospital," (Ph.D. diss., Univ. of Delaware, 1971), 101–5.

35. Minutes, Trustees of the Poor, Chester County, Feb. 20, 1799, Mar. 2, 1799, Chester County Archives (hereafter referred to as CCA). Joshua Weaver, the clerk and the treasurer for the corporation, both took the initial dimensions and drew up plans from them for the use of the contractors.

36. J. H. Battle, ed., *History of Bucks County, Pennsylvania: Including an Account of its Original Exploration* . . . (Philadelphia, Chicago: A. Warner and Company, 1887), 225.

37. Minutes, Trustees of the Poor, Chester County, Aug. 2, 1802, Aug. 3, 1802, Chester County Archives, CCA.

38. Records, Gloucester County Almshouse, 1840, GCHS.

39. Minutes, Trustees of the Poor of New Castle County, Mar. 3, 1791. Delaware Division of Historical and Cultural Affairs, Bureau of Archives and Records (hereafter referred to as DSA).

40. Minutes, Trustees of the Poor, New Castle County, July 27, 1791, DSA.

41. Ibid.

42. Russell Handsman has discussed subscription as a component of New England meeting house construction as part of both community self-definition and assertion of individual identity in the context of changing communities. See Russell G. Handsman, "Historical Archaeology and Capitalism, Subscriptions and Separations: The Production of Individualism," *North American Archaeologist* 4 (1) (1983).

43. See for example, Mast, "John Pearson's Description of Lancaster and Columbia," 54; Survey, New Castle County almshouse, Franklin Fire Insurance Company, 1855; Survey, Lebanon County almshouse, Franklin Fire Insurance Company, 1835. Records of the Franklin Fire Insurance Company, Historical Society of Pennsylvania (hereafter referred to as HSP).

44. *Delaware County Republican,* Apr. 3, 1857. The article underscored the connection between reform and cleanliness by noting the existence on the first floor of "a bath room intended for the punishment of refractory paupers."

45. Robert Mills's plans for the main buildings of the University of South Carolina, designed during the student unrest of the 1820s, which not infrequently expressed itself in acts of violence and vandalism, provided fireproof stairways for the buildings and separate entrances for the dormitories. See Paul Venable Turner, *Campus: an American Planning Tradition* (New York: Architectural History Foundation; Cambridge: MIT Press, 1984), 56.

46. *Delaware County Republican,* Apr. 21, 1854.

47. Visitors' Report, Trustees of the Poor, Chester County, 1841, CCA.

48. Visitors' Report, Trustees of the Poor, Chester County, 1826, CCA.

49. In Lancaster County, for example, the workshop was originally located in the basement of the main almshouse building, called the House of Employment. The workshops moved to outbuildings to accommodate the growth of the inmate population and to adjust to temporary changes in the use of space demanded by events such as the outbreak of cholera in 1854. See Henry A. Showalter, *Sesquicentennial of the Lancaster County (PA) Hospital, the Second Oldest Hospital in the United States in Continuous Service: A Brief Abstract from its Inception* (Compiled for the Lancaster County Historical Society, 1951).

50. Edward Strutt Abdy noted in his *Journal of a Residence and Tour in the United States of North America, from April, 1833 to October 1834* (London: J. Murray, 1835) that the mingling of the races in institutions might, depending on the temper of the administrators, be either the result of a more liberal outlook or of "a desire to make a retreat to the almshouse more repulsive and degrading to the eyes of those who might be disposed to prefer its accommodation to the scanty fare at home" (1: 187).

51. An 1854 commentator complained that this "conflicts with our idea of a complete separation of the sexes," in the *American Republican,* Jan. 31, 1854. Larger institutions, such as Lancaster County's, could often afford to house fewer inmates in each room, but on each floor the sleeping rooms opened onto a common hallway, and there seems to have been no effort to segregate specific classes of inmates on particular floors. Delaware County's second almshouse, constructed in 1856–57, provided for the separation of the sexes more successfully, by placing them in wings separated by a center structure. See the *Delaware County Republican,* Apr. 3, 1857.

52. *Delaware County Republican,* Apr. 3, 1857. It is also possible that the segregation of sleeping quarters was so obvious a necessity that the commentator who provided this description of the new building felt no need to remark upon it. Regardless of segregation at other times, the paupers would have mingled at meals.

53. See, for example, Carole Haber and Brian Gratton, "Old Age, Public Welfare and Race: The Case of Charleston, South Carolina, 1800–1949," *Journal of Social History* 21 (2) (1987).

54. Survey, Montgomery County Almshouse, 1834, Franklin Fire Insurance Company. Records, Franklin Fire Insurance Company, HSP.

55. Scharf and Westcott, *History of Delaware: 1609–1888* (Philadelphia: L. J. Richards, 1888), 1037.

56. In some institutions, these terms were also used to describe those with chronic conditions such as epilepsy.

57. The insane patients in the almshouse hospitals of Bucks, Lancaster, and Schuylkill Counties also had small enclosed yards within which to take exercise.

# PART II

# COMMUNITY

# LANDSCAPES

*Martha J. McNamara*

# From Common Land to Public Space: The Frog Pond and Mall at Newburyport, Massachusetts, 1765–1825

In March 1802 a thirty-stanza poem entitled "The Pond and the Mall" written under the pen name "Rusticus" appeared on the front page of the *Newburyport Herald and Country Gazette.* Dedicated to Captain Edmund Bartlett, the eldest son of Newburyport's wealthiest merchant for "his liberal exertions in making the Mall," the poem eulogized a twenty-acre piece of common land in Newburyport, Massachusetts, known as the "Frog Pond," where Bartlett had earlier donated labor and money to create a promenade. The landscaping of Bartlett's Mall not only illustrates the aspirations to gentility of Newburyport's elite, but it also points to a larger transformation taking place at Frog Pond. A marginal area dotted with proto-industrial buildings in the eighteenth century, after the turn of the century the Frog Pond had been altered by the removal of several nuisance industries, by the leveling of hilly terrain, and by the construction of schoolhouses,

a new courthouse, and Bartlett's Mall. After 1825 a stone prison and prison keeper's house completed the Frog Pond's metamorphosis into an "official" landscape, embracing codes of gentility and restraint.

From common land serving such disparate functions as manufacturing and poor relief to a manicured public space providing a setting for the buildings of social order, the Frog Pond offers an opportunity to examine the changing nature of late-eighteenth- and early-nineteenth-century public spaces and their physical and conceptual ties to new forms of civic buildings. Public structures, such as courthouses and prisons reconfigured and relocated from eighteenth-century commercial town centers, fit into a newly ordered landscape. A complex set of economic, social, and political factors can be traced through this transformation: squabbles over land titles, economic considerations, gentry "improvement" of the landscape, and financial speculation; yet, together these tensions point to a fundamental shift in the nature of power in the late eighteenth and early nineteenth centuries and the representation of that power in the built environment. In Newburyport, as in other Massachusetts county seats, or "shiretowns," during this period, the linking of an idealized landscape of gentility with buildings of justice and punishment outlined a new type of landscape: one of specialized, disciplined, and ordered spaces.[1]

In order to understand the landscape transformations taking place at Frog Pond, the area's changing legal and political status as common land must be examined. From the time of its earliest English settlement, the ownership of common land in Newburyport and its "parent" town of Newbury was highly contested terrain. Migrating from an area of intensive commercial farming, Newbury's English settlers were a diverse and contentious lot who brought an appetite for land ownership and set up a social structure based on rigid economic stratification.[2] Initially, a closed group of ninety-one "proprietors" claimed title to all the land in Newbury, and, because political rights flowed from land ownership, the proprietors maintained control over all aspects of town government, including land allocation. Many other New England towns employed a similar structure; as population increased and pressure to distribute common land grew, this concentration of property rights often resulted in friction between proprietors and nonproprietors. Ultimately, as land was parceled out, the "proprietor" designation narrowed to indicate those who had exclusive control over "common land": land not allocated to a specific freeholder.[3]

In addition to conflict between proprietors and nonproprietors the development of two very different settlements in Newbury—one agricultural and one mercantile—ultimately resulted in the establishment of the town of Newburyport in 1762 (fig. 6.1). Originally founded as the Third Parish in the town of Newbury, the "Waterside" or "New Town" section, which would become Newburyport, began to be laid out by the town proprietors before 1707. The first wharves and shipbuilding facilities constructed shortly after settlement along the river spurred tremendous commercial growth, and, consequently, an ideological fissure grew up between the mercantile residents of the Waterside and the agricultural residents of "Old Town."[4]

Despite their growing prosperity, Waterside residents lacked numerical strength and therefore carried little weight in town government. The absence of services such as schools, fire-fighting equipment, and a convenient building for town meetings and court sessions in the port section particularly frustrated the ambitious merchants. When a town meeting vote defeated a plan for a new town house, a group of merchants raised money by subscription to construct a building jointly with the county in Market Square, the center of the Waterside's economic, political, and social life.[5] This town house proved to be the final blow to Newbury's unity. In 1762 Waterside merchants successfully petitioned the Massachusetts General Court (or legislature) for incorporation as a separate town, arguing that "jealousy . . . and a high spirit of opposition" made it impossible for the town's rival factions to agree. The petitioners closed their appeal with a complaint about the use of public buildings. "The new Court house lately built at the Water side by the County & the people there, which altho most conveniently situated as well for the use of the town & county . . . large & capacious enough for the whole town . . . yet the town as yet have not & we suppose will not meet in it, which the Memorialists cannot but think proceeds from a party spirit which is so diffused & become so general in some parts of the town. . . ."[6] For the Waterside residents a town house representing political power they hoped would eventually match their economic power belonged in the commercial center, and if those in Newbury did not agree, founding a new town provided the only solution.

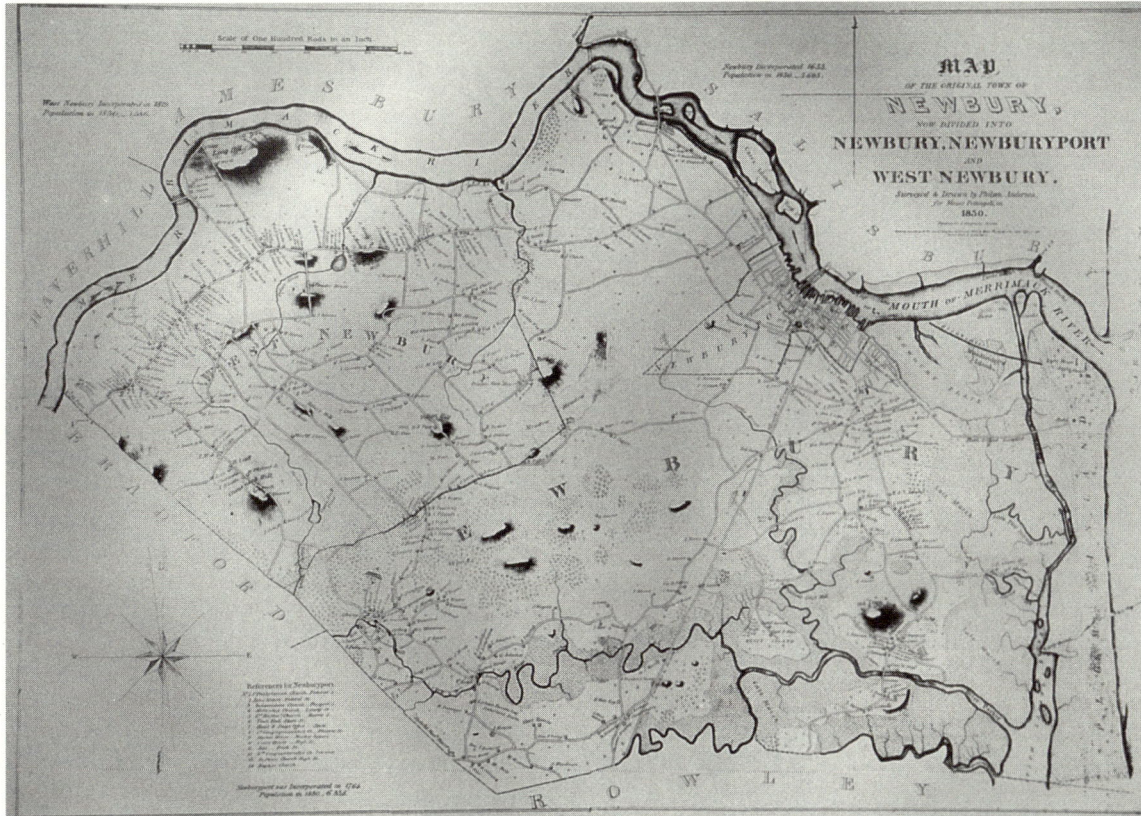

Fig. 6.1. Map Showing Boundaries of Newbury, Massachusetts, and the Location of Newburyport along the River. Surveyed and drawn by Philander Anderson, 1830. Courtesy of the Historical Society of Old Newbury.

When the general court allowed Newburyport to incorporate as a separate town, however, the committee responsible for dividing the two towns made no settlement with the proprietors for the common land remaining in Newburyport: Frog Pond and a valuable piece of land along the river known as the Middle Shipyard. As a result, these two areas became the focus of an intermittent dispute between the town of Newburyport and the newly renamed "Proprietors of Common and Undivided Land in Newbury and Newburyport," a loosely organized group comprising mostly Newbury residents. This sporadic conflict, thinly veiling the continuing animosities between merchant and farmer, lasted approximately sixty years and subtly influenced the changes taking place at Frog Pond.[7]

To assert its claim over Frog Pond and the Middle Shipyard, the Newburyport selectmen voted to survey the areas in 1766 and established them as "public ways," or highways, essentially locking the conflict into place by shifting the definition of the parcels from common land owned by the proprietors to public land open to use by the townspeople and controlled by town selectmen.[8] The survey taken for a "public way" in 1766 indicates the area's diversity of functions and its role as a mediator between city and country (fig. 6.2). Located physically and socially on the town's margins, the disputed area supported a number of economically productive activities in the mid-eighteenth century. Comprised of hilly terrain with deep ravines on either side of a glacially formed pond, it was bordered to the west by low-lying pasture land and salt marsh and to the north and east by the growing town of Newburyport. Down the road to the south a free black community had grown up, known locally as "west indies" and described by a nineteenth-century local historian as "a collection of low unpainted huts."[9] Directly to the west of the pond the Third Parish in Newbury (renamed the First Parish of Newburyport) had established a "burying place" early in the eighteenth century.[10] A windmill built atop one of the steep inclines bordering the pond in 1730 processed grains cultivated in the surrounding agricultural area, while the pond itself supplied water for grazing cattle and horses.[11] As Newburyport rapidly developed as an urban cen-

ter, therefore, the Frog Pond provided a place for the accommodation of agricultural activities to serve the townspeople.

In most New England towns, constructing buildings on common land, like those appearing on the survey of Frog Pond, required permission from proprietors or town selectmen, an indulgence easily obtained if the activity served a public good.[12] For example, when petitioning the town in 1748 to construct a ropewalk, Waterside merchant John Crocker argued that "ropemaking has been found for [some] time past very beneficial not only for the seafaring business of this Town but also as thereby many poor people are employed."[13] Ropewalks often occupied inexpensive land on the margins of town because of the

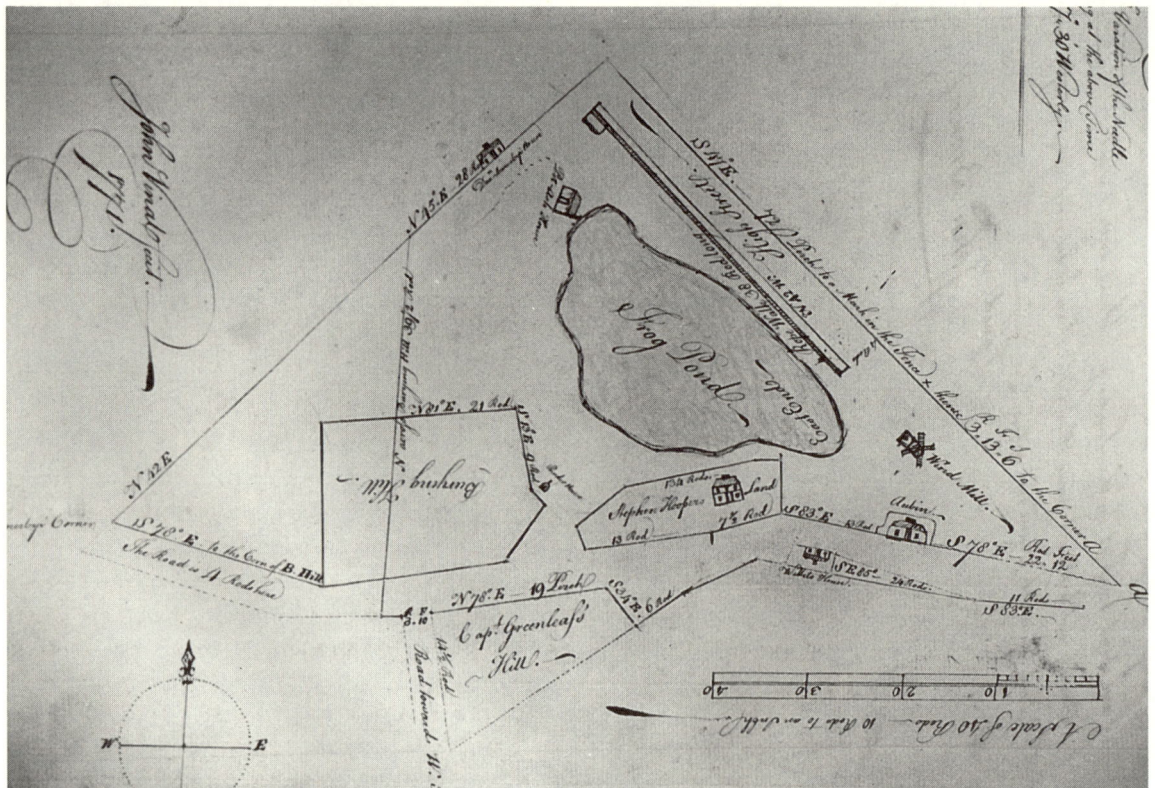

Fig. 6.2. Plan of Land and Building in the Vicinity of Frog Pond, by John Vinal, 1771. Courtesy of the City Clerk's Office, Newburyport City Hall.

amount of land required to twist continuous lengths of cordage and because they posed a threat of fire. Ropewalk builders, however, had to balance these concerns against proximity to their customers at the wharves. John Bonner's 1722 map of Boston indicates the location of a number of ropewalks at the foot of the north slope of Beacon Hill (fig. 6.3). This would have been an ideal location for cordage manufacturing because of its waterfront access to the shipping trade. Crocker's location for a ropewalk, although cleverly, cheaply, and safely sited on common land, undoubtedly presented transportation difficulties.

Not surprisingly, as Newburyport's shipping industry grew, merchants relocated rope manufacturing closer to the wharves, and Crocker's ropewalk, built "along by the windmill," disappeared from Frog Pond sometime in the 1770s.[14]

Other buildings—most importantly, the town's powder house—may also have found a home at Frog Pond because of the threat of fire, while structures such as the potash house may have been considered nuisances. Producing potash, an essential ingredient for the British textile industry as well as for soapmaking and glass production, would have been a dirty, sooty enterprise involving the

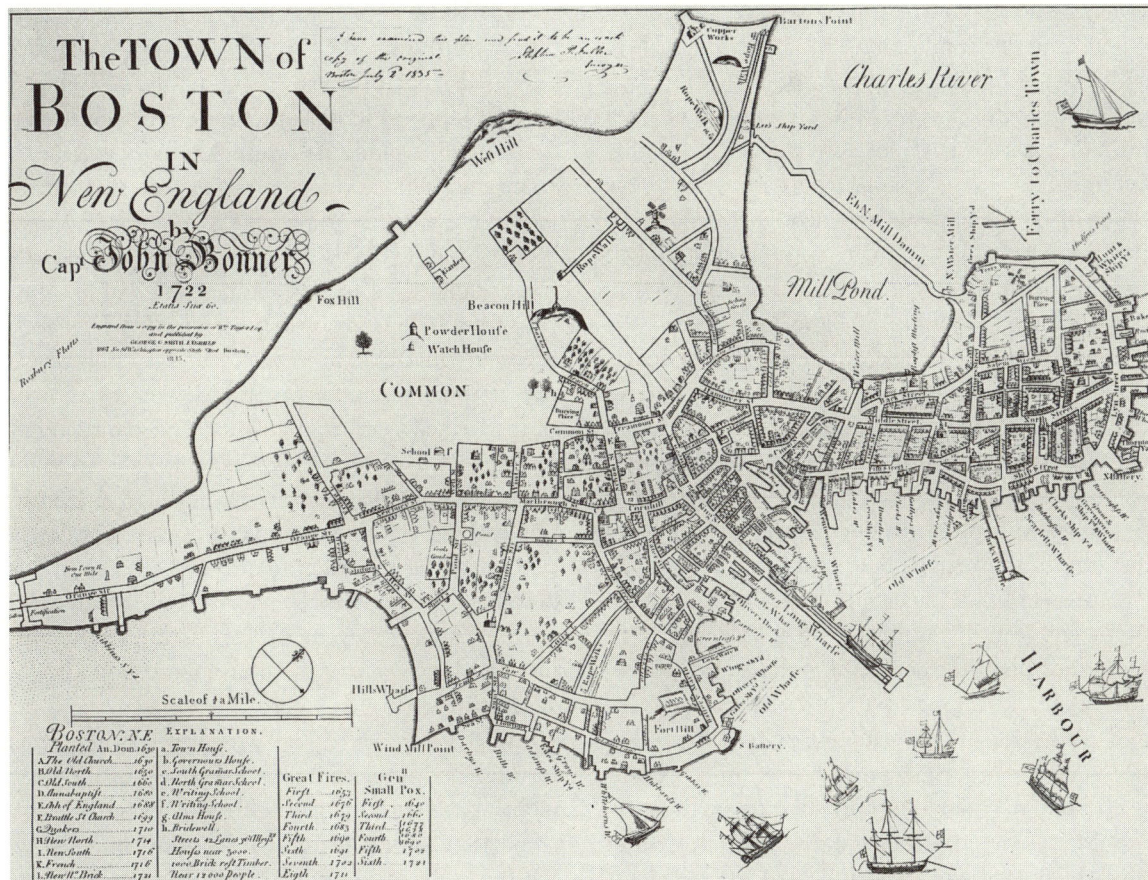

Fig. 6.3. The Town of Boston in New England, by John Bonner, 1722. 1835 facsimile by George Smith. Courtesy of the Massachusetts Historical Society, Boston, Massachusetts

soaking, refining, and packing of wood ashes, and therefore it was removed from the dense urban center.[15] Domestic buildings at Frog Pond included a two-story, center-chimney house owned by Stephen Hooper, the son of leading Essex County merchant Robert "King" Hooper of Marblehead. Small, one-story buildings allowed by the town for the benefit of Nathan Willett and Samuel Aubin occupied the southern edge of the parcel.[16] The Frog Pond area, therefore, at mid-century combined buildings for industry and agriculture, housing for merchants and the poor, and space for the living and the dead.

The 1796 construction of a new brick schoolhouse at Frog Pond, near where the windmill stood, and the landscaping of Bartlett's Mall in 1800 signal the changing perceptions of the area and its transformation from common land that housed a wide variety of activities into a highly specialized public space accommodating new types of civic buildings and new spaces for self-presentation.[17] These changes were, in part, linked to the spread of notions about refinement and improvement throughout New England in the late eighteenth and early nineteenth centuries. English historian Peter Borsay charts the progress of the impact of this "urban renaissance" through the provincial towns of England in the late seventeenth and early eighteenth centuries.[18] Richard Bushman, looking at the New World, takes a wider geographical sweep and examines the spread of "refinement" in English-speaking North America in the eighteenth and nineteenth centuries.[19] Both historians point to the rise of architectural classicism, the landscaping of urban centers with parks and walks, and the fascination with self-presentation and manners as hallmarks of this new cultural system.[20] Newburyport, like other prosperous Massachusetts towns, dared not lag behind in a stylish new world. Members of the merchant elite had begun to move their residences away from the waterfront by the late eighteenth century and to build Federal style mansion houses along

High Street on either side of Frog Pond.[21] In 1800 they turned their attention to improving the public spaces of the town by constructing Bartlett's Mall along the Frog Pond's northeastern edge, essentially substituting for the ropewalk a promenade. The *Newburyport Herald and Country Gazette* announced the benefits of such an improvement: "The liberality discovered by several gentlemen in originating and bringing forward the plan for forming and beautifying a Mall in High street reflects great honor on them. . . . So delightful a situation of a public walk has been too long neglected. When completed it will not only be useful to the people individually—but when the trees shall be grown will be greatly conducive to the health [*sic*] and highly ornamental to the town." Perhaps unsure of the public's reception of this improvement, the writer continued with a warning: "It is hoped that no depravity or an itch to do mischief will lead any to expose themselves to general execration (as well as condign punishment) by destroying or in any way injuring the trees that will be set, the railing, gates or any improvements that are in the making."[22] This concern surrounding the security of Newburyport's new promenade indicates that the gentry control of the refined landscape may have been a bit tenuous. An 1807 attempt at "improving" the town common in Hanover, New Hampshire, met with opposition from townspeople, who tore out newly planted trees in order to preserve the land for grazing.[23] In Newburyport, as well, changes in land use always ran the risk of stirring up old animosities between merchant and farmer. In 1823 a successful campaign to replace the poplars (a favorite tree of the 1790s) with more shady elms resulted in another call for protection of the trees from "boys and other mischievous persons."[24]

Bartlett's Mall provided an important venue for the refinement process: an area to show off taste and cultivation. In England, Borsay points to the rise of specialized buildings, such as coffee houses and assembly halls, and to the great proliferation of promenades for just such displays.[25] Prior to landscaping Bartlett's Mall, the Frog Pond area had already provided a place for Newburyport's elite to stroll and admire the view of the town, with the river beyond, and to take in the clean air along the ridge. Strolling, however, had social functions beyond clean air and views. As Borsay indicates, English promenades also essentially served as "marriage markets."[26] During the evening of July 29, 1788, John Quincy Adams, then an apprentice in the Newburyport law office of Theophilus Parsons, lingered at the Frog Pond with his friends. In his diary he described the use of the area by the town's young people: "Walk'd upon a sort of terass in high street. We there saw a number of young Ladies who seemed to expect to be accosted; and some who finally sat down on the grass perhaps to see if that would call our attention to them; but we were really inexorable."[27] Adams's line-a-day diary puts the point more succinctly when, in his entry for the same date, he notes: "Evening. Frog Pond. Ladies in abundance."[28] Court sessions provided a particularly advantageous setting for meeting potential suitors. When attending the Essex County courts in Ipswich, Adams recorded that he "found likewise at Ipswich a number of the young ladies from Newbury-Port, who to be sure were gallanted by their fathers."[29] The later addition of a courthouse to Bartlett's Mall logically brought together two settings for the important business of matchmaking.

Along with new construction and landscaping, the town's regulation of activities at Frog Pond also illustrates changing perceptions of the area. Despite elite improvements to the northeastern side of the parcel, the western section continued to house artisanal production, and town selectmen began to show concern for preserving the aesthetic appeal of the land and the cleanliness of the water rather than allowing its exploitation as a natural resource. A potter's kiln, established west of the pond in 1775, supplied redware for the local communities and relied on adjacent clay pits for raw materials.[30] These clay pits, in use since the seventeenth century, came under strict control in the late eighteenth century because of fears that "the Frog Pond, which is a very good and convenient watering place is in danger of being filled up and the water totally spoiled."[31] By-laws of 1794 also prohibited the townspeople from bringing their ducks and geese to the pond, and by 1814 the town also proscribed swimming and washing horses.[32]

By the late eighteenth century, therefore, townspeople began to perceive the Frog Pond as a specialized area within the urbanizing town of Newburyport that should remain unsullied by economic activity: a space that no longer served both farmer and merchant but in fact appropriated aspects of an idealized and controlled pastoral life for the urban dwellers of Newburyport. In his 1802 ode to the Frog Pond, "Rusticus" illustrates these changing attitudes. The opening stanzas of the poem describe Newburyport's commercial center as "a busy mart . . . where fortune is caressed" and as a congested place of confusion and disorder populated by cursing sailors. In contrast "Rusticus" sees Frog Pond as a pastoral space, with swimming ducks (presumably not the domestic variety prohibited by the town) and darting swallows. The writer also describes a space given over to leisurely pursuits: schoolboys sailing toy boats and young people strolling. He closes the poem by dwelling on the area's "natural" beauty:

> Now sable night; thy curtains drop,
>     And shut the pleasing view:
> The pulse of nature seems to stop,
>     Which morning shall renew.[33]

The Frog Pond's value to the town, therefore, came no longer from its associations with economic production but rather from its development as an ordered, pastoral space for refined and leisurely endeavors. Moreover, these pursuits included not the highly disordered rough and tumble of gambling, horse racing, or cockfighting, but rather the

more restrained and controlled activities of walking, courting, and the games of young children.

With these changing attitudes toward the land
came the construction of new types of civic buildings at Frog Pond. The first, an Essex County
courthouse built in 1805, differed fundamentally
from the earlier town house in its specialized use
as a building for court proceedings. Newburyport,
like other Massachusetts shiretowns, gained much
of its economic and social prestige from its position as a seat for Essex County court sessions, a
position it reluctantly shared with the towns of
Salem and Ipswich. Eighteenth-century courts in
most Massachusetts counties sat in buildings constructed jointly by the town and the county and
known variously under the names "courthouse,"
"town house," and "county house." Newbury's first
town house, built in 1730, sat near the center of
the original settlement of Newbury. The Waterside residents located the 1762 town house that
served as a catalyst for the split from Newbury in
the heart of the commercial district near the
wharves in Market Square.[34] Unfortunately, no
images survive of these early buildings, although
they probably resembled the 1758 Middlesex
County Courthouse built in Cambridge, a domes-
tically scaled, two-story, hipped-roof building
measuring approximately forty feet long by thirty
feet wide (fig. 6.4).[35] A "court chamber" given
over to court sessions and town meetings occupied the second floors of the Newburyport town
houses, and open spaces on the first floors accommodated a wide variety of town functions, including theatrical performances, militia musters, markets, and banquets. Bringing together economic
transactions with governmental and legal proceedings, these eighteenth-century buildings effectively integrated the various strands of the town's
social, economic, and political life.

Newburyport's new courthouse, however, like
others going up throughout Massachusetts during
the early nineteenth century, was stripped of its
extralegal functions and dedicated only to legal

Fig. 6.4. A Northeasterly Perspective View of Cambridge
Courthouse, by Robert Hallowell [Gardiner], Harvard
College Mathematical Thesis, 1801. Courtesy of the
Harvard University Archives.

proceedings.[36] Though occasionally used for the
very largest town meetings (specifically the annual
election of town officers), the town of Newburyport moved smaller town meetings and all other
public gatherings to a new town house, completed in 1809 and located in Market Square. The
fixed furnishings of the second-floor courtroom—
tiered spectator seating, sheriff and constable
stands, prisoner's dock, lawyers' benches, jury
boxes, and elevated justices' platform—reinforced the highly specialized nature of the space.
Moreover, the courthouse basement contained
rooms for jury deliberations, while the first floor
housed judicial offices. A central first-floor lobby
and an arcade along the front of the building constitute the only areas that may have provided
space for nonjudicial public gatherings.

Newburyport's economic prosperity enabled
the town to put significant resources into its new

courthouse. As a result, the building committee, comprising county justices and town leaders, by-passed the local building community and turned to Bostonian Charles Bulfinch for a courthouse plan (fig. 6.5).[37] Bulfinch's Newburyport court-house departed from earlier Essex County town houses in its design as well as its function. Unlike town houses in Salem and Ipswich, which were adorned with cupolas and porticoes, Bulfinch employed an arcade for Newburyport—an unprecedented design in Massachusetts courthouses—but one which fit nicely into Bartlett's Mall by extending the promenade into a sheltered space.

Most important for its relationship to the changes at Frog Pond, the Newburyport courthouse's location away from the town's commercial center broke with the colonial precedent of locating civic

buildings in the center of the town's most important street. The first town house in Massachusetts, built in Boston in 1658, occupied the site of the "market place."[38] In part because of its early function as a market, but also drawing on English town hall traditions and symbolic considerations, the building dominated the central street in Boston.[39] The two buildings constructed on the same site in 1712 and 1748 (the latter of which survives as the Old State House) followed a similar pattern, although the first floors served the merchants of Boston as an "exchange" rather than providing a market for agricultural products (fig. 6.3).[40] Closer to Newburyport, the town houses built in Salem in 1785 and Ipswich in 1794 continued this earlier tradition of town planning, which integrated the town house symbolically as well as

Fig. 6.5. Front Elevation of Essex County Courthouse, Newburyport, Massachusetts. Ink and wash on paper attributed to Charles Bulfinch, dated 1805. Courtesy of the Essex County Commissioners.

physically into the public activities of the town. Unlike these precedents, the Newburyport courthouse occupied a dominating yet removed position in the town and sat solidly within a newly created parklike landscape.

Essex County's decision in 1803 to build a new courthouse in Newburyport resulted in a two-year battle between the town selectmen and the county justices over the building's location, a battle that may have been shaped by continuing tensions between the Newbury "proprietors" and the merchants of Newburyport. The town argued for the site of the earlier town house at Market Square or in an area also close to the wharves known as Brown's Square. The county wanted the new building located at Frog Pond at the head of Green Street (fig. 6.6).[41] Ironically, a county building committee member, Justice of the Peace Ebenezer March of Newbury, had led the propri-

etors' fight for title to the Frog Pond and Middle Shipyard. Precisely how the building committee reached its location decision remains unclear, but Justice March undoubtedly understood that the proprietors could only benefit from the boost in land values that a courthouse might bring to the surrounding area if they ever secured the title. Conversely, this may also have contributed to the selectmen's great concern that the courthouse remain in Market Square. If ever required to purchase the land at Frog Pond, the location of the courthouse could inflate the price. Ultimately, the justices prevailed, and the building took its place in 1805 on Bartlett's Mall at Frog Pond (fig. 6.7).

The link between civic buildings representing social order and specialized spaces for genteel activities at Frog Pond reached its epitome with the construction of the last two buildings on the site in the 1820s: a schoolhouse at the northwesterly

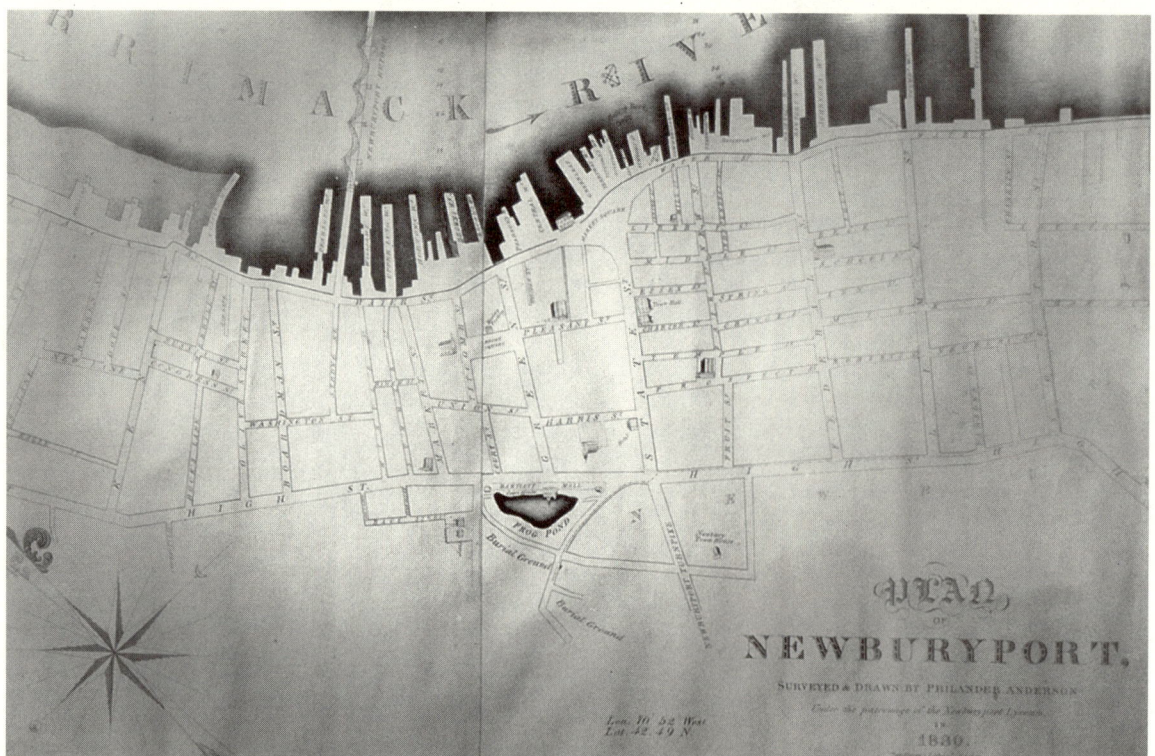

Fig. 6.6. Plan of Newburyport by Philander Anderson, 1830. Courtesy of the Boston Athenaeum.

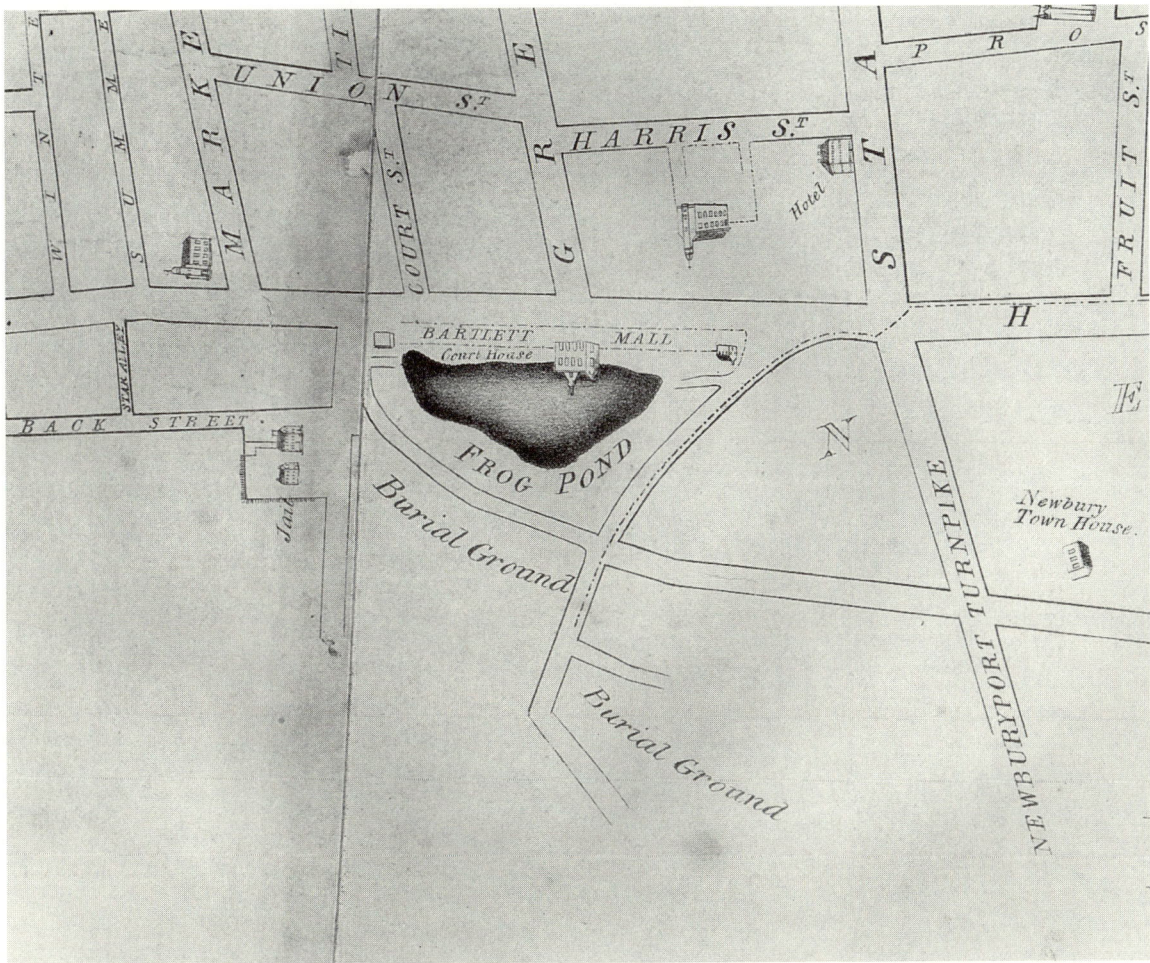

Fig. 6.7. Detail of the Frog Pond Area. From the 1830 Anderson plan of Newburyport showing location of courthouse and other civic buildings. Courtesy of the Boston Athenaeum.

end of Bartlett's Mall and a granite prison and prison keeper's house. In 1821 a town committee recommended replacing the four writing schools in Newburyport with two schools following the Lancasterian system of education, and in 1823 the town constructed a one-story brick building to accommodate the new school at Frog Pond.[42] The Lancasterian method, promoted by English educator Joseph Lancaster, looked for efficiency in education by employing one instructor and a number of older students as monitors to teach hundreds of pupils in one large, open room.[43] The Lancasterian curriculum stressed order above all and stringently regulated every detail of the students' movements in the classroom through the use of architectural elements such as desks fixed to a sloping floor and elevated instructors' platforms, which enabled close observation. Highly regimented classroom drills and routines and a series of rewards and corporal punishments further secured the students' docility.[44] Like the courthouse at Frog Pond, therefore, the new schoolhouse incorporated highly specialized spaces designed to promote disciplined activity and social order.

Essex County's new prison, raised in 1825 on the northwesterly side of Frog Pond, similarly represented the reconfiguration of an older public building form and also embodied an important aspect of the rebuilding of structures for the judiciary in early-nineteenth-century Massachusetts. Just as novel methods of education relied upon architectural forms for their efficacy, new penal systems that abandoned public punishment employed prisons to isolate criminals and monitor their behavior.[45] Moreover, building committees that began to relocate function-specific courthouses away from spaces associated with commercial transactions to areas of self-presentation and refinement also placed newly built prisons on sites aligned physically, visually, and conceptually with the courthouses. Newburyport's earlier jail was located near Market Square but not adjacent to the town house. A report on the condition of Essex County prisons in 1823 described the earlier jail: "[Built] of wood and very old, of two stories with only two rooms on each story . . . no distance can be made between debtors and criminals [and] the gaoler has been obliged to put women and men in the same room."[46] The county purchased the lot adjacent to the Frog Pond in 1824 and began construction of the prison, clustering civic buildings in the area of town most identified with gentility, leisure, and refinement. As with the courthouse, the new stone prison also differed dramatically from its eighteenth-century predecessor (fig. 6.8). Constructed of massive granite slabs and surrounded by an eight-foot wall with iron spikes protruding from the top, the prison would have been impressive notwithstanding its claim as the first granite building in Newburyport, predating Robert Mills's Custom House by ten years. Furthermore, the prison's interior differed from the earlier building by separating debtors from criminals, reserving the latter two unheated "dark cells." A prison keeper's house, also of granite, sits on the adjacent lot, reinforcing the prison's isolation and punitive message.

Fig. 6.8. Daguerreotype of 1825 Prison (left) and Prison Keeper's House, Newburyport, Massachusetts, c. 1840. Courtesy of the Historical Society of Old Newbury.

In the early nineteenth century, chastisement of criminals in Massachusetts, and throughout the United States, shifted from corporal punishment carried out as a public display to incarceration of criminals behind the walls of penitentiaries. Historians have seen in this change the rise of new forms of internalized discipline and punishment.[47] French historian and philosopher Michel Foucault argues that the removal of punishment to the prison signifies a shift in power from the demonstrative and immediate to the removed and abstracted. According to Foucault the invention of the prison merely marks a broader change in the nature of power: "Throughout the social body, procedures were being elaborated for distributing individuals, fixing them in space, classifying them [and] maintaining them in perfect visibility."[48] The change in form of prisons constitutes an important part of this power shift—allowing for prisoners to be observed, classified, and isolated, and thus causing an internalization of punishment.

The reconfiguration and relocation of civic buildings in Massachusetts shiretowns, nicely illustrated by the buildings arrayed at Frog Pond, reflect one aspect of this new "disciplinary society." Eighteenth-century town houses served a wide variety of functions and occupied prominent and accessible sites in the center of a town's active and important street. In contrast, courthouses, such as the one constructed in Newburyport, emerged in the nineteenth century as buildings dedicated exclusively to judicial proceedings, closely aligned with prisons, and set in an ordered and bounded landscape: they dominated the town, yet were not a part of it. In addition, the granite prison in Newburyport, with its separation of criminals and debtors and its punitive "dark cells," typifies the new prisons of nineteenth-century Massachusetts. Like the courthouse, it sits on a rise overlooking the Frog Pond area recently transformed from a diverse and economically productive landscape to an idealized rural area within the urbanizing town of Newburyport. As a new site for leisure, the Frog Pond fit conceptually with these buildings by embodying discipline, order, and restraint, and accommodating activities such as promenading, which both displayed and supervised those who took part.

The Frog Pond and Bartlett's Mall speak to the changing physical and conceptual landscapes of the late eighteenth and early nineteenth centuries. Civic buildings, such as courthouses, schools, and prisons, took on highly specialized forms during this period, meeting distinct and particularized requirements. Massachusetts courthouses in the early nineteenth century lost their extralegal functions, many schools adopted Lancasterian methods, and prisons incorporated new forms of individualized and internalized punishment. At the same time members of the gentry worked to refine and improve the landscape by creating idealized, pastoral settings purged of commercial activity and accommodating the newfound trappings of gentility. In shiretowns throughout Massachusetts, courthouse and prison building committees located new buildings in areas defined by plots of grass and fencing. For example, a writer in the *Columbian Centinel* described Bulfinch's 1815 courthouse and prison in Cambridge, noting that "the new buildings for the use of the County of Middlesex, at Lechmere Point, are situated on a gently rising ground, facing [the] Charles River, and in full view of Boston, Charlestown, and the surrounding country; when completed, with the proper inclosures, they will add another feature of beauty to the rich and variegated view of this vicinity."[49] Likewise, in 1821 the new courthouse for Hampden County in Springfield sat at the head of a town square also boasting the contemporaneous Hampden Coffee House, an institution that, like promenades and assembly halls, brought an air of gentility to western Massachusetts.[50] In each case, a complex mix of land speculation, aesthetic criteria, reform of the landscape, economic considerations, and political manipulations played a part in the shaping of these spaces. Yet, collectively, these competing tensions resulted in the creation of a disciplined, specialized, and abstracted landscape. New civic buildings, both symbolically and physically detached from the daily activities of the towns and removed from commercial centers to areas enclosed as parklike retreats, were thrown into high relief. Paradoxically, by being set off within a bounded and ordered landscape and by accommodating increasingly specialized functions, these civic buildings became at once both more removed and more visible.

## Notes

1. Ideas presented in this essay are further developed in the author's Ph.D. dissertation, "Disciplining Justice: Massachusetts Courthouses and the Legal Profession, 1750–1850" (Boston Univ., 1995). The author would like to thank Jane Becker, Richard Candee, Keith Morgan, Robert Blair St. George, Eric Sandweiss, Shirley Wajda, and the anonymous readers of this volume for their close and perceptive readings of this essay. In addition, Richard Gelotti, Chuck Griffin, the Essex County Commissioners, the Historical Society of Old Newbury, and the Peabody and Essex Museum were wonderfully generous with their time and resources.

Michel Foucault, *Discipline and Punish: The Birth of the Prison,* trans. Alan Sheridan (New York: Vintage Books, 1979), 3–31; 293–308. For an analysis of the transformation of urban space during the early republic and its relationship to metaphors of personal virtue and physical health, see Dell Upton, "The City as Material Culture," in *The Art and Mystery of Historical Archaeology: Essays in Honor of James Deetz,* ed. Anne Elizabeth Yentsch and Mary C. Beaudry (Boca Raton, Fla.: CRC Press, 1992), 51–74.

2. David Grayson Allen, *In English Ways: The Movement of Societies and the Transferal of English Local Law and Custom to Massachusetts Bay in the Seventeenth Century* (Chapel Hill: Univ. of North Carolina Press, 1981), 82–116.

3. Roy H. Akagi, *The Town Proprietors of New England* (Philadelphia: Univ. of Pennsylvania Press, 1924), 3–5; 129–31.

4. Benjamin Labaree, *Patriots and Partisans: The Merchants of Newburyport* (Cambridge: Harvard Univ. Press, 1962), 2–3.

5. Labaree, *Patriots and Partisans,* 2–15; John J. Currier, *History of Newburyport, Mass., 1764–1905,* 2 vols. (Newburyport: By author, 1906), 1: 13–30.

6. As quoted in Currier, *History of Newburyport,* 1: 13–16.

7. Newburyport treated the land as public space owned by the town and granted rights to build on or otherwise improve the area while the proprietors pursued legal remedies, arguing that it was "private land." The conflict was resolved in 1826 when the town settled with the proprietors for twelve hundred dollars, a sum well below that paid for the prison lot at Frog Pond two years earlier. See "Petition of Proprietors of Common & undivided lands in Newbury & Newburyport," Mar. 6, 1801, Massachusetts General Court, Senate Unenacted Legislation, Docket 2716/2, Commonwealth of Massachusetts Archives, Boston, Mass.; "Petition of the Agents for the Town of Newburyport," Feb. 11, 1801, Senate Unenacted Legislation, Docket 2716/1, Massachusetts Archives; Currier, *History of Newburyport,* 1: 119–41; John J. Currier, *"Ould Newbury": Historical and Biographical Sketches* (Boston: Damrell and Upham, 1896), 620.

8. Newburyport Town Records, 1: 60, Feb. 28, 1766, City Clerk's Office, Newburyport City Hall, Newburyport.

9. Sarah Anne Emery, *Reminiscences of a Nonagenarian* (Newburyport: Huse, 1879), 249.

10. Currier, *History of Newburyport,* 1: 214–15.

11. Ibid., 1: 119.

12. For a discussion of the archetypal New England village as a nineteenth-century creation, see Joseph S. Wood and Michael Steinitz, "A World We Have Gained: House, Common and Village in New England," *Journal of Historical Geography* 18 (1992): 105–20, and Joseph S. Wood, "'Build, Therefore, Your Own World': The New England Village as a Settlement Ideal," *Annals of the Association of American Geographers* 81 (1991): 32–50.

13. "John Crocker's Petition," Box "Deeds P–Z," Folder "Titcomb, Enoch," Manuscript Collection, Historical Society of Old Newbury, Newburyport.

14. "Crocker's Petition," Historical Society of Old Newbury; Currier, *History of Newburyport,* 1: 119–22. I am thankful to an anonymous reviewer of the essay for information concerning the siting of ropewalks.

15. William I. Roberts III, "American Potash Manufacture Before the American Revolution," American Philosophical Society *Proceedings* 116 (1972): 383–95; Harry Miller, "Potash from Wood Ashes: Frontier Technology in Canada and the United States," *Technology and Culture* 21 (Apr. 1980): 187–208.

16. Currier, *History of Newburyport,* 1: 120.

17. Ibid., 1: 317.

18. Peter Borsay, *The English Urban Renaissance: Culture and Society in the Provincial Town, 1660–1770* (Oxford: Clarendon Press, 1989), especially chap. 1.

19. Richard Bushman, *The Refinement of America: Persons, Houses, Cities* (New York: Alfred A. Knopf, 1992), especially 139–80.

20. Borsay, *English Urban Renaissance,* 41–46, 257–83; Bushman, *Refinement of America,* 181–82.

21. For a discussion of similar changes in the Essex County town of Salem, see Susan Geib, "Landscape and Faction: Spatial Transformation in William Bentley's Salem," *Essex Institute Historical Collections* 113 (July 1977): 163–80.

22. *Newburyport Herald and Country Gazette,* July 11, 1800.

23. Rudy J. Favretti, "The Ornamentation of New England Towns: 1750–1850," *Journal of Garden History* 2 (1982): 333.

24. *Newburyport Herald and Country Gazette,* May 16, 1823.

25. Borsay, *English Urban Renaissance,* 150–72; for a discussion of promenading in antebellum America, see Daniel M. Bluestone, "From Promenade to Park:

The Gregarious Origins of Brooklyn's Park Movement," *American Quarterly* 39 (Winter 1987): 529–50.

26. Borsay, *English Urban Renaissance*, 243–38.

27. *Diary of John Quincy Adams,* ed. David Grayson Allen, et al., 2 vols. (Cambridge: Harvard Univ. Press, 1981), 2: 436.

28. John Quincy Adams, Almanac Diary, July 29, 1788, Adams Family Papers Microfilm, Reel 16, Massachusetts Historical Society, Boston.

29. *Diary of John Quincy Adams,* June 19, 1788, 2: 418.

30. Joseph Chaplin, "A Plan of burying hill and lands about Frog Pond . . . ," Dec. 19, 1800, Box "Maps," Manuscript Collection, Historical Society of Old Newbury; Newburyport Town Records, 1: 233, May 15, 1775.

31. Newburyport Town Records, 1: 75, Mar. 16, 1785.

32. For ducks and geese, see "By-laws for Newburyport," Oct. 1794, Essex County Court of General Sessions, File Papers, Box 35, James Duncan Phillips Library, Peabody and Essex Museum, Salem, Mass.; for horses, see Essex County Court of General Sessions, Record Book 3: 380, Sept. 1814, County Engineer's Office, Essex County Courthouse, Salem, Mass.

33. "The Pond and Mall," *Newburyport Herald and Country Gazette,* Mar. 12, 1802.

34. John Currier, *History of Newbury, Mass., 1635–1902* (Boston: Damrell & Upham, 1902), 241–43.

35. Bainbridge Bunting and Robert Nylander, *Survey of Architectural History in Cambridge,* vol. 4, *Old Cambridge* (Cambridge, Mass.: Cambridge Historical Commission, 1973), 33.

36. For a discussion of the relationship between the emergence of function-specific courthouses and the increasing power of the legal profession in early-nineteenth-century Massachusetts, see McNamara, "Disciplining Justice: Massachusetts Courthouses and the Legal Profession," especially chap. 3.

37. Although both the Newburyport Town Records and the Essex County Court Records are silent on the hiring of Bulfinch for the Newburyport courthouse, a complete set of drawings for the building in Bulfinch's hand survives in the Essex County Engineer's Office, Salem, Mass.

38. Josiah Henry Benton, *The Story of the Old Boston Town House, 1658–1711* (Boston: Privately printed, 1908).

39. For a discussion of English town halls, see Robert Tittler, *Architecture and Power: The Town Hall and the English Urban Community, c. 1500–1640* (Oxford: Clarendon Press, 1991).

40. Sara B. Chase, "A Brief Survey of the Architectural History of the Old State House, Boston, Massachusetts," *Old-Time New England* 68 (Winter-Spring, 1978): 31–49.

41. Newburyport Town Records, 2: 255–306, Oct. 1801–Sept. 1804.

42. Currier, *History of Newburyport,* 317–21. For information concerning the Lancasterian method of education and its architectural form, see Peter E. Kurtze, "'A School House Well Arranged': Baltimore Public School Buildings on the Lancasterian Plan, 1829–1839," in *Gender, Class, and Shelter: Perspectives in Vernacular Architecture, V,* ed. Elizabeth Collins Cromley and Carter L. Hudgins (Knoxville: Univ. of Tennessee Press, 1995), 70–77.

43. Kurtze, "A School House Well Arranged," 70–71.

44. Ibid., 74–75.

45. Upton, "The City as Material Culture," 64–69.

46. "Essex County Mass. Prisons," Box 1, Folder 19, James Duncan Phillips Library, Peabody and Essex Museum.

47. Adam Jay Hirsch, *The Rise of the Penitentiary: Prisons and Punishment in Early America* (New Haven: Yale Univ. Press, 1992); Louis Masur, *Rites of Execution: Capital Punishment and the Transformation of American Culture, 1776–1865* (New York: Oxford Univ. Press, 1989); Robin Evans, *The Fabrication of Virtue: English Prison Architecture, 1750–1840* (Cambridge: Cambridge Univ. Press, 1982); Foucault, *Discipline and Punish*; Michael Ignatieff, *A Just Measure of Pain: The Penitentiary in the Industrial Revolution, 1750–1850* (New York: Columbia Univ. Press, 1978).

48. Foucault, *Discipline and Punish,* 231.

49. *Columbian Centinel,* Nov. 2, 1816, as quoted in Susan E. Maycock, *Survey of Architectural History in Cambridge,* vol. 1, *East Cambridge,* rev. ed. (Cambridge: Cambridge Historical Society and MIT Press, 1988), 130.

50. David Oliver Merrill, "Isaac Damon and the Architecture of the Federal Period in New England," (Ph.D. diss., Yale Univ., 1965), 166–72.

*Kathy Edwards and Esmé Howard*

# Monument Avenue: The Architecture of Consensus in the New South, 1890–1930

A century after its ambitious conception, Monument Avenue in Richmond, Virginia, occupies an enduring, if ambiguous, space in the perceptions and loyalties of the citizens of the former Confederate capital. Most recently for instance, the avenue has stood at the center of a political and racial controversy over the placement of a commemorative statue to tennis star and civic activist Arthur Ashe in the line of bronze and marble memorials to the champions of the Lost Cause. For those seeking to explain the past—and sometimes to define it—through their built environment, the avenue has been fertile ground for the historical imagination, offering a unique turn-of-the-century vision of progress and modernity founded in post-Reconstruction politics and memories of the Civil War.

Monument Avenue's traditional place in the canon of great American boulevards is equally enduring, though far less ambiguous. Architectural historian Richard Guy Wilson has called the avenue's "grand plan" "one of the finest illustrations of the American Renaissance and the City Beautiful Movement." When the Fourth National Conference of the Society of American City and Regional Planning History met in Richmond in the fall of 1991, the avenue was a prominent feature on the program. After a walking tour and the presentation of scholarly papers analyzing its history and architecture, conference-goers were invited to the dedication of a historic marker citing Monument Avenue as an important American landmark and "a significant planning achievement."[1] Richmonders are accustomed to such ceremonies on the avenue, and little wonder: in addition to its function as the South's grandest commemorative precinct dedicated to the heroes of the Confederacy, the avenue *itself* is a monumental urban space, a mile and a half long and fully 180 feet wide between building lines, with a tree-lined mall down its center (fig. 7.1).[2] At irregular intervals along this axis, five great bronze and marble memorials—to General J. E. B. Stuart, General Robert E. Lee, Confederate President Jefferson Davis, General Thomas "Stonewall" Jackson, and Navy Commodore Matthew Maury—define the avenue's public aspect as a shrine to a specifically southern history and identity. In spatial and architectural terms distinct yet inseparable from its commemorative program, Monument Avenue is also one of the most celebrated examples in the United States of the private residential boulevard as public amenity and civic art. Beyond broad, shaded public walks, the fabric of private residences that encloses the avenue constitutes one of the most spontaneous and sustained outbreaks of Colonial Revival architecture to be found anywhere in the United States. The coalescence of such a stylistically homogeneous and self-consciously formal enclave around so singular a theme of commemoration conveys a sense that some grand plan must be at work here, some equally singular vision of the City Beautiful (fig. 7.2).

In fact, Monument Avenue's cohesive appearance belies its making. The one-and-a-half-mile stretch of the avenue we will consider here—the extent of what is now a National Register District—developed piecemeal, in the marketplace, in several westward extensions spurred by independent initiatives between 1890 and 1930. At the same time, the controls that governed what was built in this new space were too minimal to account for the architectural homogeneity that evolved there. Instead, the parameters of appropriate scale and stylistic expression were shaped by an informal but strategic consensus devised by the residents who built over the course of the avenue's development.[3]

This architectural consensus was one manifestation of the social, economic, and political aspirations of Richmond's emerging post-Reconstruction commercial and professional elite. As early as 1876, the editor of the *Richmond Whig and Advertiser* recognized the impact upon the city of an important demographic shift: "A new race of

Fig. 7.1. Aerial View of Monument Avenue, 1927. This view shows Monument Avenue in the context of Richmond's residential Fan District (diagonal grid, to the left) and commercial Broad Street (right). Four rows of trees lining the boulevard and mall define the extent of the Monument Avenue National Register District. Courtesy of the Library of Virginia.

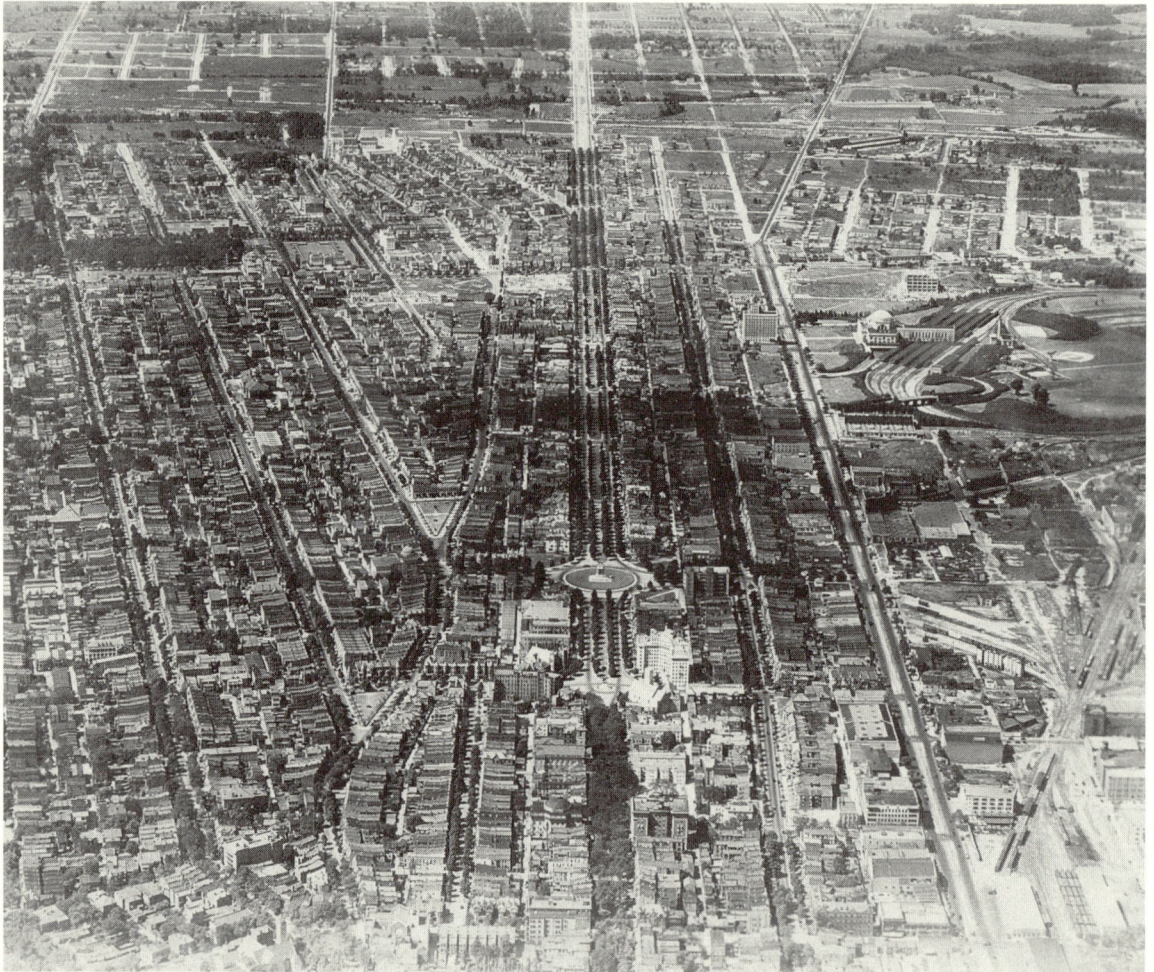

Fig. 7.2. Monument Avenue, c. 1912, Looking Northwest Past the Lee Monument (1890). This view shows development up to and just beyond the Davis Monument (1907) in the distance. Note the nearly completed streetwall of distinctively individual town houses on the north side of the 1800 block (from Lee Circle up to the first break in the mall). Courtesy of the Valentine Museum, Richmond, Virginia.

rich people have [*sic*] been gradually springing up among us, who owe their wealth to successful trade and especially to manufactures. . . .They are taking the leading place not only in our political and financial affairs, but are pressing to the front for social recognition. . . ." Speaking as one of the city's beleaguered prewar elites—the First Families of the Old Dominion—the editor ended his observation with a turn that reflected a new rate of exchange in cultural capital: "We no

longer contemn the filthy lucre. . . . Our provincial characteristics are fast disappearing, and we are not only advancing toward metropolitan development, but are losing our petty, narrow prejudices and becoming truly cosmopolitan. . . ."[4] This self-congratulatory pronouncement masked a number of ready tensions, especially in a society in which elite status had always depended upon one's colonial and (lately) Confederate lineage. In tradition-bound Richmond, according to local novelist Ellen Glasgow, "certain impon- derables were more precious than wealth." In this new social landscape, however, "imponderables might be respected, but possessions were en- vied."[5] Writing from an assured position among Old Richmond elites, Glasgow's droll, often bit- ing commentary on the city's changing social landscape reflected a pervasive unease over eco- nomic progress and over the necessity for new as- sociations that progress entailed.

Monument Avenue is testimony to the cultur- ally expedient alliance between prewar elites and the new economic power of an up-and-coming stratum. Yet, while the old order, as the cultural force behind each individual monument cam- paign, sponsored fund-raising campaigns and promoted the avenue's development as a memo- rial ground, they did not actually pay for the monuments themselves, nor did they build their homes on Monument. As the avenue's program of Confederate commemoration evolved incremen- tally over a forty-year period—sometimes leading, sometimes following the advancing line of hous- ing starts—new money derived from industry and commerce pushed residential development west- ward. The landscape that resulted was the mate- rialization of the old order's need to ground the abstract foundations of their cultural superiority in relics that represented historically "proven," popularly assumed truths: the spiritual value of public art, the courage and character of fallen Christian soldiers, the democratic affirmation of a great civic space. It was precisely the public, participatory nature of this carefully bounded theater that helped neutralize and naturalize in popular perception the contradictions between the rhetoric of universal communion in the ritu- als of a shared past and the social reality in which those rituals were acted out.[6]

The new class alliance coalesced in the 1880s around the South's first public subscription effort to finance and erect a memorial to the late Rob- ert E. Lee. The site ultimately chosen for this na- tionally heralded event was an underdeveloped parcel of land on the edge of Richmond's West End, at the terminus of fashionable Franklin Street and only a mile and a half from the state capitol. This decision was not without controversy: one of the primary arguments against it was that the site was picked for the benefit of land speculators and that Lee would be stranded "in the middle of a bare and featureless plain" until the avenue devel- oped.[7] The land belonged to the heirs of William Allen, a former bricklayer who had prospered as a building contractor before the war. His children modeled the plan of their development after Mount Vernon Place, a high-style residential de- velopment in the heart of Baltimore anchored by Robert Mills's Washington Monument. Clearly, the urban effect they envisioned was the mix of art, public space, and high property values in- spired by the European precedent of grand urban boulevards and recreated in a handful of well- known American examples, principally Common- wealth Avenue in Boston. The Allens' site proposal included the gift to the city of Lee Circle and two broad, intersecting boulevards—Lee and Monu- ment Avenues; the adjacent property was reserved for private development (fig. 7.3). This manipu- lation of their father's legacy gained the Allen heirs a boost into polite society and earned William's son, Otway, a modest political profile. In 1892—two years after the Lee monument was erected—Otway Allen changed his occupational designation in the city directory from "farmer" to "capitalist" and began a long elected tenure on the city board of aldermen, eventually chairing the powerful, growth-controlling committees on finance and street development. In 1902 he was appointed a delegate to the Virginia Constitu- tional Convention.[8]

The house Otway and Mary Allen built in 1911 at 1631 Monument Avenue, in the block bounded by the Stuart and Lee monuments, served as a model for what the family intended the avenue to become. Theirs was an elegant red-brick town

Fig. 7.3. Confederate Reunion in Allen Addition, 1896. By the time of this Confederate reunion, the Allen addition had graded avenues, fenced medians, and stakes marking proposed sidewalks. The first house to front Monument Avenue was not built until 1902. Courtesy of the Library of Virginia.

house in the Federal style, with a three-story rounded bay on the facade, a side-hall entry with a lacy fanlight, a pedimented portico, and crisp classical detailing in contrasting stone. In form and finish it evoked the cosmopolitan formality of the most exclusive Georgetown address, while it matched the scale, symmetry, and cornice lines of the town house next door, built for Mary Allen's sister. The Allen house, in other words, was an additive form, one element in a streetwall—a home owner calling attention not to himself but to his necessary and appropriate position in a particularly refined social order.

In their capacity as Monument Avenue developers, the Allens applied deed restrictions nearly identical to covenants that had been in force on Commonwealth Avenue in Boston in the 1870s. These emphasized a uniform twenty-foot setback, cohesive scale and common materials, and dictated the dimensions of allowable bays on the fa-

cades, implying the kind of undulating streetwall that developed on the north side of the 1600 block and along adjacent Grace Street and Park Avenue (fig. 7.4).[9] While the Allens were newcomers to the ranks of Richmond's elite, their program for the avenue drew heavily from a stock of conservative architectural forms that resulted in a streetscape familiar to West End inhabitants. Their singular break from traditional practice among residential developers in the city was in the systematic prescriptiveness of the restrictions they set, but the Allens made no attempt to expand their three-block development beyond its original focus on the Lee monument. By the time of the Davis and Stuart monument unveilings in 1907, the independent land traders and homebuilders who carried the boulevard scheme westward were each constructing their own vision of what was architecturally appropriate to this new environment.

Fig. 7.4. Recent View of North Side of 1600 Block of Monument Avenue. The houses along today's Monument Avenue were built between 1902 and 1926. Photo by Jack E. Boucher, Historic American Buildings Survey, courtesy of the Library of Congress.

The most prominent independent speculator in real estate immediately west of the Allen Addition was banker John P. Branch, an aggressive and notoriously acquisitive businessman, the epitome of crass "new money." Branch was the most powerful of an entrepreneurial group all too aware that the old elite was status rich but cash poor, and thus uncharacteristically open to broadening their associations. In his single-minded effort to identify his family's fortunes with the civic and commemorative program of Monument Avenue, Branch acted out an apparent obsession with achieving respectability on Richmond's stringent social terms. For his part of the bargain, he assumed the role of philanthropist and civic improver, doggedly campaigning for more and better paved streets

and donating two public bathhouses to the city. At one point he even hired his great-nephew, later a famous writer of fantasy literature, to produce a Branch family genealogy that would help establish the Branches' social legitimacy. Although Branch himself never lived on the avenue, his identification of family status with its development is evident in his gift of an entire undeveloped block to his son and daughter, with the stipulation that they build residences there.[10]

Branch reordered existing public streets through his property to conform with his independent addition to the Allen project and donated a right-of-way to the city for the extension of the avenue through this section. Covenants attached to residential deeds conveyed through Branch's Kingsland

Land Corporation often specified that a residence be of a specific value—six thousand dollars was the usual figure around 1910. Once a number of houses were built in this section, however, specific values were replaced by contextual ones: in 1912, the prospective builder at 2325 had to promise to construct a house "comparable in value to the residence on the lot immediately to the east."[11] In this way, Branch encouraged a homogeneity of residential scale and finish, but one that depended more on a competitive market standard than on a prescribed architectural character. Branch's covenants actually permitted one of the most anomalous structures on the avenue: his son John Kerr Branch's own residence. The Branch House, designed by a New York firm in 1914 and completed in 1919, contained 28,000 square feet of living space in a maze of public halls, galleries, private suites, servants' quarters, a ballroom, and designated storage rooms for carpets, china, paintings, suits of armor—all at a building cost of $160,000. This castellated Tudor Revival pile of brick and stone, parapets and gargoyles, reflected a social order far beyond Richmond, however: John Kerr and Beulah Gould Branch were world travelers who maintained households seasonally on Monument Avenue, on a farm estate in New York, and at their villa in Florence, Italy.[12]

Although the Branch House constituted an extreme example, the tendency to build big on Monument Avenue was pervasive. While initial impulse, reflected in the development in the 1600 and 1800 blocks (fig. 7.4), was to enclose the avenue between uniform streetwalls of coordinated, Victorian town houses, other early homebuilders responded to this great wide boulevard with a comparably grand scale of construction. The first houses to face the avenue dwarfed those on neighboring side streets; mansions averaged seven thousand square feet of living space, and even the first town houses averaged nearly five thousand.[13]

Ultimately, identification with the avenue was as much about respectability and propriety as it was about self-promotion. Early in the enterprise, the businessmen and professionals who flocked to build in this very public private development devised a building standard that reflected a tenuous reconciliation between these conflicting motivations. In the first frenzied flush of building between 1904 and 1910, the free-standing Colonial Revival mansion emerged as the avenue's signature form. Each incarnation was unique in its particulars, but all partook of a basic architectural vocabulary: red brick, contrasting stone trim, hipped tile roof, a three- to five-bay symmetrical facade reflecting either a center- or side-hall floor plan, a columned and balustraded front porch—all dusted with a generous portion of neoclassical ornamentation. The cream of Richmond's merchant class—or simply the more adventurous—built mansions in the new style across the street from, down the block from, or next door to business partners, family members, product suppliers—even business rivals. Among the first were real estate partners Herbert Funsten and J. B. Elam, who built red-brick mansions at 1815 and 1825 Monument Avenue in 1905 and 1907. Charles Guy of Ellington & Guy Lumber Company built his upright Colonial Revival town house at 1817 across the avenue from partner Bayard Ellington's Queen Anne/Colonial in 1908. The co-owners of the Southern Stock Yards built large, red-brick, architect-designed mansions with fine, balustraded white porches in the new fashion side-by-side at 2338 and 2340 in 1909; and R. Henry Harwood of Harwood Bros. Wholesale Oil Company built in a similar grand manner one block west of his brother and business partner, John, in 1910.

Many of these same businessmen also speculated in undeveloped Monument Avenue lots, both for profit and as a means of exercising control over property values, building restrictions, and the general character of their neighborhood—even to the extent of selecting their own neighbors. For the most part, however, speculators and developers along the avenue never aspired to any coordinated program of building there. Nearly all houses were commissioned by their future occupants, usually within a year or two of acquiring the lot. In sum, the avenue's apparently homogeneous fabric was the unlikely result of some 250 separate design projects carried through by individual property owners and their families, under the guidance and influence of a supporting cast of architects, developers, builders, and mortgage lenders.[14]

This architectural consensus reinforced Monument Avenue's dual character as both an exclusive neighborhood and Richmond's—even the South's— primary theater of public ritual. Each new monument became a cult object on this pilgrimage road emanating from the former Confederate capital and "Holy of Holies," and the number of pilgrims

was sometimes staggering. The unveiling of the Lee monument in 1890 capped a massive Confederate reunion that drew one hundred thousand celebrants and a great deal of troubled national attention to Richmond. Another reunion in 1907, this time two hundred thousand strong, culminated in the dedication of monuments to J. E. B. Stuart and Jefferson Davis and confirmed the avenue's status as the New South's National Road (fig. 7.5). By southern lights, Monument Avenue had become redeemed and sacred ground.[13]

Individual monuments also attracted their own rituals, conducted by hero cults, veterans' groups, or the United Daughters of the Confederacy.[16] But beyond Confederate celebrations and throughout the first half of the century, the avenue was Richmond's primary ground for all manner of

Fig. 7.5. The Richmond Howitzers Pass in Review Prior to the Unveiling of the Stuart Monument on Monument Avenue on the First Day of the Confederate Reunion of 1907. The dome of Beth Ahabah, two blocks east of the avenue, is visible beyond and to the right of the veiled monument. Courtesy of the Valentine Museum, Richmond, Virginia.

public celebrations, from automobile rallies to Fourth of July and St. Patrick's Day parades. Schoolchildren trooped to the avenue every Memorial Day to garland the monuments with flowers. On Easter Sunday the avenue's roadways were closed to traffic for Richmond's Easter parade, more a social than a religious event, which drew participants from all parts of the city. National events were also memorialized here, in parades welcoming soldiers home from World War I, celebrating Charles Lindbergh after his 1927 trans-Atlantic flight, and honoring Winston Churchill and General Eisenhower after the signing of the Armistice. Over time, the city's civic identity became intimately bound up in the avenue's symbolic program as its embrace expanded from an exclusive focus on heroes of the Lost Cause to include all events of civic commemoration.[17]

From its inception, Richmonders were also drawn to Monument Avenue as a promenade ground; this was local society's preferred place to see and be seen, to act out the social sorting process and refine important distinctions of inclusion and exclusion. Even in the simple family custom of taking a Sunday "turn" on the avenue in a fine carriage or—later—a motorcar, public displays of social status were as inseparable from the large and small rituals of celebration along the avenue as the facades of new homes were from the grand formal theater of this new civic space.

The avenue's combination of ritual ground and domestic space in the heart of the city represented a new era's new arrangement, an instrumental departure from the familiar scale and order of the old walking city. This instrumentality was one aspect of a larger project: the construction of a usable past, of a socially and politically expedient public memory. In post-Reconstruction Richmond, the traditional structure and values of white, Democratic Virginia society were seriously threatened—values like "governance by a responsible elite, deference on the part of a disciplined citizenry,"—white governance, black deference—"and

reverence for the customary ordering of society."[18] For a short time in the mid-1880s, Richmond's city government was controlled by a Republican Party and Knights of Labor coalition of African Americans, labor unionists, and working-class whites; the majority of this working class was made up of first- or second-generation immigrants. Unionism brought black and white workers together with enough momentum to add two blacksmiths, a cobbler, and a tanner to the city council; these joined with the few black councilmen to form a majority-controlling "labor-dominated reform coalition." Democrats rallied to elect Fitzhugh Lee, a former Confederate general and nephew of Robert E. Lee, to the governorship in 1885, and the re-strengthened party ousted the reformers from city government in 1887.[19]

The larger political reaction to the post-Reconstruction crisis was even more profound. In 1902, Virginia's conservative majority Democratic Party—including newly elected delegate Otway Allen—ratified a constitutional amendment that effectively disfranchised African Americans and most poor and working-class whites in the state. Party leaders, styling themselves as "progressives," argued that Virginia society had to be protected from its weakest elements; constriction of the electorate was vital, they claimed, to social stability, to morality, and to the prevention of "Negro domination." The new statewide mandate was immediately brought to bear upon local politics in Richmond. Jackson Ward, a commercial and residential district just east of Monument Avenue, had managed to elect black city councilmen until 1902; in 1904, just prior to a mayoral election, the ward was gerrymandered out of existence.[20]

The cultural reaction to the challenge to traditional order was less direct, but no less powerful in its effects. Old Virginia elites—allied with New South capitalists—applied themselves to the strategic tasks of public commemoration and historic preservation. The Association for the Preservation of Virginia Antiquities (APVA)—the first statewide preservation organization in the United States—was organized in 1889 and shared much of its membership with the United Confederate Veterans (organized in New Orleans the same year) and the United Daughters of the Confederacy (established in Atlanta in 1895). According to historian James Lindgren, the APVA rallied to memorialize sites that represented threatened traditions and consistently presented antebellum Virginia as an idealized social model. At the tercentennial celebration of the founding of the Virginia colony in 1907—a year coinciding with the peak of immigration from southern and eastern Europe—the settlement at Jamestown was eulogized and its ruins consecrated as proof positive that Virginians had sprung "from the flower of the Anglo Saxon race."[21] One preservationist declared that, because of Jamestown, "this country belongs to the English Speaking Race and the civilization which it represents." In more material terms, the architecture of the Jamestown Exhibition helped launch Colonial Revival as the revisionist style of choice in twentieth-century Virginia—appropriate signage for the preferred rendition of the past. The present-minded building market responded with its own fervent adoption of the style.[22]

Another strategy for the refiguring of Richmond society was the erection of monuments to the late war and the heroes of the Lost Cause. A passionate turn toward commemoration throughout the South at the end of the nineteenth century combined reactionary politics with "progressive" civic boosterism. Art historian Kirk Savage has suggested that groups promoting and financing monuments "sought to formulate a basic congruence between a 'metaphysic' of common patriotic beliefs and a 'style of life' that was ideal and elite-driven"[23]—to seize the reins of collective memory "for the public good," lest traditions codified in the past lose their currency in the new social order. The memorials placed along Monument Avenue between 1890 and 1929 symboli-

cally connected the official Confederate past with the avenue's modern incarnation of progress. By association, they also legitimated the new wealth surrounding them. Savage's conclusion from his study of the making and meaning of Civil War monuments both in the North and in the South— that "the politics of Civil War commemoration centered on race"—reflects upon a broad range of postwar "civic art." These memorials represented "the white culture's effort to cope with, and ultimately to repress, the challenges to national identity raised by black emancipation."[24] In separate works, historians Michael Chesson and Myron Berman offer evidence that, in increasingly nativist turn-of-the-century Richmond, "racial anxieties" ran deeper than the color of one's skin. Differences in language, culture, religion, even class and politics, implicated one in the larger perceived threat to traditional values.[25]

None of these social tensions were unique to Richmond, of course, but their accommodation is apparent in the fabric and evolution of Monument Avenue. Racial segregation in the city through the Reconstruction years was a matter of tradition and practice rather than law, defined in terms of block frontages, not streets or neighborhoods. Accordingly, Richmond's African-American population was scattered throughout the city in small pockets strung out along and between principal thoroughfares. By modern urban standards, black and white society were unusually integrated geographically, yet the culturally internalized rules of appropriate racial interaction held fast, subsumed and enforced in the patterns and nuances of everyday social behavior. On the eve of Jim Crow, however, in response to community pressures, black residences and businesses were increasingly concentrated in more clearly defined "Negro" areas, even as African Americans in the city realized more political and economic independence than they had ever known. Still, identifiably "Negro" areas were not monolithic; Jackson Ward, the largest of these, was at least 25 percent white even in the first decade of the twentieth century. For the most part, whites who lived in mostly black neighborhoods were Jewish and immigrant merchants and professionals who also maintained places of business in those areas, often catering to both black and white clienteles. Enforced racial segregation by block did not become official city policy until 1911.[26]

But from the beginning of its development in 1890, every deed on Monument Avenue forbade the sale of land or housing, or the rental of housing, to any individual "of African descent." Blacks might participate in public celebrations, but the only black residents allowed were servants, in appropriate quarters in the back of the house (if they were female) or in an apartment over the garage (if they were male).[27] More than 85 percent of households on the avenue in 1910 employed at least one live-in servant; nearly half had two or more. With few exceptions, these servants were female and black. Even the most modest houses on the avenue included rooms designated as maid's quarters in the builder's plans. The grander houses were designed to accommodate several domestics in service areas separated from family living quarters by a second circulation system of stairs, hallways, and back entries. The separation of spheres between servants and employers, between black and white, was also enforced in the larger landscape of Monument Avenue. Except when supervising their employers' children, servants were rarely seen in the public arena of the mall and the monuments, and they were tacitly forbidden to use the front door of a residence. For servants, tradesmen, and transients looking for handouts, the outdoor space defined by the avenue was not a grand tree-lined boulevard but rather the alleys that cut through each block between Monument Avenue and its side streets. This secondary circulation system provided for necessary behind-the-scenes household maintenance by the ice man, the coal man, the produce vendor, the "pig man" who collected

kitchen slops for his livestock, and other service and delivery personnel. Alleys along the avenue and throughout the neighboring Fan District were the infrastructure that supported the comfortable lifestyle on Monument Avenue without disturbing the avenue's pristine public landscape.[28]

The majority of homebuilders on Monument Avenue, as in Richmond as a whole, were Protestants. But perhaps the most elaborate social agenda accommodated in this new space was that of Richmond's Jews, especially Jews from Germany and western Europe. Their adoption and use of the avenue encapsulates the range of social, racial, ethnic, and economic issues worked out there. There were no deed restrictions against this group, either as homebuilders or residents, and in fact Jews constituted 30 percent of Monument Avenue's foundation families at a time when they were only 2 percent of the city's population.[29] When they began moving to the avenue after 1903, nearly all of these families were relocating from racially and ethnically mixed downtown neighborhoods, particularly Jackson Ward. On the avenue, they created an island of Jewish life anchored by two important institutions: the Jefferson Club, constructed in 1909, a prestigious men's club and educational society known as "the center of Jewish social life"; and Temple Beth Ahabah, largest of the city's four synagogues, built in 1904 in a bold Neoclassical style with a great columned portico and a dome that encompassed the entire sanctuary. Compared to residential situations in other parts of the country at this time, the degree of Jewish integration into the dominant Protestant social structure on Monument Avenue was remarkable. The Jefferson Club faced Lee Avenue one block north of the Lee monument, while Beth Ahabah was two blocks east of Stuart Circle on West Franklin Street. The only religious institutions on the avenue itself were Protestant churches.[30]

Beth Ahabah was Richmond's center of Reform Judaism, an international movement that emphasized ecumenism and assimilation, and discarded many traditional Jewish practices, including the keeping of a Kosher kitchen, the serving of unleavened bread at Passover, a strictly kept Sabbath, and bar mitzvahs. Religious services were structured much like those of Protestant churches, featuring hour-long sermons and scripture readings in English, accompanied by a choir and an organist. At one time Rabbi Edward Calisch even attempted to institute Sunday school and Sunday services, although this departure from tradition proved too ecumenical for the majority of Beth Ahabah members. Calisch was a native-born American and self-professed Social Darwinist who preached that the United States was the highest form of national evolution. Throughout his long and successful career at Beth Ahabah, he urged his congregation, in the name of patriotism and national loyalty, to disavow Zionism and to turn away, as he put it, from "those characteristics that make us aliens in occidental climes."[31]

Religious and family ties were particularly strong and complex among Beth Ahabah families, illustrating the ways in which social connections helped form both business and neighborhood communities. The Rosenbloom and Held families, for instance, demonstrated a typically cohesive pattern of Jewish development on the avenue. During the late nineteenth century, the two families lived near each other in Jackson Ward, first on West Marshall and North Second Streets, and later on West and East Clay. Irving Held married Dora Rosenbloom in 1909 in the front drawing room of her father's new three-story town house at 2012 Monument Avenue. The couple shared that address with Dora's parents, Moses and Rebecca, her four siblings, and a servant for the next nine years. In 1918 they moved en masse to the Brooke Apartments at No. 2215, and later occupied other apartments along the avenue. In 1910 Irving's parents built a Colonial Revival mansion at 3201 Monument. The Rosenbloom and Held families together occupied at least nine

Monument Avenue buildings over the years and were related by marriage to the Schwarzschilds, the Bachrachs, the Sycles, the Greentrees, and the Ullmans—all neighbors on the avenue and all Beth Ahabah families.

In many cases, family and religious ties were also business ties, establishing the basis for an offspring's later success in life. A grown son living with his parents (in both Jewish and Gentile families) often worked in his father's business and sometimes took it over after the father's death. Moses Rosenbloom's son, Abraham, worked with him in the family furniture store; after Moses died Abraham and his sister Sara each inherited a half share. Abraham's son also worked in the family business while he lived with his parents at 2002 Monument Avenue. In 1920–21 Irving Held was a traveling salesman for his father-in-law; earlier, he had worked brief stints for several different Beth Ahabah members, including the Binswangers and the Strauses. The next year, he started in the insurance business, where the experience gained through familial and social connections in his early years helped him eventually to become the leading agent in Virginia.[32]

Yet, even as a close-knit community coalesced out of shared values and aspirations, affluent Jews in Richmond often closed ranks against recent immigrants of the same faith. A particularly wide gulf developed between German and Eastern European Jews in the late nineteenth century, as Germans turned toward the Reform philosophy espoused at Beth Ahabah and Russians founded a separate Orthodox synagogue, Sir Moses Montefiore, in 1886. According to one local historian, "German Jews could not associate with Eastern European Jews on equal social terms without risking their social standing"[33]—a statement that implies an exceptionally keen awareness of both internal stratification and external scrutiny among the members of this small segment of the Richmond population. It is significant that German Jews in Richmond during this period were more inclined to accept intermarriage with elite Christian families than with Eastern European Jews. Historian Myron Berman suggests that, in reaction to the tide of anti-Semitism that spread through the United States in the 1890s, apprehensive German Jews in Richmond turned to nationalism and Reform Judaism as a means of ensuring that they would continue to be treated as fully assimilated citizens. Assimilation in this setting included coming to terms with the values and memories of the South, and many of Richmond's German Jews "adopted the legends and ceremonials of the Confederacy as their own."[34] In the first decades of the twentieth century, Richmond offered a number of more exclusive suburban residential options, but no more ready-made a setting for southern identification than Monument Avenue's self-con-

scious program of historical celebration, Colonial Revival mansions, and monumental Great Men.[35]

Beth Ahabah families on the avenue were not an innovative group architecturally. They tended, initially, to buy in rather than to build, and when they did build it was usually in a mainstream version of the Colonial Revival style (fig. 7.6). Their pattern of building suggests that their primary aims were to identify with their neighbors and to associate with other Beth Ahabah families. As we have seen with the Held and Rosenbloom families, Jews were also exceptionally loyal to the avenue, often building several residences over a lifetime, in a westward movement that reflected advancing personal and social fortunes. Rabbi Calisch, for instance, lived on Monument Avenue throughout his tenure at Beth Ahabah. His first residence

Fig. 7.6. North Side of the 2700 block of Monument Avenue, Looking East. In the foreground are the nearly twin residences of jeweler William H. Schwarzschild (2710, left) and liquor merchant Arthur L. Straus (2708), both Beth Ahabah members. The Colonial Revival–style houses were built in 1914. Rabbi Edward Calisch's second home on the avenue was also on this block. Photo by Jack Boucher, Historic American Buildings Survey, courtesy of the Library of Congress.

was a speculatively built Colonial Revival town house in the 1800 block; after 1910, he lived at 2702, in an elaborate, architect-designed mansion with an ornate Colonial Revival porch. In 1928 he retired to an elegant Mediterranean-style residence in the 3100 block.

The financial success of many Monument Avenue Jews no doubt contributed to their standing in the community. Several of the city's most prominent businessmen were Beth Ahabah members, and the number of Monument Avenue Jews who belonged to the business and political circles that ran the city is testament to their integration into Richmond's public life. Their presence on the avenue suggests that they were also part of a new social elite, for whom Monument Avenue represented "acceptance, the freedom to live where one wishes."[36] The avenue became the architectural context in which well-to-do immigrants could shed the trappings of their European past for a show of successful Americanism. But the social acceptance of Jews was not complete, and this too is reflected on the avenue. While some of the more expensively developed blocks had no Jewish residents at all, the 2800 block of apartment houses became known early on as "the Jewish ghetto." The very fact that Jews clustered on the avenue in such unusual proportions suggests that to do so served both individual and collective ends (fig. 7.7).[34]

Whether consciously or unconsciously, Jews on Monument Avenue built for the ways in which they used this new venue: for segregation from blacks and from Eastern European Jews, for consolidation as a Jewish community around their own institutions, for social and economic advancement and identification with the commercial and professional class, and especially for assimilation into Richmond's social economy. The architectural expression of these intentions was a high degree of homogeneity, the product of a more or less concerted effort to belong.

The Jewish experience summarizes how Monument Avenue functioned for a new commercial class and for Richmond society as a whole. For the initial residents who built there, the avenue was a place where crucial transformations became possible. It was, in other words, as much function as form: a highly conspicuous neighborhood, but also a strategic mechanism applied toward realizing a variety of aspirations. In the avenue's grand theater, a close relationship among material, social, and political accommodation helped Richmonders transform an emerging commercial class into a civic governing elite, crass new money into genteel privilege, successful immigrant Jews into "naturalized" Southerners, and African-American citizens—by exclusion—into an invisible servant class.

Above all else, Monument Avenue was a testament to the adaptability of Virginia's prewar elites, despite the fact that they neither lived nor built there. Richmond's social landscape before the Civil War had been geographically partitioned less by race than by interdependent affiliations of class and social group. The necessity for physically separate white and black domains was obviated by the overpowering physical and psychological authority of slavery. In the small rituals and encounters of everyday life, distinctions that enforced one's proper place in the social order were habitually reinforced at an almost intimate level: through body language, subtle behaviors, inflections of speech, and the internalized nuances of when and where certain rights and privileges of use, speech, or access pertained. The marks of class, gender, or racial difference could be as subtle as shades of variation in the texture and finish of everyday objects. But the post-Reconstruction city's expanding social economy required a very different understanding of cultural space in order to be properly managed. Monument Avenue and Jackson Ward became different aspects of this new strategy, by which threatened boundaries were rigorously maintained through the spatial demonstration of proper distinctions. On Monument Avenue, "imponderables" were *performed,* and through participation in that performance an ambitious new

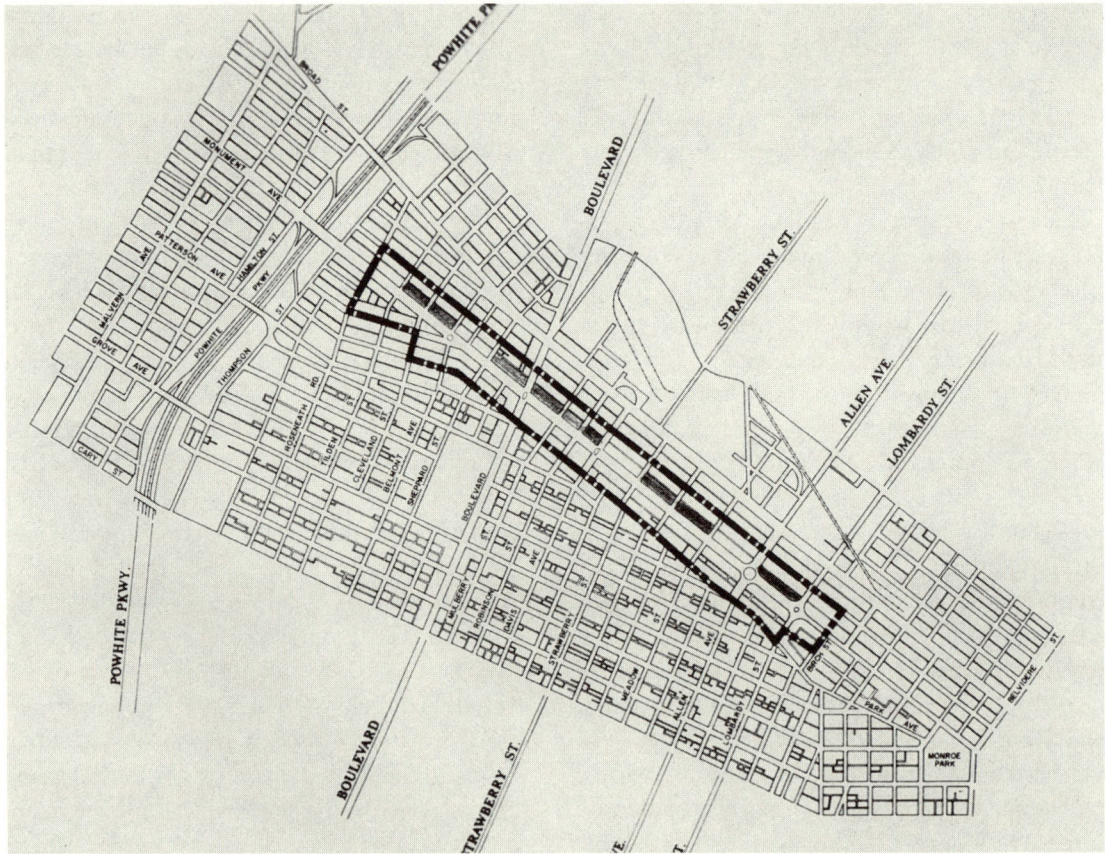

Fig. 7.7. Monument Avenue and Environs. Blocks in which Jews accounted for at least 30 percent of either initial development or first residents are marked in gray. In some of the indicated blocks, the concentration was as high as 60 percent. Because many blocks were filled in over the course of several decades, however, these figures do not reflect an actual percentage of Jews in residence at any one time. Jews also built and lived on the south side of the avenue, but for unknown reasons not in the same concentrated numbers. Drawn by Jonathan Spodek, Historic American Buildings Survey, courtesy of the Library of Congress.

group assumed the ideological trappings of the Old South, reinvigorating the status of traditional elites and, with borrowed cultural capital, transforming themselves. This process of entrenchment arranged the accommodation of individual and group agendas around a consensus on the most fundamental of principles: racial exclusion.

Material culture historian Kenneth Ames, in an introduction to a 1985 collection of essays on the Colonial Revival in America, pointed out that "many [localized] cultural accomplishments have

been propelled by a strong desire . . . *not* to be . . . associated" with groups other than one's own. Ames was not the first to call a fixation upon preserving the past "an act of cultural desperation," even "cultural retaliation." He concluded his essay by suggesting that, "while a little colonial revival may be a good thing, a great deal of it is a sign of personal or group disorder."[38] In this light, Monument Avenue might best be understood as the materialization of a pervasive social disturbance in early-twentieth-century Richmond—an architectural response to an acute anxiety.

Today Monument Avenue is protected by historic zoning and preservation regulations from the neighborhood to the federal level. Already a National Register District and a Virginia Historic Landmark, the avenue is currently being promoted by several groups for designation as a National Historic Landmark. It also remains an elite, almost exclusively white residential enclave in an economically stressed, predominantly African-American city. In 1995, amid much controversy, city leaders approved the location of a monument to Richmond-born Arthur Ashe on the avenue just beyond the western edge of the historic district. At the very least, the placement of an Ashe monument at the end of the long line of Confederate heroes will be an ironic postscript to the avenue's development. The arguments for and against it have not broken down simply along racial lines; while the black-majority city council, following the wishes of Ashe's family, approved the Monument Avenue site, other African Americans and many whites have argued that a far more appropriate location for the memorial would be in one of Richmond's primarily black neighborhoods, "where young

black boys and girls can see him."[39] The controversy highlights the complex resonances—and astonishing daily prospect—that a statue of Ashe would create on the avenue itself. A century ago, Monument Avenue inhabitants enshrined their vision of southern identity in an architectural commemoration of the Confederacy; what remained profoundly unstated, hidden just below the surface of brick, stone, and bronze, were their aspirations about both the privileges and the boundaries afforded by virtue of race, class, and wealth. The recent public discussion generated by the proposed monument to Arthur Ashe has already exposed the implicit tensions that, from the beginning, served as the foundations for Monument Avenue. The debate has also reaffirmed the avenue's strategic, symbolic place in an ongoing conflict over territory, opportunity, identity, and power that is Richmond's struggle to accommodate a new political and social reality. What remains to be seen is whether Monument Avenue can still serve its historic function as a crucible in which critical transformations become possible.

## Notes

This essay draws upon research undertaken in 1991 by the Historic American Buildings Survey/Historic American Engineering Record, a division of the National Park Service, Department of the Interior. Documentation of Monument Avenue was sponsored by the Monument Avenue Centennial Committee in Richmond and funded by the Historic Monument Avenue and Fan District Foundation, the City of Richmond, the Association for the Preservation of Virginia Antiquities, the Historic Richmond Foundation, the F. M. Kirby Foundation, Inc., the Robert G. Cabell III and Maude Morgan Cabell Foundation, and HABS. For a more thorough treatment of the avenue's social, architectural and development history, see Kathy Edwards, Esmé Howard, and Toni Prawl, *Monument Avenue, History and Architecture* (HABS/HAER, U.S. Department of the Interior, 1992). Toni Prawl's research and writing were indispensable to the HABS project, as were the maps and drawings by Jonathan Spodek. Robert Winthrop, AIA, and Drew Carneal were the project's most important resources.

1. Richard Guy Wilson, "Monument Avenue," in *The Grand American Avenue, 1850–1920*, ed. Jan Cigliano and Sarah Bradford Landau (San Francisco: Pomegranate Press for the Octagon Museum, 1994), 279. For a refreshingly ahistorical perspective on the avenue, see Allan B. Jacobs's treatment of it in his *Great Streets* (Cambridge, Mass.: MIT Press, 1993).

2. Within the area of the commemorative precinct (Stuart Circle to Roseneath Road), the roadways are each thirty-six feet wide, separated by a forty-four-foot median. Buildings are set back twenty feet from twelve-foot sidewalk allowances. In 1915, the Richmond City Council extended Monument Avenue to the city limit at Horse Pen Road, five miles west of Stuart Circle, but the avenue beyond Roseneath is very different in character, form, and function from the earlier section and bears only an incidental relation to the history we examine here.

3. The Monument Avenue National Register District, designated in 1970 and amended in 1989, extends

west from the intersection of Birch Street and West Franklin Street to Roseneath Road, encompassing both the avenue and adjacent development from Park Avenue north to Grace Street. Of the 253 surviving structures that front upon Monument Avenue, Stuart Circle, or Lee Circle, 15 were built after 1930; 12 of these are west of Boulevard. Surviving buildings include 1 hospital, 2 office buildings, 1 school (now medical offices), 9 churches and church buildings, and 240 residential structures. Residential structures include 4 rowhouses (2217–2223), 3 duplexes (2004–06, 3011–13, 3205–07), and at least 39 apartment buildings. We were able to document only 6 Monument Avenue or Stuart Circle properties that had been demolished over the years; all were constructed between 1894 and 1930.

4. *Richmond Whig and Advertiser,* Apr. 4, 1876. Quoted in C. Vann Woodward, *Origins of the New South, 1877–1913* (Baton Rouge: Louisiana State Univ. Press, 1951), 150–51; and in Christopher Silver, *Twentieth-Century Richmond: Planning, Politics, and Race* (Knoxville: Univ. of Tennessee Press, 1984), 19.

5. Ellen Glasgow, *The Woman Within* (New York: Harcourt, Brace and Co., 1954), 217–18.

6. The dates of the monuments are Lee, 1890; Stuart, 1907; Davis, 1907; Jackson, 1919; Maury, 1929. For the history of the separate monument campaigns and the evolution of the avenue's civic commemorative function, see Jay Killian Bowman Williams, *Changed Views and Unforeseen Prosperity: Richmond of 1890 Gets a Monument to Lee* (privately printed, 1969); Carden McGehee Jr., "The Planning, Sculpture, and Architecture of Monument Avenue, Richmond, Virginia," (M.A. thesis, Univ. of Virginia, 1980); and Kirk Savage, "Race, Memory, and Identity: The National Monuments of the Union and the Confederacy," (Ph.D. diss., Univ. of California at Berkeley, 1990). We are indebted to Allison K. Hoagland of HABS for providing a copy of the McGehee thesis. Mark Brack and Bruno Giberti pointed us to Kirk Savage's work. On the necessity for relics, refer to Kenneth Ames's introduction to Alan Axelrod, ed., *The Colonial Revival in America* (New York: Norton for the Winterthur Museum, 1985), 13–14. The quotation is from Savage, "Race, Memory, and Identity," 197.

7. *American Architect and Building News* 36 (829): 104. The complaint was well founded: over a decade passed between the erection of the Lee Monument in 1890 and the construction of the first residence on the avenue.

8. Brent Tarter, "Otway S. Allen: His Gift of Land Changed Richmond Forever," *The Richmond Quarterly* (12 [4] [Spring 1990]; 13 [1] [Summer 1990]; 13 [2] [Fall 1990]): 33. As for the prestige the Allen family eventually attained, it bears noting that the family burial plot in Hollywood Cemetery is on Presidents Circle, in the prestigious company of Presidents James Monroe and John Tyler.

9. The first official plan of the Allen Addition was drawn by C. P. E. Burgwyn, Richmond city engineer, consulting engineer to the Lee Monument Association, and friend of the Allen family. This document accompanied the deed in which the Allens conveyed Lee Circle to the association as the site for their monument and right-of-ways for the proposed Allen and Monument avenues to "the people of Richmond." (Richmond Deed Book 133A: 222) It is not clear to what extent the Allens participated in the plan's particulars beyond the initial scheme of crossed boulevards and monument circle, as no known documentation of the planning process survives. Given both his relationship with the family and his training, however, it is likely that Burgwyn retained at least an advisory role in the development of the scheme. Burgwyn earned degrees in architecture and engineering from Harvard University in 1873 and 1875, and was undoubtedly familiar with development underway on Commonwealth Avenue. At any rate, the Allen deed restrictions and their accompanying diagram of prescribed setbacks and allowable bays are too nearly identical to documented covenants in place on Commonwealth Avenue for the relationship to be coincidental. Bainbridge Bunting, *Houses of Boston's Back Bay: An Architectural History, 1840–1917* (Cambridge, Mass.: Belknap Press, 1967), 251–53, especially the diagram on 253.

10. The great-nephew, James Branch Cabell, even managed to dig up a couple of dubious colonial-era antecedents. See his *Branchiana: Being a Partial Account of the Branch Family in Virginia* (Richmond: Whittet and Shepperson, c. 1907). See also the Thomas Branch & Company Records, Virginia Historical Society, Richmond. Cabell himself resided at 3201 Monument Avenue for many years. In addition, John P. Branch's son, two nephews, and a granddaughter all had homes built on the most expensively developed Monument Avenue blocks. Today, Branch's great-granddaughter owns a home on the avenue one block west of the Branch House.

11. Richmond Deed Book 250A, p. 311, John P. and Mary L. Branch to Arthur L. Straus.

12. William B. O'Neal, "The Multiple Life of Space," *Arts in Virginia* 5 (Spring 1965): 2–11. Zayde Branch Rennolds, tape-recorded interview by Juanita Perry, Richmond, c. 1980.

13. For plans of houses of typical Monument Avenue scale, see chap. 3, "The Architecture," *Monument Avenue, History and Architecture,* particularly the plan of the mansion at 2304 (108–9), first-floor plans of mansions at 2601, 2714, and 2320 (111–12), and the plan of the town house at 1832 (106).

14. Prominent architects and builders in the development of the avenue are discussed in ibid. Appendix B in the same source lists the names and occupations of first owners on the avenue by address.

15. For more on the monument campaigns, see Williams, *Changed Views and Unforeseen Prosperity,* McGehee, "The Planning, Sculpture, and Architecture of Monument Avenue," and Savage "Race, Memory, and Identity." On the biblical rhetoric of the Southern "civil religion" and its role in bolstering intense Confederate feeling, see Charles Reagan Wilson's *Baptized in Blood: The Religion of the Lost Cause, 1865–1920* (Athens: Univ. of Georgia Press, 1980), especially chap. 1, "Sacred Southern Ceremonies: Ritual of the Lost Cause." For the most part, the language of Confederate mythologizing during and long after the war was drawn from the Judeo-Christian Old Testament, but the former Confederate capital was as often Mecca as Jerusalem, even occasionally some Athens-like idealization of a vanquished perfect Republic, whereas the White House of the Confederacy in downtown Richmond was the Ark of the Covenant. In the same vein, Southerners were the Chosen of God, secession was the flight from bondage, and the fallen soldiers of the Confederate Army were saints and martyrs of a holy war.

16. One such ritual, the "massing of the Flags," continues to be observed at the Davis monument every June 3 to commemorate the Congress of Secession and Jefferson Davis's birthday. The small ceremony is presided over by the local officers of the UDC and attended by a few devoted members. The fact that an address by the mayor of Richmond is a customary part of this ritual has taken on complex resonances in recent years: Richmonders have consistently elected black mayors since the 1980s, and over 60 percent of the city's present population is African American.

17. Local historian Edith Lindeman chronicled life on Monument Avenue in a number of her articles for the *Richmond Times-Dispatch,* including "Monument Avenue: Richmond's State of Mind, Shaded by Habit, Memories" (Oct. 5, 1969); "The Monuments: Stately Statues Endure Despite Periodic Debates" (Oct. 5, 1969), and "Avenue was City's Easter Parade Route" (Apr. 10, 1977), Monument Avenue vertical file, Valentine Museum, Richmond. Our thanks to Dell Upton, a former Richmond resident, for pointing out that the city has revived this Easter custom. Richmond-born novelist Ellen Glasgow occasionally employed Monument Avenue as a setting in her loosely fictional accounts of status politics in Richmond society's pell-mell rush towards modernity; see, for example, *Life and Gabriella: The Story of a Woman's Courage* (Garden City, N.Y.: Doubleday, Page and Co., 1916), 500–506. Historian Virginius Dabney occasionally referred to life and events on the avenue in his *Richmond: The Story of a City* (Garden City, N.Y.: Doubleday, 1976), see 263 on promenading and 286 on children's games around the remnants of Civil War earthworks in the 2300 block in the early 1900s.

18. James M. Lindgren, "'For the Sake of Our Future': The Association for the Preservation of Virginia Antiquities and the Regeneration of Traditionalism," *The Virginia Magazine of History and Biography* 97 (1) (Jan. 1989): 50. We are indebted to Dell Upton for the reference to Lindgren's work.

19. Michael Chesson, *Richmond after the War, 1865–1890* (Richmond: Virginia State Library, 1981), 182–88; Woodward, *Origins of the New South,* 230; Silver, *Twentieth-Century Richmond,* 42, 54. Black involvement in working-class political reform in Richmond after the war is a central theme in Peter Rachleff's *Black Labor in Richmond, 1865–1890* (Champaign: Univ. of Illinois Press, 1984).

20. Lindgren, "'Virginia Needs Living Heroes': Historic Preservation in the Progressive Era," *The Public Historian* 13 (1) (Winter 1991): 16. Lindgren's larger analysis of the public role of cultural traditionalists in Virginia is *Preserving the Old Dominion: Historic Preservation and Virginia Traditionalism* (Charlottesville: Univ. Press of Virginia, 1993). Good sources on Southern politics and disfranchisement during this period are Raymond H. Pulley, *Old Virginia Restored: An Interpretation of the Progressive Impulse, 1870–1930* (Charlottesville: Univ. Press of Virginia, 1968), and J. Morgan Kousser, *The Shaping of Southern Politics: Suffrage Restriction and the Establishment of the One-Party South, 1880–1910* (New Haven: Yale Univ. Press, 1974).

21. Lindgren, "For the Sake of Our Future," 48, 53.

22. Ibid., 72; Ames, *The Colonial Revival in America*, 10.

23. Savage, "Race, Memory, and Identity," 189.

24. Ibid., 2, 198.

25. Chesson, *Richmond after the War*; Myron Berman, *Richmond's Jewry, 1769–1976: Shabbat in Shockoe* (Charlottesville: Univ. Press of Virginia, 1979).

26. Silver, *Twentieth-Century Richmond,* 31, 110; Howard Rabinowitz, *Race Relations in the Urban South, 1865–1890* (New York: Oxford Univ. Press, 1978), 105–7.

27. Zayde Dotts (great-granddaughter of John P. Branch), Richmond, Virginia; interviewed by Esmé Howard and Kathy Edwards, Aug. 15, 1991. Drew Carneal (Monument Avenue home owner and historian), Richmond, Virginia; interviewed by Esmé Howard and Kathy Edwards, July 20, 1991. Rules about the proper place of African-American servants on the avenue were not hard and fast. Some families required married live-in servants to keep separate quarters; others did not. Some residents had stronger feelings than did others as to the "propriety" of allowing a black man to reside under the family's roof. Deeds for building lots sold by the Allen and Branch families specifically exempted black servants from the residential prohibition.

28. Zayde Dotts interview.

29. Berman, *Richmond's Jewry,* 261.

30. "The Jefferson Club," *The Owl* 14 (5) (Oct. 1902). For a detailed history of the Beth Ahabah congregation in Richmond, see Berman, *Richmond's Jewry.*

31. Berman, *Richmond's Jewry,* 249–50; Dabney, *Richmond: The Story of a City,* 260, 292.

32. Gentile families on Monument may also have been bound by the complex kinship networks that united Beth Ahabah families, but the only documented example we can offer is the Branch family (see note 8). Lewis I. Held Jr., *Held Family History, vol. 1, From Antiquity to the Generation of Irving I. Held* (privately printed, 1990).

33. Solomon A. Fineberg, a representative of the American Jewish Committee, quoted in Berman, *Richmond's Jewry,* 225 and 296–97.

34. Richmond had a long history of Jewish settlement and social participation, dating from the colonial era. Jews served in the Confederate Army and, as residents of the city during the war, endured hardships and sacrifices that forged a powerful bond of shared experience with fellow Richmonders. Berman, *Richmond's Jewry,* 246–50.

35. In conjunction with the Monument Avenue centennial, the members of Temple Beth Ahabah in 1991 organized an exhibit of photographs and reminiscences entitled "Jewish Life on Monument Avenue." Members, visitors, and avenue residents past and present contributed their own recollections to the exhibit's memory book.

36. Claire Rosenbaum, "What is it about Beth Ahabah and Monument Avenue?" Address to Congregation Beth Ahabah, Apr. 26, 1991, 11.

37. Although the context is quite different, it is hard to ignore the parallels between the Jewish congregation in certain blocks on the avenue and the Reconstruction-era pattern of racial segregation by blockfront.

38. Ames, *Colonial Revival in America,* 1–14.

39. "Leaders Disagree on Site for Arthur Ashe Statue," *Raleigh News and Observer,* June 20, 1995.

## CHAPTER 8

*Kathleen LaFrank*

# Seaside, Florida:
# "The New Town—The Old Ways"

In Jack Finney's fantasy novel *Time and Again,* Si Morley, a twentieth-century man, steeps himself in the artifacts and rituals of the past in preparation for an act of will intended to transport him into the previous century. Entering a meticulously restored apartment, the time traveler immerses himself in an accurate reenactment of everyday life in the 1880s, consciously repressing everything he knows of the contemporary world, until he has convinced himself that "in these clothes, in this room, in this building, I know I could have stood here then precisely as I stood here now."[1] At this point, Morley is ready for the actual leap across time.

In Finney's novel, the journey back is undertaken so that the hero can perform an action that will improve the future. In a similar mode today, proponents of numerous neo-traditional enterprises are pointing us backwards. From the historic preservation movement, lending a moral imperative to the reuse of yesterday's buildings, to cable TV's

*Nick at Night,* endlessly recycling outdated sitcoms as prime-time television, to The Gap, a popular middle-class clothing chain marketing blue jeans with the patina of a decade, we are being asked to take a historicist time trip, to rummage around in the attic of the past, gathering artifacts to use in the construction of a better tomorrow.

The contemporary town of Seaside, Florida, exemplifies this "Back to the Future" movement. Founded in 1979, Seaside is a community designed in the image of the past as a prototype for the future. A product of the careful study of traditional buildings and communities, Seaside is intended to be authentic, indigenous, and timeless, embodying the essential qualities of the American small town of the past.

Seaside was created by Miami developer Robert Davis. In the late 1970s, Davis had become dissatisfied with contemporary building practices. Around the same time that he inherited an eighty-acre parcel on the northwest Florida panhandle, he found inspiration in a nineteenth-century beach house. As Davis recalls, "[I]t was a dumb simple house with three exposures to catch the breezes and no tricks." Yet it stood in dramatic contrast to the International style town houses he had been building, and it prompted him to speculate about how the regional building traditions of Florida's past could be adapted for contemporary developments. Planning to develop the gulf coast site, Davis set out to tour the South in search of other models.[2]

Within a few years, the undertaking had expanded considerably. Davis had hired Andres Duany and Elizabeth Plater-Zyberk, principals in a Miami firm specializing in architecture and town planning, and the three had studied, measured, and analyzed numerous towns and buildings, selected their successful features, reassembled them in an idealized town plan, and codified them in a simple but rigorous building code.[3] In 1981, the new town opened for development. Seaside's motto— "The New Town—The Old Ways"—aptly signifies the mix of memory and idealism upon which its program rests.

It has been said that Seaside's appeal is based upon the loss of a meaningful way of life, a kind of life that no longer seems attainable in postmodern America. One way to interpret Seaside within the context of contemporary cultural issues is to look at it as a Revitalization Movement, a model for social change identified in the 1950s by Anthony F. C. Wallace. Wallace defined revitalization as a specific kind of change, "a deliberate, organized, conscious effort by members of a society to construct a more satisfying culture."[4]

Wallace defined society as an organic system that relieves stress by reinforcing the self-images, roles, and relationships of its members. He argued that when cultural systems become inconsistent, marked by repeated contradictions between cultural images and actual experiences, then cultural activities and objects lose their ef-

fectiveness in providing stability and comfort. Such chronic stress produces widespread anxiety, and when society itself is threatened by a loss of function, revitalizations are often attempted.[5]

In American society, images of home and community have long served as metaphors for and measures of security and progress. From the eighteenth-century ideal of an agrarian republic—epitomized by Monticello—through the nineteenth-century alliance between picturesque design and a high moral life—promoted by A. J. Downing—to the twentieth-century myths of mass salvation through single-family, suburban homes and urban reform through progressive design—which spawned both Levittown and Broadacre City—Americans have held to the belief that the enlightened society would be effected through the formation of good communities and the attainment of better homes. From the immigrant to the aristocrat, Americans have consistently looked to the design of home and community to give visual form to a way of life premised on self-improvement.

Yet the idea of an improvable society has lost credibility in recent years, and the cherished images of American home life are in stark contrast to the experiences of its citizens. If the American Dream is a home of one's own, then the current confrontation between the image of home and the reality of chronic homelessness significantly weakens the dream's power to inspire and comfort us. Likewise, our once-progressive image of urbanism has been corroded by a destructive cycle of poverty, disease, and violence, while the pervasiveness of fear and mistrust in contemporary urban America suggests that there is no safe place in the city.

In this context, Seaside can be seen as an attempt to relieve the prolonged stress of postmodern society by reconciling the image of home with the experience of home and community and restoring the protective power of place. If cultural ideas and objects such as the progressive city or the suburban house are no longer effective in protecting our safety or preserving our self-image, then the attempt to revitalize them at Seaside is also an attempt to reaffirm the defining ideals of American society itself.

Because Seaside also exists within the historical context of the resort, the community is particularly well suited to carry the moral imperative of cultural revitalization. Since the early nineteenth century, American resorts have traded on the promise of religious renewal and physical and/or mental rejuvenation. The perception that a vacation is also a healing experience implies that something good and necessary has been lost from everyday life and that it can be regained or replaced.

The revitalizing effects of resort life juxtapose the strange and the familiar. Resorts are defined by their contrasts with daily life, their oppositions in climate, pace, activity, and obligation, the opportunities for new experiences and the temporary relaxation of norms. Yet, resorts must also be familiar, for in some measure the solace that the vacation provides is also sustained by memory: the layering of vacation upon vacation, memories that reflect our own experiences or those of others, and the collective memory that we call tradition, as memories are selectively removed from their contexts, transformed into ideals, and blended into expectations. In a similar way, by blending the new and different with the old and familiar, Seaside's designers attempt to work their cultural cure.

In Wallace's construct, cultural revitalizations can be implemented by different methods, among them importation, revivalism, and utopianism. In import movements, features from other cultures are introduced to effect the revitalization of a local society. For example, in the decades preceding World War I, as America emerged as a world power, the importation of the grand architectural symbols of European monarchies and their redefinition as icons of democracy in the Beaux-Arts aesthetic helped to reinvigorate what had been thought of as a colonial society, while according the newly powerful nation the authority of ancient tradition.

Revivals reintroduce customs, values, and objects thought to have been present in a happier past. The American Colonial Revival movement is a good example. In post–Civil War America, massive industrialization and immigration seemed to threaten the identity of the traditional rural agrarian society. The revival of architectural forms and decoration from America's colonial era helped Americans to reconnect with what was believed to have been the simpler, purer lifestyle of the nation's early days.

Utopianism is an attempt to realize an improved cultural state for the first time. Religious millennial movements exemplify this revitalization strategy, countering threats of earthly chaos and despair with the promise of a perfect, heavenly society soon to come. Likewise, the model community is an attempt to create such a paradise here on earth.

Wallace observed that these movements rely to a large degree on historical blindness and that the different strategies are often combined. In import movements and revivals, new and traditional cultural images are redefined and improved before they are reintroduced; while in a utopian scheme, imported, existing, and traditional elements serve as unrecognized models for the new and improved product.[6] As a town that derives progressive imagery—intended to bring about positive social change—from the cultural artifacts of the past, Seaside combines a revivalist form with a utopian program. Architecture and planning are used to introduce borrowed cultural features; to abstract, ennoble, and reintroduce aspects of traditional culture; and to create a new and improved cultural ideal for the future.

Seaside was designed to evoke the form and character of a small town of the pre–World War II era, thus locating its image in a time when improvement was still thought possible. What citizens really believed in these other times and places is unknown and irrelevant. Rather, the renewal is effected through the values and behaviors that can be associated with their images now. By abstracting parts of old towns and houses, changing their content, and linking them with desirable feelings and behavior, Seaside's planners hope that these forms will seed similar feelings in us and that we will feel safe, be assured of our place in the world, and then act in positive, society-affirming ways.

But in billing Seaside as a prototype, its planners also encourage us to believe that we can take positive actions to improve life, thereby revitalizing the important idea of progress. If the reformed community is a seminal concept in American culture, then Seaside is a new version of an old idea, one in which, as one journalist put it, "the forward thing is to look backward."[7]

## The Plan

Seaside is located on an eighty-acre site. The plan was first oriented to a number of its specific features, including the Gulf of Mexico (south), undeveloped woods (north), a nature preserve (west), an existing development (east), and an east-west state highway, which bisects the southern third of the parcel. The plan dispersed development on both sides of this two-lane road, with about one-third along the beach and the rest inland, thus incorporating the highway itself into the town. Natural gorges in the dunes were used to locate the town square and the easternmost street. Diagonal streets were planned to follow existing woods, and the town grid was meshed with that of neighboring Seagrove, a small community to the east.[8]

Duany and Plater-Zyberk then imposed upon the site a balanced, orderly outline for development, an abstract and highly structured scheme with a rich symbolic content (fig. 8.1). Because Seaside's plan relies on the language of classical architecture for its forms, geometries, and perspectives, it establishes a sense of rational order in the town, structuring everyday activity within a well-known outline, reintroducing elements of time-honored symbolism, and reconnecting the community to traditional lines of authority. These cues reaffirm well-established ideas about an observable order found in nature, a permanent civilization, and a coherent world view. Yet, when Andres Duany announced that "the newest idea in planning is the nineteenth-century town," he was restating these notions as new ideas and thus reclaiming their redemptive possibilities.[9]

Although the plan of Seaside is new, its components are not, as they were derived in part from the catalog of town components identified through the planners' research and survey. More specifically, Seaside's plan was inspired by the work of John Nolen, an early-twentieth-century planner who is credited with plans for twenty-seven new towns, eight of them proposed for Florida locations in the 1920s.[10] Nolen's work falls within the broad traditions of the Progressive Era, with its focus on scientific improvement. His small-town plans provide a formula for translating a clearly defined ideological and social order into an architectural one.

Like Nolen, Duany and Plater-Zyberk created a town plan that was both unified and decentralized, defined by small, internally focused neighborhoods grouped around a dominant and highly articulated public space and linked by strong circulation systems. Seaside's plan divides the town into functional spaces, while its urban code defines building types and prototypes for each function. In general, the plan establishes a hierarchy of land use in which public space takes precedence over private, group image over individuality, and harmony over difference.

This hierarchy is clear both in plan and on site, as the relative importance of each activity is reflected in the formal complexity of its space, its location within the plan, the size of its lot, and the degree of design restriction imposed upon its buildings. For example, the town center, the most important functional and symbolic public space, is the largest and most articulated form. This octagonal feature is accorded the most prominent and visible location, marking the intersection of the central north-south axis with the highway,

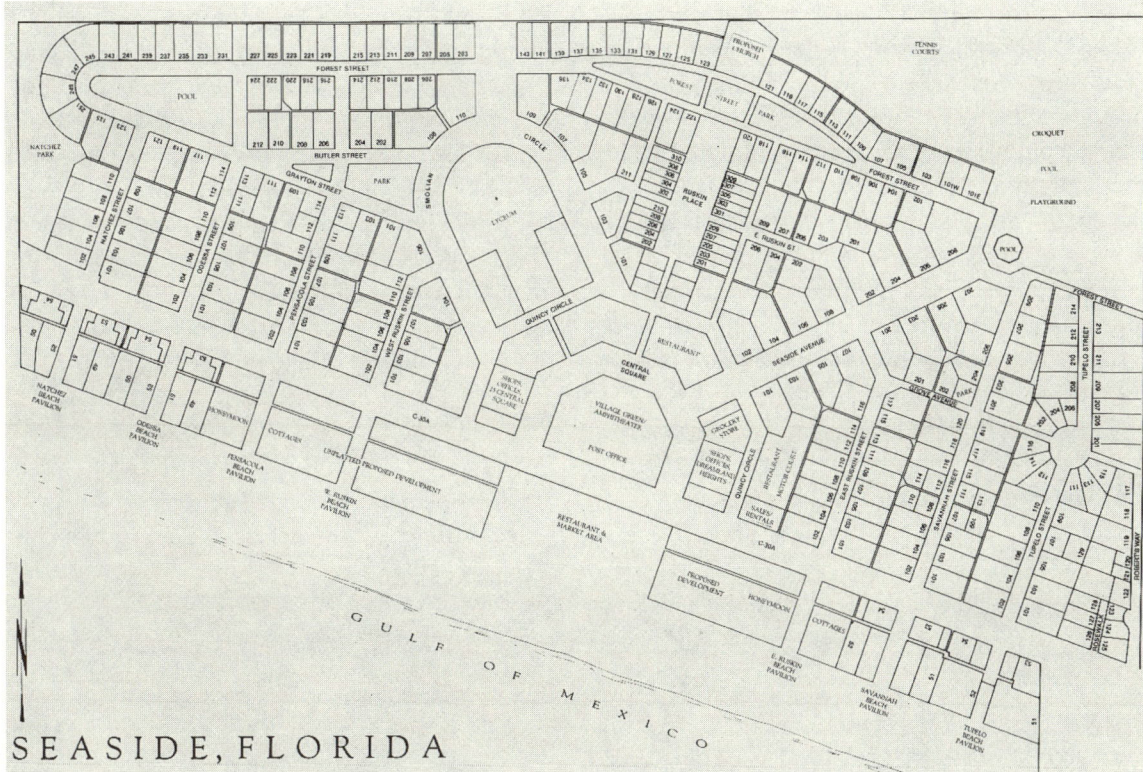

Fig. 8.1. Town Plan of Seaside, Florida, Andres Duany and Elizabeth Plater-Zyberk, c. 1981. Photo by Steven Brooke, courtesy of Seaside Group Sales and Marketing.

and the other formal components of the plan are arranged in reference to it. Likewise, buildings at the town center are to be the largest in size and scale and the least restricted in design.

Also distinctive, but slightly less prominent in placement, are the two major diagonals. These routes are reserved for the activities of select users; civic functions—the town hall and academic complex—line the northwest diagonal, Smolian Circle, and the town's wealthier residents and guests live along Seaside Avenue (to the northeast), the town's grandest residential street. Both routes were designed to be processional, and each terminates in an appropriate ceremonial feature: the town hall is at the apex of Smolian Circle and the Neoclassical pool pavilion is the focal point of Seaside Avenue.

East and west of center are seven shallow, north-south streets. These are divided into numerous small lots for middle-class residences. These streets are distinguished by their sameness: their small scale, formal simplicity, and supporting role in the town's geometry suggest the subservience of individual citizenship to the idea of community. Buildings here must also conform to strict design guidelines intended to ensure the creation of a homogeneous streetscape. In a similar manner, the plan and code provide locations and design requirements for other building types, smaller parks and focal points, service features, horizontal connectors, and pedestrian alleys.

Hierarchy was an important concept in Nolen's work as well. In his plan for Clewiston, Florida, he not only ranked streets and neighborhoods but their occupants as well (fig. 8.2). For example, Nolen laid out Clewiston's "First Residential Section" in a prominent central location. The elite position of this neighborhood is reinforced by the formal complexity of this portion of the plan, its proximity to the waterfront, and its direct line to the civic center. In contrast is an area on the far western edge of town, separated from center by business, retail, and industrial concerns, with a much simpler layout. This has been labeled "Negro Section," reserved not just for a type of use but for a prescribed set of users.

Like Clewiston, Seaside's plan is also less formal at the edges. Lots on Forest Street, the northern edge of town, are farthest from the town center and have no view of the gulf. These lots are less expensive, and designs for these locations are subject to fewer restrictions. Indeed, this hierarchy of place can be interpreted as sanctioning diversity, a desirable social condition. But in looking at Clewiston, we see that design features such as these can also ensure social control and regulate social interaction. Reintroducing these planning concepts today may also serve to revive the image of a less conflicted past, one in which social hierarchies were more acceptable and inequities more willingly tolerated.

## Architecture

In addition to locating activity within the town, Seaside's plan defines eight building types. A full range of functions is represented, including civic

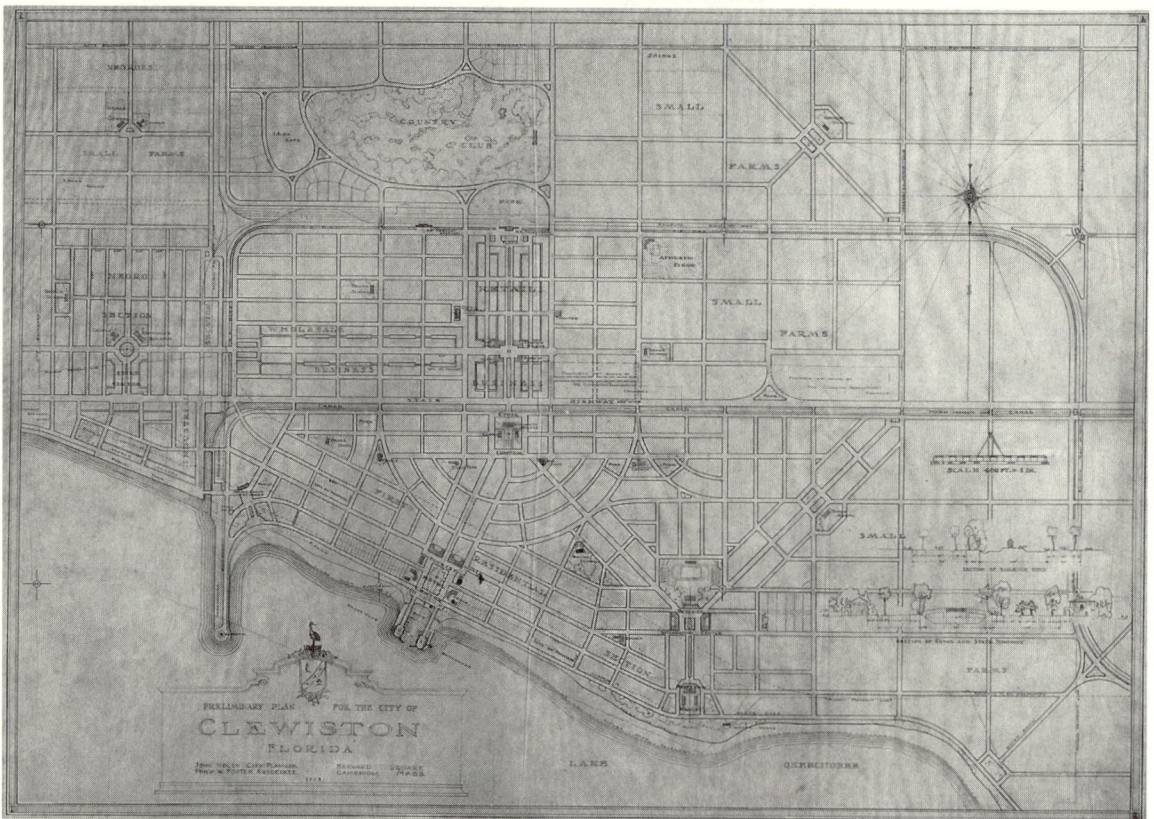

Fig. 8.2. Plan of Clewiston, Florida, John Nolen, 1923. Courtesy of Division of Rare and Manuscript Collections, Carl A. Kroch Library, Cornell University.

purposes, social activities, support services, and various residential uses. The form of each type is defined by specifications for size, scale, massing, siting, and footprint, all contained in a simple one-page diagram, which is Seaside's urban code. The code, however, is supplemented by detailed construction regulations. These outline requirements for materials, colors, trim, lighting, fences, hardware, utility enclosures, and numerous other features, down to the smallest detail. Beyond the strict requirements of code and regulations, suggested historicist models for each type guide the actual designs of buildings.

An examination of two of Seaside's residential types illustrates the use of different revitalization strategies: Type IV (fig. 8.3) is derived from an imported house type, and Type VI (fig. 8.4) revives regional forms. In each case their prototypes link them to specific cultural images, while revising the associations between images, values, and behaviors.

Fig. 8.3. Type IV Residence, Davis House, Seaside, Florida. Designed by Robert Davis with John Seaborn. Photo by Neil Larson.

Fig. 8.4. Type VI Residence, Unnamed House, Seaside, Florida. Photo by Neil Larson.

Type IVs can be built only on Seaside Avenue, the wide, landscaped boulevard that forms the town's northeast diagonal and serves as its premier residential street. Seaside Avenue also boasts the largest lots, the biggest houses, the highest prices, and one of the most elite prototypes, the Greek Revival mansion of the antebellum South. Seaside Avenue buildings must be large, freestanding houses, centered on their lots, with substantial setbacks on all sides. They are two stories tall, with full-width verandas on both stories of the facade and large outbuildings at the rear.[11]

The Type IV buildings constructed to date are characterized by their large scale and regular, symmetrical five-bay facades, most with restrained, classically derived ornamentation. At least one of these buildings, the Davis residence, has a substantial rear wing, where the classical sensibility is replaced by a more individualized and personal aesthetic. Two other Type IVs have three-story, rounded projections that serve as visual focal points and commanding lookouts. The aggrandized dimensions that characterize Type IV properties serve to set them apart from all of Seaside's other residential types. Together, their elegant boulevard siting, generous lots, full two-story heights, and dominating porches and towers serve to heighten the perceived scale of these houses, while insulating their occupants from the kind of arbitrary social interaction that is mandated everywhere else at Seaside. At the same time, their balanced facades and formal symmetry create symbols of rational, orderly, and harmonious lifestyles—desirable images for their owners and occupants.

Type IVs are intended to serve as private houses, apartments, or small inns. The plantation house was chosen as the Type IV prototype in order to inspire an architecture of grandeur, and its importation suggests that qualities of stateliness and splendor were felt to be lacking in the everyday architectural context of the panhandle.[12] Such a high-style provenance encourages the well-off owners of Type IVs to feel successful, important, and obliged—leading citizens who have a role in society and a stake in preserving it.

Yet, in the transfer of this object from the pre–Civil War South to the postmodern panhandle, certain less pleasant associations were left behind, so that we are not tempted to equate today's solid citizens (such as Robert Davis, Seaside's founder, who lives in perhaps the largest private residence in town) with the slave owners who exerted rigorous control over all aspects of human, cultural, and economic life in the Old South.

In contrast are the Type VIs, middle-class residences that are allotted the greatest number of places in Seaside's plan. Type VI development is required in the sections east and west of the town center. These streetscapes are regular, gridlike, and tight; they emphasize equality of place and maintain order through a rigid alignment of features: street, fence, setback, and porch.

Type VI buildings are closely spaced cottages on small lots. Buildings must fill a substantial portion of their lots (which are typically fifty feet by one hundred feet in size) and must be sited with a substantial front yard, an effort to preserve a view of the gulf for inland properties.[13] For the same reason, these residences are usually placed off-center within their lots, with the larger side yard on the gulf side.[14] Type VIs are low at the front—one-and-one-half stories tall—with open porches that must cover 60 percent of the facade. Many porches extend across the entire width, however, and some continue around one or both sides, substantially enclosing a small interior core within a large outdoor room. To the rears of these cottages, the code offers more flexibility, and the rigid setback line disintegrates somewhat. Buildings are allowed greater height, more volume, and a more eclectic and informal appearance. Towers and small outbuildings, which are encouraged, appear at the rears as well.

Type VIs seem to follow vernacular traditions both most faithfully and least rigorously at the same time. Many embody typical house forms and features, but display atypical, unexpected combinations of detail and color. Bungalows predominate, with their long, low forms, deeply overhanging eaves, exposed rafter ends, combinations of gable and hipped roofs, dormers, and tower-like projections. Many are strictly traditional in form, color, and decoration; yet, some are bathed in luminous postmodern color combinations, and others are overlaid with whimsical historicist embellishment.

The stated prototypes for Type VI are the anonymous vernacular houses of the rural and suburban south.[15] In the development of this typology, one finds an indigenous building (fig. 8.5), removes it from its context, purifies its form, equates it with timeless values and noble virtues—and then reintroduces a new-old version of its design as the home of the ideal citizen (fig. 8.6). Through the revival process, the real conditions of wealth, ethnicity, race, class, and climate are washed away and replaced by the heroic values and motivations of a mythic past. In this way, a small log house that may have provided impermanent shelter for a large family of poor sharecroppers can become symbolic of an experience quite the opposite: a satisfying and successful pioneer life defined by self-sufficiency, personal freedom, and economic independence. Thus, a historic resource that once had meaning within a specific local context can be reinvested with a more impersonal and inspiring content.

Type VI is thus the result of a structuralist approach, based on abstracting and idealizing vernacular architecture. By linking form to certain attitudes, behaviors, and ways of life and extending the virtues of form to the virtuous citizen, the planners have created an aggrandized icon that bears little connection to history, yet enables today's home owner to feel a link to the past that is both stabilizing and uplifting.

Fig. 8.5. Earle Plantation House, Alachua County, Florida. Photo by Ronald W. Haase.

Fig. 8.6. Revived Type VI Residence, Raeburn House, Seaside, Florida. Designed by Cooper Johnson Smith. Photo by Neil Larson, 1990.

## The Front Porch

The goals of Seaside's plan and code are reinforced by numerous smaller features. For example, one of Duany's stated objectives is "to reform society on the level of having people meet."[16] Thus, the ubiquitous Seaside front porch can be seen as an attempt to revitalize the street as a meeting place. Porches are familiar features of southern life. They had a practical function in ventilation and they were also the means by which certain social interactions took place. Seaside's porches are intended to symbolize and promote similar experiences, and their presence, placement, size, and proportion are strictly regulated.

Nearly two hundred porches are planned for Seaside and many have been built. But, by almost all accounts, the town is beastly hot in summer; air-conditioning is standard; and most of the porches remain empty. Thus, Seaside's porches fail to meet both functional and social goals, providing neither a cool outdoor room nor a catalyst to interaction. But what of their symbolic purpose? Robert A. M. Stern has observed, "in post–World War II America, public life was pushed to the back of the house . . . it may be just a gesture, but the front porch makes the street a public space."[17] Stern's comments seem to suggest that the mere presence of the porch signifies the renewal of street life—even if no one has actually returned to it.

The "porch problem" suggests one of the big questions about Seaside: Can a revival of image alone successfully revitalize a cultural system without the reinforcement of experience? We might note here that while it prospers as an upscale resort, perhaps offering temporary renewal, Seaside is a failure as a town. There are few nontourist-related jobs; there is no school, and full-time families are scarce. In fact, Seaside has been officially redefined as a vacation community.

While we might question the success of the larger cultural experiment, there is no doubt about the success of the nostalgia business as a commod-ity. Seaside's real estate values have more than tripled.[18] And, in fact, the residents of this fifteen-year-old community have already begun to recycle bits of their own history, which make great copy. A recent article in the *Seaside Times* (the town's occasional newspaper) was entitled "Do You Remember When . . ." and recounted Seaside's pioneer days—the early 1980s.[19]

Seaside has been described as a perfect memory. And, in a sense, that is exactly what it is: a wistful view of the world as it perhaps never existed, an elixir of innocence more palatable than the bitter taste of postmodern life. In today's uncertain world, as we become less hopeful for the future and less sure of our power to improve it, it is tempting to try to return to times, places, and things that may seem—from our remote and limited perspective—to have been simple, understandable, comforting, controllable, and permanent. And, as postmodern life becomes ever more fragmented, it is equally tempting to see the artifacts of the past as things that are timeless and eternal that can, perhaps, be used to help us return to those simple-seeming times.

In the construction of the particular fantasy that is Seaside, the appropriation of the artifacts of history is the means by which illusions about the past are kept alive. In a very real way, Seaside's creators and participants have distilled their memories, experiences, and expectations, extracting fears and disillusionments and enhancing the half-truths that are left. Relieved of the contradictions of the present by a convincing set design, the Seasiders stand poised like the hero of *Time and Again*—ready to make a collective leap into the past.

Seaside is an attempt to reconstruct the American Dream as we would like to believe it once existed: righteous, idealistic, optimistic, and free from even the suspicion that, by the late twentieth century, the dream itself would prove untenable for many. In that its creation was premised on the perception of cultural bankruptcy, Seaside has much to reveal about our images and experiences of home and community and about our need for comfort and how it is obtained. At Seaside, a devotion to the past has become the link between the disillusionments of the present and what was once thought possible in the future.

## Postscript

In recent years, Americans have looked increasingly to the past, rather than to the future, for their salvation. The titles of books such as *The Presence of the Past, A Future for the Past,* and *A Future from the Past* illustrate the ideological framework within which the cult of the past has flourished. In a country that was founded as a radical new experiment, the past is now defined as a progressive ideal. Today, for many of us—students and guardians of the past—understanding, preserving, and adopting the forms, designs, decorations, methods, and lifeways of the past have become tangible goals for the future. Yet, the attitudes and expectations that we bring to bear on our own interpretation and use of the past cannot be separated from our view of the present. Perhaps looking at Seaside for hints about the meanings and methods of cultural revitalization may inspire those of us who study the past to explore and interpret our own investment in history, our methodology in studying it, and our motives in preserving it.

## Notes

1. Jack Finney, *Time and Again* (New York: Simon, 1970), 97.

2. Kevin Wolfe, "Endless Summer," *Metropolis* (Oct. 1988): 84. This anecdote about Seaside's genesis is repeated in many published articles about Seaside.

3. Wolfe, "Endless Summer," 84. This description is also repeated in many articles about Seaside.

4. Anthony F. C. Wallace, "Revitalization Movements," *American Anthropologist* 58 (1956): 265.

5. Ibid., 265–67.

6. Ibid., 275–76.

7. Phil Patton, "In Seaside, Florida, the Forward Thing Is to Look Backward," *Smithsonian* (Jan. 1991): 82.

8. Andres Duany and Elizabeth Plater-Zyberk, "The Town of Seaside, Seaside, Florida," *Center* 1 (1985).

9. Quoted in Philip Langdon, "A Good Place to Live," *Atlantic Monthly,* Mar. 1988. Reprinted in "A Rediscovery of America: The Seaside Symposium 1988" (Seaside: Seaside Institute, n.d.), 77.

10. John Hancock, "'What is fair must be fit': Drawings and Plans by John Nolen, American City Planner," *Lotus International* 50 (1986). Reprinted in "A Rediscovery of America," 37.

11. Andres Duany and Elizabeth Plater-Zyberk, "A Town Plan for Seaside," in *Seaside: Making a Town in America,* ed. Keller Easterling and David Moheny (New York: Princeton Architectural Press, 1991), 102.

12. Ibid.

13. Ibid., 103.

14. Andres Duany, Interview, in *Seaside: Making a Town,* 68.

15. Duany and Plater-Zyberk, "Town Plan," 103.

16. Quoted in Joseph Giovannini, "Andres Duany and Elizabeth Plater-Zyberk: Blueprint for the Future," *Esquire,* Dec. 1988. Reprinted in "A Rediscovery of America," 87.

17. Quoted in Wolfe, "Endless Summer," 86.

18. Langdon, "A Good Place to Live," 77. Numerous articles report an increase in property values at Seaside; the amount varies depending on when they were written.

19. Carol McCrite, "Do You Remember When . . ." *Seaside Times* (Winter 1992): 7.

CHAPTER

# 9

*Gary Stanton*

# "Alarmed by the Cry of Fire": How Fire Changed Fredericksburg, Virginia

Fredericksburg, Virginia, is described in the literature of tourism and preservation as a city that retains the architecture of the eighteenth century. Yet the buildings at the core of the community that survive today are almost without exception from the second and third decades of the nineteenth century. Why was there such a complete replacement? The answer is complex but partially supported by examining fire insurance policies of the Virginia Mutual Assurance Society from 1796 through the 1820s. Through the constant documentation of standing structures, these papers report how the buildings of Fredericksburg changed from mainly detached wood structures to consolidated brick ensembles in the first quarter of the nineteenth century. Early policies depict a town of one-story or one-and-one-half-story detached wooden structures. During the second decade of the nineteenth century, the pace of rebuilding accelerated as owners sought to organize building

uses vertically and replaced frame structures with larger buildings built of brick. This rapid change occurred only in the oldest portion of the city, the commercial core. To explain how fire changed Fredericksburg, this paper traces the relationship between fire fears, the development of fire insurance in Virginia, the destruction of buildings by fire, and changes in building form and materials of buildings.[1]

In urban areas the perceived threat of destruction by fire differentially affects those people with capital assets at risk. As the concept of fire insurance developed in America during the late eighteenth century, many owners sought refuge from the high cost of rebuilding through policies covering a broad range of buildings from dwellings to stores and stables. In dispersed settlement on rural plantations where open space dominated the architecture and even within town lots surrounded by large gardens and wooden palings, the danger of

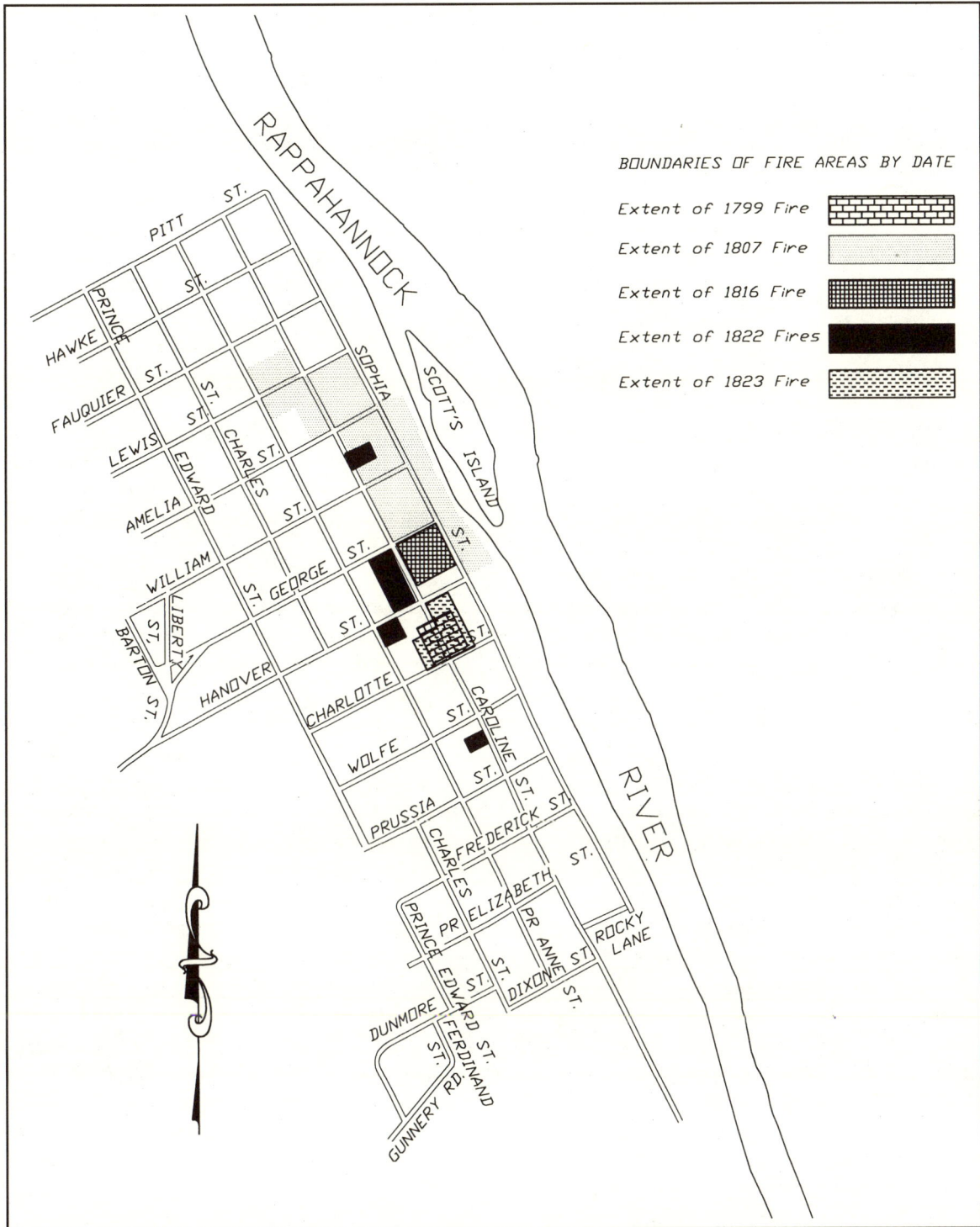

Fig. 9.1. Fredericksburg, 1828.

fire was perceived as internal to the property—the hazards of using open fires for cooking, heating, and work. Owners of these properties paid for insurance, but made few changes in the manner and materials of construction to minimize fire damage. In other areas, where urban density was achieved, the concern shifted from an internal liability involving using fire to a fear of contagion from adjoining property. The buildings most likely to receive prophylactic modifications were those housing capital-intensive, commercial-exchange activities, which were densely packed within commercial districts. As merchants in Fredericksburg, Virginia, brought these services into a downtown district closely aligned with its market square, town hall, and circuit court buildings, the threat of fire was felt to be especially severe. Each conflagration, whether modest or severe, triggered legal and material modifications to decrease the likelihood of the spread of fire. By the mid-1820s the combination of repeated fire, subdivision of downtown lots, and concern for fire created a tightly packed urban core in Fredericksburg with virtually no eighteenth-century fabric left, except at the periphery (fig. 9.1).[2]

Fear of the loss from fire damage is not alone sufficient to explain the shift in materials from wood to brick within the core area of Fredericksburg. Increasing land values, new ways of occupying buildings with vertically segregated storage, commercial and domestic space, and the prestige of substantial and permanent structures all contributed to the result. But the fire threat was certainly an important part of the calculus, and buildings with inflammable walls and roof were often described as fireproof. Fire can convincingly explain the replacement of shingle with tile and slate roofing materials in the early nineteenth century in Fredericksburg.

Fire within the urban context has not typically been considered a problem intrinsic to the building, but arises from the activities, density, and distribution of buildings. While still a calamity in less dense suburban and rural areas, fire has little influence on building practice where buildings are presumably buffered by open space. Lightning rods and brick chimneys were the principal deterrents to fire in rural areas, and beyond these actions many plantation owners found little benefit in paying for insurance. Then, too, methods for putting fires out in the early nineteenth century provided little direct control, but emphasized containing the fire, and stopping its spread. Although originally intended to provide coverage to both urban and rural properties, the Mutual Assurance Society of Virginia found that the only plantation owners who sought insurance were the social elites, and these in insufficient numbers to maintain the mutuality of benefits. The result was that the company ceased insuring properties one mile beyond a town or city boundary in 1822.[3]

Although newspaper articles described the fires, city councils passed ordinances from the ashes of fires, and volunteer fire companies were organized in response to fires, in the early nineteenth century the major documentation of the built environment before it burned was principally through the specific policies of the Virginia Mutual Assurance Society (fig. 9.2). Each policy recorded information about owners, an estimate of the cost necessary to reconstruct a building, and information about the buildings themselves. Because this was a mutual company, requiring yearly quotas of its members based upon their coverage, the insurance policies were kept by the society headquarters in Richmond, Virginia, and copies occasionally provided to owners or litigants.[4] Today the Mutual Assurance Society policies represent a collection of over thirty thousand policies from 1796 to 1865.[5] For cities in Virginia, like Norfolk, Richmond, Lynchburg, Winchester, Alexandria, and Fredericksburg, substantial documentary evidence of building size and fabric exists for a majority of the major buildings of the city. The percentage of houses and stores insured by the Mutual Assurance Society varied, but may have been as high as 80 percent for Fredericksburg at the beginning of the nineteenth century.

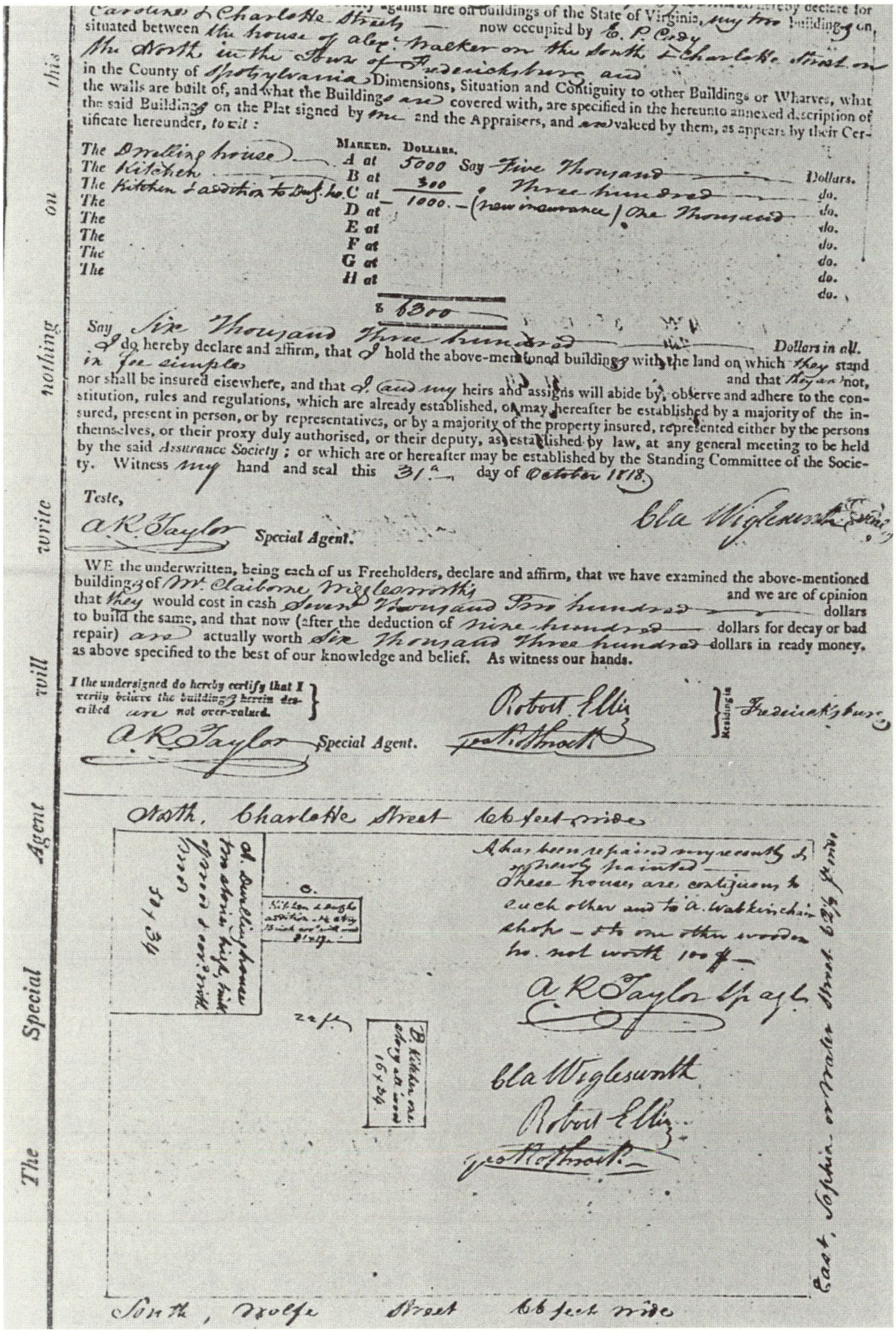
Caroline & Charlotte Streets ... against fire on buildings of the State of Virginia, ... declare for situated between the house of Alex. Walker on the South & Charlotte Street on the North in the Town of Fredericksburg — now occupied by E. P. Cody my two buildings on in the County of Spotsylvania and Dimensions, Situation and Contiguity to other Buildings or Wharves, what the walls are built of, and what the Buildings are covered with, are specified in the hereunto annexed description of the said Buildings on the Plat signed by me and the Appraisers, and are valued by them, as appears by their Certificate hereunder, to wit:

| | MARKED. | DOLLARS. | | |
|---|---|---|---|---|
| The Dwelling house | A at | 5000 | Say Five Thousand | Dollars. |
| The Kitchen | B at | 300 | Three hundred | do. |
| The Kitchen & addition to Dwel. ho. | C at | 1000. | (new insurance) One Thousand | do. |
| The | D at | | | do. |
| The | E at | | | do. |
| The | F at | | | do. |
| The | G at | | | do. |
| The | H at | | | do. |
| | | $ 6300 | | |

Say Six Thousand Three hundred Dollars in all.

I do hereby declare and affirm, that I hold the above-mentioned buildings with the land on which they stand in fee simple and that they are not, nor shall be insured elsewhere, and that I and my heirs and assigns will abide by, observe and adhere to the constitution, rules and regulations, which are already established, or may hereafter be established by a majority of the insured, present in person, or by representatives, or by a majority of the property insured, represented either by the persons themselves, or their proxy duly authorised, or their deputy, as established by law, at any general meeting to be held by the said Assurance Society; or which are or hereafter may be established by the Standing Committee of the Society. Witness my hand and seal this 31st day of October 1818.

Teste,
A. R. Taylor Special Agent. Cla Wiglesworth

WE the underwritten, being each of us Freeholders, declare and affirm, that we have examined the above-mentioned buildings of Mr. Claiborne Wiglesworth and we are of opinion that they would cost in cash Seven Thousand Two hundred dollars to build the same, and that now (after the deduction of nine hundred dollars for decay or bad repair) are actually worth Six Thousand Three hundred dollars in ready money, as above specified to the best of our knowledge and belief. As witness our hands.

I the undersigned do hereby certify that I verily believe the buildings herein described are not over-valued.
A. R. Taylor Special Agent.
Robert Ellis
Geo. Hoffman
Residing in Fredericksburg

The Special Agent will write nothing on this



Fig. 9.2. Mutual Assurance Policy for the Buildings at the Southeast Corner of Caroline and Charlotte Streets. This policy is a revaluation of an eighteenth-century property insured by Claiborne Wiglesworth. Original in the Virginia State Archives.

The Mutual Assurance Society was not the only company advertising insurance. Competitive fire insurers were present from colonial times. While local mutual companies did not develop until late in the nineteenth century, American and English stock companies began to insure in the United States after the establishment of constitutional government and the jurisdictional claims on interstate commerce were resolved. The Insurance Company of North America, Aetnea, and Franklin Fire Insurance, all of Philadelphia, wrote policies for properties in the Fredericksburg vicinity, and other companies, especially the Phoenix Fire Insurance Company of London, were active in Virginia, if not in Fredericksburg. Later, after 1880, the specificity of physical information on buildings' location and fabric declines with the development of fire insurance maps of cities, particularly those drawn by the Sanborn Fire Insurance Map Company, which provided accurate, scaled, and detailed drawings of major urban areas at frequent intervals and documented the changing fabric and structures of cities into the mid-twentieth century.

Fire insurance as practiced in the United States grew out of an earlier English fire insurance industry that developed after the great Fire of London in September 1666. The first fire insurance companies began in the 1680s, with the Fire Insurance Office begun by Nicholas Barbon, the Friendly Society, and, in 1696, the Amicable Contributors for Insuring Houses from Loss by Fire.[6] The Phoenix Fire Insurance Company is known to have insured properties in the American colonies after 1782.[7] The particular variety of fire insurance that developed in Virginia was the mutual assurance plan. In this corporation, subscribers pooled their risk and provided for their own assurance through levy of a quota each year. In America, the plan was first developed in Philadelphia in 1752 as the Philadelphia Contributionship for the Insurance of Houses from Loss by Fire, called "Hand-in-Hand" in reference to its emblem.[8] Competition ensued because of the refusal

of the Hand-in-Hand Society to insure dwellings with trees surrounding them; a rival mutual assurance society, which allowed owners to pay an extra premium and keep their trees, began to develop. In 1784, The Mutual Assurance Company was formed, using the Green Tree as its badge.[9] The Mutual Assurance Society [of Virginia] was incorporated by the general assembly in 1794. The act stipulated that no policies could be written until three million dollars in subscriptions had been accumulated, so the society did not actually organize until December 24, 1795.[10] The first policies were written in Fredericksburg in March of 1796, and, by the end of the first year, 107 policies had been written. In all over 2,300 policies would be written in Fredericksburg before 1865, 918 through December 1828, the cutoff date for the research presented in this chapter.

Each policy listed the name of the property owner holding the land in fee simple, its location, the amount necessary to rebuild each structure insured, and any deduction from that value due to decay or needed repairs.[11] The individual structure was evaluated for its risk of fire by considering its use, materials of construction—wood, brick, or stone—and the materials of its roof—wooden shingles, earthenware tiles, or slate. The buildings were estimated by three property holders in the Mutual Assurance Society, and the policy was written by the local agent with a drawing supplied showing the buildings in their principal massing, dependent massing, and giving dimensions, stories, and materials.[12] Policies were numbered sequentially upon their receipt in the Richmond office, and policy holders were required to give notice to the society when changes were made to the building that changed either the fabric or the risk of use. Certain high-risk buildings—liveries, buildings for steam engines, rope walks, or naval stores—required a separate approval from the board and a separate risk evaluation. The contents of buildings were insured separately and had their own risk structure.[13]

Fig. 9.3. Roofing Tile, Early Nineteenth Century. Owned by the Fredericksburg Area Museum and Cultural Center. Drawn by Claudette Gamache.

To be sure, not every building was insured. Even within urban areas some owners never insured their buildings or only insured those buildings in the business district. The Virginia Mutual Assurance Society only insured buildings estimated to be worth over one hundred dollars. This seemingly arbitrary threshold was common, used locally in the Federal 1798 Direct Tax assessment of buildings in Berkeley Parish, Spotsylvania County, and for state property tax assessments in Spotsylvania County. Over time, therefore, back buildings, especially outside of the business district, were not insured. No necessaries, or privies, were insured in Fredericksburg, although they are commonly enumerated in Richmond at a later date. Slave quarters were also not frequently insured. This created a significant gap in the historical record concerning slave housing, since slaves made up over 50 percent of the population in 1850. No specifically constructed slave domestic sites have survived today in Fredericksburg, and slaves' lodgings may have been an unenumerated combination to virtually all buildings in Fredericksburg. The uninsured free-standing outbuildings and dependently

massed structures—sheds and porches—must certainly have provided much of the servant space for Fredericksburg.

There are also scattered references to dwellings whose residents were listed as servants on lots at the outskirts of town. In February 1828, Philip Harrison insured a two-story brick house with wooden roof on Caroline Street north of Pitt Street (then the border of town) and listed the occupants as "my servants." In Richmond, servant rooms and quarters were combined with all manner of back buildings, from smokehouses, privies, and kitchens to stables, greenhouses, and carriage houses.

The single source of information about the density of the built environment is the enumeration of contiguous buildings, the number of structures within thirty feet, provided for each building on a policy. In 1796 the densest portion of the business district was populated with ten contiguous buildings, within thirty feet of the insured structure; by 1805 that number had mushroomed to an astonishing twenty to thirty-six contiguous buildings.

But how has fire changed Fredericksburg or any Virginia city? How would one demonstrate that fear of fire had impact on building practice? Fire may be shown to be a necessary condition for change in building materials by illustrating that zones of occupation within the town are differentiated by materials and that period documents detail these changes as being fire related. However, it is also necessary to show that these changes were not merely stylistic or fashionable, where fashion is demonstrated by high value, larger size, and better materials. Demonstrating that high-status buildings were rendered in a varieties of materials and finish and, in contrast, that buildings in the high fire-risk areas were built and trimmed in a consistent manner would show an affinity most easily explained as a reaction to the threat of fire. The most obvious example of the link between fire protection and style that contrasts commercial function with a social function is the use of slate as a roofing material. Slate is expensive in comparison with wood shingles and thus could be a status or style indicator, but it was not used that way in Fredericksburg in the late eighteenth or early nineteenth century. When slate first appeared in the early nineteenth century, it was only used in the commercial core. By the mid-nineteenth century, however, owners of these stores and shops replaced most of the slate with standing seam metal roofs, an even better fire protection, while the largest houses in surrounding residential neighborhoods replace their wooden roofs principally with slate, by then a stylish treatment.[14] It would seem that slate was a fire-related substitution in the early nineteenth century and a social distinction by the mid-century.

Numerous authors have commented on the lack of urban development in Virginia in the colonial period.[15] Major developments of Virginia's urban areas were retarded by the concentration of commercial, craft, and jurisdictional power in the hands of gentry on landed estates. These essentially agricultural industries resisted the efforts to develop rival shipping centers or supply points, and in the Chesapeake region the rural gentry often maintained direct shipping ties to port cities and England. The few towns outside of the provincial capital that did develop were usually crucially placed to facilitate shipping for plantations located beyond the fall line of major rivers. Petersburg, Richmond, Fredericksburg, and Alexandria all developed in this manner. Fredericksburg is situated immediately below the falls of the Rappahannock River, whose tributaries drain the region east of the Blue Ridge Mountains between the Potomac and James River drainages to the north and south. It began as a tobacco port in the first half of the eighteenth century, reinforced by the early location of the county government, parish church, and later the district court facilities. The town was compactly laid out in a rectangular grid on ten acres with broad streets and two-acre square blocks with four half-acre lots per block, roughly centered on a square divided

between the parish church lot and the market square. The original town plat yielded sixty-four half-acre lots for sale with four reserved for civic functions, both church and state.[16]

As important as the river was to the development of Fredericksburg, the north-south roads and later railroads, along with the east-west connectors, proved vital to binding the Fredericksburg port to the wheat-raising areas of the North Neck and the Piedmont regions.[17] Caroline Street became the main north-south business axis, reinforced by the arcaded market house at the corner of William Street. William Street, in turn, developed slowly as the principal western avenue, and, beyond the town limits, it became a toll road to Orange County and the western counties. By the 1820s, the borders of Fredericksburg had been expanded by annexing suburbs to the north, south, and west. These blocks duplicated the half-acre lots and added approximately 159 half-acre lots.

Although there is abundant and valuable building stone within the town limits of Fredericksburg, wooden buildings dominated the city at the end of the eighteenth century (see table 9.1). In this table we see the cumulative distribution of buildings insured between 1796 and 1828, grouped by seven-year intervals and sorted by the walling materials.[18] Almost 90 percent of the buildings insured in Fredericksburg during the first seven years were built of wood, and all of the buildings insured during that period were covered with wood shingles. The decline in the absolute percentage of wooden buildings is not remarkable in itself. This decline is significant when plotted against the use of the building (see table 9.2). Some special-use buildings continued throughout the period to be predominantly built of wood. When viewed over the entire period, meat houses, stables, and warehouses, approximately 25 percent of the building stock, remained predominantly wood. In other buildings, especially dwellings, kitchens, and lumber houses, wood continued to be important, but brick slowly gained in percentage, although not uniformly within the town. Buildings serving dual functions as stores on the ground floor and dwellings in the upstairs areas used the greatest percentage of brick (see table 9.3). This is confirmed when the height in stories is plotted against the function of the building, which shows that, within the urbanizing commercial area, where two-story dwellings are marginally dominant, the greater correlation is between those buildings combining the domestic and commerce functions and two-story structures. That almost half of the storehouses are also two-story suggests that many of these buildings were also dual function spaces, but not enumerated in that way.

What effect did fire, as opposed to the threat of fire, have on the development of the urban core of Fredericksburg? Between 1799 and 1824 Fredericksburg suffered a series of major fires that swept through the main business districts of the town. In April 1799, a fire began between two wooden buildings—a two-story dwelling and the silversmith shop on the west side of Caroline. It quickly spread south and was contained only at Charlotte Street, preventing the burning of Edward Herndon's wooden Indian Princess tavern. The fire did cross Caroline Street to the east and burned the "elegant range of brick buildings" completed in 1796 and owned by a prominent merchant firm, Patton and Hackley.

Table 9.1
Wall and Roof Materials Grouped by Date, Fredericksburg, Virginia

|  | 1796–1804 (%) | 1805–13 (%) | 1814–21 (%) | 1822–28 (%) |
|---|---|---|---|---|
| Wood Walls & Wood Roof | 89 | 86 | 72 | 59 |
| Brick Walls & Wood Roof | 9 | 9 | 15 | 17 |
| Brick Walls & Tile Roof | 0 | 3 | 4 | 2 |
| Brick Walls & Slate Roof | 0 | 0 | 6 | 20 |
| Stone Walls & Wood Roof | 2 | 2 | 2 | 1 |
| Stone Walls & Tile Roof | 0 | 0 | 1 | 0 |
| Totals (n) | 100(493) | 100(566) | 100(543) | 100(525) |

Table 9.2
Wall and Roof Materials Compared to Building Function, Fredericksburg, Virginia, 1796–1828

| Walls<br>Roof | Materials | | | | | | |
|---|---|---|---|---|---|---|---|
|  | Wood<br>Wood<br>(%) | Brick<br>Wood<br>(%) | Brick<br>Tile<br>(%) | Brick<br>Slate<br>(%) | Stone<br>Wood<br>(%) | Stone<br>Tile<br>(%) | Totals (n) |
| Dwelling | 81 | 14 | 1 | 1 | 2 | 0 | 100%(643) |
| Kitchen[a] | 78 | 14 | 2 | 4 | 1 | 1 | 100%(512) |
| Meat House[b] | 93 | 4 | 1 | 0 | 2 | 1 | 100%(175) |
| Stable[c] | 99 | 0 | 1 | 1 | 0 | 0 | 100%(137) |
| Store House | 80 | 15 | 0 | 4 | 0 | 0 | 100%(92) |
| Warehouse | 92 | 6 | 0 | 3 | 0 | 0 | 100%(71) |
| Lumber House | 80 | 8 | 3 | 3 | 3 | 1 | 100%(143) |
| Store & Dwelling | 29 | 17 | 19 | 31 | 4 | 0 | 100%(112) |

NOTES: [a]Includes stable and carriage house combinations.
[b]And combinations with lumber house, bake house, washhouse.
[c]Includes smokehouse.

Table 9.3
Number of Building Stories Compared to Building Function, Fredericksburg, Virginia, 1796–1828

| | Stories | | | | | |
|---|---|---|---|---|---|---|
| Function | 1 (%) | 1.5 (%) | 2 (%) | 2.5 (%) | 3 (%) | Total (N) |
| Dwelling | 41 | 4 | 53 | 0 | 2 | 100%(634) |
| Kitchen[a] | 84 | 9 | 7 | 0 | 0 | 100%(387) |
| Meat House[b] | 100 | 0 | 0 | 0 | 0 | 100%(57) |
| Stable[c] | 98 | 1 | 1 | 0 | 0 | 100%(93) |
| Storehouse | 54 | 0 | 46 | 0 | 0 | 100%(89) |
| Warehouse | 85 | 15 | 0 | 0 | 0 | 100%(55) |
| Lumber House | 70 | 2 | 25 | 0 | 2 | 100%(122) |
| Store & Dwelling | 16 | 4 | 69 | 0 | 11 | 100%(110) |

NOTES: [a]Includes stable and carriage house combinations.
[b]Includes combinations with lumber house, bake house, washhouse.
[c]Includes smokehouses, many values not reported.

Table 9.4
Old Town District Wall and Roof Materials Grouped by Date

| | 1796–1804 (%) | 1805–13 (%) | 1814–21 (%) | 1822–28 (%) |
|---|---|---|---|---|
| Wood Walls & Wood Roof | 86 | 80 | 57 | 36 |
| Brick Walls & Wood Roof | 12 | 13 | 22 | 19 |
| Brick Walls & Tile Roof | 0 | 5 | 8 | 4 |
| Brick Walls & Slate Roof | 0 | 1 | 11 | 38 |
| Stone Walls & Wood Roof | 2 | 1 | 1 | 1 |
| Stone Walls & Tile Roof | 0 | 0 | 1 | 1 |
| Totals (n) | 100(247) | 100(305) | 100(250) | 100(273) |

The fire had damaged the only brick buildings in that block, although it did not extend northward to a stone house adjacent to the brick row.[19] The fire was followed by attempts to regulate the manner in which fire coals were carried from house to house and increased the calls for fire companies.[20] Fire visited individual houses sporadically, but the major shock of vulnerability occurred in October 1807, when a chimney fire at the upper end of the original town ignited buildings during a dry and windy fall day and consumed parts of more than four blocks of the central district. William Taylor, the local agent of the Mutual Assurance Society wrote his Richmond superiors that "[f]our full squares of the thickest and best improved part of the town is now in ashes, very upwards of 200 houses are entirely destroyed, and to add to the calamity of nearly 100 families in distressed situation."[21] Although his estimates were high, his sense of calamity echoed with the people, both in Fredericksburg and elsewhere, and contributions and support flowed in for those left homeless, or for merchants left penniless. After the fire of 1807, Fredericksburg began to fear fire, and individuals and groups began to actively seek to reduce its effects.

The town suffered not only from its vulnerability to fire, but also from its inability to organize to resist fire. As early as 1792 calls had been made for a fire company in town, and again after the fire of 1799, but even with so complete a destruction as the fire of 1807, no stable long-term fire company was formed. Fire watches had been conducted in each ward of the city as early as 1790, although not without complaint that they were lax and ineffective.[22] Lacking a fire company the city council sought to remove the principal cause of contagion: the embers and burning tars emitted from chimneys when they were cleaned. In 1802 the Corporation of Fredericksburg made it illegal to fire the chimney in fair weather, charging three dollars for the offense, with half to the informer and half to the corporation.[23] Finally, in October 1813, the Hope Fire-Company was formed, with its pumps and engine stored in the lower level of the Market House.[24] Fires, however, continued to plague the city.

On Aug. 3, 1816, "the inhabitants of this town were [again] aroused with the dreadful cry of 'fire'. . . the whole row of wooden buildings between George Street on the north and Mr. Shultice's fire proof house on the south consisting of nine front tenements with all their back buildings were consumed."[25] Mr. Shultice's house was brick covered with earthenware tiles. The use of tiles as a fireproofing material began in 1808 as a direct response to the 1807 calamity. Not only were new buildings built with tiles, but old buildings, including the Fredericksburg Market House, were reroofed with tile. John Shultice's brick house, his attached dining room, and kitchen had been built new in 1812; although originally wood, three years later they were reroofed with tile.[26] Tile was associated with fireproofing in insurance policies and newspaper accounts through the second decade of the nineteenth century, when it was rapidly replaced by slate as the roofing of choice (fig. 9.3).

By charting the presence of tile and slate, the clear pattern of replacement of roofing materials becomes apparent (see table 9.1). Between 1808 and 1813, tile comprised a modest 3 percent of the roofing material in Fredericksburg. It rose to 4 percent between 1815 to 1821 and then diminished to 2 percent of the roofing material in the town.[27] Slate began to be used in 1812 and rapidly became the fireproof roofing of choice, becoming 6 percent of the roofing material between 1814 and 1821.[28] The close association with fireproofing is more vivid when it is seen that tile and slate were not used on wooden buildings, with only a single exception.[29] The inference is clear: slate and tile replaced wooden roofs as a material for protection from airborne fire. Other forms of fire protection, parapets and citywide water systems, would be added later.[30]

This movement toward fire protection was not universal throughout the town. Although shops and homes everywhere in town continued to heat with wood, and thus provide possible sources for new fires, only in the original town plan was there any concerted movement to use fireproof materials, specifically along Caroline and William Streets, bordered on the north and south by Amelia and Wolfe Streets and on the east and west by Sophia and Charles Streets (see table 9.3). The more prosperous suburb at the south end of Caroline, platted and settled by Roger Dixon in the 1750s, maintained a mix of brick, stone, and frame buildings, but did not make any movement to minimize fire hazard. The north suburb, north of Lewis Street and home to numerous small shopkeepers, several blacksmith shops, carriage shops, and taverns— all buildings in which fire was a concern—did not have a single brick building during the time frame considered in this chapter. Only in the six-block central district of Fredericksburg did the merchants feel sufficiently threatened to protect themselves (see table 9.4). By 1821, 42 percent of the insured building stock had brick walls, and 21 percent had some kind of fireproof roofing. By 1828 43 percent of the roofing would be fireproof.

After 1817 the perceived causes of fire began to

shift. Embedded in newspaper reports during the next decade were unsubstantiated reports of arson and damage by design. In 1820 John Scott's warehouse burned on Princess Anne Street. The *Virginia Herald* explained that "a general impression prevails that this fire was the work of some vile incendiary who had judiciously selected this particular point with the design of destroying all the southern section of the town."[31] By 1822 every fire had become an incendiary plot, with an extremely dry Spring contributing to five fires by the middle of July.[32] The tensions of slavery and bondage created suspicions in the minds of white men and women, even as they held the system just. April's fire demolished half a block of Caroline Street between George and Hanover Streets, devouring another stand of wooden buildings downtown. The speed and destruction of the fire reminded the newspaper of the October fire of 1807, but the cause was considered, without evidence, to be slave-based arson. The dry winds of June 1823 brought yet another fire that destroyed buildings of downtown Fredericksburg. Beginning where the previous fire had left off, it carried from the Farmer's Hotel down through the next block, blackening both sides of Caroline Street and burning again the "elegant range of brick buildings" that had burned in 1799.[33] Once more in 1824 and again in 1828, multiple building fires crept along Caroline Street, burning out the wooden core. Each began in a back building and each was supposedly the work of unseen malicious forces.[34]

Despite the common belief of the time that blamed the fires on hands bent to bad will, the evidence from the starting point of the fires directs attention to the continued existence of many wooden buildings, especially stables, along the back streets of the Caroline Street merchants. Merchants had, in their desire to protect their goods, only built substantial brick buildings with fireproof roofs close to their business/dwellings. Kitchens were more often built of brick and covered with slate than were either meat houses or lumber houses.

Both Sophia Street toward the Rappahannock River and Princess Anne Street toward the west were secondary entrances to town, crowded with wooden warehouses and stables. The decade of fires through the late 1820s came almost entirely from these back buildings, and the fires were carried not by hands of ill will, but by the strong winds of Spring. As they burned, even stables and warehouses began being replaced with brick and slate buildings. The relocation of the Market House to the west end of Market Square hard against Princess Anne Street in 1815 was the beginning of a secondary urbanization that would create a secondary north-south artery whose final remodeling would only come as churches began to move to the high ground there in the 1840s and 1850s.

So complete was the damage from the fires before 1828 that today hardly a single building from the eighteenth century survives intact within the original town plat. What survives instead are the buildings that replaced these earlier structures, dating principally from the 1820s through the 1850s. The Civil War, with its intensity, largely demolished the western edges of Fredericksburg. Only the fire insurance policies, drawn to protect the investor, not the building, have survived to speak of the old and historic district, the original town of Fredericksburg. Much more eighteenth-century architecture remains outside this early core; it was clad in fireproof roofs only in the middle nineteenth century with standing seam metal roofs, occasionally with slate, and never tile.

How did fire change Fredericksburg? By forcing attention upon the separation of civic functions into issues of commerce and social hierarchy, fire concentrated growth and the attitudes associated with urban development, an intensity of land use that denies the social segregation to which the landscape is often put. During the eighteenth century, merchants lived in the urban core, while during the nineteenth century merchants often rented out the living space above their businesses and established themselves in suburbs of domestic scale. Fire played this clarifying role in Fredericksburg's development, clearing commercial areas and forcing choices upon owners and occupants. Fire also accelerated the pace of what was a commercial inevitability given Fredericksburg's location and place within the developing transportation revolutions of the nineteenth century. In accelerating these changes, the consistency of architectural treatment gave the city's core an atmosphere of shared community that larger cities often have destroyed in their continuing development and smaller towns never achieve. In this way, fire played a role in the making of the Fredericksburg seen today by modern visitors and residents.

## Notes

1. The research for this paper was conducted with the assistance of students of the Historic Preservation Department of Mary Washington College. I want to especially thank Amy Wilkinson, Amy Cole, and Molly Gregory for their assistance. Douglas Sanford, director of archaeology at the Center for Historic Preservation, made numerous thoughtful comments that improved this presentation.

2. Earlier efforts at fire prevention included attempts to eliminate wooden chimneys and the use of night patrols and fire wards. See Edward Alvey Jr., *The Fredericksburg Fire of 1807* (Fredericksburg: Historic Fredericksburg Foundation, Inc., 1988), 4–6.

3. By action of the Virginia legislature, the town and country branches of the Mutual Assurance Society were divided in 1805. The act of Mar. 4, 1822, abolished the Country Branch, releasing members from responsibility.

4. Conversely, stock companies distributed the policies to their clients and kept only the blotter record of who had paid their premiums. The earliest stock company is the Insurance Company of North America, whose records are now part of the Cigna archives in Philadelphia.

5. The complete twenty-three volumes of policies are now deposited at the Virginia State Archives and Library and are available on microfilm.

6. Carol Wojtowicz, *The Mutual Assurance Company* (Philadelphia: The Mutual Assurance Company, 1985), 3.

7. H. A. L. Cockerall and Edwin Green, *The British Insurance Business, 1547–1970: An Introduction and Guide to Historical Records in the United Kingdom* (London: Heinemann Educational Books, Ltd., 1976), 104.

8. Marquis James, *Biography of a Business, 1792–1942: Insurance Company of North America* (Indianapolis: Bobbs-Merrill Company, 1942), 41.

9. Wojtowicz, *The Mutual Assurance Company*, 3.

10. Conley L. Edwards III, *A Guide to the Business Records in the Archives Branch, Virginia State Library* (Richmond: Virginia State Library, 1983), 105.

11. Policies could be declared invalid if the subscribers were found to hold the property in less than fee simple. A mutual company's assets were the property of its stockholders and an individual who did not own the property could not be required to sell it to meet the debts of the Mutual Assurance Society. See "Collection of the Acts of the Legislature of Virginia in Relation to the Mutual Assurance Society Against Fire on Buildings in the State of Virginia" in Virginia State Archives, Richmond, Virginia.

12. Agents were originally paid 2 percent of the value of the premium. In 1805 this was raised to 5 percent. Information is contained in a letter to General John Minor, Fredericksburg, dated Aug. 7, 1805. Letterbook of the Mutual Assurance Society, Mar. 1, 1805–July 31, 1806. Virginia State Archives, Richmond, Virginia.

13. The declarations for goods were broken down into implements and goods determined to be either hazardous or non-hazardous. See Records of the Mutual Assurance Society, "Declarations for Goods & Implements," Virginia State Archives. Accession number 28135.

14. The first policy to mention a metal roof in Fredericksburg was over a covered way connecting a kitchen with a store on the northwest corner of Caroline and Charlotte Streets in January 1826. It was policy number 3573, insured by Claiborne Wiglesworth.

15. Dell Upton, "Anglican Parish Churches in Eighteenth-Century Virginia," *Perspectives in Vernacular Architecture, II,* ed. Camille Wells (Columbia: Univ. of Missouri Press, 1986), 91.

16. Two additional lots would be taken up by civic functions when the court was moved from Germanna to Fredericksburg. See Paula Felder, *Forgotten Companions* (Fredericksburg: Historic Publications of Fredericksburg, 1982), 82.

17. William H. Siener, "Charles Yates, The Grain Trade, and Economic Development in Fredericksburg, Virginia, 1750–1810," *Virginia Magazine of History and Biography* 93:4(Oct. 1985): 409–26.

18. Table 9.1 has clustered policies in groupings dictated by the administration of the Mutual Assurance Society. The company ordered a revaluation of all policies in 1805 and with the new constitution of that year required revaluation every seven years, placing responsibility in the hands of the agent, not the owner. The major years of valuation in Fredericksburg are 1796 (135 declarations yielding 269 structures), 1805 (140 declarations and revaluations yielding 398 buildings), 1814–15 (157 declarations and revaluations yielding 408 buildings, and 1822 (189 declarations and revaluations yielding 432 buildings). Duplication that would create a statistical error was removed by eliminating revaluations of existing buildings that occurred within the clusters, but adding revaluations of buildings prior to the cluster and declarations of new buildings.

19. "Fire," *Virginia Herald,* Apr. 9, 1799. See also Alvey, *The Fredericksburg Fire,* 8–9.

20. See "Fire," *Virginia Herald,* Apr. 12, 1799; "About Fire Ordinances," *Virginia Herald,* Aug. 10, 1802; and John Moody, "Fire," *Virginia Herald,* Dec. 16, 1803.

21. Alvey, *The Fredericksburg Fire,* 15.

22. Peter Graves, *Virginia Herald,* Apr. 12, 1792. The committee was to have inspected the stove flues and chimneys of all the houses, but passed the houses of three women in the southern suburbs of Fredericksburg.

23. *Virginia Herald,* Aug. 10, 1802.

24. *Virginia Herald,* Oct. 20, 1813; "Hope Fire Company," *Virginia Herald,* Dec. 18, 1813.

25. "Fire," *Virginia Herald,* Aug. 3, 1816.

26. Mutual Assurance Policies 302 (Volume 52) and the revaluation policy 1343 (Volume 60).

27. No tile roofs survive today in Fredericksburg. From archaeological examples and four tiles removed from a demolished store in the 1960s, the tile can be described as an earthenware pan tile hung from lugs. The surviving tiles have the exterior surface glazed with Albany slip. No newspaper advertisements or identification of sources for the tiles have yet been identified, nor has any building contract identified the suppliers. The use of earthenware tile, however, provides a clue to the evolving nature of Fredericksburg. The Fredericksburg Area Museum and Cultural Center has four tiles given to them by John Ballantine from the store at the southeast corner of William and Charles Streets. For archaeological examples see William M. Kelso, "A Report on the 1985 Exploratory Archaeological Excavations at Market Square for Historic Fredericksburg Foundation"; and Douglas W. Sanford, "Market Square Archaeology, Fall 1992 Results." Both are unpublished and available at the Fredericksburg Area Museum and Cultural Center.

28. This nineteenth-century use of slate has no relation to the scattered use of slate on eighteenth-century Virginia buildings, such as Governor Alexander Spotswood's Germanna in the early seventeenth century. For that reference, see Douglas W. Sanford, "The Enchanted Castle in Context: Archaeological Research at Germanna, Orange County, Virginia," *Quarterly Bulletin of the Archaeological Society of Virginia* 44 (3) (Sept. 1989): 106.

29. See policy 2935, Feb. 9, 1822, owned by Margaret Phillips. The dwelling is a two-story house; the first story was made of stone, the second story of wood, and the house stood at the northeast corner of Frederick and Caroline Streets. Built in 1820, it was apparently reroofed in 1822. It is an unremarkable house with principal massing of sixteen-by-sixteen feet with a rear shed, doubling its first-floor space. Its revaluation in 1829 (policy 9375) again lists a wooden shingle roof. It is possible that the slate is listed in error.

30. See MAS policy 1279 written in 1814: a three-story brick tavern and dwelling owned by Godlove Hieskell at the northwest corner of Caroline and Hanover Street for the only fire parapet before 1830. It was covered with a wood shingle roof.

31. "Fire," *Virginia Herald,* Feb. 9, 1820. Three days later another fire again aroused the suspicion of arson, and the blame fell upon a black man and boy. "Incendiary Again," *Virginia Herald,* Feb. 12, 1820.

32. "Fire," *Virginia Herald,* Jan. 19, 1822; Apr. 17, 1822; "Another Fire," Apr. 20, 1822; May 8, 1822; July 13, 1822.

33. "Distressing Fire," *Virginia Herald,* June 11, 1823.

34. "Incendiaries," *Virginia Gazette,* Feb. 4, 1824; "Fire," Oct. 15, 1828.

COMMUNITIES

SHAPED BY RACE

AND ETHNICITY

*Thomas R. Ryan*

# Cultural Accommodations in the Late-Eighteenth-Century Architecture of Marbletown, New York

The three-room Hudson Valley farmhouse has long been looked upon as quintessentially Dutch by architectural antiquarians. How was it built and what makes it "Dutch"? How common was it and where did the three-room house fit within the broader range of housing options in New York's Hudson Valley? This essay draws on recent fieldwork in Marbletown, New York, and the rich documentary evidence of the 1798 Federal Direct Tax Records to establish a typology of eighteenth-century house forms in that community.[1] Next, it explores the variety of three-room plans in Marbletown and charts the rising popularity of a late-eighteenth-century three-room, center-passage plan that incorporates fashionable design elements into the regional vernacular tradition.

In 1929, Helen Wilkinson Reynolds, a pioneer of architectural study in the Hudson Valley, published her important work *Dutch Houses in the Hudson Valley*. In the introduction she announced that "the first object in preparing this book has been to learn what sort of house was built by the majority of Dutch families in the region of the Hudson River before 1776."[2] Reynolds claimed to be looking for a "Dutch average," a "general average; for the fact has been revealed that the people of the Hudson Valley, of whatever European extraction—Dutch, English, French, Teutonic, Scandinavian—all built alike."[3] The resulting work is an impressive catalog of over 150 houses covering all of the counties along the Hudson River from just north of New York City to Albany. Reynolds's search for a "Dutch average," however, obscures the subtle distinctions of ethnic diversity and architectural variety characteristic of life in New Netherland and eighteenth-century New York. Despite the presence of several northern European and African groups in the Hudson Valley since the seventeenth century, subsequent scholarship on material life in the region has remained focused largely on the Dutch cultural contribution to the region.[4]

The cultural complexity of the Hudson Valley was foreshadowed in the autumn of 1609 when Henry Hudson, an English citizen employed by the Dutch East India Company, began his third exploratory mission up the North River. Robert Juet, a Frenchman and an officer on Hudson's boat, the *Halve Maen,* described the landscape on September 25, 1609: "The five and twentieth was faire weather, and the wind at South a stiffe gale. We rode still, and went to Land to walke on the West side of the River, and found good ground for Corne and other Garden herbs, with great store of goodly Oakes, and Wal-nut trees, and Chest-nut trees, Ewe trees, and trees of sweet wood in great abundance, and great store of slate for houses and other good stones."[5] The native Esopus people, relatives of the Delaware and members of the Algonquin family of nations, successfully farmed and hunted this land at the time of Hudson's visit. By century's end, however, their imprint on the land had all but vanished.[6]

The natural topography of gentle mountains, meandering waterways, and fertile valleys observed by Hudson and Juet is part of present-day Ulster County, New York. Marbletown, New York, sits in the geographic center of Ulster County, just west of the Hudson River, about midway between Manhattan and Albany. Along the town's north boundary, the Catskill Mountains begin their gentle ascent, while in the southeast corner of the town, the Shawangunk Mountains terminate in a steep, stony outcropping. Between these mountain borders lie rolling hills and rich bottomland along the Esopus and Rondout Creeks.

Sixty years after Hudson's explorations, in 1669, a band of recently decommissioned British soldiers, the widow of one officer, and two or three Dutch settlers founded Marbletown. Within a generation, more Dutch and French immigrants, slaves from West Africa and the West Indies,[7] and the remnant of the Esopus Indians made their homes in the

town. Germans and Scots-Irish arrived in the early eighteenth century, further expanding Marbletown's ethnic composition. The interaction of people from at least seven distinct ethnic traditions as early as the 1710s raises important questions about Marbletown's culture and its material products. What kinds of houses did Marbletown's settlers build? Were they based on traditional European forms? And how did the town's domestic architecture change over the course of the eighteenth century?

A recent field survey in Marbletown revealed a landscape replete with examples of eighteenth-century houses. The survey utilized a modern topographical map depicting every building in the town. This map was cross-referenced with a 1797 map that shows ninety-seven houses on the principal roads and waterways with the owner's name written next to many of the dwellings.[8] The Federal Direct Tax "A" list for Marbletown offers detailed descriptions of each house valued at or above one hundred dollars in 1798. Included in the descriptions are house dimensions, number of stories, number and dimensions of windows, building materials, owners' and occupants' names, and the location, age, condition, and value of the houses. By comparing the two maps with the descriptions of the 171 houses in the Direct Tax "A" list, 90 surviving eighteenth-century buildings were identified in the field.[9] Thus, more than half of Marbletown's "A" list houses survive, an unusually high survival rate, underscoring the importance of studying Marbletown's architecture. Considered in the broader context of all of the housing in the town, these 90 dwellings represent 26 percent (90/334) of all houses registered in a local Marbletown tax list for the year 1800.[10] For the purposes of this study, 50 of the 90 houses were measured and documented and provide the basis for a typology of late-eighteenth-century housing forms in the town, as well as a context for interpreting the community's most common house type, the three-room plan.

The buildings in this study have been grouped

according to three characteristics: 1) the plan of the first floor; 2) the number of finished stories; and 3) the placement of chimneys and exterior doors. Attention has been given to the issue of change over time in order to distinguish original house forms from subsequent additions and transformations. Seven basic house types and several additive types survive on the Marbletown landscape. A brief description of each type establishes a context for a more extended investigation of the most prevalent type, the three-room plan, and provides a basis for future study of this late-eighteenth-century community.

The seven house types are the following: a) a one-room house with opposing entries and a large fireplace on one gable wall; b and c) a two-room plan with either a center chimney or two gable-end chimneys and one or two entrances on the principal facade; d) a two-room, two-story bank house with entrances on each level and kitchen located in the basement; e) a two- or three-room German "hall-kitchen" or *flurkuchenhaus* plan, consisting of a kitchen with opposed entries running the depth of the house, an off-center chimney with plate stove serving a front parlor *(stube)*, and often an unheated bedchamber behind the *stube*; f) a two-story, side-passage plan, roughly square, with two rooms downstairs and three rooms upstairs; g) a center-passage plan with a single room on each side of an unheated center passage with opposed entries and a chimney in each gable end; and h) a two-story, center-passage plan with two rooms in front and two in the rear (fig. 10.1). There are several additive types achieved by combining two or more of these basic forms or by adding service wings.

A general sequence of first appearances of these types can be reconstructed. Of the fifty houses surveyed, one- and two-room houses were the earliest forms, with a few extant examples dating from the late seventeenth century. Bank houses and the German hall-kitchen plan appear in the second and third quarters of the eighteenth

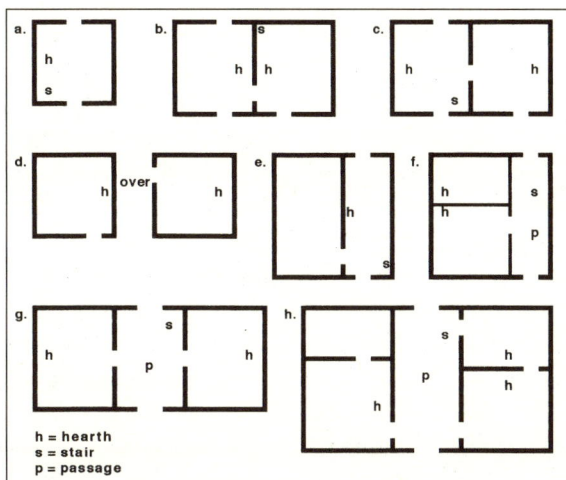

Fig. 10.1. Common Eighteenth-Century House Plans in Marbletown, New York.

century respectively, while the side-passage and center-passage plans appear immediately prior to the fourth quarter of the eighteenth century. At the time of the 1798 Direct Tax, most of the seven types were still being built with no apparent correlation between the ethnicity of the owners and the plans chosen. While a shift did occur in the second half of the eighteenth century from mostly one- and two-room houses to the inclusion of a larger center-passage plan, it would be misleading to assume that earlier types entirely disappeared as newer plans arrived. Thus, the synchronic presence of at least seven house types and seven ethnic groups in Marbletown at the close of the eighteenth century modifies previous understandings of mid–Hudson Valley architecture as predominantly Dutch in origin or as typified by a linear plan built in three phases.

The 1798 Direct Tax list of houses valued at over one hundred dollars in Marbletown provides a unique vantage point for reconstructing the late-eighteenth-century architectural landscape of the town and is an important link to a broader understanding of the original context of surviving buildings.[11] Information gleaned from Marbletown's tax list reveals that 85 percent (145/171) of Marbletown's

"A" list houses were owner-occupied. Property values on the "A" list ranged from Adam Yaple's two-room log house, valued at $151.50, to Cornelius and Cornelia Wynkoop's two-story, 13-room stone house at $2,100. The median house value was $345. A very high 97 percent of the houses were listed as one story. Three of every four houses were built of stone; the rest were either frame (33/171) or log (9/171). These statistics, however, only pertain to the 171 houses valued more than $100. Were they representative of the larger architectural landscape? A local 1800 tax list confirms that approximately 165 more houses were in Marbletown and would have appeared on the Direct Tax "B" list of houses valued under $100.[12] The surviving "B" list from the adjacent town of New Paltz suggests that Marbletown's remaining houses were most likely one-story, one-room log or frame houses, with a median value of $10.[13]

In 1952 architectural historian Hugh Morrison, leaning heavily on Helen Reynolds's fieldwork, described the common mid–Hudson Valley Dutch farmhouse as "one room deep with three rooms strung out in a row, two of them with outside doors . . . and three chimneys."[14] The type of house Morrison portrayed began as a one-room house and was later expanded by adding first one and then a second room to the gable ends. Late-twentieth-century writers, such as Lee and Virginia McAlester, reiterate Morrison's description of the additive quality of these buildings: "Dutch Colonial houses thus often show a linear sequence of two or three (rarely more) units built at different times."[15] What makes this kind of house Dutch and how common was it in the community of Marbletown? A closer look at one such house—the Broadhead-DuBois house—challenges the characterization of the three-room linear house built in phases as "typical" and raises questions about the standard "Dutch" attribution ascribed to many Hudson Valley houses.

On January 25, 1734, members of two promi-nent Ulster County families gathered to celebrate the marriage of Wessel Broadhead and Catrina DuBois.[16] Broadhead's family had been among the first settlers of Marbletown in 1668. Catrina DuBois's ancestors had helped establish the neighboring town of New Paltz in 1678. Shortly after marrying, they built a one-room house at the confluence of the Doverkill and the Rondout Creek in a remote corner of Marbletown (fig. 10.2). In their house, perched atop a hill, they had broad vistas of their fertile bottomland and the winding creek.

Their one-room house was made of native limestone, a plentiful building material in Ulster County, gathered from the land as settlers transformed it from forest to field. Atop the twenty-inch-thick stone walls was a simple roof framing system consisting of a plate, common rafters with pegged mortise and tenon joints at the peak, dovetailed and lap-joined collar beams one-third of the way down from the peak, and common purlins covered with boards or thatch. Clapboard siding sealed the gable ends of the garret where they rose above the plate. One door and one window pierced the two-foot-thick walls on the front side facing the creek. Inside the house a large fireplace, used to heat and light the room and to prepare food, occupied most of the north gable wall. The unfinished loft above served essential storage needs. In this house occurred the repetitive day-to-day activities of food preparation and consumption, washing and spinning, socializing and sleeping. Here, too, the cycles of birth, life, and death were played out against the larger seasonal backdrop of clearing land, planting, harvesting, and marketing produce. On such land and in such houses, the Broadhead-DuBois family, and many Marbletown families, made their mark on the rural landscape of the mid-Hudson Valley.

People alter buildings to accommodate their needs, to keep apace with changing fashions and social demands, and to express their sensibilities and aspirations. The Broadhead-DuBois family

Fig. 10.2. Wessel Broadhead and Catrina DuBois house, c. 1735 and before 1798. Lucas Turnpike, Marbletown, Ulster County, New York.

was no exception. In a later building phase, they added a second room to the south end of their one-room house (fig. 10.3). By the time of the Direct Tax in 1798, they had added a third room, with gable chimney, to the north end of the former one-room house. The transformation of the house from a single room measuring sixteen feet by twenty-six feet, and encompassing many activities, to three rooms measuring fifty-eight feet by twenty-six feet represents a major shift in the conception and experience of domestic space. Each sequential addition both reflected and required changes in lifestyle. The resulting plan consisted of three rooms, each with a chimney, front door, and front window, resulting in a six-bay facade. Cooking activities were relocated in the south addition. The north addition probably served as a chamber and parlor.[17] The transformation of the house yielded a dwelling with functionally specific spaces that operated in an open and accessible plan. The mixed uses common to one-room

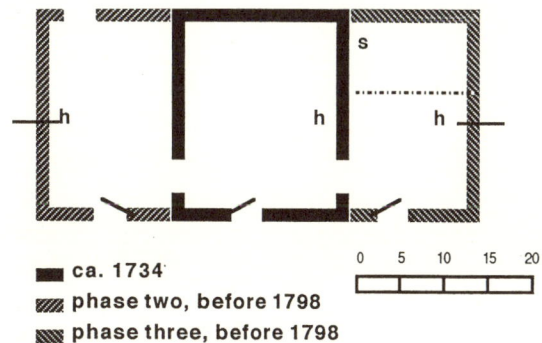

ca. 1734
phase two, before 1798
phase three, before 1798

Fig. 10.3. Broadhead-DuBois House Plan. Lucas Turnpike, Marbletown, Ulster County, New York.

houses began to dissipate with the introduction of functionally specific rooms, and the Broadhead-DuBois family would have assigned a particular function to the room that had once contained all their activities. Located at the center of the new three-room plan, it could have served as passage, parlor, dining room, or chamber.

In addition to the three-room plan, several other architectural features of the Broadhead-DuBois house are of the type often cited as typically Dutch. These characteristics include one-and-one-half stories of roughly laid up limestone walls, clapboard on the gable ends above the first floor, a protruding or "bee hive" oven, and the horizontally divided door.[18] Yet, is the Broadhead-DuBois house typical of surviving eighteenth-century houses in Marbletown? Of the fifty dwellings surveyed for this study, only the Broadhead-DuBois house has three rooms strung out in a row and built in phases.[19] Furthermore, it would be misleading to think of this house as Dutch, since Wessel Broadhead's family was from the West Riding of Yorkshire England, where three-room houses built in phases survive from the seventeenth century.[20] Likewise, the family of Catrina DuBois, Broadhead's wife, was from the Artois region of France, where three-room farmhouses, also built in phases, survive in large numbers from the eighteenth century.[21] Thus, the basic form and plan of the Broadhead-DuBois house is akin to houses from northern France, Belgium, and parts of rural England, and, while it possesses features common to many houses associated with Dutch ownership, these features are not found exclusively on Dutch houses.

If only one in the sample of fifty is of the type described by Morrison, still exactly half of the houses documented in this study consist of some sort of three-room arrangement. Leaving the Broadhead-DuBois house aside, the remaining twenty-four three-room houses may be divided into two groups: houses built in phases and dwellings built of a piece. Those built in phases were made in one of three ways: 1) a kitchen wing was built off the back of an older two-room house; 2) an "outlet" was constructed off the back of a two-room house; or 3) a center passage and parlor were added to a bank house (fig. 10.4). Three-room houses built of a piece consisted of a wide center passage with a single room to each

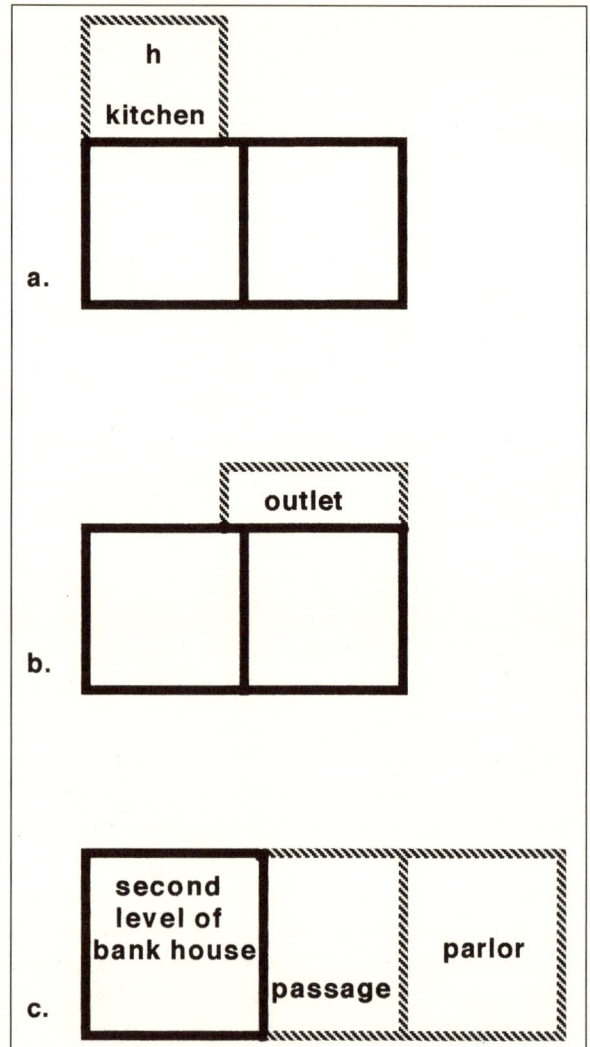

Fig. 10.4. Common Three-Room House Plans, Built in Phases, in Eighteenth-Century Marbletown, New York.

side and a kitchen off the back. Let us briefly consider the additive three-room houses and then consider three-room houses built of a piece.

Jacob Snyder and Elizabeth Wedderwax, second-generation Germans in Marbletown, lived in a dwelling with a massive, slightly off-center chimney stack, a cast-iron plate stove off the back of the stack in the parlor, and built-in wall niches, all features commonly associated with Germanic immigrants in southeastern Pennsylvania (fig. 10.1e).

Prior to 1798 they expanded their two-room house by adding a rear kitchen wing (fig. 10.4a).[22] Valued by the Direct Tax assessors in the top 30 percent of houses at $495, this house in "new and good" condition differed from the Broadhead-DuBois house in several important ways. The addition did not change the exterior appearance of the house from the street; it still had a single front entrance, whereas the Broadhead-DuBois house was lengthened and given additional entrances. The kitchen was placed several steps below the house, symbolically and practically removing food preparation and storage from the original house to an ancillary wing. This wing, with its own box stair to a loft (independent of the rest of the attic), created a distinct unit and may have provided accommodations for the Snyders' one slave.[23] Among home owners on the Direct Tax "A" list 17 percent (31/171) added this type of kitchen wing to their house.

Another way to expand to three rooms was by adding what the 1798 assessors called an "outlet," or lean-to structure, to the back of a two-room house. Although the outlet is a well-documented urban house feature, commonly used in seventeenth-century Holland and New Netherland as an entry with an occasional bed alcove or stove, Marbletown's rural farmhouses were quite different from the Dutch urban town house with its gabled end to the street.[24] Most were rectangular buildings with entrances on the long side and a smaller rectangular outlet placed at the rear of the house under an extension of the roof, sometimes creating a one-story "salt box" effect.[25]

Prior to 1798 Gerrit Van Waggenen, a man of Dutch ancestry living on the banks of the Rondout Creek, added a 6-foot-deep-by-21-foot-long outlet to a portion of the rear of his 42-foot-long-by-27-foot-deep house (figs. 10.5 and 10.4b). Van Waggenen's modest stone dwelling, with only four windows and "in need of repair" was nonetheless valued at $510 in 1798, placing it in the top 30 percent of houses. What use Van Waggenen

made of his outlet is hard to ascertain; the absence of room-by-room inventories for much of the Hudson Valley makes it difficult to draw firm conclusions concerning the practical functions of eighteenth-century outlets.[26] It is probable that Marbletown's outlets served a variety of purposes, ranging from sleeping quarters to pantries, dairies, food storage areas, or even kitchens. In 1798 13 percent of Marbletown's "A" list houses (22/171) possessed an "outlet," and no house on the Direct Tax list possessed both an outlet and a kitchen, further suggesting that the outlet may have functioned as a kitchen.[27]

The final way to expand to a three-room house in Marbletown involved combining a bank house with a passage-and-parlor addition. Around 1755 Ephraim and Magdalena Chambers, both of English ancestry, built a two-room, two-story bank house with a basement kitchen on the Kripplebush Road (fig. 10.4c).[28] In 1772 they enlarged the house with an addition consisting of a twelve-foot-wide unheated center passage equipped with chair rail and box stair to the loft, and a formal parlor/chamber at the new gable end. The presence of an original chair rail in the passage suggests that the Chambers may have lined its walls with chairs, windsors perhaps, that were called into action when it was time to entertain. In 1798 the Direct

Fig. 10.5. Gerrit Van Waggenen House, c. 1732 and before 1798. Berme Road, Marbletown, Ulster County, New York.

Tax assessors found the enlarged house in "good repair" and valued it at $570, placing it in the eighth decile of house values. This transformation from a two-room, vertically stacked house to a center-passage arrangement, with food storage and preparation in the basement and finer appointments on the principal floor, demonstrates a choice for more private and functionally specific domestic spaces.

The Chambers family was certainly aware of Cornelius and Cornelia Wynkoop's new thirteen-room, double-pile, center-passage house prominently situated on Marbletown's main road. In 1798 the Wynkoop's house, with its more that five thousand square feet of space, twenty windows to keep it well lighted, and nine fireplaces, constituted Marbletown's largest and most expensive dwelling (fig. 10.1h). With fully paneled fireplace walls in both the front and rear parlors, the extensive use of imported decorative tin-glazed earthenware tiles surrounding the fireplaces, and the large central stair with elaborately turned balusters, it would have compared favorably with an elite class of fashionably designed Georgian houses throughout the colonies.

Yet, in Marbletown's architectural landscape of single-story frame, log, and stone houses, the Wynkoop house was in a class of its own. With the construction of their house in the 1760s, the Wynkoops may be credited with introducing the concept of a formal, unheated central passage to Marbletown's vernacular tradition. The Chambers made use of this same design idea, albeit on a less grand scale, when they expanded their compact bank house into a center-passage house. The Chambers were soon joined by other prosperous farmers and merchants, who chose to build new center-passage houses that were more in keeping with local building traditions than the bookish plan of the Wynkoop house. In the post–Revolutionary War years, Marbletown witnessed a period of architectural innovation and expansion that lasted until century's end. This new architec-

ture was characterized by such features as service wings, upper-story bedchambers, a concern for exterior symmetry, refined interior finishes, and the center passage.

Indeed, almost one-fourth (12/50) of the houses documented for this study were center-passage houses built in a single phase. Those that can be reliably dated were all built in the last quarter of the eighteenth century. How do these center passage houses built of a piece compare to three-room houses built in phases like the Broadhead-DuBois house? The limestone exterior and the one-and-one-half-story height of the newer houses provided visual continuity with the older houses built in phases. However, close inspection reveals stonework on the facade to be dressed more carefully and regularly laid up. Strict attention to bilateral symmetry on building facades further sets this group apart and indicates a significant shift in local building practices as builders and clients sought to impose a different exterior order on their houses through ideas borrowed from broader national and international fashions in architecture.

On the inside, the plan is distinguished by a wide, unheated center passage with opposed entries and a boxed (or occasionally an open) stair to the garret. This passage was, in most cases, flanked by a parlor and a kitchen. If one considers the passage as merely a means for communicating between the two interior rooms or between the outside and the interior, then, strictly speaking, this is a two-room plan. As in the case of the outlet, the unfortunate lack of room-by-room inventories makes it difficult to assess the variety of functions the passage may have served. In 1757 English architectural handbook author Abraham Swan described the purpose of the center passage: "All the rooms in the house are private, that is there is a way into each of them without passing through any other room. Which is a circumstance that should always be attended to in laying out and disposing the rooms of a house."[29] While there is no firm evidence that Swan's pattern book had reached Marbletown, by the last quarter of the eighteenth century the ideas he popularized certainly had.

Perhaps the purpose of the center passage extended beyond that of social control to include such practical functions as providing a well-ventilated gathering place in warmer weather or to meet the social needs of entertainment and dancing.[30] Whatever the initial function of the center passage, the plan of a passage with a single room to each side was viewed as inadequate by its early occupants since eleven out of twelve owners chose to add a third room in the form of a rear kitchen ell within a few years of building the main block. Most likely, kitchen ells were in the mind of both client and builder from the start; they were merely viewed as the last phase of a comprehensive building project. This hypothesis is supported by the fact that in 1798 thirty-six houses, or 21 percent of all "A" list houses, were described as "new and not finished" and yet were occupied.

Perhaps the most noteworthy feature of Marbletown's center passage houses was the unusual width of the passage. Turning again to Swan's 1757 *A Collection of Designs in Architecture,* we find unheated center passages consistently depicted at approximately one half the width of their flanking rooms, or a ratio of one to two.[31] Such a narrow passage was rarely the case in Marbletown. John A. DeWitt, a farmer, surveyor, and owner of six slaves, was still in the process of building his center passage house when the Direct Tax assessors valued it at $690 (figs. 10.6 and 10.1g). DeWitt's house contained a large, room-like unheated center passage measuring twelve feet, ten inches wide. To the right was a formal parlor with cornice molding and a Neoclassical mantle. To the left was an elaborate dining room with Neoclassically ornamented paneling, built-in display cupboards, and a fashionable recess in the wall for a side board. These flanking rooms

Fig. 10.6. John A. DeWitt House, c. 1788. Route 209, Marbletown, Ulster County, New York.

were fifteen feet, six inches wide, only slightly wider than the passage. On the basement level DeWitt had two storage rooms and a basement kitchen, making this the only documented example of a basement kitchen incorporated into a center-passage house at the time of construction. At the back of the first floor passage, an open stair led to a single heated garret bedchamber.

These twelve center-passage houses built "of a piece" and documented for this study stand at a juncture between the old familiar ways of building houses and a newer approach to the arrangement of domestic space. While visually connected to the regional house forms of eighteenth-century Marbletown in their use of materials and height, they depart from the familiar additive interiors as they express a fully thought-out hierarchy of spaces with clear functional distinctions from the time of initial construction. Three-fourths of these three-room houses contain unusually large unheated center passages like the one found in John A. DeWitt's house. These were not remote, isolated dwellings, but part of a larger community of people, buildings, and meaning. Their significance can only be ascertained when considered in the more complete architectural context of Adam Yaple's log house, the Broadhead's three-phase house, Ephraim and Magdalena Chambers' bank house-turned-center-passage house, the Wynkoop's richly ornamented thirteen-room house, and the scores of one-room log and frame houses far too humble to survive into the twentieth century.

Likewise, these houses and their owners must be appraised in the larger social context of the period. By creating facades and passages similar to those found in elite urban centers, the rural gentry of Marbletown, New York, found an exciting connection to a fashionable world extending far beyond the Hudson Valley. Like their counterparts up and down America's East Coast, Marbletown's elite were captivated by an expanding marketplace full of desirable and affordable products. Only ninety miles to the south lay New York City, a rapidly expanding center of worldwide trade, with daily arrivals of cheap English creamware, expensive Chinese porcelain, beautiful Irish cut glass, and exotic printed cottons from France and India. Added to this were the locally produced redwares and stonewares, pewter plates, silver buckles, and furniture made in the latest fashion from the cabinet shops of New York, Albany, and even Kingston.

The American Republic was young and times were changing. No doubt some of Marbletown's old families felt their traditional ways of life slipping away. But a new generation of prosperous farmers and merchants was coming of age. These men served during the War for Independence and had traveled beyond the Catskill Mountains to New York, Boston, and Philadelphia. Many had seen more of America than any generation since their immigrant ancestors had arrived fifty to one hundred and fifty years earlier. In the postwar period the steady demand for agricultural products for the burgeoning metropolis to the south, as well as increased wheat exports to Europe, helped secure the financial position of many Hudson Valley farmers.[32] If they were to play their part in this fashionable lifestyle, they needed the architectural stage sets of passage and parlor to carry it off.

However, the manner in which Marbletown's late-eighteenth-century builders incorporated such fashionable design ideas as the center passage had little to do with the prescribed formulas found in pattern books. The width of these center rooms suggests that, while enticed by new architectural ideas, John A. DeWitt and others still favored a familiar open plan similar to that of Broadhead-DuBois house.[33] They retained interior aspects of a familiar past, with three large rooms on a single floor, while they experimented with symmetrical facades of regularly cut and laid stone, basement and ell kitchens, and occasionally a garret bedchamber. These young, successful farmers and merchants who were building new houses late in the eighteenth century designed homes that had the traditional open plan of their parents' houses and the social pretense of elite, fashionable architecture.[34]

During the eighteenth century, Marbletown residents built several types of houses incorporating design and construction elements from a number of European ethnic traditions. They built with logs, milled lumber, and stone. They sited their houses on flat, fertile lands, rocky hillsides, and busy village centers. Some put kitchens in basements, others out back, and still others had them in the only room in the house. To reduce these houses to one cultural designation—the Dutch three-room house—is to miss the complexity of this rural community. A closer examination of the most common group of houses, those with three rooms, revealed that there were two ways to achieve such a house: add on or build new. Those who added on did so in a number of ways, the least popular of which—"three rooms strung out in a row"—received the most attention from early-twentieth-century writers looking for Dutch characteristics.

Toward the end of the eighteenth century a prosperous, young stratum of society began experimenting with new ways of building houses and used current fashionable designs for inspiration. A few adhered closely to Georgian plans, while most translated these ideas to conform to local building traditions and the social expectations of the community. In doing so the latter group created a truly regional architecture, where the formal, bilaterally symmetrical Georgian exterior gave way on the inside to a familiar open plan.

## Notes

1. 1798 Federal Direct Tax Records for Marbletown, Kingston, and Hurley. In the Dr. George Nash Manuscript Collection on the history of Hurley, New York, at The New-York Historical Society Library, New York, New York.

2. Helen Wilkinson Reynolds, *Dutch Houses in the Hudson Valley before 1776* (New York: Dover Publications, 1965), 4.

3. Ibid.

4. Most notable is Roderic H. Blackburn and Ruth Piwonka, *Remembrance of Patria: Dutch Arts and Culture in Colonial America 1609–1776* (Albany: Albany Institute of History and Art, 1988), where Dutch influence in the material culture of the Hudson Valley is carefully researched and presented. Other sources that have contributed to our understanding of this cross-Atlantic connection include: John Fitchen, *The New World Dutch Barn* (Syracuse: Syracuse Univ. Press, 1968); Theodore H. M. Prudon, "The Dutch Barn in America: Survival of a Medieval Structural Frame," in *Common Places: Readings in American Vernacular Architecture,* ed. Dell Upton and John Michael Vlach (Athens: Univ. of Georgia Press, 1986); Clifford W. Zink, "Dutch Framed Houses in New York and New Jersey," in *Winterthur Portfolio* 22 (4) (1987); Jack A. Soban, "The Timber Framed Dutch House, A Hillsdale, N. Y. Example," (Privately printed). Contemporaries of Helen Wilkinson Reynolds include Rosalie Fellows Bailey, *Pre-Revolutionary Dutch Houses and Families in Northern New Jersey and Southern New York* (New York: Dover Publications, 1968); and Maud Ester Dilliard, *Old Dutch Houses of Brooklyn* (New York: Richard R. Smith, 1945). More recent scholarship has done a better job of addressing the cultural complexity of the Hudson Valley. For examples, see Alan Gowans, *Images of American Living, Four Centuries of Architecture and Furniture as Cultural Expression* (Philadelphia: J. B. Lippincott Company, 1964); Allen G. Noble, *Wood, Brick and Stone, The North American Settle-*

*ment Landscape, Volume 1: Houses* (Amherst: Univ. of Massachusetts Press, 1984); Dell Upton, ed., *America's Architectural Roots: Ethnic Groups That Built America* (Washington, D.C.: Preservation Press, 1986); Neil Larson, *Ethnic and Economic Diversity in Columbia County, New York,* and *The Masonry Architecture of Ulster County, New York, An Evolution, 1665–1935* (Kingston, N.Y.: Vernacular Architecture Forum, May 1986); and David Steven Cohen, *The Dutch-American Farm* (New York: New York Univ. Press, 1992). Historian Thomas J. Wertenbaker offered a thoughtful investigation of the variety of cultural and architectural traditions in the Hudson Valley in his *The Founding of American Civilization, the Middle Colonies* (New York: Charles Scribner's Sons, 1949).

5. J. Franklin Jameson, ed., *Original Narratives of Early American History, Narratives of New Netherland, 1609–1664* (New York: Charles Scribner's Sons, 1909), 23–24.

6. Marc B. Fried, *The Early History of Kingston & Ulster County, N.Y.* (Marbletown, N.Y.: Ulster County Historical Society, 1975), 85–135.

7. Prior to 1750 the majority of slaves imported to New York came from the West Indian colonies of Jamaica and Barbados. After 1750, when Spanish markets were closed to English traders, West African slaves flooded the New York market, driving prices down 50 percent. During the twenty years that this trend continued, slave traders often sold directly to customers rather than to middlemen. For more on the New York slave trade, see Edgar J. McManus, *A History of Negro Slavery in New York* (Syracuse: Syracuse Univ. Press, 1966).

8. "A Map of the town of Marbletown, County of Ulster, 1797," New York State Library, Manuscript Room, eleventh floor. I am grateful to Dorothy Pratt, the Marbletown Town Historian, for making the map available and to George Van Sickle for alerting me to its existence.

The houses of late-eighteenth-century Marbletown were far removed in time and space from their northern European roots as they expressed an aesthetic at once local and international, traditional and modern.

9. Two previous field surveys of historic properties were also consulted to help identify surviving eighteenth-century houses. The results of the survey by the Junior League between 1964 and 1968 are on deposit at the Stone Ridge Library, Marbletown, New York. Ruth Piwonka's 1989 "Reconnaissance Level Survey of the Town of Marbletown," part of a national register nomination, was made available in draft form by the author and was of great assistance in locating early houses.

10. "Assessment Roll of the real and personal Estates in the Town of Marbletown for the year 1800," Dr. George Nash Manuscript Collection, New-York Historical Society Library.

11. Others who have utilized the Federal Direct Tax of 1798 to reconstruct historical landscapes include Michael Steinitz, "Rethinking Geographical Approaches to the Common House: The Evidence from Eighteenth-Century Massachusetts," in *Perspectives in Vernacular Architecture, III,* ed. Thomas Carter and Bernard L. Herman (Columbia: Univ. of Missouri Press, 1989); Gabrielle Lanier, "Samuel Wilson's Working World: Builders and Buildings in Chester County, Pennsylvania, 1780–1827," in *Perspectives in Vernacular Architecture, IV,* ed. Thomas Carter and Bernard L. Herman (Columbia: Univ. of Missouri Press, 1991); and Peter O. Wacker, "Relations between Cultural Origins, Relative Wealth, and the Size, Form, and Materials of Construction of Rural Dwellings in New Jersey during the Eighteenth Century," in *geographie historique* (Paris: Centre National de la Recherche Scientifique, 1979).

12. "Assessment Roll of the real and personal Estates in the Town of Marbletown for the year 1800," Dr. George Nash Manuscript Collection, New-York Historical Society Library.

13. The 1798 Federal Direct Tax for New Paltz, New York. Microfilm copy in the Center for Historic Architecture and Engineering, Univ. of Delaware.

14. Hugh Morrison, *Early American Architecture: From the First Colonial Settlements to the National Period* (New York: Dover Publications, 1987), 115–16.

15. Virginia McAlester and Lee McAlester, *A Field Guide to American Houses* (New York: Alfred A. Knopf, 1984), 116.

16. Gustave Anjou, Ulster County, New York Probate Records, Rhinebeck, New York: Palatine Transcripts, 1980, 142.

17. Jane Hansen, personal communication, Marbletown, New York, Autumn 1992. Evidence of a partition indicates the probable location of the room provided for widow Catrina in her husband Wessel's will. This information comes from research conducted by Jane Hansen, the present owner of the house, who has extensively researched the history of the Broadhead family and the Rest Plaus Historic District of Marbletown, N.Y.

18. Reynolds, *Dutch Houses,* 22–25 and 189; Morrison, *Early American Architecture,* 115–16.

19. The Andries DeWitt house has four rooms built in three phases, making it similar to the Broadhead's house. Two other houses have the external appearance of the Broadhead-DuBois plan. However, permission to study them could not be obtained, making it impossible to verify either their plans or stages of construction.

20. Royal Commission on the Historical Monuments of England and West Yorkshire Metropolitan Council, *Rural Houses of West Yorkshire 1400–1830* (London: Her Majesty's Stationery Office, 1989), 119, 192, 193. Wessel Broadhead's father, Capt. Daniel Broadhead, was commanding officer of the British forces in Ulster County, New York, when Great Britain seized control of New Netherland. Captain Broadhead's grandmother, Ann Tye, was a widow, and the only woman to receive a land grant when Marbletown was laid out in 1669.

21. This assertion is substantiated by field notes, measured plans, and photographic documentation conducted by Hillary Anderson, M. Jeffrey Hardwick, and the author in Artois, France, and southern Belgium in Jan. 1993.

22. Frank and Dorothy Lynch, "The Snyder House, Cottekill, New York," unpublished essay.

23. Federal Manuscript Census for Marbletown, Ulster County, New York, 1800, Sojourner Truth Library, State Univ. of New York at New Paltz.

24. Henk J. Zantkuyl, "The Netherlands Town House: How and Why it Works," in *New World Dutch Studies, Dutch Arts and Culture in Colonial America 1609–1776* (Albany: Albany Institute of History and Art, 1987), 143–60. For a building contract that mentions a stove, see *New York Historical Manuscripts: Dutch, The Kingston Papers,* trans. Dingman Versteeg (Baltimore: Genealogical Publishing Co., Inc., 1976), 739–40. The term "outlet" may be an Anglicization of the Dutch word *uitlait* meaning "aisle" and found in early descriptions of Dutch barns. It is also close to the Dutch verb *uitlaten,* which means "to let out," and thus could refer to the outlet's function as an entryway. In northern France, the outlet was a regular feature on

eighteenth-, nineteenth-, and twentieth-century rural farmhouses and was used in both domestic and agricultural buildings.

25. Although most outlets were rectangular, some were not. Of the twenty-two in the Direct Tax, three were square and five were close to square (10 by 9 feet; 11 by 9.5 feet; 12 by 15 feet; and two at 10 by 8 feet). The remaining fourteen outlets were long, narrow rectangles. When applied to additions with square dimensions, the term "outlet" suggests that the form was more broadly conceived in the eighteenth century than it was in the seventeenth-century contracts or that the five assessors had diverse understandings of what constituted an outlet.

26. Abbott Lowell Cummings, *The Framed Houses of Massachusetts Bay, 1625–1725* (Cambridge, Mass.: Belknap Press, 1979), 28–34, offers a thorough treatment of room use for the New England lean-to based on probate inventories.

27. The Gerrit Van Waggenen house on Old Clove Road has a chimney stack of later vintage in its outlet. The 1673 DeWitt contract referred to in n. 25 above called for a stove in the outlet.

28. Others, such as Jonathan B. Davis, did the reverse and added a two-room bank house to an existing one-story, two-room house to create a main floor with three rooms similar to the Chambers house.

29. Abraham Swan, *A Collection of Designs in Architecture Containing New Plans and Elevations of Houses for General Use* (London: Abraham Swan, 1757), 2.

30 See Mark R. Wenger's "The Central Passage in Virginia: Evolution of an Eighteenth- Century Living Space," in *Perspectives in Vernacular Architecture, II,* ed. Camille Wells (Columbia: Univ. of Missouri Press, 1986).

31. According to Abraham Swan, *A Collection of Designs in Architecture Containing New Plans and Elevations of Houses for General Use* (London: Abraham Swan, 1757), the relationship in width of center passage to flanking rooms is as follows: in plates 2 and 15, 18 feet to 6 feet to eighteen feet; in plate 11, 20 feet to 8 feet to 20 feet; and in plates 12 and 13, 18 feet to 7 feet to 18 feet. In all of these illustrations, the center passages lack a fireplace or other heating device.

32. John J. McCusker and Russell R. Menard, *The Economy of British America, 1706–1789* (Chapel Hill: Univ. of North Carolina Press, 1991), 203, informs us that according to U.S. Census Schedules, New York's population tripled between 1750 and 1780 from 76,700 to 210,500.

33. Several scholars in the field of vernacular architecture have derived similar conclusions about modern architectural exteriors and traditional interior plans. Examples include Henry Glassie, "Eighteenth-Century Cultural Process in Delaware Valley Folk Building," in *Common Places: Readings in American Vernacular Architecture,* ed. Dell Upton and John Michael Vlach (Athens: Univ. of Georgia Press, 1986); Ed Chappell, "Acculturation In the Shenandoah Valley: Rhenish Houses of the Massanutten Settlement," also in *Common Places*; Bernard L. Herman, *Architecture and Rural Life in Central Delaware, 1700–1900* (Knoxville: Univ. of Tennessee Press, 1987); and Dell Upton, "Vernacular Domestic Architecture in Eighteenth-Century Virginia," in *Common Places.*

34. A comparison of the U.S. Census Schedules for Population with the Direct Tax records reveals that five of seven builders were between twenty-six and forty-four years old at the time they had their houses constructed.

## CHAPTER 11

*John Michael Vlach*

# "Without Recourse to Owners": The Architecture of Urban Slavery in the Antebellum South

In 1857 a New Yorker traveling by steamboat down the Mississippi River was heard to inquire of a native southerner: "Where's your towns?"[1] His cynically posed question points out the key problem for urban studies in the South during the antebellum era—the presumed absence of sizable towns and cities and therefore the lack of urbanism itself. There were, of course, plenty of towns during the antebellum period but they were not built to the scale that a northerner might recognize. Rather than the expected burgeoning industrial and mercantile centers, one would have found numerous crossroads villages of modest size.[2] But importantly, the major urban centers of the South could not be found by traveling through the countryside; southern cities were all established around the edges of the region.

Collectively, these places served the region as gateways that allowed people and goods in and staple crops out. Southern cities during the ante-bellum period were, in the view of historian David R. Goldfield, "urban plantations." He explains:

> Staple agriculture formed the economic base for the urban South. The proliferation of small urban places meant, among other things, that marketing staple products was the main if not the only economic activity of much of the urban South. . . . In New Orleans, visitors observed with some annoyance that conversations with residents invariably took one track: cotton planting, cotton climate, cotton soil, and cotton labor. Scarcely a shopkeeper or professional in the city was untouched by the economic vagaries of the staple.[3]

The fates of planters and urban merchants were so closely linked that Southern cities even seemed to move to an agricultural rhythm; there was, for example, not much life in them until the first arrival of new crops in the fall. Even if cities were not actually plantations, a plantation mentality was nonetheless pervasive among their residents, and chattel slavery was regarded as an indispensable urban institution. Further, the presence of slavery gave rise to an architecture of slavery.

Even though the relative number of blacks living in cities was decreasing by the mid-nineteenth century, in 1860 the largest southern cities were still 20 percent black. One-third of the people living in Richmond, Charleston, and Savannah were slaves.[4] It is not hard, then, to understand why visitors were so struck by the dark-complexioned appearance of the urban South; black people were as omnipresent in the cities as they were in plantation settings, even though they did not constitute the majority of city dwellers. It was not too great an exaggeration for Swedish traveler Frederika Bremer to claim in 1850 when she reached Charleston that "Negroes swarm the street. Two-thirds of all the people I see in town are negroes."[5] Even though her estimate was nearly double the actual number of blacks then living in Charleston, slaves were, in fact, assigned many public tasks and thus they did dominate the city's street life. A New Orleans resident similarly observed that "almost the whole of the purchasing and selling of edible articles for domestic consumption [is] transacted by colored persons."[6] The high visibility of black people was one of the distinctive marks of southern urbanism.

Simply by doing their work, slaves effectively converted southern cities into black landscapes. Visitors' repeated observations that southern cities seemed to be "swarming with negroes" make it very clear that daily life in the urban South was characterized by slave actions.[7] Because southern cities were for the most part small, crowded enclaves, the spatial domains of blacks and whites necessarily overlapped with each other. The majority of urban slaves usually lived in the homes or in the shops of their owners; a condition that was feasible since most urban slaveholders owned no more than two slaves.[8] Space was found for them somewhere in the house: in the attic, in the cellar, or perhaps in a room attached to the rear of the house. An example of this pattern can be seen in drawings of the Fearn-Garth house in Huntsville, Alabama, which indicate that the slaves were kept on the second floor of the rear-ell addition above the kitchen (fig. 11.1). At "The Maples," a residence in Washington, D.C., less than seven blocks from the capitol, William Duncanson housed his slaves at one end of his stable.[9] While his slave quarter was a two-story apartment with a large general purpose room on the ground floor and two rooms above, the usual amount of space provided for urban slaves was more confined. The slave spaces at the Fawcett house in Alexandria, Virginia, consisting of two rooms in the loft area above the kitchen, was more typical. Since the urban homes of free blacks were rarely more than tiny one- and two-room cottages, those slaves who were not allowed to live away from their masters' residences could not expect to find much more than the most meager accommodation.[10]

Urban slave owners generally wanted their domestic servants readily available, and, by keeping their slaves in rooms within their houses, masters were spared the expense of constructing and maintaining a separate building. If, however, slaveholders owned more slaves than they could reasonably accommodate within the rooms of their dwellings, the common response was to build a detached service structure, usually at the back edges of their lots. The master's house, its yard, and its servants' quarters were then the prime components of an urban compound, a gathering of buildings that was readily distinguished from the homes of city residents who owned few or no slaves.

In cities like Charleston or New Orleans, where space was severely restricted by geography or settlement density, slave compounds were carefully organized. According to historian Richard C. Wade, the slave owners in these places took particular care to insure that their buildings would clearly convey their authority over their human property. Referring to New Orleans, Wade writes: "[T]he physical design of the whole complex compelled

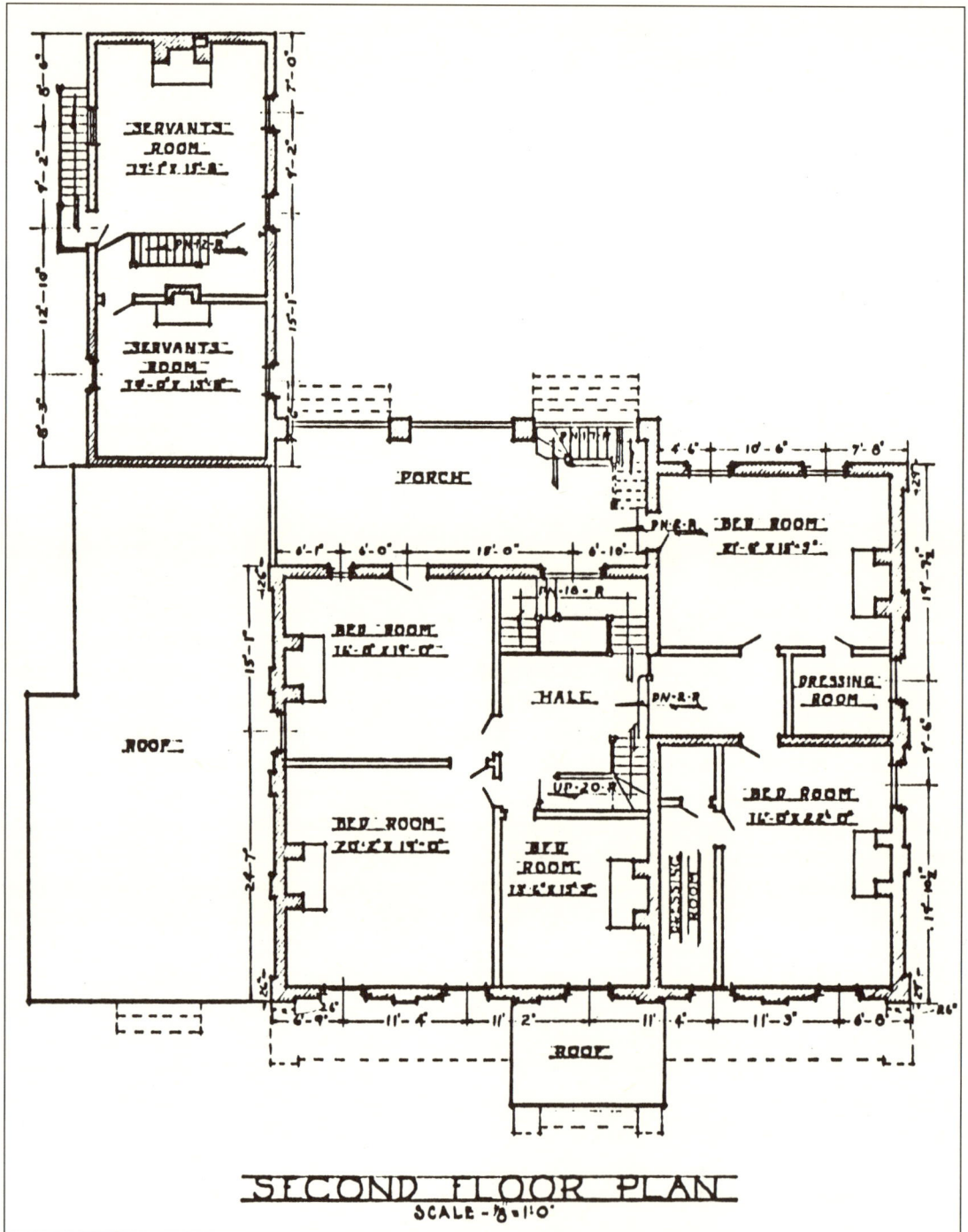

Fig. 11.1. Plan of the Fearn-Garth House, Huntsville, Alabama. The slave quarter at this house consisted of the two rooms designated as "servants rooms" in the upper left portion of the drawing. Drawn by B. F. Cole, 1935, Historic American Buildings Survey, courtesy of the Library of Congress.

slaves to center their activity upon the owner and the owner's place. Symbolically, the pitch of the roof of the Negro quarters was highest at the outside edge and then slanted sharply toward the yard—a kind of architectural expression of the human relationship involved. The whole design was concentric, drawing the life of the bondsman inward toward his master."[11] Much of his description would apply as well to slave quarters built in Mobile, Savannah, Charleston, Richmond, and Washington, D.C.

Wade's summary and interpretation are confirmed by examples of standing buildings. The slave quarters built in the 1830s as part of the Gally house in New Orleans provide a complex but relevant example (fig. 11.2). Since the house was divided into three separate residences, the quarter, at the rear of the property, was likewise divided into three separate units. Standing three stories tall like the main building, each of quarter's upper floors was, nevertheless, significantly lower than its corresponding unit in the main building. Thus, from the balconies of the quarter the slaves were compelled to look not only across a narrow space to the residences of their owners but slightly upwards as well (fig. 11.3). The slave occupants of the Gally house were put in a position that was both at the back and down, and thus their low social status was doubly underscored by their architectural context. With the three household privies on the ground floor, the kitchens on the second, and the bedrooms for the slaves at the top, the Gally house slave quarter was larger than the usual quarters-kitchen back building. More often, these structures were only two stories tall and were separated from the main house by a wider service yard, a pattern illustrated by the Staylor house slave quarter in Mobile (fig. 11.4).[12]

Even within the crowded city confines, some of the wealthier slaveholders were still able to recreate estates that were set out according to the plantation ideal; that is, a "big house" accompanied by a set of service dependencies. One of the largest,

Fig. 11.2. Gally House Slave Quarter, New Orleans, Louisiana. Photo by Richard Koch, 1936, Historic American Buildings Survey, courtesy of the Library of Congress.

and certainly one of the most elaborate, of these estates in Charleston was the residence of William Aiken Jr.[13] Laid out along Elizabeth Street, the property extended through an entire city block between Judith and Mary Streets (fig. 11.5). The house was built in 1818 for John Robinson, a fairly prosperous cotton factor. Aiken, who acquired the property in 1833, initiated an extensive program of changes to the house and its grounds. In short order he thoroughly rearranged the site. The Judith Street entrance was closed off, and the sandstone steps that formerly led up to the piazza and the front door were moved around to the back of the house where they connected the grand stair hall to a paved courtyard.[14] Along the edges of the rear yard, Aiken added several new structures and modified two extant back buildings. When his new building program was completed, the yard contained six outbuildings: a

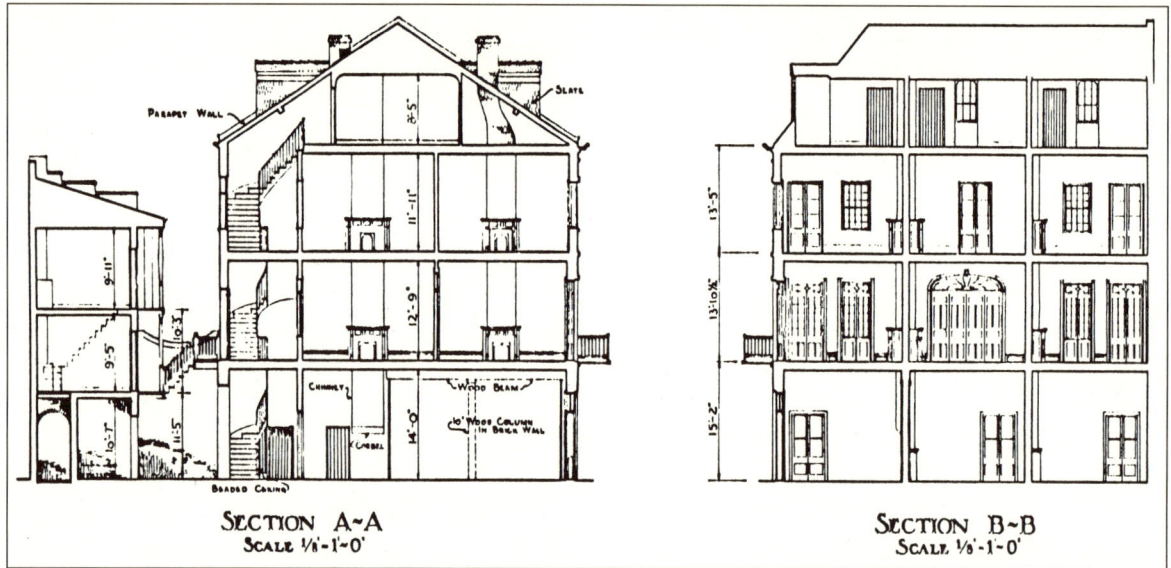

Fig. 11.3. Sectional View of the Gally House, New Orleans, Louisiana. The slave quarter is on the left with privies located on the first floor, kitchens on the second floor, and slave bedrooms on the third floor. Drawn by E. N. Maddux, 1936. Historic American Buildings Survey, courtesy of the Library of Congress.

Fig. 11.4. Slave Quarter at the Staylor House, Mobile, Alabama. Photo by E. W. Russell, 1936, Historic American Buildings Survey, courtesy of the Library of Congress.

kitchen, a stable, two cow houses or milking sheds (although one of these sheds may have served as a chicken house), and two privies.[15] Visitors could easily imagine they were approaching a country plantation as they entered the property from Mary Street and passed between two rows of magnolia trees on the way to the house.

If Aiken used the same occupancy ratios as his fellow slaveholders then he could have easily kept about thirty slaves on the property. All of Aiken's back buildings were not only substantially constructed with brick masonry but they were all, even the privies, decorated in the Gothic manner with pointed lancet windows. While such decorative touches might seem unique, if not eccentric, several other prominent Charleston estates also used the Gothic style to decorate their dependencies. It should be noted, however, that while the quarters may have been pleasant to look at, the rooms in Aiken's slave quarters were quite oppressive. Slaves living over the stable were only allowed a view of the interior yard while the exterior wall was decorated with a series of shallow niches instead of windows. Several of the rooms above the kitchen wing lacked any outside windows so that whatever light and air they received came in through the corridor that ran the length of the building (fig. 11.6). Since these spaces had only half-height windows set in a staggered alignment with the exterior windows, these rooms must

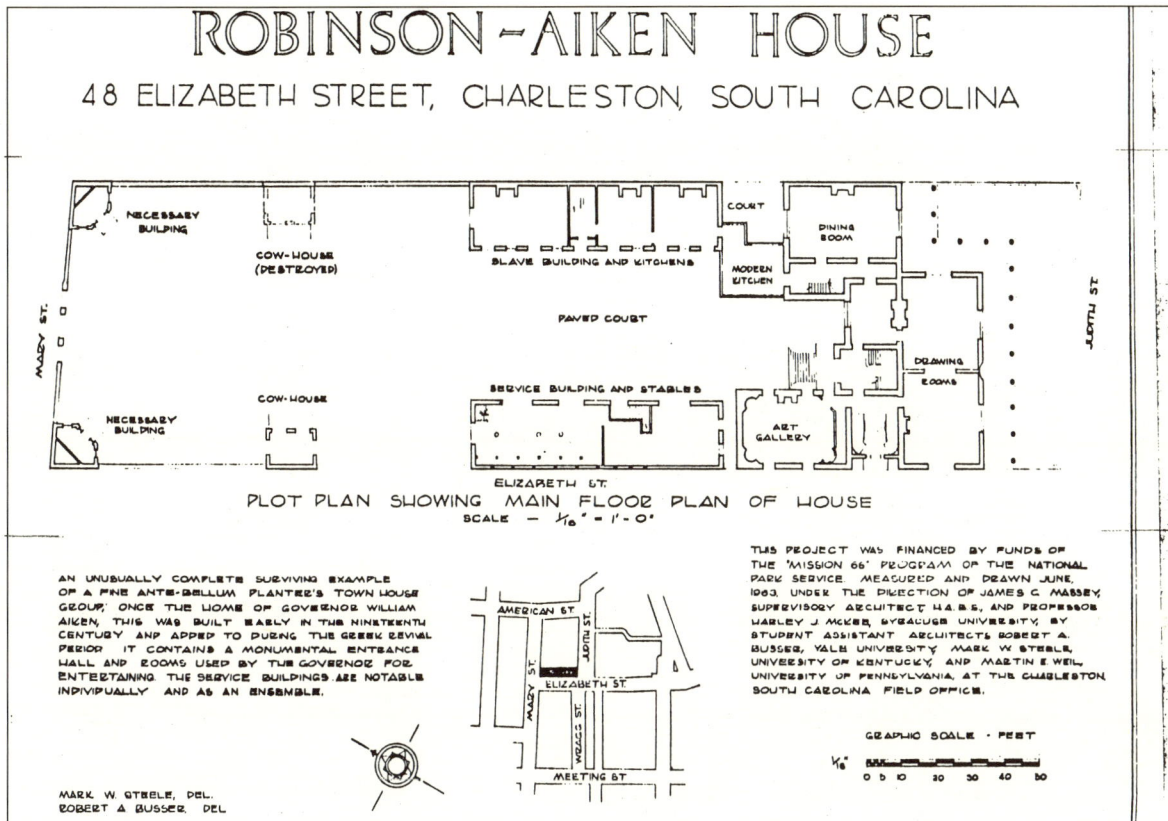

Fig. 11.5. Plan of the Aiken-Rhett House and Its Outbuildings, Charleston, South Carolina. Drawn by Mark W. Steele and Robert A. Bussser, 1963, Historic American Buildings Survey, courtesy of the Library of Congress.

have been particularly stifling during the summer months. The decorative exteriors with which William Aiken cloaked his slave quarters provided a sentimental and picturesque veneer, intended, it seems, to impart positive propaganda on behalf of chattel slavery. The overt spiritual references in the Gothic details denied the evils of the slave system. Regardless of how the gesture may have been "read," it certainly expressed Aiken's authority over his human property.

The Dargan-Waring residence in Mobile presents another case of an urban estate shaped by plantation ideals. The main house, built for Edmund Dargan in 1846, rested on a generously propor-

tioned lot that extended back almost 250 feet from Government Street, a main thoroughfare in the city. Purchased by Moses Waring in 1851, the site reflects mainly his ideas regarding slave treatment. The property was divided into three main zones; the largest was reserved for the main residence and its garden. Behind this area was a fenced yard containing the slave quarters and a privy. Presumably much of this yard was intended to be work space where his nine slaves carried out many of their required household tasks. Beyond the slave yard was a stable yard containing a well and a building that served both as a stable and carriage house. (In 1868 the Nugent house, which

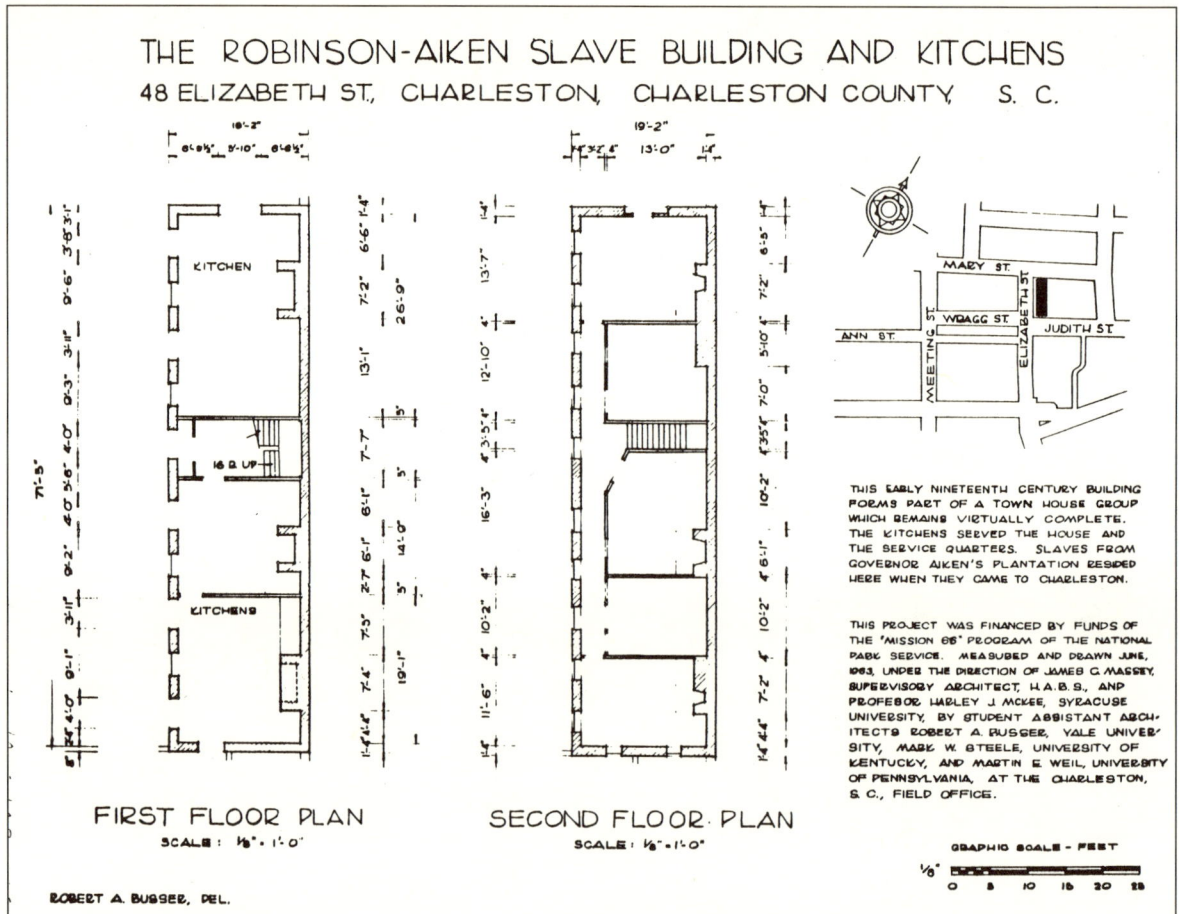

THE ROBINSON-AIKEN SLAVE BUILDING AND KITCHENS
48 ELIZABETH ST., CHARLESTON, CHARLESTON COUNTY, S. C.

FIRST FLOOR PLAN
SCALE: ½" = 1'-0"

SECOND FLOOR PLAN
SCALE: ½" = 1'-0"

THIS EARLY NINETEENTH CENTURY BUILDING FORMS PART OF A TOWN HOUSE GROUP WHICH REMAINS VIRTUALLY COMPLETE. THE KITCHENS SERVED THE HOUSE AND THE SERVICE QUARTERS. SLAVES FROM GOVERNOR AIKEN'S PLANTATION RESIDED HERE WHEN THEY CAME TO CHARLESTON.

THIS PROJECT WAS FINANCED BY FUNDS OF THE 'MISSION 66' PROGRAM OF THE NATIONAL PARK SERVICE. MEASURED AND DRAWN JUNE, 1963, UNDER THE DIRECTION OF JAMES C. MASSEY, SUPERVISORY ARCHITECT, H.A.B.S., AND PROFESOR HARLEY J. MCKEE, SYRACUSE UNIVERSITY, BY STUDENT ASSISTANT ARCHITECTS ROBERT A. BUSSER, YALE UNIVERSITY, MARK W. STEELE, UNIVERSITY OF KENTUCKY, AND MARTIN E. WEIL, UNIVERSITY OF PENNSYLVANIA, AT THE CHARLESTON, S. C., FIELD OFFICE.

GRAPHIC SCALE - FEET

ROBERT A. BUSSER, DEL.

Fig. 11.6. Plan of the Slave Quarter Located on the Second Floor of the Kitchen Wing of the Aiken-Rhett House, Charleston, South Carolina. Drawn by Robert A. Busser, 1963, Historic American Buildings Survey, courtesy of the Library of Congress.

stood at the eastern end of the stable yard, was purchased by Waring. Used as a residence for Waring's bachelor sons, it was variously referred to as "The Lodge" or the "Texas."[16])

The slave quarters and the stable were joined into a single T-shaped structure (fig. 11.7). However, the two elements while contiguous were not directly interconnected; the party wall that they shared was actually part of the boundary line between two zones of the property. The portion of the building within the slave zone was two stories tall with three rooms on each floor. Six of Waring's nine slaves were females, who no doubt

ran the laundry operation located on the ground floor of the quarters building. The sleeping rooms for the slaves were located on the second level. The other building in the slave zone, the privy, was shared by slaves and whites alike (fig. 11.8). Divided into three closets, two of them are alleged to have been reserved for the Warings and their visitors, while the third, the one with a door that opened away from the main house into a narrow space between the privy and a tall brick wall, is believed to have been used solely by the slaves. We can see in this ensemble of structures the attention given to insure that the slaves would be segregated from whites. Waring seems to have marked off with considerable care a discrete zone with fences and buildings that was understood as slave space. Even when he had to enter that space to use the privy, he continued to manipulate paths of access so that a crucial degree of separation might be maintained despite the limitations of close spatial proximity.

In urban settings blacks and whites encountered one another repeatedly and often. It could not be otherwise in a city like Mobile, where one out of every three people was black. A Charleston resident remarked of that city's slave population: "They are divided out among us and mingled up with

Fig. 11.7. Slave Quarter and Stable at the Waring House, Mobile, Alabama. Photo by E. W. Russell, 1935, Historic American Buildings Survey, courtesy of the Library of Congress.

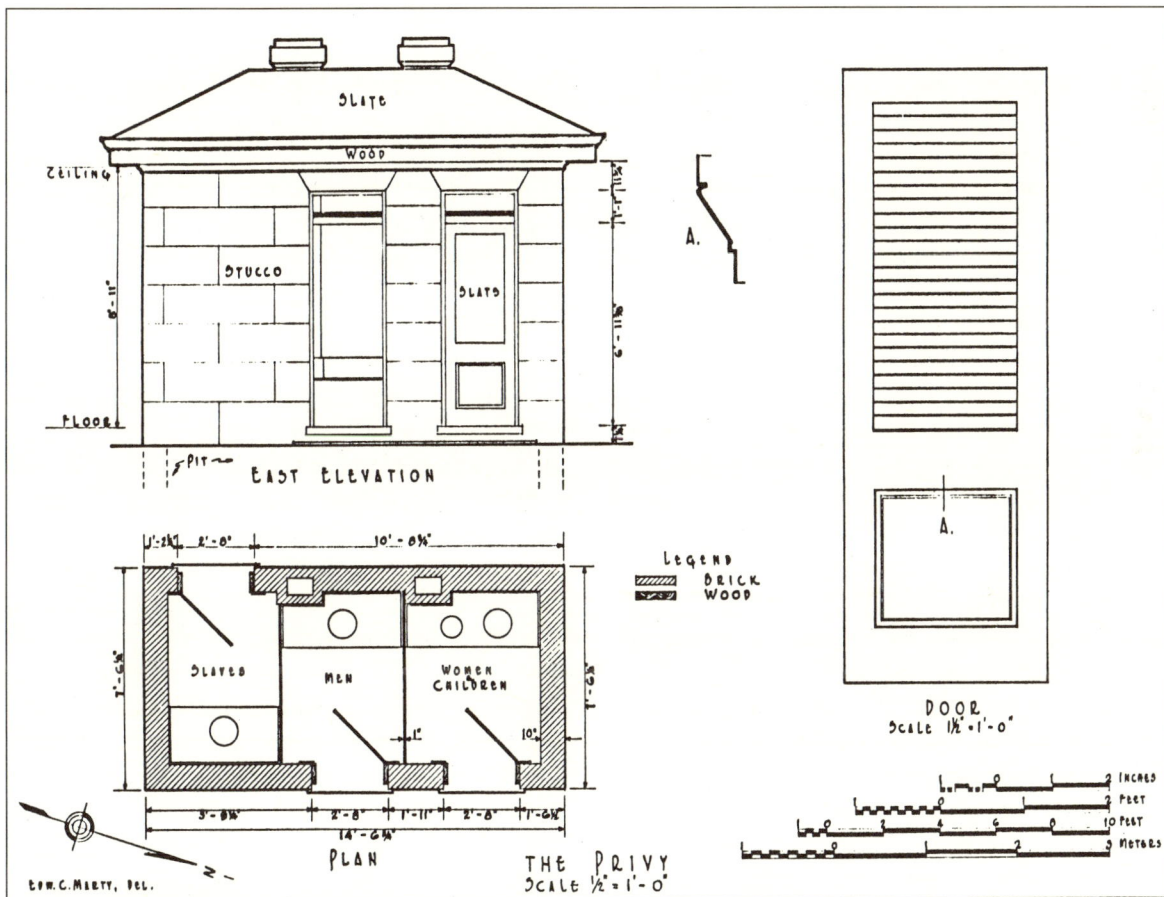

Fig. 11.8 East Elevation and Plan for the Waring House Privy, Mobile, Alabama. Drawn by Edward C. Marty, 1935–36, Historic American Buildings Survey, courtesy of the Library of Congress.

us, and we with them, in a thousand ways."[17] The same could have been said of most southern cities. Given the fact that the social routines of blacks and whites living in southern cities were so likely to overlap, Waring's efforts to keep his slaves' daily routines separate from his own reflect a circumstance that must have troubled many urban residents who were concerned with the maintaining what they considered the proper racial decorum.

While the more prosperous urban slaveholders had large homes comparable to rural plantation mansions with detached slave quarters, it was much more common for urban slaves to sleep in basement rooms, hallways, and attics. Since these were uncomfortable quarters, to say the least, the crowded conditions, which affected both the white and black members of an urban household, provided ample incentive for these slave owners to allow their bondspeople to live elsewhere. Slowly at first but then with increasing regularity, urban slaveholders permitted their slaves to "live out"; that is, to reside someplace beyond the confines of their owners' premises.

Urban slaves sought rooms wherever they might find them; all that seems to have mattered, in their view, was that they would be out from under their masters' roofs. These slaves frequently went to the shanty towns set up just beyond the city limits or to rickety tenements in which they rented rooms. Chief among the locations where urban slaves began to congregate were the expanding mercantile and industrial districts; places filled with warehouses, stables, utility sheds, and all sorts of outbuildings. "Serving commercial purposes by day," writes Richard C. Wade, "by night they attracted transients—white and Negro, slave and free."[18] Increasingly these areas were chosen by slaves as the sites for their permanent residences. Most of the structures inhabited by slaves while they were "living out" are no longer visible in the urban landscape, but they are described in the documentary record. In 1848, for example, so many slaves in Savannah were living away from their masters that one census taker complained that he was forced to enumerate them "in the place of abode, without recourse to owners."[19] In spite of the fact that slaves often endured harsher conditions while "living out" than when they remained in their masters' homes, they continued to leave. Any place, no matter how trying its lack of amenities, was considered better than living with one's owner.

Determining how many urban slaves were "living out" is difficult, but given the fact that they were able to establish well-known and easily recognizable areas—like the "Neck" north of Charleston, the Oglethorpe Ward of Savannah, or "Herring Hill" in Washington, D.C.—suggests that their numbers were significant. These places usually had, for white people, a disturbing, sinister quality. Given the hysteria over potential slave rebellions that periodically swept through the South, a large concentration of unsupervised blacks living so close at hand certainly presented them with a reason for concern if not dismay. A journalist writing in the *New Orleans Crescent* in the 1850s pondered, "Where the darkies all come from, what they do there, or where they go to, constitute a problem somewhat beyond my algebra."[20] As the numbers of slaves "living out" increased, so too did the anxiety level of whites.

Returning each night to a sizable black settlement, slaves found themselves not only in the company of their families but also interacting with free blacks, who owned and operated numerous canteens, grocery shops, gambling houses, and boarding houses. Here, while hidden within a warren of flimsy buildings, tumble-down structures, and sundry reclaimed spaces, slaves anticipated the possibility of future freedom as they saw that white man's law was often scoffed at or ignored. The twisting, mazelike streets and alleys of the black urban domain enveloped its inhabitants under a veil of protective seclusion that black people soon discovered they could well use for their own purposes. A mysterious underworld evolved, one crisscrossed with hidden passages and entered by secret passwords. While investigating the report of an unlicensed black confectionery shop in 1853, a Richmond policeman "detected a secret door in the partition, and opening it, found it led to a narrow passage. Passing through it for some distance, he came upon a large bar room, handsomely fitted up, in which one man was indulging to his heart's content."[21] The surprising lengths to which the black proprietor went to disguise his illegal business suggests the degree of independence that might be obtained by Richmond slaves while "living out."

The landscape of the urban slave owners consisted principally of their homes, their places of business, and the prominent public places and buildings, an ensemble of spaces and structures that was connected and bounded by streets and sidewalks. While slaves, too, moved through this landscape, occasionally dominating a particular place like the market, the waterfront, or the city square, their prime domains were hidden either behind their masters' houses or in a marginal section of the city that had been reluctantly ceded for their use. These black districts, filled with small, wooden structures, were noted particularly for their seedy, ramshackle appearance, an appearance that offered a marked contrast to the official decorum of the city grid and its architect-designed buildings.[22] While their settlements were criticized as squalid, miserable "dens" and feared as sources of epidemics or fires, what white city fathers feared most was the growing feeling of autonomy these settlements fostered among the slave population. This spirit was sensed in Mobile by the city's mayor, who, in 1856, wrote of the practice of allowing slaves to establish their own residences: "It is to its influence, more perhaps than to all other causes, that we are indebted for the spirit of insubordination so manifest and so much complained of in the community."[23] The existence of an independent, urban slave landscape was a portent of the freedom that would eventually mark the end of slavery.

## Notes

1. Quoted in David R. Goldfield, *Cotton Fields and Skyscrapers: Southern City and Region, 1607–1980* (Baton Rouge: Louisiana State Univ. Press, 1982), 32.

2. John R. Stilgoe, *Common Landscape of America, 1580 to 1845* (New Haven: Yale Univ. Press, 1982), 72.

3. Goldfield, *Cotton Fields and Skyscrapers*, 44, 33–34.

4. John B. Boles, *Black Southerners, 1619–1869* (Lexington: Univ. Press of Kentucky 1984), 126.

5. Quoted in Richard C. Wade, *Slavery in the Cities: The South 1820–1860* (New York: Oxford Univ. Press, 1964), 16.

6. Ibid., 29.

7. Robert Russell, *North America, Its Agriculture and Climate; Containing Observations on the Agriculture and Climate of Canada, the United States, and the Island of Cuba* (Edinburgh: A. and C. Black, 1857), 151.

8. David R. Goldfield, "Black Life in Old south Cities" in Edward D. C. Campbell Jr. and Kym S. Rice, eds., *Before Freedom Came: African-American Life in the Antebellum South* (Richmond: Museum of the Confederacy, 1991), 138.

9. See the Historic American Buildings Survey at the Prints and Photographs Division, Library of Congress, record number HABS DC-5.

10. For examples of the houses of free blacks from Richmond, see Marie Tyler-McGraw and Greg T. Kimball, *In Bondage and Freedom: Antebellum Black Life in Richmond, Virginia* (Richmond: Valentine Museum, 1988), 48.

11. Wade, *Slavery in the Cities*, 59.

12. For other examples of slave quarters in New Orleans, see Mary Cable, *Lost New Orleans* (New York: American Legacy Press, 1980), 60–61.

13. For other slave quarters in Charleston, see Albert Simons and Samuel Lapham, *The Early Architecture of Charleston* (New York: American Institute of Architects, 1927), 50, 85, 123, 133, 194.

14. William Nathaniel Banks, "The Aiken-Rhett House, Charleston, South Carolina," *Antiques* 98 (Jan. 1991): 236, 239.

15. Evidence of the earliest configuration for the Aiken outbuildings was discovered by Bernard Herman and Gary Stanton during personal fieldwork conducted in Jan. 1988 when they made measured drawings of these structures. They also measured the extant outbuildings at the second Robinson house located next door to the Aiken-Rhett house at 10 Judith Street. Finding that the two sets of buildings were constructed to the same dimensions and with very similar configurations, they concluded that the outbuildings for both properties must have built in the same period after the same design. It is reasonable to infer then that one can glimpse the original Aiken-Rhett outbuildings in the standing structures at 10 Judith Street.

16. Elizabeth Barrett Gould, *From Fort to Port: An Architectural History of Mobile, Alabama, 1711–1918* (Tuscaloosa: Univ. of Alabama Press, 1988), 126–27. The term "Texas" was used allegedly to confirm that the potentially troublesome youths, when they were in their quarters, were considered to be "in exile" in a distant place like Texas, where they would hopefully be less of a bother to their parents.

17. Quoted in Wade, *Slavery in the Cities*, 61.

18. Ibid., 73.

19. Ibid., 114.

20. Ibid., 145.

21. Quoted in Ira Berlin, *Slaves Without Masters: The Free Negro in the Antebellum South* (New York: Vintage, 1974), 242.

22. Wade, *Slavery in the Cities*, 70.

23. Quoted in Harriet E. Amos, *Cotton City: Urban Development in Antebellum Mobile* (Tuscaloosa: Univ. of Alabama Press, 1985), 146.

*Laurel Spencer Forsythe*

# Anglo-Hawaiian Building
# in Early-Nineteenth-Century Hawai'i

Upon his arrival in Hawai'i in June 1831, mission doctor Dwight Baldwin wrote, "The missionaries we found living in far more comfortable style than we expected. Mr. Bingham and Dr. Judd live in the old miss. house a convenient frame building and the printing establishment is in a stone building—In any of these you might suspect you was [sic] in the U.S.A."[1] Beginning with the arrival of the first company of missionaries to Hawai'i in 1820, American Protestants from New England introduced vernacular architecture traditions from their homeland. In Hawai'i, New England traditions were translated into new forms. In addition to building thoroughgoing New England–style structures with imported materials, missionary and Hawaiian builders developed and constructed bicultural "Anglo-Hawaiian" architectural forms, frequently incorporating Hawaiian building traditions.[2] In early-nineteenth-century Hawai'i, New England vernacular architecture served as both expression of cultural contact and as an agent of cultural change.

The Polynesians who settled the Hawaiian islands brought housing traditions and construction methods that share roots with those of central Polynesia.[3] In traditional Hawaiian society the thatched house *(hale)* was the most prevalent form of permanent shelter. Four types of thatched house predominated: houses without walls; houses with stone walls; walled houses with gabled roofs; and walled houses with hipped roofs (fig. 12.3).[4] The easily built house without walls was essentially a roof frame built directly on the ground with either straight or curved rafters. These small structures (four to six feet high) served primarily as storage space and secondarily as sleeping space during inclement weather. The house with stone walls was fundamentally a house without walls, only in this form the gable or hipped roof rested on four low stone walls rather than on the ground.

Gable-roofed houses with thatched wood frame walls were the most common form of shelter at the time of western contact; hipped-roof thatched houses seem to have gained popularity after contact.[5] As described by one missionary, these traditional Hawaiian houses were "made by fixing posts in the ground, fastening poles in the form of rafters to them, and tying in a compact manner bundles of long grass to transverse sticks."[6] Framing members were lashed together with a variety of local fibers and thatched with bundles of grasses and sedges, banana trunk fiber, or leaves such as pandanus, *ki,* and sugar cane.

Hawaiian houses varied widely in size and craftsmanship: chiefs lived in a compound of spacious and specialized houses for sleeping, separate men and women's dining, work, and worship; commoners often shared one modest-sized home per family. Archeological finds and the accounts of early voyagers indicate that Hawaiian structures ranged in size: 6-by-8-foot sheds were used mainly for storage; smaller houses averaged 18 feet long by 12 feet wide, while the larger ones approached 50 feet long by 30 feet wide. Houses with and without walls ranged in height from 4 to 6 feet for the most modest shelters to 18 to 20 feet for the homes of the chiefs. Floors were usually swept earth covered with dried grass and woven fiber mats. One low opening for a door frame was typical of enclosed structures; some houses were fitted with doors.[7] Window openings were probably not much used before western contact.

Foreign exploration and settlement of the Hawaiian islands began with Captain Cook's arrival in 1778. Use of introduced architectural forms by Hawaiians and foreigners in Hawai'i began no later than 1800, and by the time American Protestant missionaries arrived in 1820 a handful of wood frame, coral, and adobe houses lined the Honolulu waterfront.[8] Between 1810 and 1820, the resident foreign population in the Islands increased from sixty to almost two hundred with a constantly fluctuating number of transients.[9] The early-nineteenth-century foreign community was an eclectic, if exclusively male, group of American and European adventurers and entrepreneurs, including at least one escaped slave from Schenectady, New York.

Although most of these foreign residents lived in Hawaiian-made thatched houses, some began constructing more substantial stone and adobe structures roofed with thatch. The first known western-style structure in the Islands was a brick house built by foreign workmen for King Kamehameha I about 1800 in Lahaina, Maui. By 1816, several Boston merchants had erected imported house frames on the Honolulu waterfront, marking the presence (and foreshadowing the permanence) of foreign mercantile establishments in the kingdom.[10] Although foreign presence and influence in the Islands grew steadily, it was only with the arrival of missionaries in 1820 that a vision to reform the landscape and create an integrated built environment based on foreign antecedents was articulated.

The Boston-based American Board of Commissioners for Foreign Missions (ABCFM) was one of a number of societies formed in the United States and Europe during the early-nineteenth-century Second Great Awakening to support Christian evangelical work in foreign lands. The ABCFM established missions in the Middle East, India, Africa, Asia, and the Pacific, and sent missionaries across the continental frontier to convert Native Americans. Word of a potential field for mission work in the Hawaiian islands spread as Hawaiians abroad in New England caught the attention of eager young evangelicals. Between 1817 and 1826 the ABCFM sponsored the Foreign Mission School in Cornwall, Connecticut, as a training ground to prepare native peoples to introduce Christianity in their homelands. Nineteen Hawaiians attended the school during its brief existence, and four of them returned to Hawaii with the first group of American missionaries, giving important assistance as interpreters, mediators, and teachers.

In 1819, the ABCFM charged its "Pioneer Company" of missionaries to Hawai'i with the task of "filling those islands with fruitful fields, pleasant dwellings and schools and churches."[11] The board's rhetoric underscored the general reformist belief in the need for comprehensive transformation of the Hawaiians' traditional way of life through the creation of a landscape conducive to the practice and spread of the Protestant faith. The board and its emissaries preached the gospel of domesticity, arguing that the Christian faith would flourish within an orderly system of cities, towns, and farms anchored in the powerful influence of individual Christian homes. The theory offered a compelling vision to the mission and its New England supporters alike.

More than half of the nearly two hundred American Protestant missionaries who served in Hawai'i during the nineteenth century were born in New England, and fully four-fifths were from the northeastern United States. Most were young, idealistic Anglo-American men and women accustomed to some of the comforts of class privilege. Frequently, they married just prior to setting sail for the Islands, joined by their shared faith and mutual eagerness to embark on the mission's crusade. Their vision of an ideal Christian community grew out of the familiar architecture and landscapes of their homeland; the ideal domestic environment exhibited both "comfort" and "convenience," New England style. Most of these New Englanders and northeasterners, born in the small, agricultural communities of western Massachusetts, southern Vermont, central Connecticut, and upstate New York, recalled townscapes of single- and two-story frame buildings extended horizontally by various ells and outbuildings, linked by communal roads, surrounded by neatly fenced fields, meadows, and pastures, and dominated by a reaching, white meeting house spire.[12]

Along with these specific cultural memories and ideals, New England missionaries brought building skills, traditions, and tools and materials from their homeland. Yet, they had to modify their vision for reforming the Hawaiian landscape in response to their own changing circumstances. The mission's aims were complex and sometimes contradictory, and its built landscape mirrored some of its internal conflicts. From the start, scarcity of money and materials for building thwarted the fulfillment of the board's mandate to reproduce the New England townscape on Hawaiian soil. In fact, traditional Hawaiian architecture and Hawaiian labor provided the primary shelter for missionaries during their first years of settlement and continued to serve as an important housing source throughout the mission's active years, especially in rural regions.

There was consensus among missionaries on the unsuitability of such houses for permanent use. Their observations of Hawaiian thatched houses suggest that they regarded them as more suitable for housing livestock than humans. In the language of those accustomed to New England agricultural landscapes, these structures were likened to barns, haystacks, or sheds. One extremist claimed that "a native house is hazardous to the health and lives of missionaries."[13] Reverend Hiram Bingham, the mission's informal leader during its first two decades, took this criticism one step further, declaring that thatched houses were unwholesome to the spiritual as well as the physical nature of their occupants: "Such houses . . . are ill-adapted to promote health of body, vigor of intellect, neatness of person, food, clothing or lodging, and much less, longevity. They cannot be washed, scoured, polished, or painted to good purpose, nor be made suitable for good furniture, pantry, or wardrobe, nor for the security of valuable writings, books, or treasures."[14] New England ideals of "comfort" and "convenience" clearly concerned cultural definitions of cleanliness and protection of personal belongings as well.

Aided by Hawaiian builders, missionaries soon found ways to build thatched houses that could indeed be scoured. New house forms were created to satisfy American Protestant sensibilities while maintaining rigid economy and adapting to a persistent scarcity of supplies. Practical and inexpensively built thatched houses were modified with wood flooring, latches, locks, doors, and windows to mitigate missionaries' discomfort with traditional Hawaiian houses. Small adobe, stone, and coral block houses roofed with thatch also served as interim housing, and adobe and stone walls afforded highly valued protection and privacy. In the traditional stone-walled Hawaiian house, the three-foot-high stone walls, fitted without mortar, served primarily as a base for the thatched roof structure. Use of mortar and dressed coral block was a departure from the Hawaiian practice of fitting together loose lava stones. Stone houses built for the mission featured larger, full-size walls, eight to ten feet in height, and were sometimes two stories high. Like the houses of Hawaiian chiefs, houses built for missionaries were larger than common houses. Thus, the earliest structures at the mission's Honolulu headquarters—thatched houses known as "mis-

sionary row"—ranged in size from 28 by 20 feet to 20 by 14 feet for the dwelling houses, 30 feet square for the storage room, and 8 by 10 feet for the cookhouse (fig 12.1).

Anglo-Hawaiian mission houses often made eclectic use of materials and style, such as in a compound of interconnected buildings that was at once both alien and familiar to missionary wife Maria Patton Chamberlain, a native of Lancaster County, Pennsylvania: "Mr. Clark and we live in the same enclosure. Our houses are between 30 and 40 feet apart, but are connected by *lanais* (Open thatched sheds) and a cook house in the middle. The cook house is built of large unburnt clay bricks white washed has a grass roof and a stone chimney in the middle, and somewhat resembles the house in which Ingham Kinsey used to live [in the U.S.]"[15]

Such bicultural houses were transitional; generally, they were used only until replaced by frame and stone buildings. Few missionaries felt truly at home even in modified thatch and adobe structures, and the need for "permanent" (i.e., wood and stone) houses was portrayed to the mission's

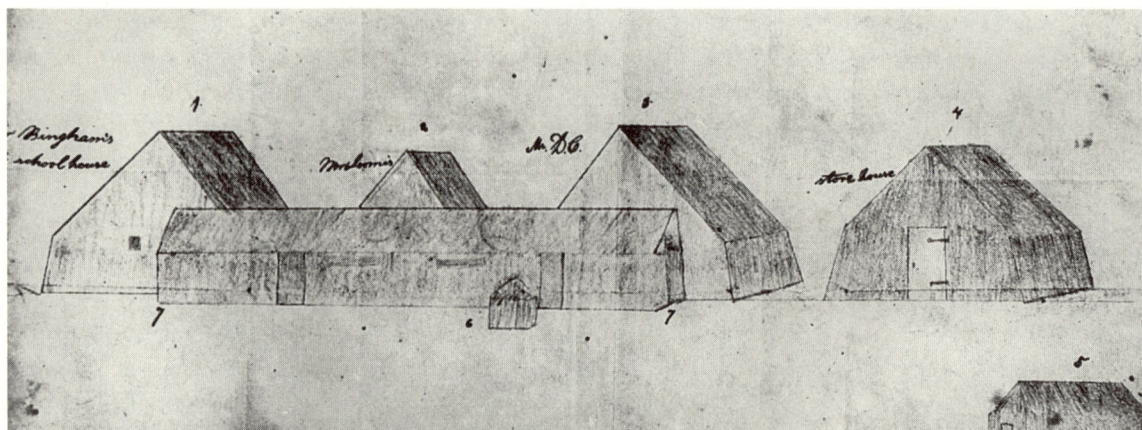

Fig. 12.1. Sketch by Dexter Chamberlain of "Missionary Row," Honolulu, 1820. The cluster of thatched houses custom-built for the mission by the Hawaiian government departed from traditional forms of Hawaiian building. Missionary row featured three attached dwelling houses with a long thatched shed to the rear (7); a mud-covered cookhouse sheltered the imported cookstove (6); and a sturdy strap-hinged door secured mission provisions in the thatched store house (4). Hawaiian assistant John Honoli'i resided in a small, separate thatched house within the compound (5). Courtesy of HMCS Library Collections, Mission Houses Museum.

sponsors as urgent. In spite of the board's emphasis on fostering an Americanized landscape for Christian Hawaiians, the mission argued that its long-term aims of "Christianizing and civilizing" Hawaiians could only be accomplished if missionaries first acquired proper shelter themselves. Health, and especially the well-being of mission women, were offered as principal reasons for building western-style mission houses in Hawai'i. Mission business agent Levi Chamberlain carried on a lively discourse with the mission board's secretary over the need for materials for building permanent houses, urging the board to send funds and supplies sufficient for providing each family with "a substantial and comfortable dwelling house."[16] Chamberlain's arguments proved successful: in 1848 he reported to ABCFM Secretary

Rufus Anderson that some ninety thousand dollars had been expended for building mission houses in three decades. Ultimately, a major part of the mission's funds were expended in materials and labor for building mission houses.

The mission's headquarters at Kawaiaha'o lay nearly a mile from the nucleus of the largely foreign port town of Honolulu. Outlying stations established throughout the islands eventually numbered seventeen. Through the secular agent at the Honolulu headquarters, the mission received supplies from Boston, including materials for building and articles of trade for obtaining local labor and supplies. The mission's "Pioneer Company" was supplied with the means for building a model mission house for its headquarters, including a precut post-and-girt frame, window glass, weath-

Fig. 12.2. Honolulu Mission Houses and Kawaiaha'o Church. Engraved by Eveleth for a Sunday school certificate, c. 1825. In 1821 the mission raised a house frame sent from Boston by its governing board. Beyond the imported frame house still stood the large thatched houses of missionary row. Other thatched and adobe outbuildings included temporary dwelling houses, storage houses, a blacksmith's workshop, and a shaving house. The compound was encircled by a seven-foot-high coral block wall. Courtesy of HMCS Library Collections, Mission Houses Museum.

erboards, lumber, and hardware. The house frame was sent in response to the "plan of taking females [from the United States] to live or die among the barbarians of Hawai'i"; it was shipped free of freight charge by a Boston mercantile firm whose owners thought that Hawaiian thatched houses were unsuitable accommodations for American women abroad.[17] Prevented from building the house for some months, mission families at Honolulu resided in the thatched houses called "missionary row," which were custom-made for the mission by the Hawaiian government. Missionary wife Maria Loomis gave an account of these early dwellings in her diary: "The three dwelling houses, standing in a line about ten feet apart, are connected together by what in America would be called a long shed, but what is here called a Ranie [lanai or open porch]. Answers all the purpose of hall, dining room, kitchen and is thatched like the houses in the style of this country."[18] In accordance with traditional Hawaiian methods, earth floors covered with dried grass and then laid with Hawaiian-made mats served as flooring in these earliest mission houses (fig. 12.2).

This cluster of houses continued in use after Liholiho (King Kamehameha II), who controlled all foreign building, permitted the mission to raise its imported house frame. As soon as it was complete, primary residence shifted to the one-and-one-half-story wooden house, and the vacated thatched houses were used as outbuildings, as temporary dwellings for visitors, and as the Islands' first printing office. Hawaiian John Honoli'i, an assistant to the mission and a former Cornwall Foreign Mission School student, did not remove to the frame house but remained in a separate thatched house that had been built for his use and that he shared with other Hawaiians and Tahitians, both students and visitors. Meanwhile, four missionary families and several lodgers shared the ground floor and unfinished chamber of the frame house, occupying rooms that averaged fourteen by twelve feet. As many as fifty took meals in the

cellar at a communal "long table."[19] In spite of these crowded conditions, the familiar frame structure was overwhelmingly the preferred dwelling, especially for the sick. Mary Mercy Moor Ellis, the ailing wife of a visiting London Missionary Society minister, stayed in one of the remaining thatched houses of missionary row while her husband traveled to outlying islands, but she was transported by her mission sisters to the overcrowded frame house whenever her health worsened, rather than being left to languish in a supposedly unwholesome thatched house.

Although communal housing was accepted as a necessity in the early years, as the mission became established and children were born, mission families appealed for individual family homes. Apparently, the shared work of communal living did not adequately offset their discomfort with conditions they found crowded and unmanageable. Mission women, most of whom were well-educated and experienced teachers who hoped to pursue their vocation in the mission field, often wrote of the heavy toll of their domestic duties. They struggled to maintain unwieldy households overflowing with endless visitors and lodgers in houses that they deemed very difficult to superintend. These women gave testimony to the advantages of imported homes like the Honolulu frame house. One relieved woman declared: "We have a new framed house & it is really one of the greatest temporal comforts we have, we were injuring our health by living in a damp [?] house. . . . It seems quite like civilization to live in a comfortable house with white walls."[20] Another described the salutary influence of a similar frame dwelling in Kailua, Kona, in equally enthusiastic terms: "The wooden house, in which we are now established, has been to me as the shadow of a great rock in a weary land. To obtain it has been a great tax upon you, as well as upon us, and it is in itself, in a land like this, truly valuable."[21] Still, one weary woman remarked on the burden of her domestic responsibilities even in a newly erected frame house: "Such is our situation, that it is double the work to provide for a family to what it would be in [a] convenient house in America."[22] Dust, insects, and other discomforts continued to plague mission households even when they were settled in more familiar surroundings.

Many of the laborers employed for building permanent frame and stone (or coral) mission houses were Hawaiians. Hawaiian men worked on the full range of mission building projects, from construction of traditional and modified *hale* to work on raising post-and-girt frames, clapboarding, shingling, plastering, and laying up masonry. With axes supplied by the mission's business agent, Hawaiian men hewed coral blocks from the exposed reef flats and dragged them ashore for building houses and walls. Hawaiian builders were paid for their labor either in cash or in supplies from the mission's depository—mostly cloth, books, and slates. Churchgoing Hawaiians sometimes contributed labor and materials for building mission houses as part of their donation to the monthly "concert of prayer."[23]

As they sought more permanent dwellings for themselves and paid Hawaiians laborers to construct them, missionaries also urged Hawaiian parishioners to adopt sturdier shelters. The Reverend C. B. Andrews wrote: "We have been wishing to

Fig. 12.3. Thatched House of Princess Ruth Keʻelilolani at Kailua, Kona, Hawaiʻi. Courtesy of HMCS Library Collections, Mission Houses Museum.

get the people building stone houses, and unkennel from their grass huts. To begin with I have been helping a poor but choice woman with a little family and blind husband to build a stone house or cottage."[24] Andrews noted that the house would be finished with glass windows, plastered walls, and a thatched roof. Even on remote Molokaʻi island, in 1845 four Hawaiian-owned houses were finished with glass windows. Yet, Reverend Elias Bond on the island of Hawaiʻi remarked on the slow rate of change in the rural district of Kohala: "We have indeed five or six small wooden dwellings in the district, but in the style of domestic and social life, generally, there has been, if any, the slightest possible progress. The dwelling houses are in no sense superior to those of twenty years since. Neither are the real comforts of domestic life in advance of those then possessed. A Forty dollar bedstead occupying one third or more of the space in the small thatched house and standing upon the earth floor, an object to be looked at and never used by the family, is far enough from adding to the comforts of the family."[25]

As efforts to establish comfortable and convenient mission stations were realized, mission architecture was modified to suit increasingly complex social circumstances. Couples who had set out from New England as newlyweds and began to have children in Hawaiʻi grew concerned with maintaining a strong collective identity as Christian Americans and with perpetuating that identity in their offspring. Some mission families strictly segregated their children from contact with Hawaiians (excepting domestic workers and chiefs), especially forbidding them to speak the locals' language. They particularly feared the influence of Hawaiian sexual customs on their children. At the same time, missionaries actively cultivated relationships with Hawaiian chiefs to gain their support and improve the chances of the mission's success. By the mid-1820s a group of high-ranking chiefs had converted to Christianity and were enthusiastically promoting the faith to the commoners.

Design and use of houses, outbuildings, and enclosures became a means of establishing and
maintaining separate spheres between missionaries and the different classes of Hawaiians. Missionaries adapted house forms, outbuildings, and
enclosures to facilitate their friendships with
chiefs by allowing them special access to their
homes; at the same time, the structures were built
to achieve segregation from commoners, or at
least to restrict them from ingress to the core of
mission households. At Kailua, Kona, the Thurston
family planned its compound to ensure segregation of the children from Hawaiians by means of
an intricate labyrinth of walls, fences, and structures. Lucy Thurston stated emphatically that
"no intercourse whatever should exist between
children and heathen," and, with her husband,
Reverend Asa Thurston, she carefully planned a
compound that would prevent any such fraterni-
zation. Separate yards, divided by six-foot-high
stone walls, segregated Hawaiian domestics and
Hawaiian visitors from the Thurston children.
"Our yard is capacious, surrounded and divided
by stone walls 6 feet high—As few doors as possible, as the natives are like children, ready to
press through every gap."[26] Further, Lucy Thurston
designed a plan for building a new ell that would
allow chiefs into her family's sanctum through a
passage into the chamber of the main house. This
arrangement, Lucy said, would allow "chiefs [to]
be conducted to the sitting room, which lies in the
chamber of [the main] house, without having an
avenue below opened, through which their linger-
ing trains would press and swarm like bees in
those very parts of an establishment which we
would fain *tapu* [forbid] to children."[27]

As missionaries designed and developed permanent compounds, the architecture of the mission stations became increasingly specialized. Another way to control access to family dwellings
was to establish a place for seeing day-to-day visitors. Frequently, mission ministers used ells or
free-standing outbuildings to serve as both a study

and a receiving room for Hawaiians. "Native
rooms" in detached outbuildings, or in an ell with
a separate entrance, enabled ministers to interview Hawaiians outside the interior, domestic
sphere. At the remote mission station 'Iole in the
Kohala district on the island of Hawai'i, Reverend Elias Bond added a study and "Native room"
with a separate entrance onto an existing house
to accommodate Hawaiians who sought his ad-
vice. At Kalua'aha on Moloka'i, the two resident
ministers each had separate, free-standing studies;
and at Hana on Maui, the "native room" stood
quite apart from the mission house (fig 12.4).

Fences and palings, integral to the cultural
landscape of New England, found new uses in
Hawai'i. Beyond definition and protection of
property, fences provided an important social bar-
rier (fig 12.5). Separation of the missionaries from
unregulated contact with Hawaiian society was
instituted with the first housekeeping effort. Even
before the construction of a permanent dwelling,
the mission families built "a light fence paling of
slender poles set perpendicularly in close order in
the earth having two horizontal ranges of poles
tied to them with bark or vines." Hundreds of
Hawaiians gathered outside this fence daily to
watch mission women cook and heat irons on an
imported cookstove.[28]

In rural New England the ubiquitous stone
wall made practical use of an abundant resource.
In Honolulu fieldstones were scarce, and an uncommon effort had to be made to procure material for building sturdy walls. Hawaiian workers
armed with axes from the mission's supplies cut
coral blocks out of reef flats along the Honolulu
shoreline and dragged them to the mission premises. Within two years of its establishment, the
mission compound at Honolulu was enclosed
with 170 fathoms of coral wall more than seven
feet high, nearly twice the height of the average
four-foot New England stone wall. A missionary
son who grew up surrounded by this substantial
structure recalled that it was built "in order to

Fig. 12.4. Engraving of Mission Station, Kaluaʻaha, Molokaʻi. Made at Lahainaluna School, c. 1845. At the remote station of Kaluaʻaha each of the two ministers had a study that stood apart from his family's house where Hawaiian parishioners visited and work was done. A large house for Hawaiian domestic workers stood at the center of the compound. Single missionary teacher Lydia Brown occupied her own house nearby. Courtesy of HMCS Library Collections, Mission Houses Museum.

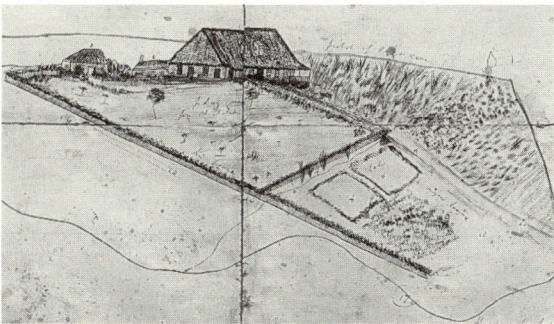

Fig. 12.5. Mission Station, Wailuku, Maui, c. 1832. Drawn by Clarissa Armstrong. Missionary Clarissa Armstrong's sketch of her family's residence delineates the children's kapu (forbidden) play yard. Courtesy of HMCS Library Collections, Mission Houses Museum.

keep the place *kapu* (or forbidden) to the natives and the children from undue familiarity with them."[29] He failed to mention that the wall was built by those whom it was intended to exclude.

Even when missionaries and Hawaiian domestics had "equal" housing—that is, when missionaries and their servants alike resided in thatched houses—their homes stood in separate yards, bounded by symbolic *ki* fences, which were made of slender plant stalks, or by sturdy stone and mud walls. Although Hawaiians who worked in mission households generally lived in separate thatched houses, they sometimes lived within the main mission house, such as at Waimea, where the "house for domestics" was part of the attached stone cookhouse, and at Honolulu, where Hawaiians lived in the cellar.[30] In at least one case, a Hawaiian family resided in the lean-to ell of the mission house occupied by the Judd family at Honolulu (fig. 12.6). In many mission households, however, separation of mission children and Hawaiian workers and visitors was carefully arranged: "Our House occupied about an acre of land, half of it in yards for our native *ohuas* [servants], and for domestic animals, cows, pigs, and poultry. The other half where the children played was surrounded by a high wall topped by a projecting paling to barr [sic] out native intruders" wrote missionary son Sereno E. Bishop.[31]

By the 1840s the major mission stations had developed a uniformity of appearance. Most were encircled by high stone walls and featured one or more stone or frame houses with a stone or wood cookhouse ell, attended by various specialized outbuildings, including thatched houses for Hawaiian domestics, studies, woodhouses, workshops, bathhouses, and privies. Meticulous landscaping contributed to a growing air of permanence and prosperity at the mission stations. More than one observer noted with irony the manorlike appearance of the larger stations. As early as 1833, a newly arrived mission physician remarked on the impropriety of the elaborate mission stations he found:

"The *large houses, numerous domestics,* and *extensive tenanted* domains, possessed by individuals of this mission exhibit an appearance of prosperity and worlding inconsistent with the self-denying spirit, which we profess, and is at variance with every effort we may make to secure the assent of the natives to our benevolent and disinterested motives in living among them. The chiefs are already jealous of our acquisitions, and have diminished greatly their favors, and the common people can conceive of no wealth to be desired above fields well stocked with men and food."[32]

Hawaiian chiefs, often eager to adopt western modes, studied the mission stations and other foreign examples and patterned their buildings after these models, ordering precut house frames and building materials from America, and filling their homes with up-to-date foreign furnishings. The brick house constructed about 1800 for Kamehameha I

Fig. 12.6. Sketch by Reverend Hiram Bingham of the Judds' House at Honolulu, c. 1835. The mission physician's family lived in a framed house with an attached thatched roof ell for Hawaiian domestic workers. In most other mission houses, Hawaiian domestic workers resided in free-standing thatched, adobe, or frame outbuildings; these often stood within a separate yard. Courtesy of HMCS Library Collections, Mission Houses Museum.

in Lahaina was likely the first western-style building in the Hawaiian islands.[33] When Liholiho (Kamehameha II) established the official seat of government in Honolulu in 1821, just a year after the missionaries' arrival added to the growing foreign presence, he appointed his spacious, thatched Pakaka Palace with cut-glass chandeliers, mahogany furniture, and Chinese sofas and chairs upholstered in crimson. Upon visiting the palace in 1823 Reverend Charles S. Stewart observed: "It is a large and fine house for one of the kind; perhaps fifty feet long, thirty broad, eight feet high at the sides, and thirty at the peak of the roof. The exterior is entirely composed with a thatch of grass; and in its whole appearance is strikingly like the Dutch barns seen in many parts of our country. There are two large doors, one at each end, and several windows without glass, but furnished with Venetian shutters."[34] Nearby, principal chief Kalanimoku possessed a two-story, "European built" stone house praised by London missionary William Ellis in his journal: "Several [Hawaiians] have forsaken their grass huts, and erected comfortable stone or wooden houses, among which, one built by Karaimoku [sic], the prime minister, is highly creditable to his perseverance and his taste."[35]

By the mid-1820s, Kalanimoku and other principal chiefs who had converted to Christianity settled a compound just a short distance from the Honolulu mission premises. Here Kauikeaouli (King Kamehameha III) furnished a "large straw house," or palace, with "beautiful mats chairs, tables and other furniture."[36] The palace, a "fine, lofty building," stood forty feet high and measured over one hundred feet in length, with a breadth of about sixty feet. The floor was paved with stone and mortar "having all the smoothness of marble," then covered with fine mats "forming a carpet as delightful, and appropriate to the climate, as could be selected."[37] Regent Ka'ahumanu, a frequent overnight visitor at the mission's Honolulu

frame house, built a two-story frame house near Honolulu harbor and frequently lodged overnight at the mission's frame house; yet, she ultimately preferred a traditional *hale* for her own use.[38] In general, stone, coral block, and frame houses became more prevalent in the port towns of Honolulu and Lahaina.

As religious enthusiasm and fervor diminished toward mid-century, secularism stole into even the most pious of mission families. A handful of former missionaries, now successful in business or enjoying positions of prominence in the kingdom's government, built large, well-appointed houses in Honolulu's most desirable sections, such as cool Nu'uanu Valley. After private land ownership became possible as a result of the foreign-inspired *Mahele* (land division) of the late 1840s, many of the mission's properties were sold to individual mission families. Missionaries and former missionaries alike exhibited an eagerness for private property ownership as evidence of a spirit of acquisitiveness grew. By mid-century one missionary printer-turned-businessman revealed that "religion is not always uppermost in my thoughts and affections."[39] A few years later at the old Honolulu mission station a boundary dispute arose between Mrs. Chamberlain, widow of the mission's business agent, and Mr. Cooke, her neighbor. Cooke, who had inherited Chamberlain's mantle as mission business agent, left the mission to open a business with another former secular agent of the mission, using the old mission depository as the warehouse for his mercantile firm, called Castle and Cooke. The Cooke family became the owner-occupants of the mission's old frame house. Mrs. Chamberlain objected to the proximity of a commercial establishment to her household, and especially disliked the signs—in both English and Hawaiian—and brightly colored flags set near her house to attract business to the store. Unable to dissuade her late husband's former colleagues to cease advertising, she soon sought to claim a one-story, two-room coral block house that stood between her large house and the old mission frame house. The mission ultimately decided the case in favor of the Cookes, leaving Mrs. Chamberlain rather dissatisfied.[40] The episode exposed the strong sentiments about property ownership held by at least a few former mission members.

By 1848, the American Board of Commissioners for Foreign Missions planned for the mission's transition from a foreign-sponsored entity to a home-based operation. Over the next fifteen years, the mission came to a gradual end. The board encouraged American ministers to turn over their churches to a Hawaiian pastorate and, at the same time, urged them to remain in the islands to support the organizations they had worked to establish. In 1854 the Hawai'i Evangelical Association was formed to oversee the Protestant ministry. As the mission ended in 1863, the board's aims for transforming Hawai'i's landscape were still largely unrealized. Wealthy Hawaiian chiefs built mansions to rival those in large U.S. cities, while Hawaiian church members labored to build their own meeting houses and schools. Traditional native Hawaiian houses still predominated in all but the most urban areas, and traditional Hawaiian building methods continued to inform the construction of homes, churches, and schools. Yet, westernization spread apace throughout the islands, affecting all aspects of Hawaiian culture, including building practices and land use. As the nineteenth century drew to a close, the Honolulu cityscape increasingly resembled its American counterpart, while immigration of Asian laborers to Hawai'i's sugar plantations contributed to the creation of a unique Pacific-American architecture in suburban and rural districts. The traditional Hawaiian thatched house grew so scarce that one was preserved and exhibited in Honolulu's Bishop Museum just after the turn of the century.

By this time, Hawaiians' traditional ways of life had changed dramatically and tragically. Since the beginning of western contact, introduced disease had brought death to many Hawaiians, and depopulation continued throughout the nineteenth century at an appalling rate: population estimates before contact range from 300,000 to over 800,000 Hawaiians; the first official census in 1832 counted 130,000 Hawaiians; by the end of the century, the indigenous population was numbered at fewer than 40,000. The land division of the late 1840s led to utter dispossession for Hawaiians, since it inherently favored western customs and views of land ownership; except for the crown lands, the few parcels that transferred into Hawaiian hands at mid-century were quickly bought out by nonindigenous residents. Throughout the century cultural traditions diminished, disrupted by missionary censure and the wholesale transformation of their contexts.

More directly influential on the transformation of Hawaiian society than the mission's efforts to reform the landscape was the involvement of former missionaries and their children in Hawaiian government, law, education, and commerce. As early as the 1830s, former mission minister William Richards became "Chaplain, Teacher and Translator" for King Kamehameha III and aided in the drafting of the kingdom's first constitution. Mission physician Gerrit Judd held cabinet positions in Kamehameha III's government for a dozen years. A mission son and grandson were key players in the unlawful removal of Hawaiian Queen Lili'uokalani from her throne in 1893 and the subsequent annexation of Hawai'i to the United States in 1898. By the end of the century, the life of the land, so essential to order and balance in traditional Hawaiian society, had indeed been transformed, at least in part as a result of the mission's agency and legacy.

## Notes

1. Journal of Dwight Baldwin, June 14, 1831, Journal Collection, Hawaiian Mission Children's Society Library, Honolulu, Hawai'i (hereafter referred to as HMCSL).

2. My thanks to Barnes Riznik, retired director of Grove Farm Homestead and Waioli Mission House on Kaua'i, for introducing me to the term "Anglo-Hawaiian" architecture.

3. Te Rangi Hiroa (Sir Peter H. Buck), *Arts and Crafts of Hawaii: Houses* (Section II) (Honolulu: Bishop Museum Press, 1957, reprinted in separate sections, 1964), 75.

4. Ibid., 78–99. David Malo, *Hawaiian Antiquities* (1903; reprint, Bernice Pauahi Bishop Museum, 1951; reprinted 1951, 1971, 1976, 1980, 1987, 1991), 118–22.

5. Ibid.

6. Levi Chamberlain to Rufus Anderson, Jan. 21, 1836, Missionary Letters, HMCSL.

7. Te Rangi Hiroa, *Arts and Crafts of Hawaii,* 102–5. Malo, *Hawaiian Antiquities,* 121.

8. Charles Peterson, "Pioneer Prefabs in Hawai'i," *Hawaiian Journal of History* 5 (1971): 25–26.

9. Donald D. Johnson, *The City and County of Honolulu: A Governmental Chronicle* (Honolulu: Univ. of Hawai'i Press), 7, 12.

10. Peterson, "Pioneer Prefabs in Hawai'i," 25–26.

11. *Instructions of the Prudential Committee of the ABCFM to the Sandwich Islands Mission* (Lahainaluna: Press of the Mission Seminary, 1838), 27

12. John R. Stilgoe, *Common Landscapes of America, 1580–1845* (New Haven: Yale Univ. Press, 1982), 56–58.

13. J. D. Paris to Levi Chamberlain, Ka'u Station Report, Apr. 20, 1842, HMCSL.

14. Hiram Bingham, *A Residence of Twenty-One Years in the Sandwich Islands* (1847, 3d rev. ed., 1849; reprint, Rutland, Vt.: Charles E. Tuttle Co., 1981), 116.

15. Maria Patton Chamberlain to Isabella Patton, Honolulu, Oct. 29, 1830, HMCSL.

16. Levi Chamberlain to Rufus Anderson, Jan. 21, 1836, Missionary Letters HMCSL.

17. Bingham, *A Residence of Twenty-One Years,* 61–62.

18. Journal of Maria Loomis, 54–55, Journal Collection, HMCSL.

19. Sybil M. Bingham, n.d., Box 3, Bingham Family Papers, HMCSL.

20. Betsey Lyons to Emily Bliss, Waimea, Apr. 29, 1836, HMCSL.

21. Lucy Thurston to Levi Chamberlain, Kailua, Dec. 25, 1833, ABCFM Papers, Houghton Library, Harvard Univ.

22. Journal of Maria Loomis, 156.

23. Paris to Chamberlain, Ka'u Station Report, Waiohinu, Apr. 20, 1842, HMCSL.

24. C. B. Andrews to family, Lahaina, May 19, 1845, HMCSL.

25. Ethel Damon, *Father Bond of Kohala: A Chronicle of Pioneer Life in Hawaii* (Honolulu: The Friend, 1927), 157.

26. Lucy Thurston to Mr. Goodell, Oct. 16, 1829, ABCFM Papers, Houghton Library, Harvard Univ.

27. Lucy Thurston to Levi Chamberlain, Dec. 25, 1833, HMCSL.

28. Bingham, *A Residence of Twenty-One Years,* 96.

29. HMCS Annual Report, 1910, vol. 7: 7.

30. General meeting minutes, 1848. HMCSL; Lorenzo Lyons to ABCFM, Waimea, 1836, ABCFM Papers, Houghton Library, Harvard Univ.; Martha Goodrich to Nancy Ruggles, Dec. 7, 1928, HMCSL.

31. Sereno Bishop, *Reminiscences of Old Hawaii* (Honolulu: Hawaiian Gazette Co., 1916), 15.

32. Alonzo Chapin to Rufus Anderson, Hilo, Oct. 6, 1833. Missionary Letters, vol. 8, HMCSL.

33. David W. Forbes, *Encounters with Paradise: Views of Hawaii and Its People, 1778–1941* (Honolulu Academy of Arts, 1992), 76.

34. Walter F. Judd, *Palaces and Forts of the Hawaiian Kingdom: From Thatch to American Florentine* (Palo Alto, Calif.: Pacific Press, 1975), 30–31.

35. William Ellis, *Journal of William Ellis* (1825; reprint, Rutland, Vt., and Tokyo: Tuttle, 1979), 12.

36. Andrew Bloxam, *Diary of Andrew Bloxam* (Honolulu: Bishop Museum, 1925), 28.

37. Judd, *Palaces and Forts,* 35.

38. Jane L. Silverman, *Kaahumanu: Molder of Change* (Honolulu: Friends of the Judiciary History Center of Hawaii, 1987), 75, 143.

39. Henry Dimond to brother Isaac, Dec. 12, 1850, Hawai'i State Archives.

40. A. S. Cooke Journal, vol. 9: 25–26, 50–52, 124, HMCSL; Maria P. Chamberlain to daughters, June 4, 1851, Aug. 1851. HMCSL; Maria P. Chamberlain Journal May 23, 1853. HMCSL.

*Alison K. Hoagland*

# Totem Poles and Plank Houses: Reconstructing Native Culture in Southeast Alaska

In June 1940, the southeastern Alaska town of Wrangell celebrated the dedication of a new tribal house with a potlatch. Ironies abounded: the potlatch was a ceremony practiced by Northwest Coast Indians such as the Tlingit who lived in Wrangell, but this potlatch was sponsored by non-Native city fathers. The U.S. Forest Service and the Office of Indian Affairs signed on as co-sponsors, although the government had discouraged potlatches in the past. The house that was being dedicated was designed by a white architect in the form of the traditional Tlingit dwelling discarded by the Tlingit fifty years before. And the totem poles that were raised for the celebration had been seen by missionaries, government officials, and Christianized Natives only a generation earlier as a symbol of Native "backwardness."

These conflicting roles and abruptly changed policies reflect the complexity of totem-pole and plank-house preservation. The Forest Service as-

sumed stewardship responsibility for these Native artifacts and saw opportunities for Native employment in their preservation. Many of the Natives, though, sought social and economic advancement in other arenas and did not see their future so closely connected to their past. By looking first at the Forest Service's motivations, and then at the Natives' historical and evolving relationship to these artifacts, we can begin to understand the complexity of the potlatch in Wrangell in 1940.

The plank house and totem poles that were being dedicated were products of one of the more unusual Civilian Conservation Corps endeavors. Impoverished Natives who wanted a piece of the federal jobs program joined with Forest Service attempts to salvage the irreplaceable Native architecture and artifacts found in the vast stretches of Southeast Alaska land that it managed. From the point of view of the government officials, this was a jobs program, but it was a preservation effort as well.

In 1905 the Forest Service was charged with administering most of the land in Southeast Alaska. While the harvest potential of the vast spruce and hemlock forests was its primary concern, the Forest Service also found itself the guardian of numerous villages abandoned by the Indians. In some cases disease had decimated their populations. In other cases the lure of schools or jobs emptied whole communities, leaving behind only the traditional houses and totem poles. The Haida village of Old Kasaan was a particularly tragic example of neglect. Abandoned by its residents in about 1902, the village boasted an impressive array of totem poles and plank houses. In 1915 the Forest Service, supported by the National Park Service and the Smithsonian Institution, asked that Old Kasaan be declared a national monument. Shortly after, a fire swept the abandoned village, leaving few houses intact, but this fact was not communicated to government officials in Washington, D.C. A little more than a year later, the president created the Old Kasaan National Monument. The remains of the village, however, were not maintained, and the poles and other artifacts continued to deteriorate and disappear. Finally, in 1955, national monument status was revoked.[1]

By the late 1930s, southeast Alaska's traditional Native houses and totem poles were in imminent danger of disappearing. The Forest Service, which was given responsibility for administering the CCC in Alaska, initiated a totem-pole preservation program after it was forced to admit Natives into the previously segregated jobs program. Between 1939 and 1941, three plank houses were reconstructed in Wrangell, Kasaan, and Totem Bight, near Ketchikan—large, single-room dwellings framed with heavy logs and covered with vertical planks. At the same time, 116 totem poles—carved images in a vertical arrangement—were repaired or replicated. Most of them were erected in the populated villages of Hydaburg, Klawock, and Saxman.[2]

The young Natives employed by the CCC, however, were well assimilated into Euro-American culture and knew nothing about carving or traditional construction. That knowledge rested with the older Natives. So, although the national CCC program was limited to men between the ages of eighteen and twenty-three, in Alaska the Forest Service also employed older men—Natives who remembered how to carve—to teach the younger ones. Because an important aspect of carving a totem pole is understanding the images that are portrayed, the young Natives also learned the legends and traditions that they had not been previously taught (fig. 13.1).[3]

The Forest Service's strategy was to obtain permission of owners of the totem poles, move the poles to populated areas, and create "totem parks." Their arrangement in circles and avenues was highly artificial, given that they would have originally lined the shore, set in front of houses (fig. 13.2). The craftsmen replaced deteriorated pieces of the poles, and, if the pole was too far gone, replicated it entirely. They also painted the poles—far too much so, according to some critics.[4] The highly accomplished Northwest Coast Indian carving appeared not only on tall outdoor totem poles, but also on house posts, the interior structural members of plank houses. In order to display this form and to provide an appropriate

Fig. 13.1. Tlingit Carvers Repairing and Replicating Totem Poles at the USFS Workshop in Saxman, c. 1940. Courtesy of the National Archives.

setting for the totem poles, three traditional plank houses were reconstructed, two of them based on measurements of the only surviving houses of their type.

The first of these ventures was in the Haida community of New Kasaan, the mining town to which the villagers of Old Kasaan had moved. In about 1880 Chief Son-i-hat had built a traditional plank house, with principal purlins supported on elaborately carved interior house posts, platforms on two levels, central firepit, and smokehole. The side and rear walls were of vertical planks, mortised into sills, but the house front was nontraditional clapboard, with windows and paneled door. Measuring about forty-five by forty-five feet, the

building housed seven families totaling thirty-one people, who slept in small cubicles or curtained-off areas.[5] By 1938, the house was in ruins, with only its house posts and principal purlins standing (fig. 13.3). Linn Forrest, an architect for the Forest Service, designed a traditional plank building to be constructed around them, specifying that old members be reused. Chief Son-i-hat's son, James Peele, not only gave permission for this reconstruction but advised the foreman on proper techniques as construction proceeded.[6] The reconstruction survives today: the broad gable front of vertical planks is pierced by only one opening, a small door. Inside, the carved totem poles support the structure of the roof (fig. 13.4).

Fig. 13.2. Totem Poles Brought from Nearby Abandoned Villages Formed the "Totem Park" at Klawock, 1941. Photo by Joseph Yolo, courtesy of the U.S. Forest Service.

Fig. 13.3. Haida Chief Son-i-hat's House before Reconstruction, 1938. The house posts and some of the framing were all that remained of this house near Kasaan before reconstruction. Photo by Otto Schallerer, courtesy of the U.S. Forest Service.

Fig. 13.4. Haida Chief Son-i-hat's House after Reconstruction, 1941. The restored house posts and an unusual center post dominate the reconstructed house. Photo by C. M. Archbold, courtesy of the U.S. Forest Service.

Concurrently with the house in New Kasaan, Chief Shakes's house in Wrangell was reconstructed. Whether the modern clapboard front was original to the house or whether it had been added later is not known, but the forty-by-forty-three-foot house was traditionally constructed (fig. 13.5). The house's carved interior house posts and the carved screen that they flanked had been used in previous tribal houses on the site and dated from at least the early nineteenth century (fig. 13.6). By the 1930s the house had deteriorated considerably. Linn Forrest had the existing building removed and a new one reconstructed on its footprint, again using the dimensions and details of the previous house. The historic posts were re-installed in the new building. The screen had been sold off in the early twentieth century, but Forrest designed a replica and placed it on the front of the building, not inside (fig. 13.7).[7]

Fig. 13.5. Front of Chief Shakes's House in Wrangell, 1893. Although built with traditional methods, the front of Chief Shakes's house had modern windows and doors in a clapboard-covered wall. Courtesy of Anthropological Archives, Smithsonian Institution.

Fig. 13.6. Interior of Chief Shakes's House. The carved screen and house posts were reused from a previous tribal house on the site. Courtesy of the Wrangell Museum.

In a reconstruction that was more fanciful than scholarly, Forrest designed a third house at Totem Bight, near Ketchikan. It was not based on an existing house but instead combined both Tlingit and Haida conventions. The house and accompanying poles were executed by both Tlingit and Haida carvers. A whole village of new plank houses was intended to accompany them, but with the onset of World War II the carving program was terminated.

As picturesque and appealing as the totem parks were to government officials and tourists, the tribal houses and totem poles had a different set of meanings to the Natives whose culture they represented. A brief examination of three interrelated elements of Tlingit and Haida culture—plank houses, totem poles, and potlatches—reveals

Fig. 13.7. Chief Shakes's House after Reconstruction, 1940. The house was reconstructed with vertical planks and an ornamental screen on the front. Photo by Otto Schallerer, Courtesy of the U.S. Forest Service.

the complex nature of Indians' changing attitudes. Each of these elements of traditional culture faced changing attitudes due to a variety of external and internal pressures, including the spread of Christianity and concerns for legal and economic status.

To the Tlingit and Haida, the tribal house was both a piece of architecture and an idea. Architecturally, the tribal house was traditionally constructed of heavy log framing consisting of vertical posts and principal purlins, which supported the gable roof. The exterior walls were planks, split from logs. The only entrance was through a door in the center of the gable front. The house contained one large open room, with flooring that rose in several levels from a central firepit. Positioned above the fire, a smokehole with windscreen provided the only ventilation, as there were no windows. The interior house posts, the screen that ran between them, and sometimes the front of the house displayed carvings.

Transcending its physical appearance, the tribal house was the primary unit of government. Tlingit and Haida society was divided into two moieties, Raven and Wolf or Eagle, which were exogamous, matrilineal, and totemic. Each of these was divided into about thirty clans (also exogamous, matrilineal, and totemic), and these into various house groups. The house group was composed of several families, and the tribal house was the center of social life and social values. The house reflected the Tlingit and Haida world view, in which status was extremely important. The house itself symbolized the world, with status within the dwelling reflecting the occupant's place in the world order. The head of the house and his family would always occupy the space at the back of the house behind the screen, with status diminishing nearer the door. The firepit was the center of the universe.

Totem poles were a second and even more visible manifestation of traditional culture. Totem poles were composed of carved images that re-ferred to a story or legend that was known, related the history of the clans that occupied a house, or memorialized a person or event. For example, the mortuary pole in fig. 13.8 depicts three adventures of Raven. At the top, Raven has outstretched wings and a sun halo. During the flood that covered the earth, Raven flew up to the Sun, and the Sun's three children are depicted on his breast. The second image is the Fog Woman, who had the ability to attract salmon, which are also shown. Raven treated her badly and she left; he tried to stop her, but she was like fog, and he could not hold her. The third story concerns Frog, who took Raven to the bottom of the ocean. They

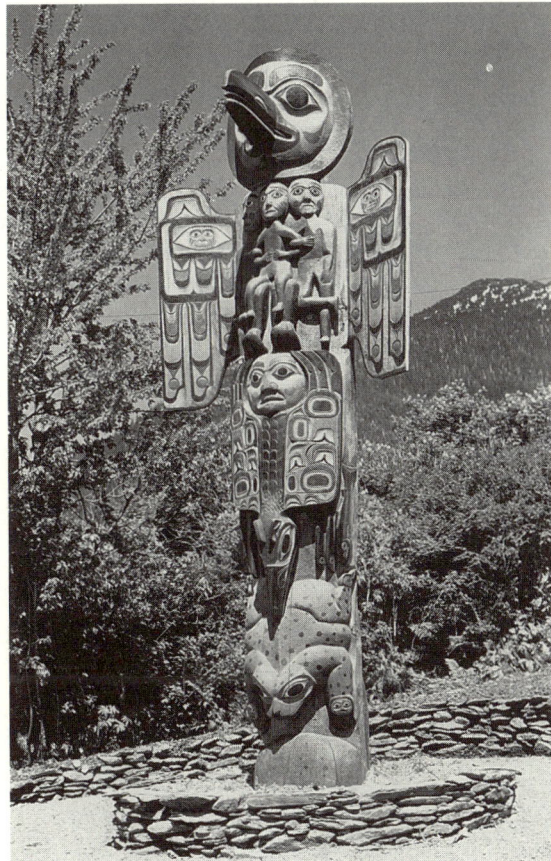

Fig. 13.8. The Sun and Raven Pole at Saxman. This photo was taken shortly after its restoration in 1939. Courtesy of the National Archives.

are shown diving. This pole was carved in 1902 by Kahctan, a Tlingit, as a memorial to two sons of a woman of the Raven moiety, and it was restored in 1939 by the Forest Service as the first pole in the totem park at Saxman.[8] In general, the images on totem poles were of certain animals or birds, reflecting the animistic nature of Tlingit beliefs—that everything has a soul. Animals, geographic features, and ancestral spirits were social and moral forces to be reckoned with, but they were not worshipped.

Construction of a house or the carving of a totem pole could be performed only by members of the opposite moiety. To pay off the debt of building a house or carving a pole, the one who commissioned the house or pole would hold a potlatch, which involved a public acknowledgment and absolution of the debt, the lavish distribution of gifts, and feasting and dances, all oriented to the recognition and maintenance of the status of the potlatch-giver and his guests. The potlatch was an intricate form of redistribution of wealth, an investment that would return, as well as a public payment of debt. In addition, the potlatch was used to commemorate the dead and to pass on the responsibilities of a tribal house. Thus, the survival of the tribal house was dependent on the survival of potlatching.[9]

The Natives faced pressures to assimilate into Euro-American culture from missionaries, government representatives, and economic forces. Presbyterian missionaries, who arrived in Southeast Alaska in the late nineteenth century with the aim of Christianizing and civilizing the Natives, were strikingly successful in converting many of the southeast Alaska Natives. One aspect of Native culture that anthropologists often prefer to overlook is the Natives' devout Christianity. The church played an important role in most communities, far beyond the activities of missionaries who rotated in and out. The Christian church became a social institution and moral force, and we have no reason to doubt the sincerity of its adherents. And, in the late nineteenth and early twentieth centuries, the missionaries in Alaska, as well as throughout the American West, linked Christianity to assimilation: a Native could not become a good Christian unless he or she had relinquished traditional customs.[10]

The missionaries looked at the tribal houses and saw not a unit of government, but a large plank house accommodating a number of families in unsanitary and immoral conditions. Because the smoke from the central fire was not drawn out by a chimney, a layer of soot covered everything in the house. Without windows, the houses were stuffy and smoky, fostering tuberculosis and other pulmonary diseases. Mixing several families together without separate rooms threatened the "purity" of young girls, in the missionaries' view.[11] The missionaries campaigned to replace the traditional multifamily plank houses with single-family, American-style residences, believing that a different house type would change traditional patterns of living.

The missionaries were equally dismissive of totem poles and potlatches. Although they were said to have mistaken totem poles for objects of worship, the missionaries were in fact both awed and impressed by the poles. As symbols of a heathen and backward way of life, though, the poles had no role in the assimilationist future that the missionaries foresaw for the Alaskan Natives. They also disapproved of potlatching, which in their view was a foolish disposal of goods and the accompanying dances a pagan ritual.[12] Not until the plank houses and totem poles were threatened with extinction would it become socially acceptable to missionaries and government officials to save them—and then only as isolated works of art, not as evocations of a way of life.

John Wallace's history is a poignant illustration of the conflicting pulls of tradition and Christianity. Wallace, a Haida, was born in 1857 and learned carving from his father. He joined the Salvation Army—which in Alaska is more of a church than a service organization—in order to convince his neighbors to stop drinking, and he managed to convert his whole village. He gave up carving and became a lay missionary, encouraging two Haida villages to move to a new site, forming the town of Hydaburg. The extent to which he embraced Protestantism is seen in an account of his life, which claims that "he encouraged his people to destroy their fine carvings and helped cut down and burn totem poles in Klinkwan."[13] Late in life he returned to carving, producing poles and objects for a commercial market before becoming, in his eighties, one of the chief carvers on the CCC project. His journey away from carving to Christianity and finally back to carving is emblematic of the changes sweeping the Native communities in the twentieth century.

The Natives also received governmental pressures to assimilate. Alaskan Natives were never forced onto reservations, as in the rest of the United States. By the transfer act that made Alaska a U.S. possession, certain rights would be imparted to "civilized" Natives—although no Tlingit or Haida qualified as "civilized."[14] Once the Natives had attended the Presbyterian school in Sitka, could read and write English, held jobs and earned money, they expected U.S. citizenship. That these rights did not naturally ensue caused intense legal wrangling until Congress granted citizenship to all Natives in 1924.

For Natives, U.S. citizenship was viewed as hugely important, for with it came considerable economic power that they could not otherwise possess. One result of the lack of citizenship at the turn of the century was that Natives could not file mining claims. Fishing rights were also significant, as the proliferation of salmon canneries threatened the primary resource of Indians' subsistence. Most important were land claims, including the disposal of timber on that land, an issue not fully resolved until the Alaska Native Claims Settlement Act of 1971. But in the early part of the century, assimilation held the promise of citizenship and civil rights.[15]

Also, in looking at the Natives' view of their houses and totem poles, it is important to remember their attitudes toward material wealth. This was a society in which members ritualistically distributed their wealth in order to demonstrate their status. They did not disregard wealth, but material possessions were far less important than status and reputation. Such a society had no place for sentimental attachment to works of architecture, enabling them to leave a village of plank houses and totem poles to establish a new village if they foresaw long-term improvement in their lives.

Faced with the social upheaval brought on by the introduction of Christianity and by their precarious legal and economic standing, the Natives began a process of acculturation that was at times selective, such as with the construction of tribal houses.[16] Because of the dual nature of the tribal house—as idea and as object—the Natives were able to forsake their traditional dwellings in a superficial way. Plank fronts were rapidly replaced with new clapboard-covered fronts with windows and doors, an innovation that had been adopted by the Indians even before the Presbyterians arrived in Alaska.[17] Yet they were only fronts—the same multifamily tribal house persisted behind. New fronts and new houses built in the American style became fashionable just as the Tlingit and Haida were gaining prosperity, due to the cash income provided by salmon canneries throughout southeast Alaska. Although there was a gradual shift toward single-family houses, tribal houses—communally owned and serving a specific social function—continued to be built, although not in the traditional plank-house form. Tribal houses thus survived as idea but not as architecture; by the 1930s, no traditional plank houses remained intact in southeast Alaska.

Totem poles disappeared even faster than plank houses. In the view of Tlingits and Haidas, totem poles were erected to commemorate an event and their survival was not important. Earth-fast and standing outdoors, they deteriorated rapidly.[18] With the various pressures to assimilate, totem poles fell out of favor, and few new totem poles were raised after about 1900. Yet the carving tradition continued, on a reduced scale.

Despite the Natives' apparent willingness to abandon their totem poles, the perception that missionaries chopped down the poles persists.[19] The story of the Tlingit village of Kake demonstrates the divisions within the Native community, not autocratic actions of missionaries. Four men, encouraged by the Presbyterian missionary George Beck, organized a town government. One of their first actions was to rebuild the plank sidewalk—a symbol of progress—and cut down and burn the totem poles. As witness John Bean described it, the four men "organized work parties to cut down all the totem poles in front of the village, took the bones of the dead from the boxes and in the mortuary poles, and blew them to bits with dynamite while the older people wept." Charles Newton, the youngest of the four men, recalled, "The sidewalk was the symbol of a new life. The old totems were cut down and the new sidewalk dedicated January 8, 1912. There was a parade and a band and speeches." He also noted, however, "Some old still did not agree." Missionary George Beck claimed to be taken by surprise at the assault on the totem poles: one morning he woke up, and "rushing out I found the place covered with smoke and nearly all the poles blown up and burned. . . . The whole village took part in the work but no one would admit giving the orders."[20] Here at Kake, as in other villages, progressive young Natives sought a modern way of life, one with a democratic government and new plank sidewalks. Reminders of traditional ways, such as totem poles, were destroyed.

With this history of changing attitudes toward traditional plank houses and totem poles, it is not surprising that the Forest Service's carving program met with a mixed reaction among the Na-

tives. Some younger Indians thought that more worthwhile projects could be undertaken.[21] Others thought that the carving program's products were inauthentic: Tlingit Frances Paul described a pole erected in Auke Bay as a "barbecue" pole—a white man's invention. The Forest Service hastened to assure the public that that pole had been based on a traditional Tlingit legend, and that it had been carved by a Tlingit carver, Frank St. Clair.[22]

Other Natives viewed the carving program as an opportunity to develop marketable skills. Some of the older carvers had been carving new poles for a small market that had developed.[23] Recognizing this opportunity, the Bureau of Indian Affairs, in another Alaskan New Deal program, established a clearinghouse to identify markets for Native arts and crafts. Some Natives, such as Charles Brown, the head carver of the Saxman workshop, saw the value of revived interest in Tlingit heritage. Some of the younger carvers had never been exposed to the legends and associations of the poles and gained an insight into their heritage that may not have been intended by the Forest Service.[24]

But the Forest Service program did not instigate a sustained renaissance in traditional arts and crafts. Most of the newly trained carvers returned to other means of income when the carving program was abruptly terminated. The totem poles and plank houses were not maintained and again deteriorated. It was not until the 1960s that another traditional plank house was constructed in Alaska, and a concerted program to preserve the remaining totem poles was instituted.[25]

The pendulum has swung again. The situation today is probably best portrayed by the Tlingit village of Saxman, which operates the 1930s totem park. The village constructed a traditional plank house in 1990, carved under the direction of Nathan Jackson, a Tlingit. The village interprets the site to visitors, presenting programs on Tlingit heritage and traditional dances in the plank house. In addition, the village sponsors a carving workshop on the premises, where one of the featured carvers is Lee Wallace, grandson of Haida carver John Wallace.

It would be easy to interpret the Forest Service's preservation program as a well-intentioned but ultimately misguided scheme if it were not for the artifacts that were preserved. Chief Shakes's house in Wrangell and Chief Son-i-hat's house in Kasaan were the only traditional plank houses remaining, albeit in altered states. And, although today we might choose a different strategy of preservation, the reconstructions that stand in their places are the only houses built according to actual measurements, copying existing examples of construction methods. The totem poles are a fragile resource; today no totem poles dating from before the 1930s remain standing outdoors in Alaska.

Although we may have a justifiable wariness of government programs that emanate from the top down, it is important to remember that one artifact can mean many things to different people and at different times. The potlatch in Wrangell in 1940 can be interpreted in many ways: as a celebration of a successful jobs program; as a resurgence of Native pride; as a calculated bid for more tourism by town officials; as an exploration of new job opportunities by the Tlingit; or as an attempt to recognize the aesthetic value of Native arts and crafts. Plank houses and totem poles were symbols of a traditional past that many Natives were struggling to escape, making the reconstruction of the Wrangell tribal house and its attendant ceremonies a complex turning point in the "culture wars" of Native heritage and assimilation.

## Notes

1. T. T. Waterman, "Observations Among the Ancient Indian Monuments of Southeastern Alaska," *Explorations and Field-Work of the Smithsonian Institution in 1922* (Washington: Smithsonian Institution, 1923); H. W. Krieger, "Archeological and Ethnological Studies in Southeast Alaska," *Explorations and Field-Work of the Smithsonian Institution in 1926* (Washington: Smithsonian Institution, 1927); Lawrence Rakestraw, "A History of the Forest Service Role in Totem Pole Restoration and Preservation and an Index of Sources for the United States Forest Service Work in Reference to Totem Poles, 1906–1971," typescript, n.d. (1971), U.S. Department of Agriculture, National Agricultural Library.

2. The basic history of USFS activities is Rakestraw's *A History of the United States Forest Service in Alaska* (Anchorage, Alaska Historical Commission, 1981). Numbers from attachment to C. T. Brown, "Memorandum of Forest Service Accomplishments in the Restoration of Totem Poles in Southeast Alaska," July 12, 1967, typescript, Alaska State Museum. Integration of the program in 1936 was due to Senate hearings in Ketchikan and Juneau. Conner Sorensen, Lawrence Rakestraw, Robert R. Martin, Sr., "Alaskan Native Participation in the Civilian Conservation Corps: A Finding Aid to the Sources," Alaska Historical Commission Studies in History No. 206, 1986, 6–9; (Juneau) *Daily Alaska Empire*, July 15, 17, 1936. While as many as four hundred Natives worked on the usual village improvement programs of new sewer lines, improved harbors, or airstrip construction, more than two hundred were diverted into the totem-pole restoration program after it started in 1939.

3. Robert R. Martin Sr. interviewed by Conner Sorensen, Apr. 3, 1986, typescript, Alaska State Library. The USFS hired an ethnographer, Viola Garfield, to record the legends associated with the poles. Some of these appeared in Viola E. Garfield and Linn A. Forrest, *The Wolf and the Raven: Totem Poles of Southeastern Alaska* (Seattle: Univ. of Washington Press, 1948; reprint, 1961). Others are recorded in Garfield's field notes at the University of Washington Archives.

4. Some of the earliest criticism of the USFS project was by Katharine Kuh, "Confidential Report, Part I: Preservation of Indian Art in Southeastern Alaska," 1946, typescript, Alaska State Library, 2, and repeated in Kuh, "Alaska's Vanishing Art," *Saturday Review,* Oct. 22, 1966, 26. Her criticism of the use of paint was echoed by Haida carver Lee Wallace, interviewed by author in Saxman, Aug. 18, 1992, and in Ketchikan, Aug. 19, 1992.

5. Linn A. Forrest, "Memorandum for Mr. Heintzleman," Nov. 22, 1938, typescript in National Archives, Record Group 95, entry 146, Civilian Con-

servation Corps, correspondence of Region 10, 1937–1942. Forrest relates that three slaves were included in the total of thirty-one people, although slavery had been abolished by the U.S. government more than a decade before this house was built.

6. C. R. Snow to C. M. Archbold, Feb. 15, 1939, typescript in National Archives, RG 95. Because Haida society is matrilineal, James Peele was not heir to his father's house, and the Forest Service was careful to obtain permission from James's son, David Peele, as well.

7. Nora Black-Rinehart of the Wrangell Historical Society and Museum provided a number of historical photographs and helped piece this chronology together. The historic screen was placed on the front of the building at one point, as it was photographed there (Garfield Papers, Univ. Archives, Univ. of Washington [hereafter referred to as Garfield Papers, UW]). The historic totem poles have been removed from the house and placed in the Wrangell Museum for safekeeping. Replications stand in their place.

8. Garfield and Forrest, *The Wolf and the Raven*, 13–17.

9. Frederica de Laguna, "Tlingit," *Handbook of North American Indians, Volume 7: Northwest Coast* (Washington: Smithsonian Institution, 1990), 212–13, 220–21; Kalervo Oberg, *The Social Economy of the Tlingit Indians* (Seattle: Univ. of Washington Press, 1973), 29–52; and Viola E. Garfield, "The Tlingit, Haida, and Tsimshian Indians of Southeastern Alaska," 1945, typescript in Garfield Papers, UW.

10. Margaret B. Blackman, *During My Time: Florence Edenshaw Davidson, a Haida Woman* (Seattle: Univ. of Washington Press, 1982; rev. ed., 1992), xvii. In the preface to the revised edition, Blackman notes that if she were writing the biography anew, she would place more emphasis on Davidson's Christianity. Sergei Kan notes a general neglect of Indian Christianity in "Russian Orthodox Brotherhoods Among the Tlingit: Missionary Goals and Native Response," *Ethnohistory* 32 (3) (1985): 216n. 2. Numerous biographies of Natives reflect the importance of Christianity. See, for example, Carol Feller Brady, *Through the Storm Towards the Sun: A Personal Account of Life in Transition in Southeast Alaska* (privately printed, 1980); Walter A. Soboleff, interviewed by Margaret Deck, May 23, 1987 (tape in Presbyterian Historical Society); and Blackman. Missionaries' insistence on

changing behavior is discussed in Joseph Bettridge, "Tlingit Christianity," (Ph.D. diss., Fuller Theological Seminary, 1979), 15.

11. "The Gospel and the Sawmill" [1880?], Sheldon Jackson Collection, Scrapbooks, Presbyterian Historical Society, Box 18, vol. 7: 12; Eva Clark Waid, *Alaska: The Land of the Totem* (New York: Women's Board of Home Missions of the Presbyterian Church, [1910]), 93.

12. Philip Drucker, *The Native Brotherhoods: Modern Intertribal Organizations on the Northwest Coast,* Smithsonian Institution, Bureau of American Ethnology, Bulletin 168; Washington: GPO, 1958, 59. The missionaries objected most vehemently to mortuary poles, which contained ashes of the deceased; they encouraged interment.

13. Garfield and Forrest, *The Wolf and the Raven,* 10. If true, Wallace omitted this fact from his autobiography. "Life of John Wallace," attached to letter from Charles W. Hawkesworth to C. J. Rhoads, May 27, 1932, typescript in National Archives, Record Group 120, Office of the Territories, Classified Files, 1907–1951, 9-1-36.

14. Drucker, *The Native Brotherhoods,* 44–45; Ramona E. Soza, "Alaska Natives and Federal Indian Policy," (Ph.D. diss., Univ. of Washington, 1988), 54.

15. The significant role of the Alaska Native Brotherhood should not be overlooked. Founded in 1912 by southeast Natives who had attended the Presbyterian mission school in Sitka, the ANB was the most influential voice for Native civil rights and progressivism until the 1960s. See Drucker, *The Native Brotherhoods.*

16. Margaret B. Blackman, "Creativity in Acculturation: Art, Architecture and Ceremony from the Northwest Coast," *Ethnohistory* 23 (4) (Fall 1976): 387–413.

17. Joanna Scherer pointed this out to me, citing Eadweard Muybridge's photographs of Wrangell in 1868, which show modernized fronts on plank houses.

18. Repair or repainting of a totem pole would require the services of the opposite clan, and payment through a potlatch; thus, such effort was reserved for new totem poles.

19. No evidence can be found that missionaries chopped down poles in Alaska. Marius Barbeau, *Totem Poles* (Ottawa: National Museum of Canada, 1950), 2: 819, erroneously relates that missionaries chopped down poles in Kake.

20. Bean interviewed by Philip Drucker, c. 1951, transcript in Drucker's field notes, Box 1, folder 5, p. 4 of Philip Drucker Papers, National Anthropological Archives, Smithsonian Institution. Newton interviewed by Viola Garfield, c. 1940, transcript in Garfield's field notes, Box 8, Garfield Papers, UW. Beck's account in Beck to Keithahn, Jan. 22, 1946, typescript, Alaska State Library, reiterated in *American Anthropologist* 63 (6) (Dec. 1961): 1337–38.

21. C. M. Archbold, "Totem Pole Restoration," 1939, typescript, Alaska State Museum, 7. This was apparently a draft of an article for *Alaska Sportsman* 5 (Mar. 1939): 16, but the reference to disagreement was omitted from the published article.

22. Barbeau, *Totem Poles,* 1: 409–10.

23. For example, Secretary of Interior Ray Lyman Wilbur ordered two totem poles from the governor of Alaska in 1931. Gov. George A. Parks gave John Wallace the commission. Parks to E. K. Burlew, Feb. 5, 1931, National Archives, RG 95. Today the poles frame the door to the secretary's office in the Department of Interior building in Washington, D.C.

24. *The Alaskan* (publication of the Civilian Conservation Corps program), Feb. 20, 1940. Tlingit civil rights activist William Paul also praised the program at the Wrangell potlatch. *Alaskan,* June 20, 1940.

25. William Wallace, John Wallace's son and a carver at the Hydaburg workshop, for example, gave up carving after the war. Lee Wallace interview. The deterioration is mentioned in Kuh, "Confidential Report." A plank house was erected in Haines between 1957 and 1964 by Alaska Indian Art, Inc. Beginning in the late 1960s, the Alaska State Museum, in partnership with the Alaska Native Brotherhood, undertook a totem retrieval project that resulted in the opening of the Totem Heritage Center in Ketchikan in 1976.

COMMUNITIES

SHAPED BY

COMMERCE

*Bryan Clark Green*

# The Structure of Civic Exchange:
# Market Houses in Early Virginia

The landscape of Virginia in the eighteenth and early nineteenth centuries was predominately rural, punctuated by the development of a rather small number of towns. At the center—both physically and socially—of these places stood market houses, the most important civic structures of Virginia's early towns. The market house occupies a position of primary importance in the urban and social landscape of the early Virginia towns of economic or political consequence. Politically, the market house (through the courts and council chambers housed within) symbolized the emerging importance of these towns as the landscape of Virginia became more densely populated, and as cities (such as Richmond and Alexandria) began to challenge the former economic, political, and social hegemony of the agrarian countryside. On another level, market houses were the commercial, legal, and social center of the town. They were places where merchants, beggars, and farmers selling their produce all vied for attention; where carts displaying vegetables rested against lockups and whipping posts; and where in the evening the market yard might be swept and the upper rooms become the setting for an elegant assembly or ball, welcoming only the most wealthy.[1]

Market houses emerged as common urban civic structures in late medieval England.[2] Prominent features in the English urban landscape during the sixteenth century, they were being erected in Virginia by the early eighteenth century. From that date, they persisted with little architectural modification as models for more functionally specialized urban, civic architecture, such as courthouses, town halls, and firehouses, through the nineteenth and into the early twentieth centuries. The transformation of community structure and values and a multifaceted technological shift (the development of truck farming, refrigeration, and the neighborhood grocery store) removed the market house from the economic, administrative, and social center of Virginia's towns.[3]

By the second quarter of the eighteenth century, towns acquired a more prominent position in the social landscape of Virginia.[4] Of particular importance to this study is the legal method by which Virginia towns were officially incorporated. While in all colonies (and later states), incorporation granted a town additional economic, judicial, and administrative authority, in Virginia incorporation was a much more comprehensive act. In each county a number of justices of the peace (members of the established local gentry) were empowered to sit collectively as the county court. Each county court held an amalgam of economic, judicial, and administrative authority, including authority over unincorporated towns.[5] Through incorporation, however, individual towns largely removed themselves from the authority of the county court. The charter of incorporation conferred upon the town a package of rights including the right to form an independent town government and judicial system, the power to levy taxes, and the ability to regulate commercial exchanges within the town. For example, the charters granted to Norfolk and Williamsburg, the first two towns incorporated in Virginia, established town governments consisting of a mayor, recorder, aldermen, and a common council, all of whom were known collectively as the common hall. The common hall exercised some administrative powers and regulated certain internal affairs, including the construction of market houses and the establishment of market regulations, but the bulk of authority was granted to the hustings court, which consisted of the mayor, recorder, and the aldermen, but not the common council. The hustings court held additional regulatory powers (typically over liquor and flour prices) and, in Norfolk and Williamsburg, decided civil cases arising within the borough involving less than

£20 or four thousand pounds of tobacco.[6] This system was adapted with minor modifications in all towns incorporated in Virginia through the early nineteenth century.

Constructing a market house and drafting market regulations were generally among the first actions undertaken by the common hall of a newly incorporated town. The primary reason was economic, in that the taxes generated in the market were the lifeblood of the incorporated town. Delays in the completion of a market house, the focal point of trading activities, could result in a loss of revenue. This loss was particularly acute in Virginia, as the incorporated town had few economic, judicial, and administrative ties with the county that surrounded it and relied heavily on revenue generated through the market house.

In addition to the other rights obtained through incorporation, a newly created town obtained the right to tax commerce within its legal boundaries, and the market house (and sometimes the market square) became the area within which the exchange of foodstuffs was strictly confined and carefully regulated. So important were the taxes generated by the market house that the construction (or rebuilding) of a market house and the establishment (or revision) of market regulations were often the very first official acts of a newly created common council. For example, the first act of the common council of Norfolk consisted of two parts: the first ordered the construction of a market house and the second established a set of market regulations to be enforced as soon as the market house was completed.[7] Virginians incorporated seven towns before 1785: Williamsburg (1722), Norfolk (1736), Alexandria (1779), Winchester (1779), Fredericksburg (1782), Richmond (1782), and Petersburg (1784); all seven can be documented as having market houses.[8]

Once a municipality committed itself to the construction of a market house, many elements needed to be put into place. An orderly and profitable market required many components, both legal and physical, in order to function properly. Such elements as a carefully drafted set of market regulations, a public clock and bell to keep and enforce market hours, a public scale along with a set of official weights and measures to insure equitable exchange in the market, and a series of sheds, stalls, and benches to shelter goods and facilitate trade all needed to be considered. These various elements of the market house will be discussed in turn.

Market regulations set up the two basic elements of commercial exchange within the incorporated town: 1) they established the days and hours during which the market operated, determined the legal boundaries of the market, and enumerated the items required to be traded at the market, and 2) they created the position of clerk of the market, who was charged with managing the daily affairs of the market.[9]

The first section of a set of market regulations generally established the days and hours of the market, the articles that must be sold at market, and the legal spatial boundaries of the market. The regulations also established penalties for selling during market hours within the town at places other than the market house. Following the establishment of market days and hours, the regulations established the legal boundaries of the market yard or square surrounding the market house. At Fredericksburg, the market square behind the market house—clearly defined by the edges of the buildings that surrounded and defined the space—was by custom understood to be the legal bounds of the market. This understanding was so clear that the drafters of the 1809 Fredericksburg regulations did not feel the need to point the boundaries out. This is in sharp contrast to the situation in Staunton, where—in the absence of a defined market yard or formalized market square—the drafters of the 1813 regulations describe the boundaries of the market in excruciating detail. The regulations ordered that

the limits of the Market for the Corporation of Staunton shall be within a line drawn as follows, Viz. Beginning at the North east corner of the Jail, and from thence across New Court house Street, in a direct line to the railing enclosing the Courthouse yard, thence along the same westwardly, in a direct line to the West side of Augusta Street, thence down the same, in a direct line Southwardly to the crak [sic], thence down the crak [sic], to a point opposite the South west corner of the Jail; and from thence in a direct line to the South West corner of said Jail, and with the walls thereof to the place of Beginning.[10]

Following the sections that legally define the market, most regulations established what items must be sold at market. The same 1813 Staunton market regulations, for example, stipulate "[t]hat all and every person or persons who shall have any articles or provisions to sell or dispose of on the Market days aforesaid, to wit: flesh, fish, fowl, butter, eggs, cheese, vegetables, roots, fruit and other articles usually bought and sold in well regulated markets; shall bring them to the Market house in the Corporation of Staunton, on the Market days aforesaid, and there offer them for sale."[11] There were items that, as exemptions, could be sold elsewhere, and market regulations very carefully enumerate those items. The selling of fish, for example, was not only prohibited by law within the market house of Staunton itself, but was also not covered by market restrictions, although fish selling was regulated in some other markets, such as Portsmouth.[12] Other exceptions, noted in the 1813 Staunton regulations, allow the purchase of small amounts of provisions, "necessary for their families use," that may be purchased outside of market hours.[13]

Penalties for the violation of market regulations could be strict. For example, in Fredericksburg, the penalty for forestalling, or hindering free trade, for a free white citizen was forfeiture of the value of the goods involved for the first offense. The second offense resulted in the forfeiture of double the value of the goods. If the offense was committed by a slave, the penalty was "20 lashes on their bare back at the public whipping post, unless the master or owner [and only the master or owner] pays the penalty."[14]

The market regulations also created the position of clerk of the market, who was charged with the day-to-day administration of the marketplace. The clerk, neither a gentleman nor a member of the common council but always a man, was selected by the gentlemen who made up the council to represent its interests at the market. The clerk was generally charged with such duties as safeguarding the corporation's weights and measures, verifying the weights and measures of shopkeepers within the market, issuing certificates stating the weight of articles weighed on the public scale, inspecting the quality of meat and produce sold at the market, collecting tithes on articles sold at market, collecting fines from those violating market regulations, and physically maintaining the market house. He was generally paid a salary by the council and/or received a percentage of the tithes collected at the market house. The clerk of the market was in a complex social position: while he was neither councilman, sheriff or deputy, nor justice of the peace, he was charged with upholding corporation laws. Thus, when faced with a violation of those laws, the clerk was often forced to go to great lengths to enforce them. For example, under Fredericksburg law, the clerk was required to "inspect the quality of all provisions brought into public market during market hours," to condemn those found to be "unsound or unwholesome," and to see to it that the condemned articles be "either burnt or thrown into the river."[15] Condemnation, however, required "calling on a magistrate whose opinion shall be had before condemnation," thus reinforcing the social hierarchy of the town: the clerk may enforce corporation law, but that law was ultimately created and interpreted by the gentleman magistrates.[16]

While the clerk of the market was charged with the day-to-day management of the market house, his authority was very tightly circumscribed by the corporation.

While market regulations clearly state at what hour the market would open for business and at what hour it would close, clocks were owned by a small minority. Before the railroads introduced standard time, the keeping of the hours was still very much a public function of each individual town, and the hours were made known to the town largely through the ringing of the town bell.[17] It was not so much the hour itself that opened trading in the market, but the ringing of the public bell, which informed the townspeople as to the beginning and ending of trading hours. Clocks and bells were important devices owned by the municipality: if a clock were present, such as at Alexandria (fig. 14.1), it was important that it be elevated so that it could be seen through the town, and, as for the bells, it was important that they be heard at a great distance. The town clock in Alexandria, while exceptional—rising high above the city in the lower part of a two-part hexagonal cupola—typifies the public act of keeping time. Travelers noted the remarkable visibility of the clock: "The squares of the cupola present six faces of a single clock, which show the hour of the day to a vast distance."[18] In an age in which each town kept its own time, the town clock, hovering above Alexandria in its cupola, its place marked in the skyline by the steeple soaring from the cupola, was an important regulator of life. While church bells rang in tune with an ecclesiastical schedule (interrupted to ring for the deaths of parishioners or exceptional events such as fires), the town bells rang the schedule of secular, urban life. Town bells (such as Alexandria's, which rang "so loud as to be heard over the town") were used not only to mark the hours, but to announce slave curfews, meetings of court and council, and emergencies such as fires, as well as the opening and closing of the market and other events deemed necessary by civic authorities.[19] There was a special language to the bells, as well. In Alexandria, the bells defined the schedule of the market day: "Market begins at day-light and usually ends at ten o'clock everyday, except Sunday, which is out an hour sooner. At nine o'clock A.M. on Sunday, you hear a small bell ring for about a minute, this is succeeded by a peal from the great market bell. The first is to give notice to those in the market, to pick up his or her unsold articles, and be off. . . ."[20] Town clocks and bells, whether located in the market house itself or in the market yard, performed the vital role of spelling out the hours and their important punctuations in an age in which time and the sounding of the hours remained was very much in the public realm.

The market house precinct consisted of two basic components: the market house itself and the yard or enclosure surrounding it. The market house was made up of an open, arcaded lower story for the display and sale of foodstuffs and an enclosed upper story or stories, used as meeting rooms for such civic functions as the town council or the corporation court. The scale of the market buildings varied with the wealth and needs of the local government, ranging from the Alexandria example discussed earlier, to the single-story example at Lynchburg (fig. 14.2). The market yard also varies,

ranging from the formal market square at Fredericksburg to an informal area demarcated by benches and stalls surrounding the market house at Petersburg and Richmond (figs. 14.3 and 14.4).

Fig. 14.2. Market House, Lynchburg, Virginia. From Frank Leslie's Illustrated History of the Civil War. New York, 1895, 555.

Fig. 14.1. Town Hall (before 1820–c.1880), Alexandria, Virginia. Courtesy of the Library of Virginia.

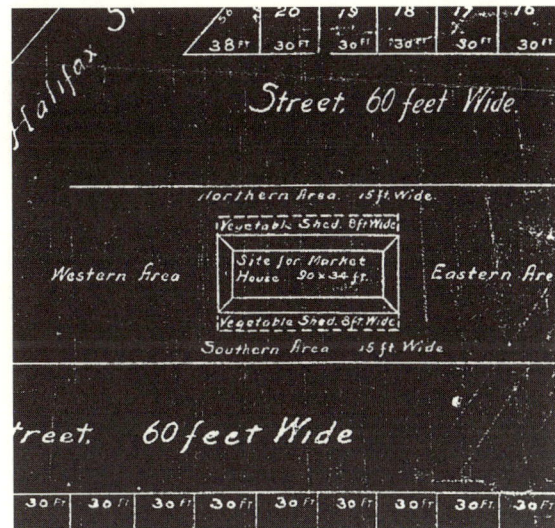

Fig. 14.3. Market House, Petersburg, Virginia. 1853. From Petersburg Plat no. 1, Feb. 26, 1853. Courtesy of the Virginia State Library.

Fig. 14.4. Second Seventeenth St. Market, Richmond, Virginia. From Frank Leslie's Illustrated Newspaper, Nov. 7, 1868, 708.

The market house was at its most basic a building built to facilitate the commercial exchange of farm products brought into town for sale. An array of utilitarian sheds, stalls, and benches were needed, as well as such official accouterments as a public water supply, scale, and the town's official weights and measures. While no examples of the many sheds, stalls, and benches that once filled these markets survive, a composite picture emerges from an examination of the surviving market house records. Sheds were erected to protect meats, cheeses, and milk from the elements, and the interiors of both the market house and the attached sheds were subdivided into stalls. These stalls were either rented out on a quarterly or yearly basis or, in some cases, reserved for the use of those who could not afford or did not need

to enter into a long lease.[21] The general layout of the typical market is clearly illustrated by a plat of the second Petersburg market house and by a visitor's description of a market in Philadelphia, Pennsylvania. The market house on Market Street, Philadelphia, is described as "a double row of the finest looking vegetables, a mile in length, viz. on both sides of the market-house, with every thing else that can be named for the table; and then the butchers' meat, filling the whole length of the space between."[22] The plat of the second Petersburg market house corresponds to the same pattern described at the Philadelphia market house: vegetables were sold from sheds appended to the sides of the market house, and meat and dairy products were sold from within. This pattern was typical of Virginia's market houses. Fish, it should be added, were generally sold (by law) at a distance from the market house in a small shed (or sometimes, as at Alexandria, in a small market house devoted solely to fish) for obvious reasons; without refrigeration—and with the offices of town government above—nothing was to be gained by too closely associating city politics with the aroma of rotting fish. In time, the stalls of many market houses came to be dominated by butchers. In Portsmouth, for instance, an 1817 city council order established a committee "to lay out the Market House into five Butchers stalls" and then ordered the "erection of benches around the Market House as well as to extend the sheds thereof," indicating that others who had previously used the stalls inside were now without a place to operate in the market.[23] While one visitor noted that at the Alexandria market house "the benches and stalls are kept remarkably clean, being washed every day," the number of times city councils across Virginia issued and reissued orders to clean market houses and yards indicate that, in terms of cleanliness, either the description was charitable or Alexandria was very much the exception.[24]

Often, as was the case in Fredericksburg and Alexandria, the market house was the most expensive municipal building in a Virginia town. While it was usually not finished as elegantly and expensively as some of the wealthier churches and private homes of a given town, the market house was finished more expensively than the majority of buildings. The importance of maintaining the market house as a symbol of the town is evidenced by the citizens of Fredericksburg having committed $6,250 and 6,000 feet of plank in 1817 to rebuild the market house in brick.[25] In contrast, the average value of houses insured by the Mutual Assurance Society of Virginia in Fredericksburg from 1810 to 1820 was $3,703.06, and the average value for the year 1817 was $2,664.28.[26] The market house was therefore a substantial civic investment in the urban landscape of Fredericksburg.

The manner of construction and quality of finish of these buildings was in keeping with that of the houses of substantial and prosperous townspeople. It was important that the buildings be substantial and (if necessary) imposing, yet neither ostentatious nor frivolous. The specifications of the market house built in Norfolk in 1736 called for a "Thirty foot long fifteen foot Wide six foot overjet each side the body of the House to be seven foot pitch the overjet the same to have four good Posts each side to support the Overjet the body of the House underpinned with Brick three Brick high from the Surface of the Earth, the body of the House to be done with good feather edged Plank and the Roof to be well Shingled."[27] The Alexandria market house of 1779 represents a marked increase in both scale and quality of architectural finish from the Norfolk market. Not only is the Alexandria market much later, but it represents a much more complex and highly embellished building.

Changes in the scale and finish of market houses reflect the expansion of the social, economic, and political base of Virginia's towns and cities. In 1736 a two-story planked building sufficed as a marketplace and municipal center for one of Virginia's largest towns. By 1779, however, when the thriving port town of Alexandria sought to build a market house, the vast changes in scale of the town demanded an increase in both the scale and capital invested in the materials and finish of the building. The Alexandria market house of 1779 is the largest, most expensive, and most highly architecturally embellished market house of the period under study. Behind its three-story, seventeen-bay masonry façade was not only a market but a town hall, courthouse, city council chamber, library, and even museum, representing the citizens' aspirations and the economic power of Alexandria to realize these aspirations.

Most markets went through several remodelings, and in many cases several markets were built on the same site, each one more expensively finished than the one preceding it. For example, the second Norfolk market house (1784) included the specification that "the Commissioners shall only agree for the Outside work, Windows, doors, laying of the floors and a staircase to be finished for the present, and this Hall [the common council] will at a future day provide means for Elegantly compleating the inside work."[28] Records also indicate that, although the town might aspire to elegance, financial reality often circumscribed such aspirations. Norfolk's "future day" appears to have been a long time in arriving: by 1798 they were offering use of the market house in exchange for basic repairs. The Baptist Society gained use of the building provided they "put a new Sill under the door, mend the plaster + glaze all the Windows."[29] High aspirations and low finances often led to the erection of a wooden market house, which was later to be replaced by a larger brick market house, both of which were frequently repaired and added to and ultimately replaced again by a yet larger market house. Richmond's wooden market house of c. 1780 was replaced in 1794 by a two-story, brick market house, the brick work of which cost £139.18.6. Seventeen years later, the council authorized the expenditure of $200 to improve "the upper part of the market house," and, one year after that, in 1812, the council authorized spending $1,000 "to convert the upper part of the Market house into a Court house for the Court of Hustings."[30]

Market houses were the settings of many diverse civic and social activities, ranging from essential civic functions to diversionary social activities. Markets bustled daily around fire-fighting equipment, and corporation courts shared rooms with city council meetings; in the evenings, militia drills might alternate with assemblies, and elegant balls could be staged over lockups holding revelers from a tavern of decidedly different social standing. These myriad economic, civic, and social functions were all accommodated in the same building, and sometimes in the same rooms.

After a brief discussion of the interior spaces that served as settings for some of these functions, the three general categories of civic functions will be discussed: public punishment of crime, fire-fighting, and social gatherings.

Little is known about the interior spaces of the market house itself. Among the few references to the finishing of the interiors of market houses are some rather vague references to the completion of the market house at Staunton, Virginia. During construction (1802), the city council of Staunton agreed to turn over the lower story of the market house to the district chancery court of Augusta County, while the city council was to retain the upper floor for its own use. The corporation then agreed to spend one hundred pounds to finish the lower story for the county.[31] Though the building itself was not used for a market, a later order for repairs gives some clue as to the interior fittings of the rooms used for civic gatherings. An order of 1807 called for "a new Roof, inside paved and surrounded with sound sills, and boards as high as the benches."[32] The repair order, which most likely refers only to the lower story (and in this case corresponds to the upper story of all other market houses in Virginia), indicates that the room was likely wainscoted in the area of the justices' bench, but, at best, this entry indicates only the broadest contours of the interior finish.

A chance reference in the Portsmouth city records reveals the only evidence of the furnishing of the upper rooms of market houses. The trustees' accounts for the years 1801 to 1804 record the purchase of a dozen chairs and a table for the market house; the chairs were purchased for $18.00 and the table for $7.00.[33] While the account says nothing about the kind of chairs ordered, an entry of nearly ten years later does. On July 25, 1814, the town sergeant was ordered to call upon a townsman who had borrowed some furniture from the market house and never returned the pieces. The sergeant was ordered to call on this gentleman and return with "two

Windsor chairs and a pine table belonging to the Trustees."[34] In all likelihood, these pieces were part of the same set of furniture purchased for the market house between 1801 and 1804. While Windsor chairs were regularly used in taverns and public buildings in northern cities in this period, in Virginia they seem to have been restricted to use in the homes of Virginia's wealthy.[35] This indicates that Virginians were willing to spend significant sums of money on the finishing of the corporation's court and council rooms in the market houses to reflect and express the authority vested in that body, a situation that parallels the contemporaneous developments occurring in Virginia's county courthouses.[36]

Among the diverse activities arrayed at market houses was the punishment of criminals. A malefactor was generally punished in public, with the guilty party frequently being locked into the stocks, whipped, or, in some cases, hanged by the neck. The idea that people could be incarcerated and thus do penance for their crimes (e.g., in a penitentiary) was still an emerging notion in this period. Market houses frequently had what was called a lockup, or "cage," which was a public cell for the temporary restraint of miscreants. But the lockup was strictly a temporary restraint: punishment was generally meted out swiftly and always in public. Common structures in the market yard surrounding the market house were whipping posts and stocks. The 1813 market regulations for Staunton, Virginia, explicitly mention the public whipping post, at which slaves who violated market hours were to be punished.[37] Stocks and whipping posts were an essential component of the municipality's functional and symbolic display of the powers gathered unto it by the act of incorporation.

The most prominent component of an incorporated town's approach to punishment was the lockup or cage.[38] A traveler in 1814 defined one cage as "a small room on the ground floor of jails for the confinement of unruly persons. It is gener-

ally in a public part of town, and the gate being formed of iron bars, the culprit is of course exposed to the view of the passengers [passersby]."[39] Much more elaborate than most was the lockup constructed at the second Seventeenth Street market house in Richmond, Virginia (fig. 14.5). Constructed by 1814, this lockup was a three-story circular building measuring fifty-eight feet in circumference and surmounted by a dome. In his memoirs, a resident of Richmond later described the cage of the second Seventeenth Street market as follows:

> "The cage" is, I believe, a term peculiar to Richmond, as applied to the receptacle for offenders. It originated from a structure, so called, erected at the north-east end of the market bridge, some fifty years ago when it terminated close to the market-house; its long, parapet-wall of brick, surmounted by a capping of free-stone. This cage, of octagonal form, had open iron gratings on three sides, about ten feet above the street, and the floor of this prison was arranged ampitheatrically [*sic*] so that each occupant could see, and what was worse, be seen from the street.[40]

These two passages make clear the essential fact that the punishment meted out for the violation of corporation law was a public act: both accounts emphasize that the offenders can be seen in the cage and that this public shaming was an essential part of the punishment. It is also important that this punishment took place in what was perhaps the busiest public place in the town: the market.

Perhaps the most important civic function of the market house was that of housing the corporation's fire-fighting equipment. Even a cursory glance at the Fredericksburg city council records reveals the dramatic impact of the devastating fire of October 19, 1807, which quickly translated into city council action. Town councils clearly understood that among of the most important civic functions they could perform were the

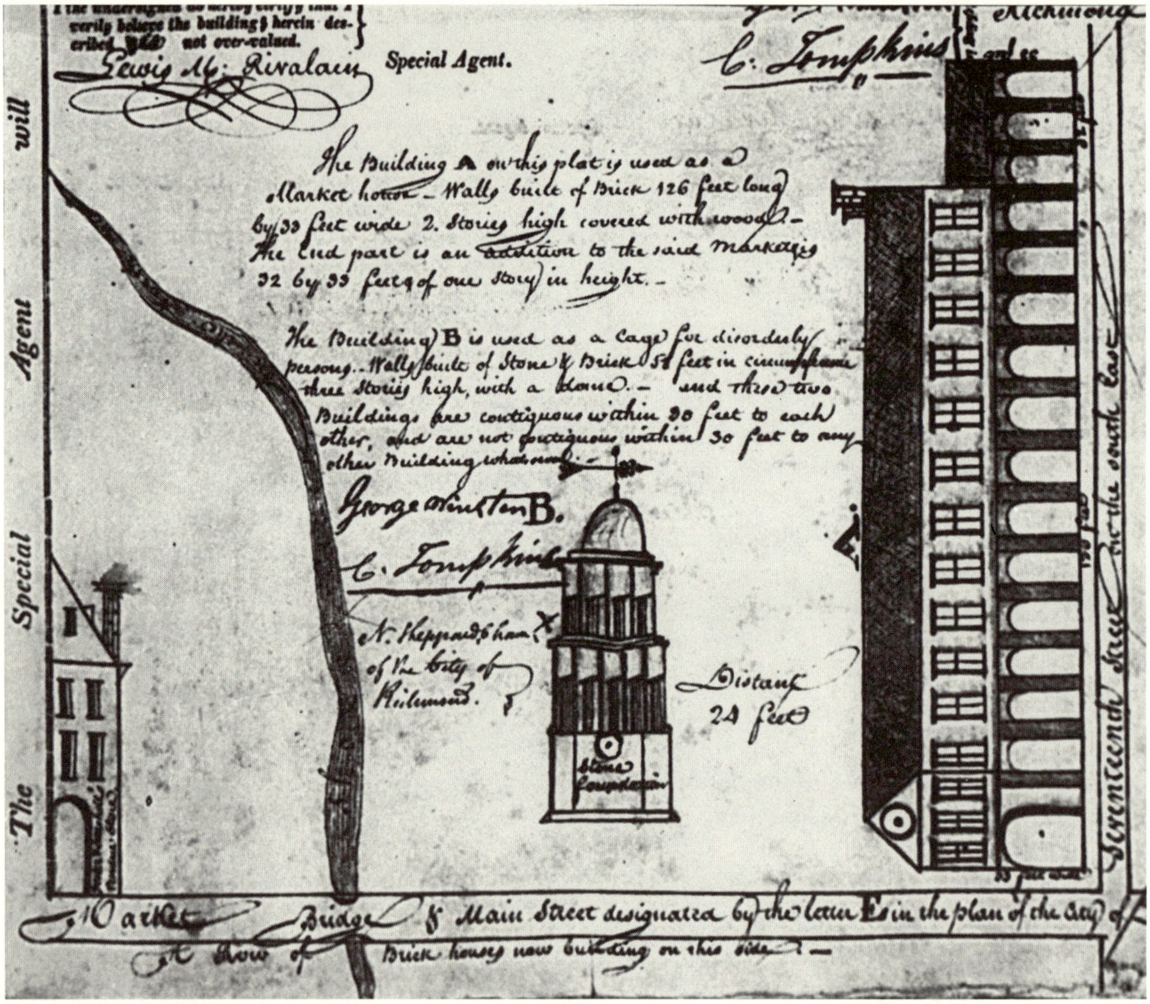

Fig. 14.5. Seventeenth Street Market House, Richmond, Virginia. 1814. Mutual Assurance Society of Virginia Collection, courtesy of the the Library of Virginia.

prevention of fire (through laws requiring masonry chimneys, slate on new roofs, and ladders on the roofs of existing houses with wooden roofs, etc.) and the fighting of fires through the purchase and maintenance of such fire-fighting equipment as leather buckets, hooks, axes, ladders, and fire engines.[41] This link between the corporation and fire fighting led to the close association of the market house with the housing of fire-fighting equipment long after the engines ceased to be actually stored in the market house.

At Fredericksburg, the market house became the place in which the fire engine as well as the fire hooks and axes were stored. In 1807 the council passed a resolution "to inspect and receive the engine now under repair together with the axes + fire hooks directed by the body corporate to be procured + see that the usual room in the Market House be in a fit state for their same keeping in."[42] Of particular importance are the words "the usual room in the market house," indicating that this was a practice that had become traditional. The following year, the trustees of the market, in addition to their regular duties, were required "to take care of the fire hooks ladders and Engines" and were later that year required to "Superintend the Hogsheads of water and the fire hooks, that they keep always in readiness to see that they are brought to the fire with the greatest dispatch and to superintend the management at the fire."[43]

The connection between fire fighting and the market house in Virginia is clear in Benjamin Henry Latrobe's unfinished 1798 sketch of the first Shockoe Hill market in Richmond (fig. 14.6). The Latrobe sketch shows the Shockoe Hill market to the right; to the left, it shows two men pulling a cart towards the market house.[44] The cart that the men are pulling is in fact a fire engine; the curving elements extending from the cart are pump handles, and the square object resting on the cart houses the pump itself. The link between fire fighting and market houses extends far beyond the life span of the market houses themselves. Market houses remained associated with fire fighting, and later designs for town halls, such as the Manassas, Virginia, Town Hall (fig. 14.7), incorporate formal elements borrowed from the market house, as well as civic associations between the city council and fire fighting. The market house, in short, is the model for many if not most fire stations of the nineteenth century (such as the Alexandria Military fire house and the United States Arsenal fire house at Harper's Ferry) and for many others built well into this century.

In addition to the many economic and political functions fulfilled by the market house, in many towns the market house proved to be a very important public meeting place. In a few towns, the market house was at the very center of urban social life. The upper floor or floors of market houses were used for such diverse social functions as libraries, museums, dancing rooms, card rooms, Masonic halls, assembly rooms, dissenting religious services, schoolrooms, political meetings, militia

Fig. 14.6. Market House (Shockoe Hill), Richmond, Virginia, by Benjamin Henry Latrobe, 1798. Benjamin Henry Latrobe Collection, courtesy of the Library of Congress.

Fig. 14.7. Town Hall, Manassas, Virginia. Architect, Albert Speiden. Photo c. 1915, courtesy of the Manassas Museum.

drill halls, and theaters.[45] That the market house fulfilled important social functions in the life of a town should not be surprising. After all, the only other large, open spaces available for public meetings were taverns and churches.[46] For functions such as town meetings, taverns were not always large enough, nor were they appropriate for other functions, such as for schools or religious meetings. For other purposes, such as card playing, a church was an equally inappropriate space.

The importance of these diverse social functions of the market house is revealed by two passages about the first and second Fredericksburg market houses, respectively. A traveler from Pennsylvania, passing through Fredericksburg in 1777, wrote of the town: "Even this small Town affords a Proof of the Luxury & Extravagance of its Inhabitants, for a House has been erected by private Subscription, which is entirely devoted to Dissapation. It is of Brick (not elegant) & contains a Room for Dancing & two for Retirement and Cards."[47] A more approving sentiment is expressed in a later resolution passed by the city council of Fredericksburg, which reads: "We the Subscribers having a due sense of the great utility afforded the Country in general as well as the inhabitants of the Town of Fredericksburg by the commodious situation of the Town House in the said town, which rendered accommodation, not only to polite, and numerous assemblies, by which youth were greatly benefited, but also to all sorts of ancient and modern societies of Fellowship. . . ."[48] As illustrations of the variety of uses to which these rooms were put, the upper floor of the market house at Portsmouth was used both as a schoolhouse and a meeting place for a local Baptist society, the upper floors of the market house at Alexandria were used as a museum and library, and the upper floor of the second Seventeenth Street market in Richmond was used as a theater.[49] Clearly, the market house performed

a vital role in the social life of the Virginia town.

As an integral component in the day-to-day life of Virginia's towns and cities, the market house was a place of social stratification, where the levels of Virginia urban society were literally visible: in the market yard were common merchants and farmers displaying their products, while inside the market house was the clerk—the common council's agent—insuring the fairness of the ensuing transactions. Also "below" were the lockups, stocks, and whipping posts, used in the enforcement of corporation law; these were not primarily used for the punishment of transgressors among the gentry, whose punishments were financial, not physical. Also, literally above the market floor were the council chambers, in which the town leaders—invariably members of the local gentry or well-heeled local merchants—controlled the corporation's finances and made its laws. Also above the market floor were the corporation courts, in which the laws made by councilmen were applied to the people "below." On this level were found the various high social functions located in the building, such as assemblies, balls, and the like, also reserved for the upper classes. Finally, "above" this, were found the town clock, bells, and cupola, which (both visually and aurally) represented the town and its authority and the rule of law extended over all citizens of the town below. Citizens from all levels of society experienced the market house, and, while for each of them it may have held a different meaning, it was nonetheless one of the focal points of the Virginia urban experience.

## Notes

The author would like to thank Catherine Bishir, Charles E. Brownell, Carl R. Lounsbury, Carroll William Westfall, Camille Wells, and anonymous readers for their many suggestions, comments, and ideas.

1. For an excellent synopsis of literature on the architecture of early Virginia, see Dell Upton, "New Views of the Virginia Landscape," *The Virginia Magazine of History and Biography* 96 (Oct. 1988): 403–70.

2. The most thorough discussions of English market houses are found in two recent works: Robert Tittler, *Architecture and Power: The Town Hall and the English Urban Community c. 1500–1640* (New York: Oxford Univ. Press, 1991), especially chaps. 1 and 2; and Peter Borsay, *The English Urban Renaissance: Culture and Society in the Provincial Town, 1660-1770* (Oxford: Clarendon Press, 1989). On the connection between

market houses and Virginia county courthouses, see Carl R. Lounsbury, "The Structure of Justice: The Courthouses of Colonial Virginia," in *Perspectives in Vernacular Architecture, III,* ed. Thomas Carter and Bernard L. Herman (Columbia: Univ. of Missouri Press, 1989), 214–26.

3. Whereas all Virginia towns of consequence once had a market house, only one antebellum market house remains: the second market house at Fredericksburg. American market houses have received little scholarly attention. Exceptions to this are James M. Mayo, "American Public Markets," *Journal of Architectural Education* 45 (Nov. 1991): 41-57; Catherine Bishir, *North Carolina Architecture* (Chapel Hill: Univ. of North Carolina Press, 1990), 172-73, 226-28; Lounsbury, "The Structure of Justice"; and Marian Card Donnelly, *New England Meeting Houses of the Seventeenth Century* (Middleton, Conn.: Wesleyan Univ. Press, 1968), 46, 85, 94-98, 99-100, and 106-8.

4. On Virginia's early towns, see Carville Earle and Ronald Hoffman, "Staple Crops and Urban Development in the Eighteenth-Century South," *Perspectives in American History* 10 (1967): 13. See also Joseph A. Ernst and H. Roy Merrens, "'Camden's turrets pierce the skies!': The Urban Process in the Southern Colonies during the Eighteenth Century," *William and Mary Quarterly* 3d Series, 30 (Oct. 1973): 549–74; and Charles J. Farmer, *In the Absence of Towns: Settlement and Trade in Southside Virginia, 1730-1800* (Lanham, Md.: Rowman & Littlefield, 1993).

5. For an account of the division between city and county authority in Virginia that concentrates on the late nineteenth and twentieth centuries, see Weldon Cooper, "Virginia Local Government, 1776-1976," *The University of Virginia Newsletter* 52 (11) (July 1976): 41-44. For a more extended account, see Chester W. Bain, *"A Body Incorporate": The Evolution of City-County Separation in Virginia* (Charlottesville: Univ. Press of Virginia, 1967). See also E. Lee Shepard, "Courts in Conflict: Town-County Relations in Post-Revolutionary Virginia," *The Virginia Magazine of History and Biography* 85 (Apr. 1977): 185.

6. Shepard, "Courts in Conflict," 186.

7. Minutes of the Common Council of the Borough of Norfolk, Dec. 20, 1736.

8. Shepard, "Courts in Conflict," 186 and 188; and Cooper, "Virginia Local Government," 41. See also Bryan Clark Green, "The Market House in Virginia, 1736–c. 1860," (Master's thesis, Univ. of Virginia, 1991), appendix 1.

9. See Green, "Market House in Virginia," appendices 2 and 3.

10. Minutes of the Council of the City of Staunton, July 24, 1813, Sec. 2.

11. Ibid.

12. Records of the Town & City of Portsmouth, Virginia, Mar. 2, 1811, Sec. 1.

13. Minutes of the Council of the City of Staunton, July 24, 1813, Sec. 13. Certainly many foodstuffs were sold—both informally and through grocers—beyond the market, but this trade often existed despite official legislation.

14. Fredericksburg City Council Minutes, Jan. 12, 1809, Sec. 10.

15. Ibid., Sec. 4.

16. Ibid., Sec. 1. The Portsmouth clerk was required to go through a more complicated if less hierarchical process to condemn provisions thought to be unsound. Upon inspecting "any kind of bad meat or poultry, or meat or poultry that may be spoilt by long keeping," the clerk was required to gather together "three or more house keepers to inspect the same" and arrive at a judgment as to its quality. Records of the Town & City of Portsmouth, Mar. 2, 1811, Sec. 5.

17. For a discussion of the public nature of time and clocks, see Daniel J. Boorstin, *The Discoverers* (New York: Random House, 1985), 24-78.

18. Anne Newport Royall, *Sketches of History Life and Manners in the United States* (New Haven, 1826), 108.

19. Ibid., 108.

20. Ibid., 110.

21. A typical references to the renting out of stalls in the market house is found in the Records of the Town & City of Portsmouth, Aug. 12, 1805. Two references to the reserving of certain stalls for the use of the general public are included in Fredericksburg City Council Minutes, Aug. 22, 1782, and Fredericksburg City Council Minutes, Jan. 12, 1809, Sec. 11.

22. Royall, *Sketches,* 208.

23. Records of the Town & City of Portsmouth, July 20, 1817.

24. Royall, *Sketches,* 110.

25. Fredericksburg City Council Minutes, Mar. 28, 1812, and Apr. 23, 1814. The market house was built with a brick and stone lower story measuring 97 feet by 33 feet, above which was a brick two-story portion of 49 feet by 33 feet housing a town hall and a council chamber, to be flanked by two one-story wings each 24 feet by 33 feet.

26. Figures computed from Mutual Assurance Policies, Virginia Department of Historic Resources.

27. Minutes of the Common Council of the Borough of Norfolk, Dec. 20, 1736.

28. Minutes of the Common Council of the Borough of Norfolk, June 30, 1784.

29. Minutes of the Common Council of the Borough of Norfolk, June 24, 1798.

30. City of Richmond, Records of the Common Hall, Apr. 24, 1794, June 16, 1794, Feb. 18, 1811, and Mar. 16, 1812.

31. Minutes of the Council of the City of Staunton, Oct. 29, 1802.

32. Ibid., Mar. 11, 1807.

33. Records of the Town & City of Portsmouth, Aug. 11, 1806.

34. Ibid., July 25, 1814.

35. Mark R. Wenger, "The Central Passage in Virginia: Evolution of an Eighteenth-Century Living Space," in *Perspectives in Vernacular Architecture, II,* ed. Camille Wells (Columbia: Univ. of Missouri Press, 1986), 148.

36. On the interiors of Virginia's county courthouses, see Lounsbury, "The Structure of Justice," 222-25.

37. Minutes of the Council of the City of Staunton, July 24, 1813, Sec. 3. Many other market regulations (such as Portsmouth's) spelled out in great detail the number of lashes slaves who violated market regulations were to receive, and it seems certain that these—and probably all—market towns had public whipping posts at the market house.

38. For a discussion of county jails in Virginia, see Lounsbury, "Structure of Justice," 217.

39. John Cook Wyllie, ed., "'Observations made During a Short Residence in Virginia': In a Letter from Thomas H. Palmer, May 30, 1814," *The Virginia Magazine of History and Biography* 76 (Oct. 1968): 395.

40. Samuel Mordecai, *Virginia, Especially Richmond, in By-Gone Days: With a Glance at the Present: Being Reminiscences and Last Words of an Old Citizen,* 2d ed. (Richmond, 1860), 23.

41. On the technology of fire fighting in the eighteenth century, see E. L. Jones and M. E. Falkus, "Urban Improvement and English Economy in the Seventeenth and Eighteenth Centuries," *Research in Economic History* 4: 123-24. While Jones and Falkus specifically discuss English towns, they discuss provincial towns that are analogous in scale to the incorporated towns of Vir-

ginia. This fact, combined with the fact that the technologies of fire fighting were virtually the same throughout the settled areas of Great Britain (including Virginia), means this essay provides an excellent approach to understanding urban improvements throughout the English-speaking world in the eighteenth century. A standard account of the firehouse, Rebecca Zurier, *The Firehouse: An Architectural and Social Profile* (New York: Abbeville Press, 1991), does not mention the market house as a possible precedent for the design of the firehouse.

42. Fredericksburg City Council Minutes, Oct. 27, 1807.

43. Ibid., Mar. 21, 1808, and June 2, 1808.

44. Despite the close proximity of a fire engine, Quesnay's theater—the building in the center of the sketch with the gable end facing the square—burned on Jan. 23, 1798, within the same month Latrobe began the sketch referred to above.

45. On Virginia churches used as social gathering places, see Dell Upton, *Holy Things and Profane: Anglican Parish Churches in Colonial Virginia* (New York: Architectural History Foundation, 1986), 199-232. On Virginia Taverns as social spaces, see Jane Carson, *Colonial Virginians at Play* (Williamsburg: Colonial Williamsburg, 1965), 109-14; and Elise Lathrop, *Early American Inns and Taverns* (New York: R. N. McBride, 1926), 215-23. On assemblies in eighteenth-century England, see Borsay, *English Urban Renaissance,* 150-62; and Daniel Defoe, *A Tour Through the Whole Island of Great Britain, 1724–1726,* ed. Pat Rodgers (Harmondsworth: Penguin, 1971), especially 49, 76, 108, 170, 192, 214, and 360.

46. Ebenezer Hazard, "The Journal of Ebenezer Hazard in Virginia, 1777," *The Virginia Magazine of History and Biography* 62 (Oct. 1954): 403.

47. Fredericksburg City Council Minutes, Sept. 4, 1782. The reality of the situation, however, was very different, as the market house was "in need of very considerable repair," and since there was no "Fund within the powers of the Corporation" sufficient to repair the building and "the abilities of the inhabitants of the Town being inadequate to a tax for that purpose," the Corporation turned to private donations to repair the market house. See Fredericksburg City Council Minutes, Sept. 4, 1782.

48. Fredericksburg City Council Minutes, Sept. 4, 1782.

49. Records of the Town & City of Portsmouth, June 6, 1803, and June 24, 1798; Joseph Martin, ed., *A New and Comprehensive Gazetteer of Virginia, and the District of Columbia* . . . (Charlottesville: J. Martin, 1835), 479; Mordecai, *Virginia, Especially Richmond, in By-Gone Days,* 142; and Mary Wingfield Scott, *Old Richmond Neighborhoods* (Richmond: Whittlet and Shepperson, 1950), 64 and 67.

## CHAPTER 15

*Lisa Tolbert*

# Commercial Blocks and Female Colleges: The Small-Town Business of Educating Ladies

In 1860, a newspaper editor in Columbia, Tennessee, marveled at the town's recent architectural transformation. "Within the past five years," he observed, "there has been almost a complete renovation of the town. . . . Upon the crumbling foundations of old frame houses, new and beautiful houses have risen," along with "new and commodious business houses."[1] Emboldened by the economic potential of the expanding railroad, town residents throughout Middle Tennessee made huge investments to improve their homes and businesses. But local entrepreneurs did much more than simply build bigger, more fashionable houses upon the "crumbling foundations" of the old. Their architectural choices document profound spatial reorganization—the creation of a distinctive new townscape.

With fewer than two thousand residents, these small county seats of Middle Tennessee were hardly urban places at the beginning of the 1850s. Yet, like their urban counterparts in Philadelphia and New York, Middle Tennesseans increasingly divided domestic from business space and completely reorganized town commerce by differentiating retail from wholesale zones. Warehouses and commission stores, built near the railroad, removed wholesale commerce from town center to periphery, while the public square became primarily devoted to nonmanual professions and the retail trade.[2] These new, specialized urban spaces have chiefly been interpreted as a consequence of industrialization that had profound implications for gender roles. The workplace became redefined as aggressive, competitive, masculine, while the home became the site of a new domestic female ideal.[3]

The timing of this process in the South has been the subject of considerable debate. Elizabeth Fox-Genovese has argued that the household remained the dominant unit of production throughout the antebellum period, preventing the development of an autonomous domestic ideology. By contrast, Suzanne Lebsock has shown that an identifiable women's culture in antebellum Petersburg, Virginia, was shaped by the ideology of separate spheres, which she describes as "a temporary and uneasy solution" to the new division between household and workplace.[4] In broad terms, this debate concerns the increasingly distinctive roles of rural and urban women. As plantation mistresses in an overwhelmingly rural region, nineteenth-century southern women are believed to have been less influenced by the division between domestic and work space that reshaped so many urban dwellers' lives. Overlooked in the region are the small towns that Fox-Genovese admits were "ubiquitous."[5] The lives of these small-town women were shaped by a distinctive dynamic, neither fully urban nor completely rural.

The division between residential and commercial space occurred dramatically in the antebellum county seats of Middle Tennessee during the course of a single decade, and it proceeded hand-in-hand with the emergence of a new female ideal. Throughout the architectural renovation of the 1850s, Middle Tennesseans repeatedly pointed to the accomplishments of female residents, measuring town progress and urbanity by a particular version of the domestic ideal—the refined and genteel "Lady." The Lady's influence extended beyond the household to other town regions. In particular, two entirely new types of buildings embodied the influence of the new gender ideal in the renovated townscape. Commercial blocks on the public square and college campuses designed for elite young women reveal that concerns over gender were deeply intertwined with concerns about town business.

Murfreesboro merchant Legrand Carney wholeheartedly joined the building boom that effectively redefined town space in the decade before the Civil War. Six blocks from the public square, in the northern limits of town, he built an imposing brick home in the early 1850s (fig. 15.1). A neighbor described the Carneys as "the richest people" in town, with "much the finest house."[6] Though surrounded by acres of lawn, orchard, and garden, the house stood out. Its dominant feature—double, two-story, white-columned porticos—declared the family's fashionable allegiance to the Greek Revival. During the decade, Legrand Carney also built a new dry goods store on the public square and invested heavily in Soule Female College, where his daughter, Kate, studied painting and practiced the guitar.

Kate Carney was a small-town lady through and through. In 1859, she had lived all of her seventeen years in Murfreesboro. More noteworthy than her musical or artistic skills was the regularity with which Kate reported her activities to her diary. The document that survives is remarkable not for its self-reflection or probing analysis of small-town life, but for its straightforward description of what Kate did almost every day in 1859. Her fondest employment was walking—not just in her own expansive yard, but all over town and not just on warm, sunny days, but on cold winter ones, too. One day in January she "walked up to town four times, . . . three times this morning, and once this evening."[7] It was the frequency and duration of these walks to which her mother, Katherine, objected, and not the fact that Kate wandered

Fig. 15.1. The Carney House Was Known as "The Crest." The Carneys sold the house after the Civil War; it was torn down in 1910. From Mary B. Hughes, Hearthstones: The Story of Historic Rutherford County Homes (Murfreesboro, Tenn.: Mid-South Publishing Co., 1942), 59.

unchaperoned through town streets. The problem was that Kate's chores often went unattended as a result of these daily expeditions. One day an exasperated Katherine Carney admonished her peripatetic daughter that she "must stop walking," because there was "enough to do at home for exercise. She must be right," Kate admitted, "but it is not only for exercise, but for pleasure; for I enjoy those walks very much."[8] Luckily, Katherine Carney did not enforce her rule, and her daughter's pleasure in walking never waned.

Kate's walks were a declaration of her status, her freedom from household chores. Every evening, she recorded her itinerary in her diary, which became a small-town travelog of sorts—a remarkably descriptive record of small-town life. Occasionally she found herself completely overwhelmed by the task of recording the places she had visited and the people she had seen. "Mary Spence and I took quite a long walk, and I got a little tired before getting home. We went by the store, and, but pshaw! I cannot think of telling everywhere we went, & ever body [sic] we saw for it would take to[o] much time."[9] But most nights, Kate did take the time to record her itinerary.

On a typical afternoon in March 1859, she "went up town" after midday dinner with her friend and cousin Nannie Black. Before their excursion ended, Kate and Nannie had spent the day in the company of other young ladies visiting the two town regions most visibly influenced by the new gender ideal. In the simple act of an afternoon walk, they affirmed their position among the most conspicuous inhabitants of the renovated townscape—as refined and accomplished ladies.

The girls walked six blocks, passing Soule Female College and several houses along their way, to the public square (fig. 15.2). Nannie and Kate zigzagged around the square from store to store. "We first went to Mr. Neilson's & Crichelow's store, then to Pa's, & then back to the same one, & then across to Jordan's & Elliott's." Each of these stores advertised that same year in Murfreesboro

newspapers as dry goods establishments.[10] Having finished their business on the square for the time being, the girls retraced their steps three blocks down the Lebanon Pike "to call" on some friends boarding at the College. "We staid [sic] some time," Kate wrote, "when Nannie saw Ellen & Mary [Spence] going by." So Kate and Nannie "bid the [College] girls good bye, & went out & caught up with them." The group of girls returned to the public square, where their number would be enlarged once again.

"Nannie & Ellen walked together, & Mary & I until we came to Crockett's store & we all went in except Nannie," who had business at another store. The three girls soon met Nannie at "Mr. Neilson's & Crichelow's," where they also "found Misses Sallie Neilson [and] Jennie James. . . . We all then went to Reed's Bookstore (quite a number six in all) from there we [went to] Mr. Elliott's then walked down Main Street and turned across to College St., stopping only to bid Miss Sallie & Miss Jennie good evening."[11]

Kate Carney's description of the public square seems incongruous with nineteenth-century photographs that show men lounging on street corners and posing proudly in front of their stores (fig. 15.3). Such photos rarely pictured women, even as shoppers. These images reinforce the notion that the public square, dominated by the courthouse, was a uniquely masculine region. Certainly the space was owned by men—Messrs. Neilson & Crichelow, Jordan & Elliot, for example. Then enter Kate and Nannie and their four female friends parading around and through the square, and the scene changes dramatically. The band of girls roamed freely, though not indiscriminately, through the space. Significantly, they patronized particular dry goods stores, owned by family and friends in the same social circle, avoiding businesses that were inappropriate for young ladies to enter, such as groceries that sold liquor. Though they observed such implied restrictions on their movements, the girls nevertheless traversed town

**N**

0            500 feet

LEBANON PIKE

Carney
House

Soule
Female
College

County
Female
Institute

Murfreesboro
Female
Institute

COLLEGE STREET

PUBLIC
SQUARE

MAIN

MAIN

*Basemap source*: Murfreesboro, Rutherford
County, Tennessee, 1878. D.G. Beers & Co.

*P. H. Neumann*

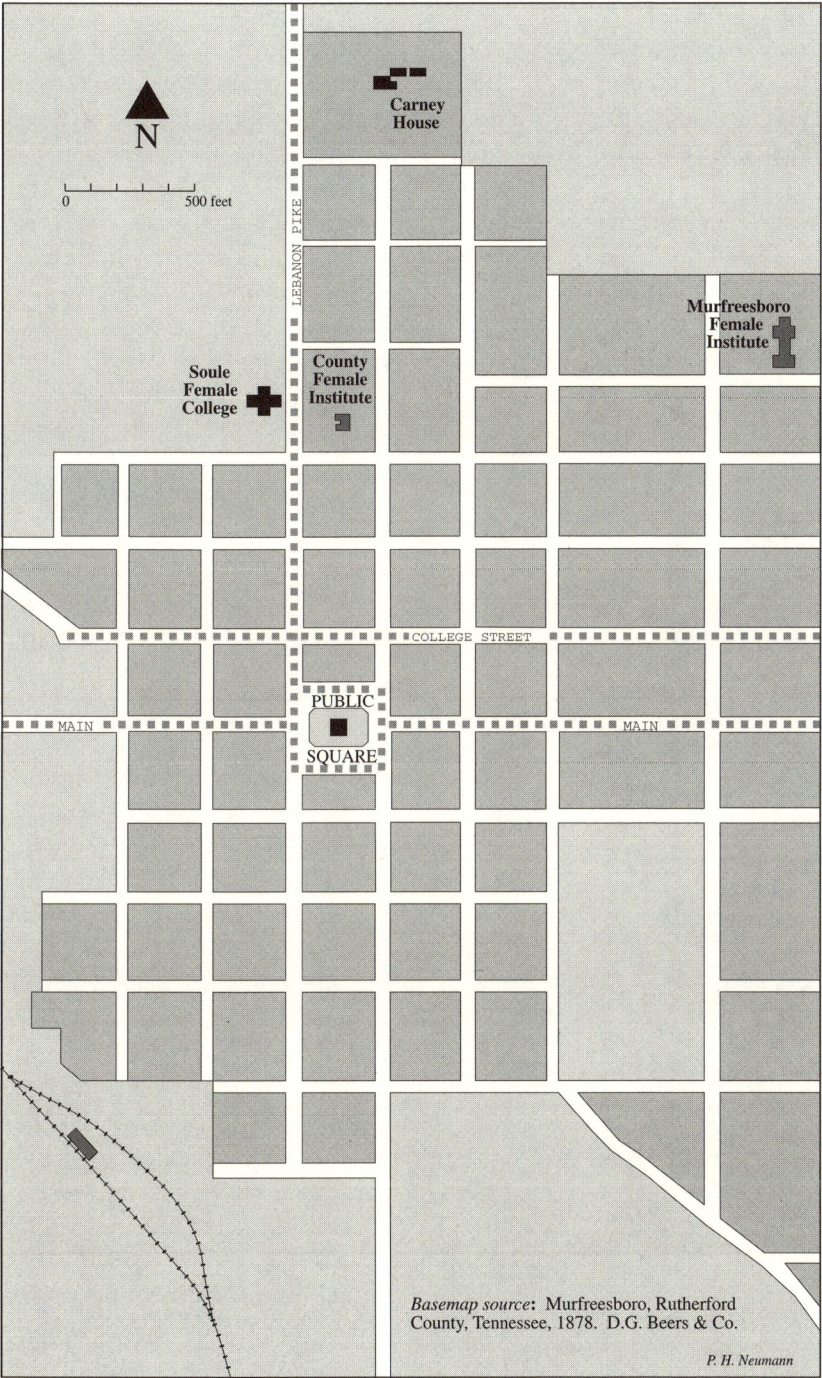

Fig. 15.2. Map of Murfreesboro, 1850s. This map shows the route Kate Carney
and her friends took on their afternoon walk. In addition to Soule Female College,
the map also shows the location of two other female colleges built during the 1850s.

streets unaccompanied by parent or guardian. Kate Carney and her friends represented a new class of leisured young women who began to make their afternoon walks about the same time that commercial changes in retail sales patterns were reshaping the public square.

Between 1846 and 1861 (when he sold his business), house carpenter Nathan Vaught profited from commissions to build or modify nine stores on or near the public square in Columbia, Tennessee.[12] Urban models could not have been far from the minds of merchants who continued to travel every year to Philadelphia and other northern cities to buy products for the small-town market. In

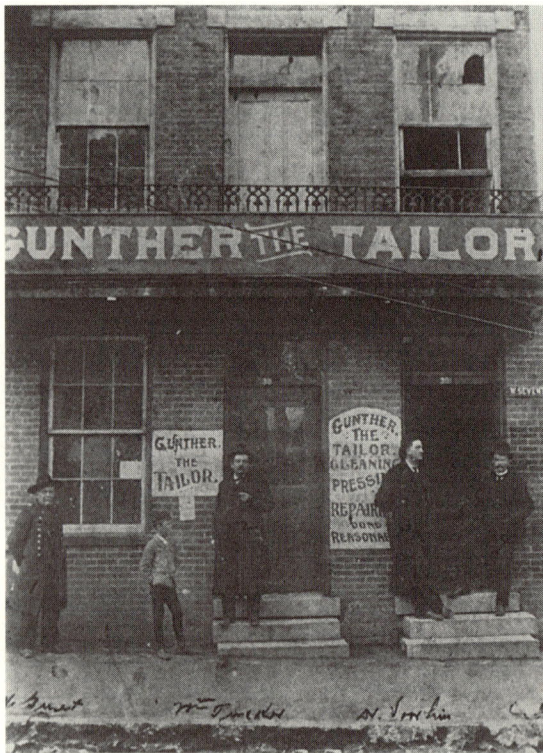

Fig. 15.3. "Gunther the Tailor." This shop was located one block from the public square in Columbia, Tennessee. From First Autumn Carnival Given Under the Auspices of Columbia Lodge, No. 686 Benevolent and Protective Order of Elks, Columbia, Tennessee, September 16 to 21, 1901 [Nashville, Tenn.: Press of Foster & Webb, n.d.].

1846—the same year that A. T. Stewart opened the first department store in New York City, a "marble palace" with a ladies' parlor on the second floor—Nathan Vaught built the first commercial block in Columbia. Considerably more humble than a "marble palace," Vaught recalled that the building was "a very deep and extra wide brick storehouse . . . 2 doors from the corner of the public square [with] the first open front in town."[13] The size of the commercial block alone signaled a revolution in town commerce. Murfreesboro merchant John Spence declared in amazement that businessmen who had formerly been content with "a twenty feet square room . . . are now making store houses twenty by eighty feet long, still feeling a little crouded [*sic*]."[14]

These stores embodied new ways of doing business. The commercial block was particularly suited to retail specialization in the renovated townscape. Although the dry goods store, which sold everything from hoes to hats, remained an integral component of the public square, it was joined by specialized stores that exclusively sold drugs or books or some particular type of merchandise. The principle of retail specialization achieved full expression in the commercial block Vaught built in 1859, thirteen years after he had installed the first plate-glass window on the public square in Columbia. In a single unit, the new commercial block contained three distinct stores, each with large glass windows at the ground-floor level (fig. 15.4).[15] Vaught altered the roofline and window styles to define clearly the three separate stores incorporated into the block. The design enabled merchants to differentiate types of merchandise—for instance, the corner store in the Vaught block specialized in furniture.[16]

Such retail specialization has been interpreted from the perspective of changes in business organization, but it was also compatible with the selective shopping patterns of new female customers like Kate Carney and her friends. Commercial success on the square substantially depended on

Fig. 15.4. Commercial Block Nathan Vaught Built in 1859 on the Square in Columbia, Tennessee. Courtesy of Mrs. Jill K. Garrett.

female patronage. This principle was most evident during what local newspapers called the "Fall season," when merchants announced the arrival of the latest merchandise from New York and Philadelphia. In the fall, as at no other time of the year, merchants noticed that "Main Street is alive with ladies visiting and shopping. From morning to night their gay and pleasant faces enlivening its walks." Such pointed observations of ladies thronging the small-town commercial avenue suggest the newness of this habit. More importantly for the businessmen, female shoppers did more than promenade along Main Street. Women began to "congregate every day in their stores, to pass sentence upon the styles, to purchase" all manner of goods, from the luxurious to the utilitarian.[17] When merchants redesigned their stores, replacing cramped, one-room "storehouses" with large "commercial blocks," they intended to attract this refined female clientele. Local merchants were aware that Nashville, the urban center of Middle Tennessee, drew ever closer to small-town shoppers with improved turnpikes and an expanding railroad network. As she walked past the "open front" of plate-glass windows that literally opened up the interior of the small-town commercial block, some casual shopper might be enticed to enter and purchase a fancy item that happened to catch her eye.

Plate-glass windows and retail specialization signaled technological and business innovations only partially related to the new gender ideal. Perhaps the subtle rearrangement of the old-fashioned dry goods store within the new commercial block most clearly demonstrated the direct influence of the refined female consumer. These small-town merchants rearranged their store interiors with an eye for "convenience" and "elegance," cardinal principles of small-town gentility.[18] One Columbia newspaper editor took his readers on a tour of "two large business houses" that were "connected with each other by large doors between," located "on the North corner of Main Street and the Square." The interior arrangement made spatial distinctions between storage and display. While the basement was "thickly crowded," the second floor glittered "with every imaginable species of glassware, china, etc.," and the third floor was "closely packed with articles, of which samples are to be seen below." After examining "the entire establishment," he "pronounce[d] it in every way most elegantly arranged."[19] No longer did ladies have to climb over saddles and farm implements to view the latest china patterns.

The same businessmen who were building commercial blocks on the public square also sponsored an architectural revolution to house female education. In the renovated townscape, the accomplishments of young "ladies" like Kate Carney increasingly became the ultimate measure of urbanity. The reputation of the entire community hung in the balance, and businessmen set out to assure that young women would be prepared for their essential role in the refined townscape. The result was the female college, a new town industry devoted to the production of ladies.

The female college was architecturally and intellectually distinct from earlier town academies. Before the 1850s, strangers to town would have been hard-pressed to single out the "academy," where local girls learned "all the useful and ornamental branches of an English Education" from reading, writing, and arithmetic to French and Italian languages, needlework, and painting.[20] Indeed, private citizens often opened such schools in their own homes. In the early 1830s, the first session of the Shelbyville Female Academy commenced "in a large commodious room in a retired part of town." The new school informed parents of potential students that "young ladies from the county can be accomodated [sic] with boarding in respectable families on reasonable terms."[21] The difference between this humble academy and the female college was much more than a matter of semantics, particularly when the college is viewed as part of a larger renovated townscape in which domestic and commercial space were newly divided.

When it opened in 1852, the Columbia Athenaeum, with its multibuilding arrangement, became the most architecturally ambitious college for women in Middle Tennessee. The rectory, adorned with an exotic Moorish portico, set the tone for a campus that would become a catalog of eclectic mid-nineteenth-century revivalisms (fig. 15.5). In 1860, local carpenter Nathan Vaught enlarged the central building, known as the auditorium, or "Athenaeum Hall." He described its most impressive feature as "a very heavy portico at the north and south ends," supported by Doric columns rising a full two stories.[22] The auditorium was accompanied by two octagonal brick rotundas, each connected by a series of two-story, rectangular brick buildings—the whole embellished with Italianate bracketing and colonnaded walks, and crowned by fleurs de lis (fig. 15.6). On the hill above Columbia, the enlightened residents of this new "Athens of the West" displayed their knowledge of the great architectural traditions of history.

Though often less architecturally exuberant than Columbia's Athenaeum, female colleges became a standard, conspicuous feature of renovated townscapes across Middle Tennessee.[23] In Murfreesboro, a group of prominent businessmen, including Kate Carney's father, organized Soule Female College in 1853 (fig. 15.7). A few blocks from the public square, on a campus of about four acres, they built a substantial three-story brick building with

Fig. 15.5. Athenaeum Rectory. Originally built in the mid-1830s for Samuel Polk Walker, nephew of James K. Polk, the house became the residence of Athenaeum founder and president Franklin Gillette Smith in 1852.

Fig. 15.6. Columbia Athenaeum Campus, Showing the Auditorium and Rotunda. The Athenaeum stood until 1915, when it was torn down to make way for a public high school. Courtesy of Mrs. Jill K. Garrett.

two recessed wings. The trustees assured their patrons that this structure had been "constructed expressly for a female boarding school." In particular, it was designed with attention "to the convenience and . . . health" of the students. Inside, the rooms were "large, airy, and well ventilated" and the halls were "spacious and well adapted to indoor exercise in bad weather." Outside, the campus, with its grove of trees, provided "ample room for pleasant and healthful recreation."[24]

Then the trustees of Soule Female College revealed the major distinction between their school and the old-fashioned academy: "To protect our

reputation and ensure the objects of our school," they announced, "the trustees have found it necessary to pass an ordinance making it an absolute requirement, that all boarding pupils shall board in the College."[25] No longer were girls from the country expected to board with respectable town families. This was one of the reasons that town residents built such large school buildings: they were essentially dormitories. But this decision was significant in the context of the larger townscape for two reasons: first, it indicated a new ambition to extend cultural influence far beyond small-town borders; and second, it produced highly specialized town regions of gender segregation.

In contrast to their academic predecessors, female colleges targeted an audience far beyond the town and contiguous countryside. Among the students at the Columbia Institute in 1850, 32 percent came from states other than Tennessee. Unlike the teachers, who were primarily of northern origin, the students arrived from southern states, especially Alabama and Kentucky, but also Mississippi, Louisiana, and Virginia.[26] By boarding these out-of-state students together in dormitories, female colleges became highly specialized town regions defined by gender more explicitly than any other town space. But this was class-based segregation as well, for these colleges were designed for young "ladies" in particular.

Spatial segregation made college campuses the appropriate sites for highly regulated female performance. Students displayed their accomplishments in public exams and concerts at the end of each school session. The Athenaeum regularly gave "soirees," "devoted to Vocal and Instrumental Music, conversation, etc." On such evenings the study hall was "open for promenades," and "friends and patrons of the school" were encouraged to come and "meet the teacher and pupils."[27] These events demonstrated more than the skills of individual students; they reflected the level of refinement of the entire town. Soule College trustees

Fig. 15.7. Soule Female College. The college was named for Methodist Bishop Joshua Soule of Nashville. After the Civil War, Kate Carney took charge of the academic department for a short time. Courtesy of Mrs. Mabel Pittard.

even argued that Murfreesboro itself was one of their school's chief assets. Their list of local resources included "the healthfulness of the locality, the refinement of the surrounding citizenship, [and] the neatness and accessibility of the town, being immediately on the Nashville & Chattanooga R. R." These "external commendations and facilities," they declared, were "equal to those enjoyed by any school in the South."[28] Competition among towns produced considerable hyperbole; nevertheless, local businessmen reinforced their boosterism with substantial investments. The quality of the female colleges they built could help distinguish one town from another in the race for economic advantage.

The trustees of female colleges spent impressive sums to build these schools at precisely the same moment they were investing heavily in railroads, commercial blocks, courthouses, and elaborate additions to their homes. Even Kate Carney worried that her father was "in debt a great deal," noting that "our expenses have been very heavy for the last six or seven years."[29] Soule Female College cost Murfreesboro subscribers about $25,000; while in Columbia, Methodists confidently sought $10,000 in subscriptions from "the people of Maury and the adjoining counties," to build the female seminary they sponsored.[30] This "preoccupation with buildings" demonstrated more than the trustees' intention to create permanent institutions; they fully expected a return on their investment.[31]

Female colleges occupied a prominent place in the renovated townscape because their male designers defined them as integral to larger economic and cultural town goals. In Columbia alone, three female colleges were educating seven hundred scholars by 1860. A local newspaper editor ranked these schools among the town's most important businesses.[32] Phil P. Neely, a spokesman for Columbia's Methodists, described the church's proposed female seminary as "an enterprize [*sic*]" that would ultimately benefit the "temporal interests" of the entire community. Significantly, Neely based his claims on a broad argument emphasizing the economic benefits of education—especially female education. He encouraged residents to support these schools because they would "enhance the value of your town property—your lands—will open up a fine market in your county town and put in circulation, annually thousands of dollars . . . which but for them, would be confined to other sections."[33] One Columbia paper went so far as to claim that "were our schools permanently to suspend operations, Columbia would be a place of no very great importance in any point of view. Indeed, the rapid growth of the town would be greatly retarded, and business, now so lively, would materially fall below its present standard."[34] The female college had become a new kind of town industry in which the production of ladies was a key element of generalized communal prosperity. Town residents considered these colleges essential to their cultural reputation and economic progress—integral to population growth, improved property values, and commercial success.

The same editor who listed female colleges among Columbia's most important business ad-

vantages also boasted that the town offered "the best location for a home" to be found "anywhere in the broad limits of the South."[35] Female colleges occupied a strategic position at the center of a new division between commerce and domesticity in the renovated townscape of the 1850s. While they contributed substantially to the economic prosperity of the community, these institutions were ultimately designed to train young ladies in their proper domestic roles. Thus, commerce and domesticity converged in the female college, making it the appropriate symbol to represent dialectical town roles—town as marketplace and town as home.

Ironically, the age that created a privatized, idealized domesticity also redefined female education as a lucrative town business. Viewed in the context of townscape renovation, it is clear, however, that gender was central to both economic and cultural ambitions in the county seat. The simultaneous development of the female college and the commercial block was not coincidental. Though many factors influenced the redefinition of town space during the 1850s, these two town regions incorporated distinctive spatial strategies for capitalizing on a new gender ideal. Dependent on the patronage of a refined female clientele, business owners on the public square designed their commercial blocks to showcase specialized merchandise, arranged with an eye for display. The same entrepreneurs displayed their daughters' accomplishments in female colleges, which became highly specialized regions of gender segregation. As appropriate sites for the traffic of "ladies," both the college and the commercial block embodied the complex intertwining of gender and commerce that marked spatial reorganization in the renovated townscape of the 1850s.

## Notes

1. *Maury Press,* Mar. 7, 1860.

2. John Spence, *The Annals of Rutherford County,* vol. 2: 1829–1870 (Murfreesboro, Tenn.: The Rutherford County Historical Society, 1991), 102. Spence describes the creation in Murfreesboro of "Depot Hill" just after the arrival of the first train. Stuart Blumin examines the development of urban retail centers specializing in nonmanual business interests of the middle class. See his *The Emergence of the Middle Class: Social Experience in the American City, 1760–1900* (Cambridge: Cambridge Univ. Press, 1989), 83–107.

3. The literature that examines this transformation is vast. Barbara Welter made the now classic statement of the ideology of separate spheres in her article "The Cult of True Womanhood, 1820–1860," *American Quarterly* 18 (1966): 151–74. Subsequent research has explored the efforts of nineteenth-century women to expand their sphere of influence beyond the household. See, for example, Mary P. Ryan, *Women in Public: Between Banners and Ballots, 1825–1880* (Baltimore: Johns Hopkins Univ. Press, 1990). The impact of this ideology on architectural and spatial change has been examined by Gwendolyn Wright, *Building the Dream: A Social History of Housing in America* (New York: Pantheon, 1981).

4. Elizabeth Fox-Genovese, *Within the Plantation Household: Black and White Women of the Old South* (Chapel Hill: Univ. of North Carolina Press, 1988); Suzanne Lebsock, *The Free Women of Petersburg: Status and Culture in a Southern Town, 1784–1860* (New York: W. W. Norton, 1984), 224.

5. Fox-Genovese, *Within the Plantation Household,* 5.

6. Virginia Shelton to her aunt, May 15, 1856, Campbell Family Papers, Special Collections Department, William R. Perkins Library, Duke University. The house no longer stands. For a description and photograph, see Mary B. Hughes, *Hearthstones: The Story of Historic Rutherford County Homes* (Murfreesboro, Tenn.: Mid-South Publishing Co. Inc., 1942), 59.

7. Kate Carney Diary, Jan. 12, 1859, Southern Historical Collection, Wilson Library, The University of North Carolina at Chapel Hill (hereafter referred to as SHC).

8. Ibid., Feb. 21, 1859.

9. Ibid.

10. See *Murfreesboro News,* Feb. 2, 1859, in which Neilson & Crichelow advertised their new partnership. Jordan and Elliot's dry goods store is also advertised in that issue of the *Murfreesboro News.* Kate's father, Legrand Carney, had recently built a new building for his dry goods store on the square. He had previously been a partner in one of the town's first drugstores, see *Murfreesboro Telegraph,* Nov. 13, 1845.

11. Kate Carney Diary, Mar. 19, 1859, SHC.

12. From the "Reminiscences of Nathan Vaught," transcribed in Nancy C. Tinker, "Nathan Vaught, Master Builder of Maury County: A Study of Middle Tennessee Greek Revival Architecture," (M.A. thesis, Middle Tennessee State Univ., 1983).

13. Ibid., 113–14. See also Harry E. Resseguie, "A. T. Stewart's Marble Palace—The Cradle of the Department Store," *New York Historical Society Quarterly* 48 (1964): 131–62.

14. Spence, *The Annals of Rutherford County,* 2: 114.

15. Tinker, "Reminiscences of Nathan Vaught," 118. On Apr. 11, 1860, the *Maury Press* noted that "[a] beautiful block of three large stores is just completed on the square near Nelson's Hotel"—this comment is in reference to Vaught's project.

16. *Maury Press,* May 2, 1860, advertisement for new furniture store, corner building of W. J. Dale's new block, north side public square, includes list of furniture for sale and advertises related undertaking business.

17. *Maury Press,* Sept. 26, 1860.

18. *Maury Press,* Apr. 4, 1860.

19. *Maury Press,* Apr. 4, 1861.

20. *Western Freeman,* Mar. 6, 1832.

21. Ibid.

22. Tinker, "Reminiscences of Nathan Vaught," 118.

23. Residents in all four county seats examined built female colleges during the 1850s: the Athenaeum and the Methodist Female College in Columbia; Soule College and Eaton Female College in Murfreesboro; the Franklin Female Institute; and the Shelbyville Female College, built in 1858 at a cost of fifteen thousand dollars. See the Goodspeed histories of Maury, Williamson, Rutherford, Wilson, Bedford, and Marshal Counties of Tennessee, reprinted from *Goodspeed's History of Tennessee* (1886; reprint, Columbia, Tenn.: Woodward & Stinson Printing Co., 1971).

24. *Murfreesboro News,* Feb. 2, 1859.

25. Ibid. Eaton Female College in Murfreesboro also made "ample arrangements . . . for boarding in the Institution" (*Murfreesboro News,* Sept. 26, 1860). By contrast, the Murfreesboro Military Academy, located in a building opposite the Methodist Female College in Murfreesboro, informed potential male students that boarding "can be had with private families on reasonable terms." See *Murfreesboro News,* Feb. 2, 1859.

26. Manuscript census for Columbia, 1850.

27. *Columbia Mirror,* Nov. 12, 1857.

28. *Murfreesboro News,* Feb. 2, 1859.

29. Kate Carney Diary, Feb. 22, 1859, SHC.

30. *Columbia Beacon,* Jan. 15, 1847.

31. Shirley Ann Hickson, "The Development of Higher Education for Women in the Antebellum South," (Ph.D. diss., Univ. of South Carolina, 1985), 79. Hickson discovered that the time and effort trustees spend on property management was second only to their responsibilities for managing school finances, but she simply interprets this as part of the evidence that female colleges were intended to be permanent institutions. On the other hand, in her book *Alma Mater,* Helen Lefkowitz Horowitz offers thorough and insightful architectural analysis, but considers female colleges in isolation rather than in the context of a townscape. See *Alma Mater: Design and Experience in the Women's Colleges from Their Nineteenth-Century Beginnings to the 1930s* (New York: Knopf, 1985).

32. *Maury Press,* Mar. 7, 1860.

33. *Columbia Beacon,* Jan. 15, 1847.

34. *Maury Intelligencer,* Jan. 4, 1849.

35. *Maury Press,* Mar. 7, 1860.

# 16

*Shirley Teresa Wajda*

# The Commercial Photographic Parlor, 1839–1889

Anthropologists point out that architecture, broadly conceived, creates boundaries where they do not exist in nature, and that the resultant types of space depend on the culture and the time in which these spaces are created. Given this, architecture and space interact, or, rather, humans, space, and architecture interact, and it is this interaction that engages anthropologists in the search for clues to culture. Indeed, anthropologists as a matter of course believe that culture influences the use of space, which in turn influences architecture—a reversal of what tradition-minded architectural historians study as "big C" (i.e., high style) culture.[1]

Now, this is an obvious point, but one well worth asserting when we study that part of the built environment we commonly call *commercial*—shopping plazas and malls, urban business districts, strips, markets, bourses, exchanges, and the like. One would think that the study of commercial buildings has no place in vernacular ar-

chitecture, with its emphasis on the folk, the craft-built, the community origins of architectural style and building practice. Yet, what does the word *commercial* signify but exchange, communication, and social intercourse—the essential components of community? According to Dell Upton and John Michael Vlach, a high "intensity of social representation" characterizes those buildings we deem vernacular, and commercial buildings certainly meet this criterion.[2] Architectural historian Richard Longstreth has noted that, despite this breadth, the relationship of architecture to consumer culture has not been adequately analyzed. Seeking the "full value" of a given architectural style, Longstreth noted, requires the inclusion of commercial buildings as a comparative, contextualizing extension of the study of domestic dwellings, churches, meeting houses, and civic buildings that constitute the bulk of current scholarship.[3]

Because the purpose of a commercial building may change, and change rapidly, over its existence, people experience a given commercial space not necessarily as a whole nor as a type of architectural style, but in very specific ways related to market activities. Interior functions more often serve to define the building for its users. As Longstreth points out, a building's mass may be related more to lot configuration, and floor plans are often irrelevant due to constant alteration or merely to the fact that most buildings were constructed with open plans to be fitted for occupants.[4] Semipermanent architectural features therefore prove critical to our understanding of commercial spaces.[5]

We might suggest how these features "work" through a preliminary consideration of commercial spaces as experienced in one nineteenth-century incarnation: the American commercial photographic parlor. Before George Eastman perfected his Kodak system in 1888, which ushered in amateur photography, commercial daguerreotypists and photographers and their patrons had adopted an architectural code designating their aspirations and concomitant behaviors. Portrayal was first and foremost a business, and enterprising practitioners quickly converted bare rooms of commercial structures into inviting environments of contemplative repose.[6]

Although the parlor is most often associated with the domestic dwelling, the study of its commercial incarnation necessarily rests (if you'll pardon the pun) on slightly different premises: we must assess the roles of the producer and the consumer, the type of service or goods proffered by an establishment, and the constraints or benefits of location. Yet, because of the very nature of change inherent in commercial activities, extant physical evidence of photographic parlors is difficult to find. Nevertheless, we may be able to study them through other means. We can fruitfully utilize written and photographic evidence to construct a history of how photographic parlors as spaces were experienced by their temporary inhabitants. After all, capitalist consumer culture requires constant novelty to maintain itself; it must offer ready, quick lessons to potential consumers who must learn how to read novel and ever-changing cues to social behavior. These cues do not always have to be learned on site; rather, informative advertisements, testimonials, and word of mouth offer ancillary lessons in appropriate behavior and may approximate historical actors' understanding. The architectural design of a given space may not necessarily teach but need only remind temporary inhabitants of the appropriate rules of behavior; after all, individuals must negotiate many types of space in the course of a modern day. Architecture in this case serves as a mnemonic device to facilitate use and, in some instances, to assert power relations in a given society at a specific time.[7]

Such was the case of photographic parlors. Enterprising photographers, wishing to situate their nascent profession within the Romantic definition of genius (embodied in the Artist), sought elite status (if not always an elite clientele) through the employment of fashionable room embellishments and the stratification of space. As astute consumers themselves, these photographers utilized the material expressions of power to appeal to the socially eminent and to shore up their claims to emulative, if not equal, social status. Pierre Bourdieu's concept of a "structuring structure"—that which is both a medium and the resultant of social practices—is wholly applicable here, as semipermanent architectural elements of photographic parlors intimated to knowledgeable visitors expected behaviors, defined aberrant ones, and reinforced the genteel practices associated with literacy, the use of time, cleanliness, and hospitality.[8] In this sense, the photographic parlor, like its domestic counterpart, constituted what archaeologist Linda W. Donley-Reid has described as a "ranked space"—one which does not determine use, but one which aids in reifying and sustaining power relations through form and through formalized social performances.[9] Thus, an analysis of the commercial photographic establishment rehearses architectural appointments, technological improvements, and business practices. Although the basic physical character of this commercial space changed little, its lexical and social referents did. Known in the early 1840s as *rooms,* then generally as *galleries, parlors,* and *saloons* in the 1850s and 1860s, and finally as *art studios* by the 1870s and into the early years of the twentieth century, this commercial, "middle" space, not quite public but not private, tells us much about the relationship of class consciousness, consumption practices, and the power of architecture in the nineteenth century.[10]

The daguerreotype, introduced into the United States in 1839, was ill-suited to portraiture, but portraiture tellingly served as the mainstay of daguerreotypists.[11] The capricious process of daguerreotypy required bright sunlight, variable and lengthy exposures, and patient sitters. Although daguerreotype-manual authors overwhelmingly preferred expensive skylights, many early daguerreotypists set up their operating rooms in the great outdoors or on city rooftops or built glass houses. More often, upper-story rooms with sidelight windows, with a northern or northwestern exposure, were utilized. The word "DAGUERREOTYPES" painted on the side of a building or on an affixed signboard signaled that a building housed that service. Persons promenading on Broadway, the national center for commercial photography, or on Washington, D.C.'s "Photographers' Row" (Pennsylvania Avenue between Sixth and Seventh streets), could glance up at unfurled banners announcing establishments located in upper-story rooms.[12] Advertisements often located daguerreotypists' rooms in relation to ground-floor enterprises: one could find in 1850, for example, J. E. Martin's "Excelsior Rooms" over the Odd Fellows' Hall in Detroit, and the Daguerreian Galleries of Clark Brothers, & B. L. Higgins were located over the "Regulator," in the Franklin Building, in Syracuse. By at least 1844, and in increasing numbers afterward, enterprising daguerreotypists were combining with their operating rooms picture galleries and elaborately furnished and embellished reception rooms in which visitors could be accommodated while waiting. Such an addition was worthy of notice: The *Daguerreian Journal* noted with delight that Buffalo, New York, daguerreotypist McDonnell in the spring of 1851 had "fitted up a room adjoining his former place of business, with carpets, furniture, &c., as a 'show room,' around whose walls are pendant the portraits of many of our citizens." Because of the unreliability of the sun and of developing chemicals in the antebellum years, many daguerreotypists discouraged appointments and created waiting rooms to encourage a walk-in trade.[13]

Although more often considered an attribute of the domestic dwelling, the parlor appeared in commercial spaces. Enterprising daguerreotypists' establishments and later photographers' shops could vary greatly in size and quality of appointments, but the term *parlor* denoted a specific set of material and behavioral requirements. In both realms a division of manual from nonmanual, "handwork" and "head-work" tasks corresponded to the production of goods and the facilitation or practice of consumption.[14] The commercial parlor was thus the natural medium in which to introduce innovations to the consuming public. Indeed, the term *parlor* was employed to characterize those spaces that dealt with the comfort, care, and display of the consuming body. The new Gothic, Italianate, and bracketed styles accompanied at mid-century the bodily comforts provided by the latest heating, ventilation, and sanitation technologies. Pullman cars and steamship staterooms, employing new transportation technology softened by layers of textiles, trim, and spring seating, cosseted the better sort by means of beautiful surroundings and the personalized, expert care of liveried conductors, stewards, and porters, among others. Fashionable hotels, as opposed to the reviled "caravansaries" of travelers' reports, offered ladies' parlors fitted with comfortable chairs, worktables, and writing desks. Porters, bellmen, maitres d'hôtel, and other appropriate personnel attended to the personal care of hotel "guests." Even personal grooming became a genteel performance: middle-class men could seek out the upscale tonsorial parlor.[15]

Photographic parlors were no exception. Dodge's Daguerrean Gallery, like many others across the country, offered female visitors in Augusta, Georgia, a "tastefully furnished parlor, in which is an elegant piano, where they may beguile their time pleasantly, while friends whom they accompany, or others who are in advance of them, are sitting for their likenesses."[16] These entrepreneurs participated in the major cultural reform movement of the mid-nineteenth century, known to architectural historians as the Romantic Revival. The Romantic revelation and display of one's self through both performance and portraiture helped to define the possessive individualism at the core of genteel identity, an identity accessible through commercial means.[17]

Because urban photographic establishments were housed in the top floors of buildings, proprietors often advertised by displaying select specimens at ground-floor doorways. Thieves, however, are rarely genteel, and in 1850 Clark Brothers offered a five-dollar reward for the return of a full-size "View of a Gothic Cottage" stolen from their door at 551 Broadway.[18] Display cases or windows were quickly substituted to protect free-hanging specimens. The crowds who gathered around display cases could become visitors to the parlor and potential "candidates for portraiture" (i.e., candidates for proper social performance)[19] once they ascended the stairs. The function of the porch and the hall in defining appropriate domestic parlor occupants and behavior was performed by the street-level entrance and the set of stairs ascending to the photographic rooms. No servant

with a card tray could announce the visitor while ushering him in the parlor, nor could the words "not at home" be spoken to turn away an unwanted guest.[20] The stairways served to characterize the caliber of the establishment, yet, conversely, scenes describing stairway activities delineated the type of visitor to be expected at the photographer's door. "Upon the stairs is a deafening racket," wrote "Y.T.S." in the *Daguerreian Journal* in October 1851, presaging the appearance of an "Alabama planter and matron, with their tribe of little ungovernables," and requiring this Northern proprietor to watch carefully the accouterments of his reception room and to endure "cake-crumbs, nut-shells, and candy-papers . . . lavished at will upon [the] carpet."[21]

Those accouterments could dazzle and were advertised as appealing to persons of good taste. Matthew Brady's Broadway establishment in 1853, for example, advertised photographic specimens in street-level rosewood-and-gilt showcases. Up two easily ascended flights of stairs, patrons found through folding doors reception rooms carpeted with highly colored velvet tapestry, satin- and gold-papered walls, and a frescoed ceiling from which a "six-light gilt and enamelled chandelier" threw "enlivening colors in abundant profusion." Windows were draped in "costly needle worked lace" festooned with damask. Patrons could rest in "superb rosewood furniture,—tetes-a-tetes [*sic*], reception and easy-chairs, and marble-top tables, all of which are multiplied by mirrors from ceiling to floor."[22]

Philadelphia "heliographer" Marcus Aurelius Root suggested that "books sufficiently various to interest the majority" be supplied to patrons. "Such works, abundant in our day, might do much, both for staving off ennui and for awakening better moods." Tabletops should be covered with "an ample variety of the finest engravings, prints, &c., . . . together with curiosities of different kinds, more especially such as have classic, romantic, and historic associations connected with them—e.g., medals, coins, vases, urns. . . ." If the patron was still bored, he or she may be entertained by "several cages of singing-birds," which "tend to awaken emotions and call up recollections and associations which impart to the face an amiable, genial expression."[23] A beautifully appointed room's decor, in Romantic theory, naturally elicited beautiful thoughts in the minds of the inhabitants willing (or schooled) to accept this inculcation. These parlors shared a sensibility with the domestic counterparts—to effect a calming influence on and provide a restful haven for its enumerated inhabitants.[24] One European visitor noted the "peculiarities which characterize[d] American photographers": "their rooms . . . are palaces worthy of comparison with enchanted habitations. . . . Everything is here united to distract the mind of the visiter [sic] and give to his countenance an expression of calmness and benevolence. The manufacturer, the physician, the merchant, the politician even, here forgets his labors."[25]

By contrast, in his 1871 survey of several establishments, Hartford, Connecticut, photographer H. J. Rodgers found social distinctions declared through the type and use of space and quality of merchandise proffered. Intrigued by a sign advertising "twelve tin-types for twenty-five cents" over an entrance, he entered "as a matter of curiosity." He recalled, "I had not ascended more than six flights of stairs when I met great numbers and varieties of people coming down. . . . [A lady] hoped she would know enough next time to go where comfort, cleanliness and convenience were regarded. . . . I commenced feeling and winding my way through the dirty, dismal halls, and up squeaking, dilapidated stories till at last I came to the door."

Rodgers's six-story meander through a dark labyrinth foreshadowed (as we by now should know from the normative descriptions of genteel parlors) the appearance of an unacceptable establishment. Rodgers equated the "promiscuous crowd" there with the products they indiscrimi-

nately desired. Tintypes produced by cut-rate operators on street corners and in unkempt shops were cheaper than daguerreotypes and even photographs; no self-respecting person would, presumably, purchase these portrait types. "The scene which met my eye forcibly reminded me of a side-show at a circus, where they were passing them in and out," Rodgers exclaimed. This place, "a disgrace to the art," was "generally well patronized by the ignorant and illiterate." The lack of decorum in this tintype establishment was Rodgers's major concern. Revealingly, Rodgers in a visit to another lowly tintype room described observing (if not meeting) crowds only known by their crude physical features: "turn-up noses, bottle noses, long and crooked noses, ugly faces, large mouths, and blear-eyes," all of whom were devoid of "any respect for themselves, or regard for taste, beauty, and convenience."[26]

If worthy of the designation of parlor, a commercial establishment sought through material cues a clientele who would comport themselves with decorum. Much like the exacting practice of calling on friends, neighbors, and relatives codified in contemporary etiquette guides, consuming in commercial parlors required individuals to attend to rules of genteel performance. A commercial parlor celebrating "head-work" proposed—but could not guarantee—genteel society. As Root observed, "a single day may bring . . . a host of persons, comprising almost every type of organization: the ignorant and the stolid, the flippant and conceited, the fastidious, the difficult, &c."[27] Such traits were equally applicable to rich and poor, but Rodgers's observations dispute just whom Root had in mind. Americans of all social and economic strata sought their portrait photographs. Yet, reception rooms represented the proprietor as a host who selected his guests and reflected his own claim to genteel status—a status that, in the abstract, ignored class and physical differences. *Gleason's* took notice that Mr. Ball's choice of appointments for his establishment in Cincinnati reflected his care for the patron and commended that "enterprising proprietor" as "the very essence of politeness."[28] And a proprietor offered himself not only as a decorous and egalitarian host, but as an artist as well. As the *Photographic Art Journal* observed of Matthew Brady: "Brady is not an operator himself, a failing eyesight precluding the possibility of using the camera with any certainty, but he is an excellent artist nevertheless—understands his business so perfectly, and gathers around him the first talent to be found."[29] The photographer as artist and capitalist, as a steward and as an embodiment of Romantic sensibilities, offered the quintessential model of genteel behavior. No less important was the deportment of employees in contact with the patron. Manhattan photographer J. Gurney's operators and assistants "of both sexes" in his establishment at Fifth Avenue and Sixteenth Street were promoted as "gentlemen and ladies, dressed as such."[30]

Art work displayed in commercial parlors also fixed the meaning of photographic portrayal within canons of art and history. Art also implied customers who shared that knowledge and sensibility. Ball's Daguerrean Gallery of the West boasted a room twenty feet by forty feet, the walls "tastefully enamelled by flesh-colored paper, border with gold leaf and flowers." Noteworthy was the collection of ideal figures arrayed along panels on the south wall. These classical statues represented the goddesses of Poesy, Music, Science, Religion, and Purity. On the ceiling was a depiction of Venus, "sitting recumbent on a splendid throne," attended by the Three Graces: "Aylia holding a casket of jewels, from which Thalia is culling gems to deck her rich hair, while Euphronsuna holds a shining mirror before her." Hovering doves and adoring cupids surround the tableau. Eighty-seven specimens of Mr. Ball's work "ornamented" the north wall: "Babies and children, young men and maidens, mothers and sires look you in the face. Jenny Lind, with other distinguished personages, and five or six splendid views

of Niagara Falls are among the collection." These images were surmounted by "six of Duncanson's finest landscapes."[31] Galleries thus adorned provided the means for what anthropologist Mary Douglas has called a "naming" or "proving" strategy, by which the practice of consumption allows not only the proving of one's status through proper use of understanding or use of a good, but allows also for the "sharing [of] names that have been learned and graded." As Douglas concludes: "This is culture."[32]

This naming strategy, considered in its vulgar sense, could produce tragic consequences, assuring its success for social stratification. "I was over in your city the other day," "a Jerseyman" wrote to *Harper's* in 1858, "and I dropped in at a gallery of daguerreotypes":

> There I saw a picture, an Irish hod-carrier standing at the side of his hod, pipe in mouth. The poor fellow looked wearied enough with his toil, and I appreciated the fanciful title written underneath, "The Greek Slave By the Powers!"
>
> Just then a dandyfied [*sic*] fellow happened to spy it, and taking out his eye-glass, gave it a critical examination and drawled out, "Ah, yes! Greek Slave! Powers's Greek Slave: very fine, saw the original; very good copy this is; fine specimen of the art." And being perfectly satisfied that he had seen a copy of the Greek Slave, he walked on to study the next.[33]

Not only was the Irish hod-carrier ridiculed, portrayed while laboring (engaged in "hand-work"), rather than as the result of Romantic contemplation of the self through purposeful portrayal as genteel practice mandated (inherent in the patron-occasioned portrait), the image was misread by a social rube pretending to cosmopolitan knowledge. His unfitness as an authentic "parlor person" was revealed. Postbellum etiquette guides codified gallery behavior: "If you are visiting a picture gallery, or an artist's studio, do not meddle; make no loud comments; do not seek to show superior knowledge in matters of art by gratuitous criticism. If you are a connoisseur of art, you will seek modesty of expression; while if you are not, you will only give publicity to your ignorance."[34]

The photographic specimens displayed in galleries could beguile, but to cognoscenti they offered a continual means of testing for impostors. These images could reinforce the real and "imagined" communities constituted by the visitor and these "counterfeit presentiments." Brady, for example, advertised his establishment only to those who would appreciate the portraits suspended on the walls: "the Daguerreotypes of Presidents, Generals, Kings, Queens, Noblemen—and *more nobler men*—men and women of all nations and professions."[35] Visitors to photographic parlors possessed the leisure to avail themselves of the entertainment and education offered by the changing exhibition of photographic images. Through a familiar cosmopolitanism, they also reinforced their "people"-hood. The *Newark Journal* reported that the "Beautiful art galleries of Messrs. Thomas & Co." were "fast becoming a fashionable lounging place during the afternoons. A visit to this storehouse of photography will regard all lovers of the beautiful. Photographs of all sorts of people may be found there, from the prominent statesman to the most humble citizen."[36] Mr. Edsall's Manhattan reception rooms in 1889 were "filled with fine specimens of portraiture, among which many faces may be seen which are familiar to the residents of Harlem."[37] Photographic parlors provided "schools" for cosmopolitan knowledge.

The best clues to how photographic parlors worked are found in the constant attention to social performance within the space. The parlor's "spell" must be acknowledged through the correct negotiation of the parlor accouterments by the performer to prove that he or she is indeed part of the performance.[38] The intrepid Hartford photographer H. J. Rodgers condemned those among his own patrons who put their feet upon chairs, missed the spittoon, or left the door open in winter. One poor customer, "extremely black with dirt," wished fifty cents' worth of likenesses. After ruining toiletries set out for patrons, the bumptious young man attempted to sit for his portrait. "Coming up stairs he seats himself violently down in the operating chair, and leaning backward lost his equilibrium, and stove through a twenty-five dollar back ground, suddenly appearing behind the scenes, where in the photographic drama this class 'look well'"—that is, according to Rodgers, this unfortunate fellow should not have thought of posing for his likeness at all.[39] The individual in such a situation is usually not fully schooled nor forewarned of the details necessary for proper conduct.[40] Tragic consequences may be forgiven if the performer is a student; in this case, the well-meaning but dirty patron may have attended to his appearance, but his clumsiness—his failure to navigate properly the space—revealed his unfitness. By comparison, a gentleman could easily size up the social occasion and space and act accordingly, in an "easy, pleasant, home-like manner," protecting his claim to genteel status.[41]

Photographic parlors were not restricted to urban locations. Itinerant photographers were not exempt from the social necessity of a reception room. One "DAGUERREOTYPE SALOON, on wheels" was advertised for sale in *Humphrey's Journal* in 1851. The use of the word *saloon*, a permutation of the French *salon*, offers at least a hint that the interior was in part "genteel."[42] *Anthony's Photographic Bulletin* printed a cut of a portable photographic gallery in 1871, measuring thirty-six feet long and fifteen feet wide, with a display case of specimens hung at the door. Despite a weight of nearly three tons, it could be broken down into eight-foot-wide sections, and moved on flatbed railroad cars. The floor plans included a fourteen-by-fifteen-foot reception room.[43] Many "photographic boats" traveled western rivers at mid-century. Mr. John P. Doremus, a Paterson, New Jersey, photographer, built and maintained a gallery on a Mississippi River flatboat. "The boat is a little palace in itself," exclaimed *Anthony's Photographic Bulletin* in 1876. "The deck is 18 × 76 feet, on which there is a miniature house. Upon entering the inside of the boat one is ushered into the reception room, 8 × 16 feet, fitted up handsomely with marble-top table, water color and oil paintings, chromos, carved brackets, etc., showing taste and lavish expenditure."[44]

Competition helped to create these reception rooms. Parlors provided an especially effective strategy when cheap operators could produce likenesses that compared favorably to those produced by upscale photographers. The proof of Romantic consumption, never found solely in the goods, was to be found in the sensory and performative circumstances surrounding acquisition. The British photographer John Werge noted that, despite the bareness of cheap American daguerreotype "factories," the results he acquired were satisfactory, regardless of the fact that no one person attending him fit the artist ideal and that comfort and leisure were not proffered by the surroundings:

> I was shown into a waiting room crowded with people. The customers were seated on forms placed around the room, sidling their way to the entrance of the operating room, and answering the cry of 'the next' in much the same manner that people do at our public baths. . . . having had my number of "sittings," I was requested to leave the operating room by another door which opened into a passage that led me to the "delivery desk," where, in a few minutes, I got all my four portraits fitted in "matt, glass, and preserver,"—the pictures having been passed from the developing room to the "gilding" room, thence to the "fitting room" and "delivery desk," where I received them. Thus they were finished and carried away without the camera operator ever having seen them. Three of the four portraits were as fine Daguerreotypes as could be produced anywhere.[45]

That enterprising photographers would disparage these establishments by calling them "factories" reveals their own claims as artists who controlled each aspect of the creative process. Moreover, the term reveals the premium placed on the use of time and the treatment of the patron implied by the parlor. "Factory" does indeed describe these establishments, where the photographic process is based on a machine (the camera), is reduced to discernible steps, and takes on the appearance of an assembly line (the labor revealed in "hand-work"). Importantly, the patron fully participates in the work process, aware that he or she is merely one equal part of the activity. Parlors, on the other hand, offered a relaxing atmosphere in which the patron's time was to be used as he or she saw fit. Beyond posing in an operating room (later called a skylight room or studio), the patron was protected from the actual work of developing, printing, coloring, refinishing, burnishing, and framing a portrait daguerreotype or photograph.

Photographic establishments, like genteel houses, employed a front/back syntax, carving out public spaces (reception rooms and/or galleries), private spaces (in the form of a ladies' parlor or boudoir, and business offices), and production spaces (operating room and dark room, closets and storerooms).[46] Reception room visitors were protected from the actual production process. Kurtz's New York establishment, erected in 1874, was notable because it contained two stairways. The accessway, which reminded visitors of that in a "public institution" (defining—importantly—this commercial activity as "not public"), was contrasted with the "stairway especially provided for the employees": "by which ingress and egress from each of the apartments occupied by operatives from cellar to roof is secured without contact with the patrons. Certain doors, also, are to remain closed to all but the proprietor, thereby effectually preventing any intercourse."[47] Again, the divorcement of labor and leisure, "hand-work" and "head-work," is evident. Sociologist Erving Goffman has observed in particular the "sorting out" that occurs in commercial enterprises, pointing out that "it is expected that those who work backstage will achieve technical standards while those who work in the front regions will achieve expressive ones."[48]

Postbellum establishments, such as Kurtz's, often occupied entire buildings (effectuated by incandescent light) and not only replicated the front/back syntax of domestic dwellings, but also featured architectural elements which reflected an increasing desire for suburban locations and accompanying views. The notion of "homey-ness" was featured in the design of these street-level concerns. Harman & Verner, of Bay City, Michigan, constructed a fifteen-foot-wide show window in which more than photographic goods were displayed: "Opposite this there is a finely carved mantel, with a grate." The symbolic importance of a mantel and fireplace, the hearth of the house, evoked the comfort associated with domestic parlors.[49] And Kurtz's "New Art Gallery," located on Twenty-third Street across from Madison Park in Manhattan, possessed a suburban-like location, "facing as it does the shrubbery and lawn of the Park, overlooking which are the reception room and both of the glass rooms." The immense glass fronts made the building "unmistakably photographic," and provided for a spectacular view for patrons: "the light in all the principal apartments has a peculiarly soft and pleasing effect, increased by the verdure beyond, while constant streams of pedestrians and other moving objects give variety and animation."[50]

As a matter of fact, by the 1870s space was utilized more effectively to symbolize exclusivity, even to the point of uncertain legibility. The word *studio* was employed increasingly in the 1870s to signal photographers' adaptation of new theories of light and new technologies in photographic production. The partnership of Julius Ludovici and Thomas Lord in 1883 occupied a former

brownstone of a "wealthy broker," located at the corner of Twentieth Street and Fifth Avenue in New York City. That private dwelling had been converted "into one of those aristocratic marts for which New York's avenue of palaces is fast becoming noted." This establishment at first puzzled the visitor, being the most "unconventional place of business. . . . What struck us so strangely was the utter absence of anything outside or in to indicate even the existence of a photographer—neither word nor work of camera or brush was anywhere in view." Prepared to find the formulaic architectural clues of street-level showcase or display window, banners, or other signage, and a richly embellished parlor, the visitor was greeted with a "marble floor amply covered with persian rugs and tiger skins, and a stately, richly carved bench . . . in the hallway." An elevator, rather than stairways, conveyed visitors to the proprietors' "offices," indicated only by brass door plates. Even specimen photographs were scarce. "Not until we reached the approach to the office was there a picture to be seen, and but very few of them there." This apartment served as the reception room, and "negligently scattered" about were the "occasional portrait or view."[51] Overt merchandising was not necessary in what had been a private residence in an upscale neighborhood; yet, the fact that this private residence had been rehabilitated into a commercial space seems to have both charmed and confused the visitor. The parlor idea possessed a reassuring fixity for its knowing inhabitants—patrons and proprietors—and Ludovici and Lord's studio, while presenting a certain departure, still adhered to the expected physical attributes marking the parlor.

Did patrons actually understand the mnemonics of this commercial space? Our resources—diaries, letters, advertisements, travel accounts, etiquette guides, and periodicals—do not merely supply an objective "window" on the commercial photographic parlor—or any parlor. As Katherine

C. Grier has pointed out in her fine study of domestic parlors, *Culture and Comfort,* the means by which nineteenth-century consumers usually acquired information—mass-circulated periodicals and newspapers—were new and urban phenomena at mid-century. Thus, "public" parlors offered by hotels, steamships, railroads, and photographers constituted model rooms in which middle-class patrons could "try on" parlor living.[52] No doubt this was true for many Americans; travelers' accounts and diaries detail the excitement elicited by these spaces. Yet, these spaces were quickly elaborated in very specific ways by specialty journals and in popular magazines such as *Harper's* or *Gleason's* or *Godey's.* Although we would do well to heed Grier's astute observation that the vagaries of the early dissemination of information about parlors constitute a factor in interpretation, we need not dismiss print's instrumental role in teaching "parlor culture" to its readers. Print evidence is more than a window on a reality—it is part of that reality, framing it in critical ways. Acknowledging the parallel redaction of parlors in print and in commercial architecture impels the historian to explore in tandem these cultural practices.

This is all to say that, although we should heed the evidence at hand, we should equally seek what goes unstated or unenumerated by our informants; such muteness, like architecture in and of itself, supplies clues to understanding the "metapolitics" of commercial parlors.[53] It might seem difficult to believe that the camera in the hands of the professional photographer was not a democratic tool. Some were excluded from the experience. Yet, as historian of technology Langdon Winner observes, the power of technology and its objects resides not in the things themselves, but in the power structures in which they are created: "[O]ne must say that the technological deck has been stacked in advance to favor certain social interests and that some people were bound to receive a better hand than others."[54] Strategies of

ranking are evident in the use of the parlor, complicating our reading of the architectural elements of this commercial space. That popular literature, descriptive advertisements, and articles in professional and domestic journals offered rules for behavior along with detailed depictions of room furnishings should direct us not only to offer typologies of the physical structures, but correspondent typologies of mental structures as well. That the Englishman John Werge was surprised to find that a "factory" could produce as good a daguerreotype as a "parlor" does not devalue this point; rather, his assumptions about space and behavior argue for the power of "structuring structures" in a consumer society.

Mary Chesnut's characterization of her repeated visits to a Charleston, South Carolina, photographic parlor offers an example of reading mute evidence. That wealthy and prominent lady took the "cars" from Camden to Charleston, South Carolina, in 1861 to socialize with friends, confiding to her diary these activities. "We have a round table together," she penned in her diary on March 26, "Louisa Hamilton took me shopping. Then to Quinby's, bought 2 dozen cartes de visite of all the celebrities." She also confided: "I am to have my carte de visite made."

Two days later, Mary Chesnut again visited Quinby's photographic establishment: "Made Mr C[hesnut] dress & go with me—had his taken. Bought an album. Gen. Means gave me his. Met at the artist's rooms Hal Fraser & his sister, Mrs. Frederick Frazier, Mr. Manning & Gen. Simons. Mr. M. promised me his likeness. Saw there also Miss Susan Alston & her brother. Sally Rutledge walked up with me—& I met Mrs. Keitt, so affected and absurdly dressed."

On March 29, Mary Chesnut received her small photographic portrait, as did her husband his. "Mr. Chesnut very good—mine like a washer woman." Once again, Mary returned to Quinby's: "Mr. Manning took me to Quinby's—where I met Gov. Richardson & Col. Beaufort Watts & Hal

Fraser. Had a good time. Then we drove to Mrs. Izard's and talked art, &c. Saw pictures & all sorts of foreign things."[55]

Mary Chesnut repeatedly met individuals of repute and of acquaintance at Quinby's. Her visits to Quinby's were not only to sit for her likeness; she first bought an album and collected likenesses of her friends and purchased those of "celebrities." Yet, she also reinforced her social standing in other ways. She used a class-based reference ("like a washer woman," conveying physical and personal coarseness) to characterize her displeasure with her likeness. Simply, Mary Chesnut sought in her carte de visite a portrait fitting her status as a cultivated lady who could and did "talk art." And one is left to wonder just who she left out of her lists of persons met at Quinby's—no mention of slaves, servants, or strangers, not even a crowd.

One could easily make the case that Chesnut did not bother to list strangers—who would? Diaries served as registers of social interaction for future reference. No crowds of the unkempt or ignorant seem to have visited Quinby's. Photographic parlors offered a quasi-private space in which appropriate persons knew their place and performed genteel activities comfortably. Contemporary etiquette guides confirm that such behaviors were not to occur on the street—indeed, women were not to acknowledge men on the street—but within what was considered the private sphere, among social equals.[56] Indeed, a friend, not a servant, was twice sent on hapless errands to secure Mary Chesnut's unacceptable portraits.[57]

Technology in the form of the camera could make the portrait, traditionally the prerogative of the aristocrat or the celebrated, available to the many. Yet, the creation of the photographic parlor demarcated a new aristocrat—the genteel patron. Importantly, the parlor idea masked the very fact that photography was a mass medium, that the product itself was not unique, as a painting was; the parlor promoted, through physical cues, the photographer as an artist and protected patrons from the realization that they were purchasing a consumer good that many others could readily possess as well.[58] Anthropologists have observed that nonreligious rituals have become all the more necessary in the West because of the increasing number of strangers who engage in collective secular activities. Ritual provides a means to contain the drift of cultural meaning, and consumer goods are especially useful as ritual adjuncts in this attempt to fix meaning in the culture of consumption.[59] Early enterprising daguerreotypists and photographer, seeking—by helping to create—a genteel clientele, distanced themselves from cut-rate "cheap Johns" or "blue bosom operators"[60] by adopting marketing strategies (call them fashionable fictions) to tap the overwhelming desire to affirm social claims to bourgeois individualism through portraiture. It was not that anyone was denied one's portrait photograph in theory—indeed, parlorization occurred simultaneously on different, local levels and on cultural, natural ones as well, from the lowly itinerant saloon to the Broadway palaces—but enterprising photographers of all stripes employed material cues to expected behaviors, an invisible ink strategy to test successful "candidates for portraiture," to allow for and reward character-confirming conduct, and to ward off pretenders. Through this process, proprietors and patrons became conscious of a widely varying notion of class, as they themselves redacted, through architecture and through print, traditional aristocratic privilege. As historian David Waldstreicher has recently observed, there exists a "homology, or structural parallel, between rhetoric and ritual. . . . Rhetoric works like ritual in that it persuades through invocation of reliable, repeated movements. Ritual, like rhetoric, brings us into communion with the performer and the performance."[61] Class as an abstraction, as a fiction, is made visible through ritual (repeated architectural appointments creating a stage on which patrons perform) and through print (a performance of reading about the performance). Proprietors and patrons privatized spaces in decoration, in action, and in word in which the rituals of group affirmation and exclusion could be performed in the process of consuming. What constituted accepted behaviors and knowledge went unspoken. And only the irredeemably vulgar and rude (those "ignorant" found in "factories") were ignored or rejected. Those who affected gentility—those bumblers who enter the frame of these parlor stories—were considered at least to be possible future members of the respectable classes. It was difficult for the middle class, Richard Bushman observes, "not to shun those who failed to appreciate the beauties of parlor life. Without so intending, the unwonted consequence of the democratic movement to spread parlor culture was to draw an indelible line between the middle and lower classes in American society and to make rudeness a cause for shame."[62] This privatization—a physical withdrawal from the world that corresponded to a cultural privileging of certain emotions, sentiments, and tastes—distinguished an "us" from a "them"[63] and was celebrated and endorsed in ceremonial spaces such as commercial photographic parlors. Portrait photographs provided proofs of class inclusion. Mary Chesnut's "round table"—derived romantically from the mythical tale of King Arthur and his knights—was secure for those who believed it to be.

## Notes

1. See Susan Kent, ed., *Domestic Architecture and the Use of Space: An Interdisciplinary Cross-Cultural Study* (Cambridge and New York: Cambridge Univ. Press, 1990), especially "Activity Areas and Architecture: An Interdisciplinary View of the Relation between Use of Space and Domestic Built Environments," 1–8.

2. Dell Upton and John Michael Vlach, "Introduction," in *Common Places: Readings in American Vernacular Architecture,* ed. Dell Upton and John Michael Vlach (Athens: Univ. of Georgia Press, 1986), xvii. See also Sally McMurry, "Women in the American Vernacular Landscape," *Material Culture* 20 (1) (Spring 1989): 33–49, and, in contrast, Kingston Wm. Heath, "Defining the Nature of Vernacular," *Material Culture* 20 (2) (1988): 1–8.

3. Richard Longstreth, "Compositional Types in American Commercial Architecture," *Perspectives in Vernacular Architecture, II,* ed. Camille Wells (Columbia: Univ. of Missouri Press, 1986), 12.

4. Longstreth, "Compositional Types," 14.

5. Amos Rapoport, "Systems of Activities and Systems of Settings," in *Domestic Architecture and the Use of Space,* 9–20.

6. This essay is based on my Ph.D. dissertation, "'Social Currency': A Domestic History of the Portrait Photograph in the United States, 1839–1889," (Univ. of Pennsylvania, 1992), especially chap. 5, in which I explore the role of the portrait photograph as a consumer good in the first half century of photographic practice. For works on the history of photography in the United States and on consumption and consumerism, see notes below. For this essay, I consulted both professional photography journals and domestic periodicals for descriptions and images of photographic parlors. *Daguerreian Journal* (1850–51) became *Humphrey's Journal* in 1852, and remained in publication until 1870. I then analyzed *Anthony's Photographic Bulletin,* which began publication in 1870 and continued into the early years of the twentieth century. I also consulted *Godey's Lady's Book, Gleason's Drawing-Room Companion,* and *Harper's New Monthly Magazine.*

7. These are Rapoport's assertions. See "Systems of Activities." See also Dell Upton, "The Preconditions for a Performance Theory of Architecture," in *American Material Culture and Folklife: A Prologue and a Dialogue,* ed. Simon J. Bronner (Ann Arbor: UMI Research Press, 1985), 182–85.

8. Linda W. Donley-Reid, "A Structuring Structure: The Swahili House," in *Domestic Architecture and the Use of Space,* 114–26.

9. Ibid., 115.

10. On "flight-and-pursuit" consumption, consult Grant McCracken, *Culture and Consumption: New Approaches to the Symbolic Character of Consumer Goods and Activities* (Bloomington and Indianapolis: Indiana Univ. Press, 1989). This process, I argue, is reflected in the many terms employed to demarcate this commercial space based on the activity of photographic portrayal. *Gallery* may seem more appropriate than *parlor,* but *gallery,* most often employed by proprietors in

their enterprises, describes in this instance the collection of specimens worth showing, with the hand of the artist—the proprietor's name—ensuring quality. The reception rooms—*parlors*—were seen as a separate but related entity. See discussion about "public" parlors and parlor culture, below.

11. General histories of photography relating the technological, artistic, and entrepreneurial aspects of early commercial photography include Beaumont Newhall, *The History of Photography from 1839 to the Present Day,* 5th ed. (New York: Museum of Modern Art, 1982); Helmut Gernsheim and Alison Gernsheim, *The History of Photography from the Camera Obscura to the Beginning of the Modern Era* (New York: McGraw-Hill, 1969); Floyd Rinhart and Marion Rinhart, *American Daguerrian Art* (New York: Clarkson N. Potter, Inc., 1967); Rinhart and Rinhart, *The American Daguerreotype* (Athens: Univ. of Georgia Press, 1981); and Reese Jenkins, *Images and Enterprise: Technology and the American Photographic Industry 1839 to 1925* (Baltimore: Johns Hopkins Univ. Press, 1975). Robert Taft, *Photography and the American Scene: A Social History, 1839–1889* (1938; reprint, New York: Dover Publications, 1964); Alan Thomas, *Time in a Frame: Photography and the Nineteenth-Century Mind* (New York: Schocken Books, 1977); and Richard Rudisill, *Mirror Image: The Influence of the Daguerreotype on American Society* (Albuquerque: Univ. of New Mexico Press, 1971) consider the cultural meanings of photographic images.

12. Beaumont Newhall, in *The Daguerreotype in America,* 3d rev. ed. (New York: Dover Publications, 1976), concludes in his chapter "The Broadway Galleries" that the sun dictated the necessity for a gallery; fashionable promenaders would seek speedy sittings elsewhere (55–56). Washington's "Photographers' Row" is discussed in Laurie A. Baty, "On the Trail of Nahum S. Bennett (ca. 1816–?)," in *The Daguerreian Annual 1990,* ed. Peter E. Palmquist (Eureka, Calif.: The Daguerreian Society, 1990), 25–28.

13. Martin's rooms advertised in *Daguerreian Journal* 1 (2) (Nov. 15, 1850): 61; Clark Brothers, and B. L. Higgins in ibid., 62; "McDonnell," *Daguerreian Journal* 1 (11) (Apr. 15, 1851): 339. See also "Our Daguerreotypes," *Daguerreian Journal* 1 (8) (Jan. 1, 1851): 114, for a celebration of the St. Louis daguerreotypist Fitzgibbon's newly fitted rooms. Such notice was standard even later in the century. See, for ex-

ample, "Newly Fitted Galleries," *Anthony's Photographic Bulletin* 6 (Aug. 1875): 253.

14. On "hand-work" and "head-work," see Stuart M. Blumin, *The Emergence of the Middle Class: Social Experience in the American City, 1760–1900* (Cambridge: Cambridge Univ. Press, 1989), and Paul E. Johnson, *A Shopkeeper's Millennium: Society and Revivals in Rochester, New York, 1815–1837* (New York: Hill and Wang, 1978).

15. On parlors, see Katherine C. Grier, *Culture and Comfort: People, Parlors and Upholstery 1850–1910* (Amherst and Rochester: Univ. of Massachusetts Press and the Margaret Woodbury Strong Museum, 1989). On the evolution of domestic space and room designation, consult Abbott Lowell Cummings, *Rural Household Inventories, Establishing the Name, Uses and Furnishings of Rooms in Colonial New England* (Boston: Society for the Preservation of New England Antiquities, 1964); Dell Upton, "Vernacular Domestic Architecture in Eighteenth-Century Virginia," *Winterthur Portfolio* 17 (2/3) (1982): 95–120; Clifford E. Clark Jr., *The American Family Home 1800–1960* (Chapel Hill: Univ. of North Carolina Press, 1986).

16. "Dodge's Daguerreian Gallery," *Daguerreian Journal* 1 (11) (Apr. 15, 1851): 339.

17. See, of course, Clifford E. Clark Jr., "Domestic Architecture as an Index to Social History: The Romantic Revival and the Cult of Domesticity in America, 1840–1870," *Journal of Interdisciplinary History* 7 (1) (1976): 33–56, and A. J. Downing, *The Architecture of Country Houses* (New York: D. Appleton and Co., reprint, New York, Dover Publications, 1969). On the Romantic and consumerism, see Colin Campbell, *The Romantic Ethic and the Rise of Modern Consumerism* (London: Basil Blackwell, 1987).

18. Clark Brothers advertisement, *Daguerreian Journal* 1 (1) (Nov. 1, 1850): 27. See also thefts from Gurney, *Daguerreian Journal* 2 (1) (May 15, 1851): 19, 28; and Lawrence, *Daguerreian Journal* 1 (7) (Feb. 15, 1851): 212.

19. The term "candidates for portraiture" is Oliver Wendell Holmes's. See his "Doings of the Sunbeam," *Atlantic Monthly* 12 (6) (July 1863): 8.

20. On domestic rituals and the uses of space, see Kenneth L. Ames, "Meaning in Artifacts: Hall Furnishings in Victorian America," *Journal of Interdisciplinary History* 9 (1) (Summer 1978): 19–46; John F. Kasson, *Rudeness and Civility: Manners in Nineteenth-Century America* (New York: Hill and Wang, 1990); Karen

Halttunen, *Confidence Men and Painted Women: A Study in Middle-Class Culture, 1830–1870* (New Haven: Yale Univ. Press, 1982).

21. "Y.T.S.," "Life in the Daguerreotype. No. 1. The Reception Room," *Daguerreian Journal* 2 (10) (Oct. 1, 1851): 310.

22 "Brady's Daguerreotype Establishment," *Humphrey's Journal* 5 (5) (June 15, 1853): 73–74. Compare "M. M. Lawrence's New Heliographic Establishment, 381 Broadway," *Humphrey's Journal* 5 (1) (Apr. 15, 1853): 10–11, and "Daguerreotype Galleries of Meade Brothers," *Gleason's Drawing-Room Companion* 4 (1853): 21.

23. Hence "watch the birdie." Marcus Aurelius Root, *The Camera and the Pencil; or the Heliographic Art* (Philadelphia: M. A. Root, 1864), 47–48. See also Henry H. Snelling, *The History and Practice of the Art of Photography* (New York: G. P. Putnam, 1849; facsimile reprint, Hastings-on-Hudson, N.Y.: Morgan and Morgan, 1970).

24. See Grier, *Culture and Comfort*, 5, 46, for a discussion of the "domestic environmentalism" of the parlor.

25. "Daguerreotyping in New York," *Daguerrean Journal* 3 (1) (Nov. 15, 1851): 19, reprinted from *La Lumiére*.

26. H. J. Rodgers, *Twenty-three Years Under a Sky-Light; or Life and Experiences of a Photographer* (Hartford, Conn.: H. J. Rodgers, Publisher, 1872) 213–14; 219. Similar stories may be found: "Bobbing Around, or Visiting Galleries. By a Rambler," *Anthony's Photographic Bulletin* 2 (Nov. 1871): 400–402; and "Wounded in the Heart and Pocket," *Humphrey's Journal* 4 (16) (Dec. 1, 1852): 252–53.

27. Root, *The Camera and the Pencil*, 38.

28. "Daguerrean Gallery of the West," *Gleason's Drawing-Room Companion* 6 (3) (Apr. 1, 1854): 208. The cultural power of gentility—in that it was perceived as "natural" behavior—is discussed in Pierre Bourdieu, *Distinction: A Social Critique of the Judgement of Taste,* trans. Richard Nice (Cambridge: Harvard Univ. Press, 1984). See especially 100.

29. *Photographic Art Journal* 7 (1854): 103.

30. "Gurney's Gallery," *Humphrey's Journal* 20 (26) (Nov. 1, 1869): 412. This establishment boasted twenty-six rooms.

31. "Daguerrean Gallery of the West." Both the proprietor James M. Ball and his employee Robert S. Duncanson were African American. On Ball, see Valerie Hollins Coar, *A Century of Black Photogra-*

*phers, 1840–1940* (Providence: Rhode Island School of Design, 1983), 10; Deborah Willis-Thomas, *Black Photographers 1840–1940: A Bio-Bibliography* (New York: Garland Press, 1987); David S. Lubin explores Duncanson and his work in *Picturing a Nation: Art and Social Change in Nineteenth-Century America* (New Haven: Yale Univ. Press, 1994).

32. Mary Douglas and Baron Isherwood, *The World of Goods: Towards an Anthropology of Consumption* (New York: Basic Books, 1979), especially 75–76; McCracken, *Culture and Consumption,* 34, considers this an "invisible ink strategy" to cast out pretenders.

33. "Editor's Drawer," *Harper's New Monthly Magazine* 17 (99) (Aug. 1858): 425. Of course, this humorous story could be apocryphal, but its moral worth lies within the humor elicited by boundaries broached and broken.

34. Prof. Walter R. Houghton, A.M., et al., *American Etiquette and Rules of Politeness* (Indianapolis: A. E. Davis, 1882), 124–25.

35. "Brady's Daguerreotype Establishment," 73–74. Emphasis in the original. I am playing, of course, with Benedict Anderson's term in his study of modern nationalism, *Imagined Communities,* 2d ed. (London: Verso, 1994). Ronald J. Zboray has explored the role of technology in increased antebellum book production and dissemination as related to the changes in writing and reading in the United States, finding that in the shift from letter to novel, "identity itself blurred into fictional types. . . . This 'fictive people' through the exchange of correspondence, periodicals, and books, saw the world of print itself become a surrogate for community on a national scale." See *A Fictive People: Antebellum Economic Development and the American Reading Public* (New York: Oxford Univ. Press, 1993), 121.

36. "A Popular Art Gallery," *Anthony's Photographic Bulletin* 16 (11) (June 13, 1885): 351.

37. "Views Caught With a Drop Shutter," *Anthony's Photographic Bulletin* 20 (24) (Dec. 28, 1889): 768. Edsall had added to his former parlor, expanding to 246 and 248 West 125th Street in New York City.

38. Sociologist Erving Goffman has noted that the physical attributes of a space become associated within the space. Along with the performers, the "decorations and permanent fixtures" of a given space "tend to fix a kind of spell over it." See *The Presentation of Self in Everyday Life* (Garden City, N.Y.: Doubleday, 1959), 124.

39. Rodgers, *Twenty-three Years Under a Sky-Light,* 151–52. Women's behaviors in reception rooms were

not discussed by Rodgers; presumably, women by their very natures knew how to behave in such spaces. His use of dialect in the work displays ethnocentric bias. Cleanliness indicated moral rectitude in nineteenth-century America. See Richard L. Bushman and Claudia L. Bushman, "The Early History of Cleanliness in America," *Journal of American History* 75 (4) (Mar. 1989): 1213–38.

40. Goffman, *Presentation of Self in Everyday Life,* 73.

41. Rodgers, *Twenty-three Years Under a Sky-Light,* 152.

42. Advertisement, *Daguerrean Journal* 1 (11) (Apr. 15, 1851): 349.

43. "A New Portable Gallery," *Anthony's Photographic Bulletin* 2 (Aug. 1871): 213.

44. E. I. Stewart, "Photography Afloat" (letter to the editor, Clarksville, Mo., Nov. 15, 1875), *Anthony's Photographic Bulletin* 7 (Jan. 1876): 27. See also "Art Afloat—How a New Jersey man is to 'Do' the Mississippi Valley," *Anthony's Photographic Bulletin* 5 (Sept. 1874): 345–46, reprinted from *St. Paul News.*

45. John Werge, *The Photographic News,* Apr. 13, 1866, 172.

46. Halttunen discusses the use of a spatial front-back syntax in the nineteenth-century domestic parlor in *Confidence Men and Painted Women,* 104–5.

47. "Mr. Kurtz New Art Gallery," *Anthony's Photographic Bulletin* 5 (Apr. 1874): 151.

48. Goffman, *Presentation of Self in Everyday Life,* 122.

49. "Views Caught With a Drop Shutter," *Anthony's Photographic Bulletin* 21 (10) (May 24, 1890): 320. On the symbol of the hearth, see Clark, *American Family Home,* 114–16. For other postbellum parlors, see "A Photographic Palace (North & Oswald)," *Anthony's Photographic Bulletin* 7 (June 1876): 182–83 (reprinted from *Toledo Blade*).

50. "Mr. Kurtz New Art Gallery," 151.

51. "Ludovici's Photographic and Crayon Studios," *Anthony's Photographic Bulletin* 14 (Sept. 1883): 312–13. See also "Another Step Forward," *Anthony's Photographic Bulletin* 14 (June 1883): 176 (on Klauber of Louisville, Kentucky); and "Mr. Fitz Guerin's New Establishment," *Anthony's Photographic Bulletin* 14 (Mar. 1883): 80.

52. Grier, *Culture and Comfort,* 19–20.

53. "Metapolitics" as it relates to the individual and cultural nationalism is discussed in Michael Warner, *Letters of the Republic: Publication and the Public Sphere in Eighteenth-Century America* (Cambridge: Harvard Univ. Press, 1990).

54. Langdon Winner, "Do Artifacts Have Politics?" in *The Whale and the Reactor: A Search for Limits in an Age of High Technology* (Chicago and London: Univ. of Chicago Press, 1986), 19–39.

55. C. Vann Woodward and Elizabeth Muhlenfeld, eds., *The Private Mary Chesnut: The Unpublished Civil War Diaries* (New York: Oxford Univ. Press), 47–53.

56. Kasson, *Rudeness and Civility,* and Lawrence W. Levine, *Highbrow/Lowbrow: The Emergence of Cultural Hierarchy in America* (Cambridge: Harvard Univ. Press, 1988). For a discussion of the relationship between late-nineteenth-century etiquette and fiction, see Guy Szuberla, "Ladies, Gentlemen, Flirts, Mashers, Snoozers, and the Breaking of Etiquette's Code," *Prospects: An Annual of American Culture Studies,* 15, ed. Jack Salzman (New York: Cambridge Univ. Press, 1990): 169–96.

57. Woodward and Muhlenfeld, *The Private Mary Chesnut,* 52–53.

58. Sarah Burns finds a similar relationship between artists' studios and department stores. See her "The Price of Beauty: Art, Commerce, and the Late Nineteenth-Century American Studio Interior," in *American Iconology: New Approaches to Nineteenth-Century Art and Literature,* ed. David C. Miller (New Haven: Yale Univ. Press, 1993), 209–38.

59. Sally F. Moore and Barbara G. Meyerhoff, "Introduction: Secular Ritual: Forms and Meaning," in *Secular Ritual,* ed. Moore and Meyerhoff (Amsterdam: Van Gorcum, Assen, 1977), especially 3–4.

60. "Blue bosom operators" refers to the rapidity of exposing the plate: the white shirt fronts of the sitters were rendered bluish in the finished plate, evidence of an assembly line–style photographic enterprise.

61. David Waldstreicher, "Rites of Rebellion, Rites of Assent: Celebrations, Print Culture, and the Origins of American Nationalism," *Journal of American History* 82 (1) (June 1995): 49.

62. Richard L. Bushman, *The Refinement of America: Persons, Houses, Cities* (New York: Knopf, 1992), 279.

63. I borrow this from Raymond Williams, *Keywords: A Vocabulary of Culture and Society,* rev. ed. (New York: Oxford Univ. Press, 1983), see "Private," 242–43.

## CHAPTER 17

*Janet Ore*

# Jud Yoho, "the Bungalow Craftsman," and the Development of Seattle Suburbs

In the early twentieth century, domestic landscapes in the United States underwent a dramatic change. No longer did Victorian houses dominate new neighborhoods. Instead, low, unpretentious bungalows lined America's streets. In explaining this transformation, architectural historians generally maintain that architectural reforms that originated in planned, professionally designed suburbs somehow filtered down through society.[1] But such communities constituted only a minor part of the urban landscape. Their influence can only partially explain the vast neighborhoods of ordinary builder-produced bungalows that characterized urban landscapes.

The common houses of early-twentieth-century suburbs represented more than the influence of a reform-minded upper class. They were symbols of America's transition to a modern consumer economy and culture. After 1900, as the nation shifted from a producer to a consumer economy based on mass-produced goods and services, cultural values changed as well. Consumption-oriented concepts of self-gratification, leisure, and debt gradually overtook nineteenth-century ideals of hard work, thrift, and self-denial. As artifacts of this cultural reorientation, bungalows reveal how consumption and its values reached deeper into the populace, beyond the wealthy, drawing new groups into a twentieth-century consumer economy and society. Thus, the bungalow landscape was more a landscape of consumption than a landscape shaped by domestic reforms or design principles.[2]

In ordinary bungalow neighborhoods, salespeople, not professional architects or planners, exerted a major influence on the built environment. Small businesspeople who actively dabbled in all phases of building sought out new buyers, helping to create an expanded market for houses. These agents designed, constructed, and sold small houses that addressed the needs and concerns of people with only moderate means. Through modern advertising methods and installment purchasing, building entrepreneurs ushered median-income families into a twentieth-century consumer society. Unlike developers of elite, planned suburbs, small housing dealers did not place a high value on Arts and Crafts–inspired naturalism or the community control of architectural and neighborhood form. Instead, housing sellers articulated a suburban ideal that appealed to the desire for technological efficiency and family independence.

Seattle's Jud Yoho was the epitome of the ambitious housing entrepreneur who promoted the consumption of houses (fig. 17.1). Yoho typified a large group of businesspeople who helped create the city's extensive early-twentieth-century suburbs. Like most of Seattle's smaller dealers, Yoho performed a variety of functions, acting as real estate broker, contractor, and designer. Working outside of professional organizations, he prided himself in his "modern" business outlook. Although he billed himself as Seattle's spokesman for the Craftsman bungalow movement, Yoho was no idealistic housing reformer intent on moral reform. Rather, he was the quintessential self-promoter, capitalizing on the "bungalow craze" to increase his profits. He wanted, as he said, "every bungalow built from my plans to prove a lasting advertisement" for his firm. To Yoho, Craftsman bungalows were products to be sold, not symbols of a reform impulse associated with a larger Craftsman movement.[3]

Although he sometimes called himself an architect, Yoho had no professional training in design. He was, in fact, a shrewd and flamboyant businessman who gained his knowledge through practical experience. Yoho learned the art of selling from his father, John Yoho, a restless man with little or no formal education who aspired to the dream of entrepreneurial success. After years of moving throughout the American West, John

Fig. 17.1. Jud Yoho, c. 1913. Courtesy of the Seattle Public Library.

and his family settled in Seattle around 1896, drawn by business opportunities from the city's Klondike gold rush boom. John soon established an office selling mines and real estate. As a teenager, Jud worked in his father's Seattle real estate office for several years, surely imbibing the ethic of opportunistic salesmanship. Then in 1906, Jud, only twenty-three years old, opened his own real estate and insurance business. Like his father, Jud took advantage of another period of economic expansion, this time the city's massive 1906 building boom. At first he sold real estate, insurance, and even furniture, further honing his skills. By 1911, Yoho had branched into constructing "cottages" on speculation in the growing Wallingford district of Seattle. From his upbringing, Yoho knew how to profit when economic opportunity presented itself.[4]

Smart salesman that he was, Yoho cleverly discerned how to tap into contemporary housing trends. After the 1907 depression, Yoho made a series of marketing changes that coincided with a surge of interest in California bungalows. In 1911, he and two associates incorporated the Craftsman Bungalow Company and he began calling his houses "bungalows" instead of "modern cottages." As a showcase, he erected a model bungalow in Wallingford where he moved with his wife, Elsie, and son John in 1911 (fig. 17.2). Understanding that the Craftsman fad would help him sell houses, Yoho astutely included the Craftsman image in his advertising schemes.[5]

Yoho and others like him conducted their business in a climate of fierce competition. After 1901, Seattle experienced growth, especially in residential construction, "of the 'mushroom' order. . . . Here and there and everywhere," the *Seattle Post-Intelligencer* stated in 1904, "new residences and homes are going up like magic." Such rapid expansion attracted myriad construction-industry operators—contractors, architects, and real estate dealers. The wealthier and more powerful members of these fields attempted to quash their smaller but threatening competitors by professionalizing into associations and pushing for licensing laws.[6]

Despite such regulatory efforts, ambitious small dealers like Yoho worked to win a portion of Seattle's housing market by widening the group able to participate in home ownership. They focused their attention on people of moderate means—the largest group demanding housing and one usually ignored by professional architects and large contracting firms. Yoho realized that to extend the housing market to these people, he needed to develop new ways to reach the public and induce them to buy. Being primarily a businessman, Yoho and others like him utilized "modern" selling techniques to encourage more people to purchase homes.[7]

One selling innovation Yoho used to attract people of moderate means was the stock plan sold through a plan book. Yoho was one of Seattle's most prolific plan book purveyors. In 1911 he issued his first "booklet" on bungalows with new or updated editions in 1913, 1915, 1917, 1920, and 1921. From these, customers could purchase a complete set of plans and specifications for bungalows. Calling himself "The Bungalow Craftsman," Yoho implied he had some sort of specialized training in design. In the 1913 "edition de luxe," he stated that "the designing of an artistic bungalow of the true type requires as much skill and education as does any other branch of the architect's work. The man with the experience and training is the one to give you the best results. All of the designs in this book are bungalows pure and simple. Most of them are my own ideas."[8]

Yoho, however, obviously borrowed many of his plans directly from other sources. Numerous photographs included bungalows with palm trees, a plant suited to California but not Washington (fig. 17.3). The backgrounds in these photographs were suspiciously blanked out. Historian Rob Anglin found that the "Bungalow Which was Awarded the Prize" in Yoho's plan

Fig. 17.2. Yoho's Home at 4718 2nd Avenue NE, Seattle. Featured in *The Bungalow Magazine*, July 1913. Courtesy of the Seattle Public Library.

book was actually a slightly altered version of architect Arthur S. Heineman's 1909 California house (fig. 17.4).[9]

By liberal use of the term "craftsman," Yoho hoped to gain attention for his products and services through association with the Arts and Crafts movement and Gustav Stickley's popular magazine and furniture line. But rather than espousing the handicraft ethic promoted in the *Craftsman Magazine,* Yoho merely co-opted it for commercial purposes. This was most graphically shown in the formation of the Take Down Manufacturing Company in 1915 by Yoho, his wife, Elsie, and Ralph and Loraine Casey. The new firm got started by issuing a booklet entitled "Craftsman Master Built Homes" (fig. 17.5). The houses depicted were not,

as the title implied, bungalows erected by master carpenters, but instead were prefabricated "portable" houses. For as little as $300 to $450, families could order small dwellings in panelized sections that, the proprietors claimed, could be "erected by any one by following our simple directions without it being necessary to hire skilled labor" (fig. 17.6). According to the company, "Craftsman Master Built" actually meant a "method of construction" in which houses were factory produced, eliminating expensive hand work. "We have learned from experience," the owners stated, "that power driven machines can do better work at a lower cost than hand labor. This has resulted in a factory equipment that does every bit of the work with the most modern machin-

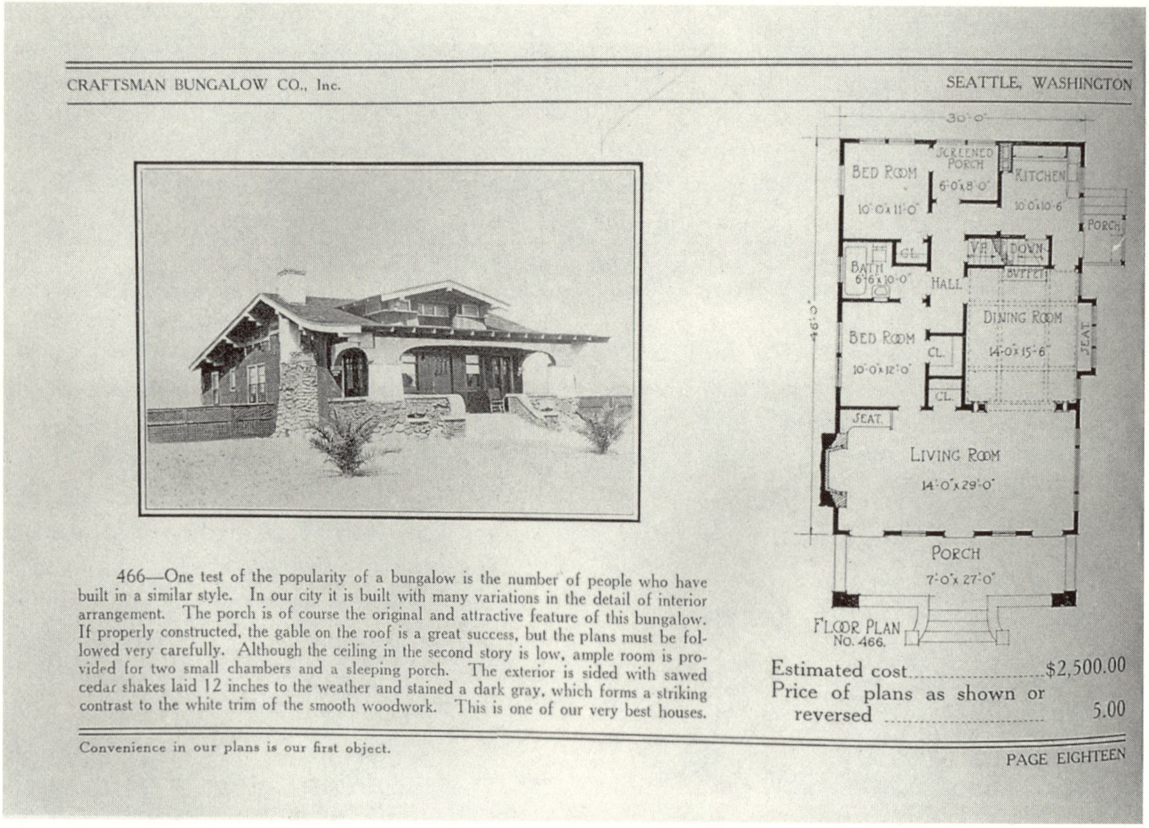

Fig. 17.3. An Illustration from Yoho's 1913 Plan Book. The plan appears to be doctored. Note the palm trees. Courtesy of the Seattle Public Library.

CRAFTSMAN BUNGALOW CO., Inc.                                    SEATTLE, WASHINGTON

BED ROOM
10'-0"x10'-6"

BED ROOM
10'-6'x12'-0"

PORCH
6'6'x7'6

CLOSET

CLOSET

HALL

BATH
6'-6'x8'-0"

KITCHEN
12'-0"x12'-0"

BUFFET

DINING ROOM
12'-0"x14'-0"

LIVING ROOM
14'-0"x16'-0"

PORCH
13'-0"x16'-0"

FLOOR PLAN
No. 418

Estimated cost...................$2,400.00
Price of plans as shown or
reversed ............................ 5.00

Houses are built to live in as well as to look at.

418—This bungalow is the house shown on the front cover of this book. It is a perfect example of bungalow architecture, and has proved to be one of the most popular styles ever designed. The unique feature of the exterior is the introduction of cobblestones for the massive porch columns. The well-proportioned roof and wide overhanging eaves lend an individuality to this design that has met with favor in every part of the United States. The siding used should be rough from the saw and stained a golden brown to complete the scheme. The principal rooms of this house are models of convenience and comfort. The dining room has beam ceiling and panel walls, with a large built-in buffet. The bed room arrangement is good and affords ample closet space. This house will be a continual delight to a lover of a good home.

PAGE TWENTY-ONE

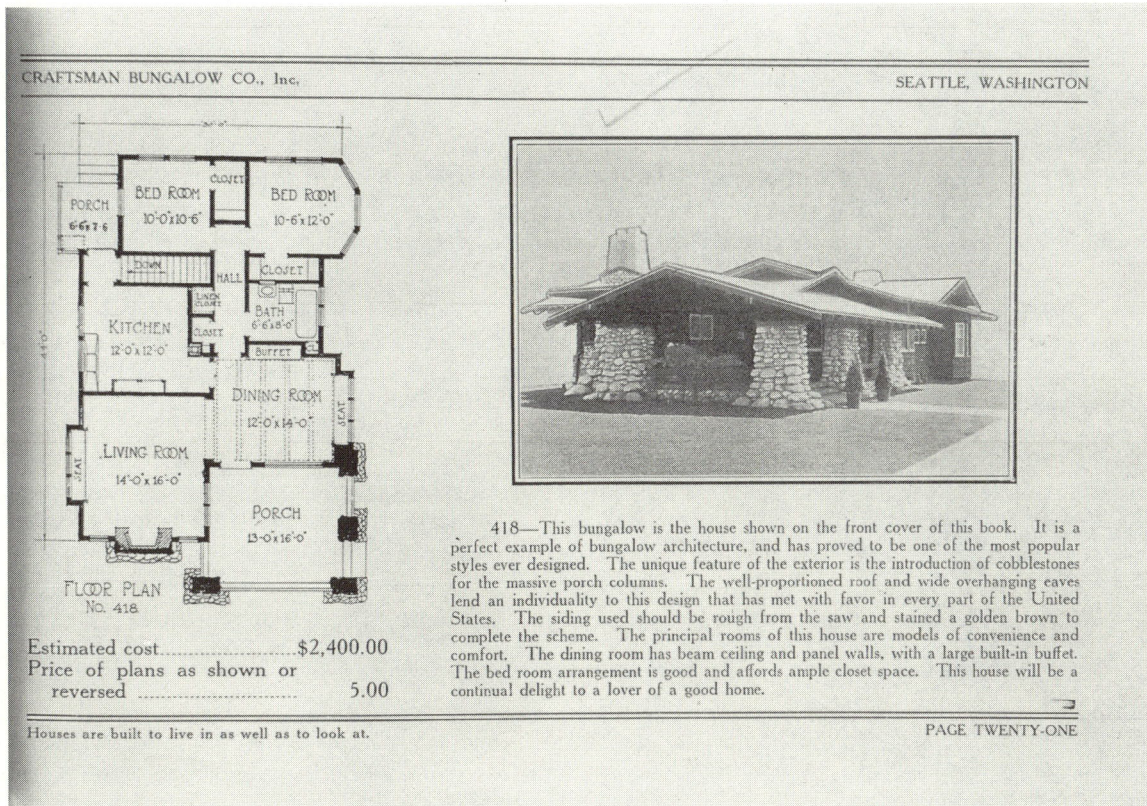

Fig. 17.4. Yoho's "Bungalow Which was Awarded the Prize." Depicted in his 1913 plan book. Courtesy of the Seattle Public Library.

ery." Yoho and his partners thus successfully converted William Morris's original glorification of the traditional craftsman into a marketing slogan for factory-made houses. They took symbolism that began as a critique of industrial capitalism and used it to support, and even extend, a modern economy based on mass production and consumption. In this sense, Yoho's advertising strategy hastened a disintegration of the essential meaning of the Craftsman ideology.[10]

Magazines were another tool that entrepreneurs like Yoho used to spread consumption of their products and services. Capitalizing on the Arts and Crafts momentum and the simultaneous explosion in residential construction, Yoho helped establish *The Bungalow Magazine,* a glossy monthly that basically served as promotional advertising. Briefly published in Los Angeles between 1909 and 1910, the journal moved to Seattle in 1912 under the ownership of the Bungalow Publishing Company, which Jud Yoho headed. In format, the periodical was similar to Stickley's *Craftsman* magazine. Well-illustrated with photographs, it mostly featured Seattle bungalows and articles about California residences, many lifted directly from the *Craftsman*. With these came recommendations for interior decorating, built-in furniture, landscaping, and technical systems appropriate to bungalows. Each month's issue included a supplement that consisted of complete plans, elevations, and a materials list for a specific bungalow (fig. 17.7). Unlike Stickley's

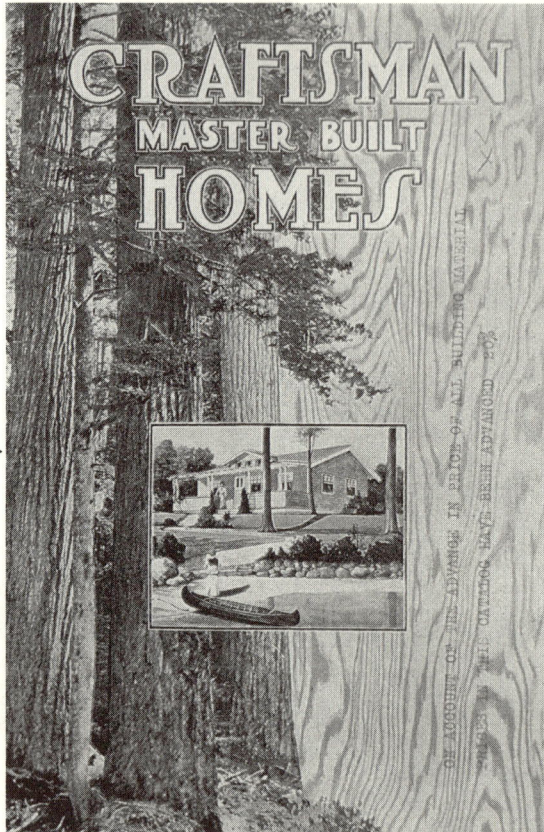

Fig. 17.5. Cover of the Take Down Manufacturing Co.'s Plan Book. Note the naturalistic setting. Courtesy of the Seattle Public Library.

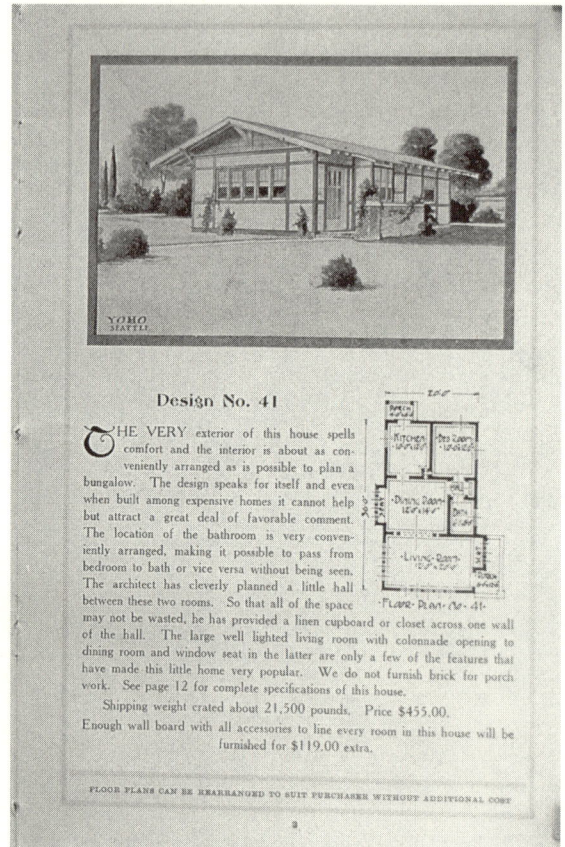

Fig. 17.6. Rendering and Plan for a "Portable House." From the Take Down Manufacturing Co.'s plan book. Courtesy of the Seattle Public Library.

*Craftsman, The Bungalow Magazine* omitted articles about the broader ideology of the Arts and Crafts movement. It never, for instance, included editorials promoting social reform or lauding William Morris's socialism or his glorification of the master craftsman. The Seattle journal merely advocated the pleasures of bungalow living and sought to acquaint the buying public with the sellers of bungalows.[11]

While calling itself "an illustrated monthly magazine devoted exclusively to artistic bungalow homes," the journal's real purpose was to promote a commodity in which its creators, especially Yoho, had a major financial interest. In 1913, when Yoho was president of the Bungalow Publishing Company, he was also president of the Craftsman Bungalow Company and had helped form the Take Down Manufacturing Company, both advertising their plan books in the magazine. At the time, Yoho and his firm were actively constructing speculative housing in Seattle's northern neighborhoods. The magazine subtly advertised these houses by featuring them with Yoho's name prominently displayed as the building's "architect."[12]

*The Bungalow Magazine* served as a new advertising source for a group of businessmen like Yoho—Seattle's bungalow builders, small architects, and real estate developers. Each issue included glowing descriptions and numerous pho-

Fig. 17.7. A "Supplement Bungalow" by Jud Yoho, "Architect." Featured in *The Bungalow Magazine,* Jan. 1914. Note the similarity to the house in fig. 17.3. Courtesy of the Seattle Public Library.

tographs of Seattle bungalows with the architect, designer, or builder's name and address. While some articles mentioned a client or home owner, others revealed that the houses had been constructed on speculation. Through its advertising section and its articles, *The Bungalow Magazine* spread information about professional services that otherwise would have reached only a limited audience. For instance, the "free plan service" it offered gave customers sources for purchasing the many house plans shown in the journal. Through these efforts, *The Bungalow Magazine* worked directly to unite firms producing a marketable commodity with potential consumers.[13]

Yoho's periodical epitomized a new type of popular magazine that helped usher in what historian Christopher Wilson has called a "consumerist re-

orientation" in the early twentieth century. Managed by men fluent in the organizational skills of a sales economy, mass-produced periodicals encouraged consumer behavior throughout American society. As promotional material, *The Bungalow Magazine* espoused a certain "taste" in domestic architecture that not coincidentally benefited the magazine's owners and advertisers. Through their journal, Yoho and his partners tried to sway consumer choice by featuring only one architectural style—the bungalow—in which they had a direct financial stake. Yoho's periodical both attempted to initiate its readers into a consumer ethic and promoted a specific consumer product.[14]

Yet another technique that evinced the spread of the "consumerist reorientation" was Yoho's offer of easy home financing. Taking advantage of new attitudes toward debt, Yoho and other housing en-trepreneurs extended home ownership to people who previously could not have afforded new homes. Beginning in the early twentieth century, lending institutions began increasing the avail-ability of mortgages and invested larger amounts of money in real estate. By 1920, more middle-income buyers were signing mortgage papers. Just as important, real estate dealers like Yoho began using an innovative method of financing that al-lowed people with only limited savings to pur-chase houses. In a "contract for deed," the buyer simply signed a legal contract in which he or she agreed to pay a small down payment and monthly installments to the seller. Upon final payment, the purchaser received the deed. Judging from adver-tisements, by 1910 Jud Yoho and his cohorts commonly sold houses and land on contract. Through installment plans, small dealers brought a new group of buyers into the consumption of houses—first-time home owners who had been renting their dwellings. As one of Yoho's counter-parts asked, "why pay rent when such homes can be bought on easy monthly payments?" The ac-ceptance of debt and the extension of credit re-flected a shift away from a mid-nineteenth-cen-tury value system based on self-sufficiency and frugality to a twentieth-century mindset of acqui-sition and personal fulfillment.[15]

To attract their potential clientele, Yoho and his colleagues featured a particular suburban ideal in their advertising. It emphasized the independence and freedom individual families could obtain through controlling their own small environment. This view of suburban life was quite distinct from the version articulated by corporate developers of elite communities. Promoters of exclusive, planned neighborhoods, like Seattle's Laurelhurst or Mt. Baker Park, sold customers not just a house, but the vision of a socially and visually homogenous suburb set in a gardenlike park. Yoho advanced a different ideal. He sold only small pieces of a neigh-borhood—individual lots and houses—already laid out in the grid system, so he did not guaran-tee his customers community control over neigh-bors or residential architecture. Nor did he strongly emphasize a naturalistic setting. He did, however, promise his consumers secure homes where they could retreat from the outside authority of land-lords. For families fleeing apartment living, this was alluring. Most important, Yoho stressed an image of individual homes closely tied to technol-ogy and the larger consumer economy. Yoho's houses were "modern," meaning they contained the latest household technology—full plumbing and sewerage, electricity, furnaces, and gas for cooking. These technical systems further bound home owners to consumption by compelling them to purchase their heat, light, and water and encouraging them to buy household appliances.[16]

Yoho's and his colleagues' advertisements also minimized a naturalistic setting, instead empha-sizing access to urban systems such as streetcar lines and convenient locations near workplaces, schools, and the city center. Outwardly, his houses expressed a rustic Craftsman "natural-ism," but they stood on small lots in densely built blocks of logged-off land. Magnificent views and beautiful landscaping were less important than neighborhood "improvements," such as concrete sidewalks, paved streets, and water mains. Yoho stressed the proximity of his houses to Seattle's urban center rather than their distance from it.[17]

Yoho's central advertising theme emphasized the affordability of an individual, technological house—a major concern of moderate-income people. As an opening lure, salesmen usually placed the price or the small monthly payment on the first line of the announcement. Yoho declared "EASY TERMS" on his 1908 "Modern Cottage" for sale, asserting that this vision of comfort and convenience could be obtained with payments the "same as rent." Clearly, Yoho aimed his message at people just entering the housing market.[18]

Yoho himself represented the people to whom his suburban ideal appealed. With his wife and two young sons, Yoho lived and worked in Wallingford, a Seattle neighborhood that contained mostly bungalows constructed between 1906 and 1915. There, in 1920, the occupational groups that most often selected bungalows were salespeople, accountants, clerks, and agents like Yoho. Although many occupational groups—professionals, managers, and skilled workers, for instance—also lived in bungalows, they did not choose them as exclusively as did the sales class. Like Yoho himself, many Wallingford residents were probably first-time home owners. Wallingford neighbors took advantage of easier home financing, incurring a large debt to purchase their dwellings. In a sample of homes in 1920 within a portion of Wallingford, 44 percent of the families held mortgages on their homes. From firsthand experience, Yoho understood these new consumers and addressed his advertising to their needs. People involved in a sales economy responded to his appeal. Together, they created a neighborhood that reflected not so much Progressive reform movements as new attitudes about the changing economy and their position in it.[19]

Yoho's Seattle career lasted only as long as the city's Craftsman bungalow craze. When World War I began curtailing residential building in 1915, Yoho divested himself of his interest in *The Bungalow Magazine*. It discontinued publication in 1918. The Take Down Manufacturing Company reincorporated as Factribilt without Yoho. In 1917, Edward L. Merritt, a trained architect, took over the Craftsman Bungalow Company with Yoho as an associate. Perceiving waning interest in Craftsman houses, the two published their last plan book of Craftsman bungalows in 1920. By the next year, they had moved on to the newest popular style, producing the plan book entitled "Colonial Homes, A Collection of the Latest Designs featuring the new Colonial Bungalow." In 1920, during the painful post–World War I recession, Yoho moved to Akron, Ohio, where he opened another architectural and build-

ing firm with D. E. Hooker, his Seattle partner and former editor of *The Bungalow Magazine*. His departure and the publication based on colonial bungalows signaled that the heyday of craftsman bungalows was over.[20]

When Yoho's bungalow business ended, so too did his marriage. His wife, Elsie, had been an active participant in Jud's enterprises. In 1913, she was secretary-treasurer of the Craftsman Bungalow Company and in 1915 served as a trustee for the Take Down Manufacturing Company. But when Jud's Seattle ventures folded around 1920 and he left for Ohio, the couple apparently separated. Although Elsie and her sons may have accompanied him for a short time, Akron city directories never mentioned Elsie or her sons. By 1922 they listed another woman, Maud R. Yoho, as Jud's wife. Though reformers may have intended Craftsman homes for family togetherness, the principle failed to work for the Yoho family.[21]

Although he promoted himself as an architect, Jud Yoho in fact epitomized the consummate twentieth-century salesman whose goal was to promote and extend a new consumer culture. He represented an entire group of ubiquitous small, diversified operators who worked outside of powerful professional organizations and large corporations. Through shrewd salesmanship and a multiplicity of business ventures, Yoho and others like him commodified the Craftsman ethic, rendering virtually meaningless its original utopian conception. While using Craftsman rhetoric, Yoho advanced an individualized, technological vision of family independence. His advertising appealed especially to people much like himself—salespeople, clerks, and accountants finally able to move out of their rentals and willing to accept a large debt for their first homes. Together, Yoho and his customers created neighborhoods that reflected their relationship to a transforming economy. They did not passively absorb ideals of architectural reform filtered down from society's elites. Through their own agency, they actively defined their urban spaces through their participation in the burgeoning consumer culture.

Thus, the meanings attached to exclusive planned communities do not necessarily extend to the suburban landscapes of Jud Yoho and his associates. More than professional architects, salespeople like Yoho shaped ordinary bungalow neighborhoods. While using reform rhetoric to line their own pockets, they helped extend the consumer economy and culture that has so characterized the twentieth century. It was this landscape of consumption, not planned communities, that dominated the early-twentieth-century urban environment.

## Notes

I wish to acknowledge and thank those people who generously helped me with this chapter, especially Roger Roper, Peggy Pascoe, JoAnn Fenton, Elaine Schmid, and four anonymous reviewers. Above all, I am particularly grateful to Mark Fiege, who carefully critiqued every draft and helped me to better articulate my ideas.

1. Most architectural historians have written about early-twentieth-century suburban form as originating from reformers, professional architects, planners, or corporate developers. See, for example, Clifford Clark, *The American Family Home, 1800–1960* (Chapel Hill: Univ. of North Carolina Press, 1986); Gwendolyn Wright, *Moralism and the Model Home: Domestic Architecture and Cultural Conflict in Chicago, 1873–1913* (Chicago: Univ. of Chicago Press, 1980); Marc A. Weiss, *The Rise of the Community Builders: The American Real Estate Industry and Urban Land Planning* (New York: Columbia Univ. Press, 1987); Mary Corbin Sies, "Toward a Performance Theory of the Suburban Ideal, 1877–1917," in *Perspectives in Vernacular Architecture, IV*, ed. Thomas Carter and Bernard L. Herman (Columbia: Univ. of Missouri Press, 1991). Little has been written on the activities of small early-twentieth-century real estate agents, building contractors, or residential designers (including plan book architects) who operated outside professional organizations, trade associations, or large corporations. See Michael Doucet and John Weaver, *Housing the North American City* (Montreal: McGill-Queen's Univ. Press, 1991), for a discussion of building entrepreneurs in an eastern Canadian context. Dennis A. Andersen and Katheryn H. Krafft, "Plan and Pattern Books: Shaping Early Seattle Architecture," *Pacific Northwest Quarterly* 85 (Oct. 1994): 150–58, show the influence of pattern book architecture on Seattle's residential neighborhoods.

2. The historiography of the early-twentieth-century transition to a consumer economy and society is extensive. Of particular value to me were Ronald Edsforth, *Class Conflict and Cultural Consensus: The Making of a Mass Consumer Society in Flint, Michigan* (New Brunswick: Rutgers Univ. Press, 1987); Daniel Horowitz, *The Morality of Spending: Attitudes Toward the Consumer Society in America, 1875–1940* (Baltimore: Johns Hopkins Univ. Press, 1985); T. J. Jackson Lears, *No Place of Grace: Antimodernism and the Transformation of American Culture, 1880–1920* (New York: Pantheon, 1981); and Richard Wightman Fox and T. J. Jackson Lears, eds., *The Culture of Consumption: Critical Essays in American History, 1880–1980* (New York: Pantheon, 1983). For an overview that synthesizes consumer society into the narrative of early-twentieth-century American history, see Michael E. Parrish, *Anxious Decades: America in Prosperity and Depression, 1920–1941* (New York: Norton, 1992).

3. Rob Carson, "Ode to Bungalows," *Pacific Northwest* (June 1986): 23; Rob Anglin, "Briefing Paper on Bungalows in Seattle," report submitted to the Seattle Landmarks Preservation Board, 1982; Jud Yoho, "Craftsman Bungalow Co.," Seattle, 1913 Edition De Luxe, 3. Because Yoho's plan books exist in several collections (Seattle Public Library and the National Archives, among others), Yoho is cited in a variety of architectural histories, including Alan Gowans, *The Comfortable House: North American Suburban Architecture, 1890–1930* (Cambridge, Mass.: MIT Press, 1986), 228; Deryck Holdsworth, "Regional Distinctiveness in an Industrial Age: Some California Influences on British Columbia Housing," *The American Review of Canadian Studies* 12 (1982): 71; Holdsworth, "House and Home in Vancouver: Images of West Coast Urbanism, 1886–1929," in *The Canadian City: Essays in Urban and Social History,* ed. Gilbert A.

Stelter and Alan F. J. Artibise (Ottawa: Carleton Univ. Press, 1984), 197–98. Not only his plan books, but Yoho himself apparently reached Vancouver. The *Pacific Builder and Engineer* reported that Yoho had "invaded the Vancouver territory," opening an office there in 1911. See *Pacific Builder and Engineer*, 12 (Aug. 5, 1911): 41.

4. John F. Yoho and family probably arrived in Seattle in 1896. A 1908 advertisement for Jud Yoho and Co. stated "est. 1896," when Jud would have been only fourteen years old. The Polk City Directories, however, first noted John in 1898. See *Seattle Post-Intelligencer*, May 10, 1908, Sec. 2, 5, and Polk Seattle City Directories, 1894–1925. Both John and his wife, Esther, were born in Ohio and married in 1877 when John was twenty years old and Esther only thirteen. The next year, the Yohos had their first child in Texas. Two more children were born in Texas, including Jud, and another in Colorado between 1882 and 1885. *Twelfth Census of the U.S.*, 1900, vol. 8, Washington, E.D. 118, Sheet 30, Line 8 (Manuscript); *Thirteenth Census of the U.S.*, 1910, Washington, E.D. 68, p. 16 (Manuscript); *Seattle Post-Intelligencer*, May 17, 1908, Sec. 2, 5. Jud may have been compelled to open his own business by the fortunes of his father. In the 1905 city directory, John was listed as "inventor" rather than real estate agent, and, by the next year, Jud's occupation had changed from an employee—bookkeeper—to independent real estate and insurance agent. The directory listed no occupation for John in 1907, and he died in 1908 at age fifty-one. I speculate that ill health possibly sidelined John, forcing Jud to venture out on his own. John apparently had some limited success as an inventor. In 1904, the *Pacific Builder and Engineer* reported that he had "invented a new style of instantaneous heater" to be manufactured in Vancouver "by the Yoho bath heater co., ltd." *Pacific Builder and Engineer* 2 (Apr. 23, 1904): 1.

5. "Articles of Incorporation for The Craftsman Bungalow Company," no. 15477 and no. 15525, located in Puget Sound Branch of the Washington State Archives, Seattle; Anglin, "Briefing Paper on Bungalows in Seattle." In 1908, Jud Yoho married Elsie Romestch of Portland, Oregon, when he was twenty-five and Elsie twenty-three. Elsie's connection to Portland may explain the Portland branch office of Yoho's Take Down Manufacturing Company. Polk Seattle City Directories, 1894–1921; Take Down Manufacturing

Co., "Craftsman Master Built Homes," 1915; *Thirteenth Census of the U.S.*, 1910, Washington, E.D. 68, p. 16 (Manuscript); *Fourteenth Census of the U.S.*, 1920, Vol. 23, Oregon, E.D. 132, p. 9 (Manuscript).

6. *Seattle Post-Intelligencer*, Aug. 14, 1904, 12. For a more detailed discussion of how burgeoning professional organizations in Seattle attempted to regulate their industries and exclude small competitors, see Janet Ore, "Constructing the Modern Home: Domestic Architecture and Cultural Change in Seattle Neighborhoods, 1890–1940," (Ph.D. diss., Univ. of Utah, 1993), chap. 2, "Selling the Home." See Dell Upton, "Pattern Books and Professionalism: Aspects of the Transformation of Domestic Architecture in America, 1800–1860," *Winterthur Portfolio* 19 (Summer/Autumn 1984): 107–50, and Robert Gutman, *Architectural Practice: A Critical View* (Princeton: Princeton Architectural Press, 1988): 61–69, for a discussion of how architects used professionalization to distinguish themselves from builders and exclude other building occupations from design.

7. Professional architects have never concerned themselves much with the design of small houses but left this to carpenters and builders. See Michael Doucet and John Weaver, "Material Culture and the North American House: The Era of the Common Man, 1870–1920," *Journal of American History* 72 (Dec. 1985): 560–87. In Robert Gutman, *The Design of American Housing: A Reappraisal of the Architect's Role* (New York: Publishing Center for Cultural Resources, 1985), 15–17, the author claims that "the [architectural] profession did not achieve a major role in housing production for the mass of the population until fairly recently. The designs for most speculative housing built in cities and suburbs in the United States before World War II came from pattern books or arose out of the cumulative experience of the speculative builders and developers themselves."

8. *Pacific Builder and Engineer* 11 (Dec. 9, 1911): 424; Yoho, "Craftsman Bungalow Co.," 3; Building Permit no. 119746 for 4207 Corliss Ave. N., located in the Microfilm Library, Department of Building and Construction, City of Seattle. For an example of Yoho's title of architect, see *The Bungalow Magazine* 3 (Jan. 1914): 3. Until the 1919 Washington law requiring architects to be licensed, anyone could call him or herself an architect. Yet, Yoho sometimes seems to have been careful about using the term. In his catalogs, Yoho

called himself a "specialty bungalow designer" and in his journal often used "Craftsman Bungalow Company, architects." This may have reflected his awareness of the Washington AIA's ongoing attempts to pass legislation that would prevent untrained entrepreneurs like him from using the title. This did not stop him from claiming himself an architect in other places, however.

9. Anglin, "Briefing Paper on Bungalows in Seattle," 7; Andersen and Krafft, "Plan and Pattern Books," 158. I suspect that Yoho and the Craftsman Bungalow Company got their "ideas," if not outright designs, directly from southern California architecture. For instance, in 1912 the *Seattle Post-Intelligencer* reported that Virgil Hall, "connected with the Craftsman Bungalow Company" and associate of Edward L. Merritt (perhaps his brother-in-law) had "returned from a five-week sojourn throughout California . . . travel[ing] a greater part of the distance from Southern Oregon throughout California by means of a motor car." My guess is that this was more than just a pleasure trip. See *Seattle-Post Intelligencer*, Mar. 24, 1912, Real Estate Sec., 6.

10. "Articles of Incorporation of Take Down Manufacturing Co.," no. 18947 and no. 21432, located in Puget Sound Branch Archives; Take Down Manufacturing Co., "Craftsman Master Built Homes," 1; T. J. Jackson Lears, "From Salvation to Self-Realization: Advertising and the Therapeutic Roots of the Consumer Culture, 1880–1930," in *The Culture of Consumption*, ed. Fox and Lears, 21. For a particularly illuminating discussion of the commodification of the craftsman ideal, see chap. 2, "The Figure of the Artisan: Arts and Crafts Ideology," in Lears, *No Place of Grace*, 59–96.

11. Anglin, "Briefing Paper on Bungalows in Seattle," 6; Andersen and Krafft, "Plan and Pattern Books," 156; Doucet and Weaver, *Housing the North American City*, 234. For example, *The Bungalow Magazine* 7 (Mar. 1918): 21, included an article entitled "Three Charming Little Colonial Bungalows," by Charles Alma Byers that the *Craftsman* had published in 28 (July 1915): 409–14 under the title "The 'Colonial Bungalow': A New and Charming Variation in Home Architecture."

12. Title page of *The Bungalow Magazine* 2 (May 1913); title page of *The Bungalow Magazine* 4 (Jan. 1915); title page of *The Bungalow Magazine* 4 (May 1915): 295; Polk Seattle City Directories, 1891–1928;

Anglin, "Briefing Paper on Bungalows in Seattle"; Clarence Bagley, *History of Seattle from the Earliest Settlement to the Present Time* (Chicago: S. J. Clarke Publishing Co., 1916), 3: 843–44.

13. *The Bungalow Magazine* 7 (Jan. 1918): 20; *The Bungalow Magazine* 2 (Dec. 1913): 70.

14. Christopher P. Wilson, "The Rhetoric of Consumption: Mass-Market Magazines and the Demise of the Gentle Reader, 1880–1930," in Fox and Lears, eds., *The Culture of Consumption*, 42–43.

15. Weiss, *The Rise of the Community Builders*, 32; John M. Gries and Thomas M. Curran, "Present Home Financing Methods," Department of Commerce (Washington, D.C.: Government Printing Office, 1928), 7–9; John M. Gries and James S. Taylor, "How to Own Your Home: A Handbook for Prospective Home Owners," Department of Commerce (Washington, D.C.: Government Printing Office, 1923), 4–9.

16. *Seattle Post-Intelligencer*, Aug. 28, 1910, Classified Sec., 2; *Seattle Post-Intelligencer*, Jan. 14, 1912, Real Estate Sec., 4; Thomas J. Schlereth, "Conduits and Conduct: Home Utilities in Victorian America, 1876–1915," in *American Home Life, 1880–1930: A Social History of Spaces and Services*, ed. Jessica H. Foy and Thomas J. Schlereth (Knoxville: Univ. of Tennessee Press, 1992), 238–39.

17. For example, see the *Seattle Post-Intelligencer*, Aug. 27, 1911, Classified Sec., 3.

18. *Seattle Post-Intelligencer*, Aug. 28, 1910, Classified Sec., 1.

19. *Thirteenth Census of the U.S.*, 1910, (manuscript), shows Yoho renting his dwelling at 1639 King Street, Seattle. My conclusions about who lived in bungalows derives from a sampling of homes in four Seattle neighborhoods—Ballard, Fremont, Green Lake, and Wallingford. Using detailed descriptions and photographs compiled by the Works Progress Administration in 1937 for tax assessments, I created an architectural data base of 20 percent (approximately 800 residences) of the houses within sample areas. To the houses constructed before 1920 (most of the bungalows), I added 1920 manuscript census data. From this, I was able generally to group heads of households according to their occupation and associate these groups with the type of houses each chose. In Wallingford, I sampled 20 percent of the houses between North Forty-fifth, Bagley, Woodlawn, and North Thirty-fourth. Among the salesmen, accountants, clerks, and

agents, 73 percent selected bungalows. The rest picked four-squares and a solitary Dutch colonial.

20. Polk Seattle City Directories, 1913–17; Gowans, *The Comfortable House,* 228. Yoho's associates typified small, aspiring entrepreneurs who brought a modern sales-oriented mindset to the building industry. Merritt graduated with an architecture degree in 1900 at the University of Minnesota. In 1904, he joined his father, Charles, a general contractor in Seattle. With Virgil Hall (probably Charles's son-in-law), the Merritts formed the Merritt-Hall Investment Company in 1904. The firm constructed both private and speculative houses, specifically bungalows, by 1910. After 1914, Merritt began designing residences from his own office. Merritt's houses often appeared in *The Bungalow Magazine.* He maintained the Craftsman Bungalow Company from 1917 until 1928. For information on Edward L. Merritt, see *Pacific Builder and Engineer* 10 (Oct. 22, 1910): 160; *The Bungalow Magazine* 2 (May 1913); C. H. Hanford, ed., *Seattle and Environs, 1852–1924* (Chicago and Seattle: Pioneer Historical Publishing Co., 1924), 2: 521–22; Polk Seattle City Directories, 1918–42. The *Seattle Post-Intelligencer,* Mar. 24, 1912, Real Estate Sec., 6, noted that Virgil Hall was connected with the Craftsman Bungalow Company. With passage of the architect certification law in 1919, Yoho could no longer bill himself independently as an architect. This may explain his association with Merritt. Yoho and his partner, Dolph E. Hooker, were opportunists who knew how to cash in on a region's prosperity. Hooker had been Yoho's associate since about 1907 when he had arrived during Seattle's building boom. Hooker was a versatile businessman who conducted a number of activities simultaneously. An "architect" with Jud Yoho in 1909 (and living just down the street from Yoho), he became editor of *The Bungalow Magazine* between 1913 and 1915 while also treasurer of the Bungalow Publishing Company. Meanwhile, he conducted an import-export business, advertising in *The Bungalow Magazine.* In 1912, he took the job of assistant city superintendent of buildings and used his position to officially endorse Yoho's Take Down Manufacturing Company's "Craftsman Master Built Homes." Hooker left Seattle around 1918 when residential building reached a standstill. By 1920, Yoho had joined him in Akron, Ohio, where they established Yoho and Hooker Company, selling architectural and building services and lumber supplies. Both Hooker and Yoho bought homes on the same block. By 1930, Yoho had left Akron while Hooker continued to operate "Yoho and Hooker, The Akron Company" until at least 1935. Apparently, Yoho continued his association with Hooker but had moved on to greener pastures. *The Bungalow Magazine* 4 (Jan. 1915): 4-A; Polk Seattle City Directories, 1898–1930; Burch Directory Co., Akron City Directories, 1920–35; Take Down Manufacturing Co., "Craftsman Master Built Homes," n.p.

21. Polk Seattle City Directory, 1913; Articles of Incorporation, Take Down Manufacturing Co. I surmise from census and city directory evidence that Jud and Elsie had separated. See Akron City Directories, 1920–35, and *Fourteenth Census,* 1920, Vol. 194, Ohio, E.D. 187, Sheet 20, line 73 (manuscript); *Fourteenth Census,* 1920, Vol. 23, Oregon, E.D. 132, Sheet 9, line 4 (manuscript).

*Richard Longstreth*

# The Mixed Blessings of Success: The Hecht Company and Department Store Branch Development after World War II

Retail development in the United States experienced profound changes during the half dozen years following the Second World War when locations on the urban periphery emerged as important focuses of trade. Prior to that time, most merchants purveying apparel, accessories, furniture, and a host of other products that lay outside routine consumer purchases continued to concentrate in the city center. A new wave of remodeling and sometimes expansion had widespread impact on city centers after the worst years of the Depression. Retailers' collective investment in the urban core was already enormous, and much of it had been made only a decade or two earlier during a period of unprecedented downtown growth. Even without that intensity of development, the belief remained strong in the late 1930s that the downtown alone afforded the critical mass and scope of merchandise to attract volume patronage. The leading proponents of this

view were the huge department store companies, which both dominated downtown retail activity and provided the draw upon which so many other merchants depended. As long as the department stores remained anchored to the city center, most other emporia held fast.[1]

By 1950, the situation had changed dramatically. Downtown remained by far the largest retail center in size and sales volume in metropolitan areas nationwide, but it was no longer seen so much as a place of the future. If not already broken, the core's dominance in trade was seriously threatened. Retailers were making much greater investments in outlying areas that just a few years previous were inconceivable as surrogates for downtown. The major department stores led this shift, some of them beginning their preparations before the war's end. Six years later, most of these companies either were operating or in the advanced stages of planning at least one sizable facility well removed from the core.[2]

A variety of factors contributed to the shift, foremost among them the intensifying lateral spread of residential districts inhabited by the middle class, which comprised the big stores' principal market. This trend began decades earlier, of course, but even in the early 1920s a large percentage of consumers still lived within a two- to three-mile radius of the core retail district and still relied on centralized public transportation systems for many activities, shopping included. By the decade's end, however, an increasing amount of new residential development was oriented to the motorist, a trend that continued after the Depression and gained great momentum following the war. New residential tracts situated ten miles or more from downtown were common by the early 1950s in large metropolitan areas and in some smaller ones as well.

The increasing reliance on cars for everyday as well as for recreational use likewise was a key factor that began over two decades earlier and became especially pronounced during the postwar era. Automobiles brought traffic congestion and parking problems to the core, problems that seemed almost insurmountable by the 1940s. But even had these difficulties been less, expansion in the city center was fraught with hurdles. Land was expensive and in short supply where it was most needed by the big stores. Many of these emporia literally had nowhere to expand without so dispersing their sales floors as to undermine the operation.

By contrast, outlying areas were closer to the homes of a large share of the department stores' clientele and were easily reached by car. Land was much less expensive than in the core. The labor pool was cheaper, too, and considered more dependable. Moreover, competing chain companies were already staking out the territory, a trend that began in the 1920s and grew at a rate many downtown firms viewed with alarm. Sears, Roebuck & Company pioneered this initiative when

it entered the retail field in 1925; within a few years, others followed, including variety, clothing, and accessories chains. After the war, the consumer market experienced a new surge. More people had more disposable income. The average work week was shorter, while more emphasis was given to efficient use of time, including time spent on purchasing goods.[3] If the department stores were to take advantage of the growth and maintain their prominence in the retail field, they had to take the initiative, adapting some chain methods in the process.

Among downtown department stores, few were more ambitious in branch expansion during the immediate postwar years than the Washington-based Hecht Company. When the company's second big suburban facility opened in 1951, Hecht's boasted over half a million square feet of retail space beyond the city center, almost as much as its downtown emporium, and one of the largest totals anywhere in the country save Los Angeles.[4] This program was spearheaded by Hecht's chief operating officer, Charles B. Dulcan, who saw branch development not only as a means to maintain the company's existing share of the market, but also as a way to increase it and propel the store into the forefront regionally.

Founded in 1895, Hecht's was the youngest of Washington's department stores and among the least prestigious during its first three decades of operation. Its target audience came from the lower end of the market: white- and blue-collar people of moderate income. Beginning in the 1920s, Hecht executives sought to broaden that base without neglecting core constituents. Greater reliance on well-known brands, coupled with aggressive merchandising, lay at the core of this strategy. To accommodate larger crowds as well as to symbolize its rising stature, Hecht's built an ornate new store in 1924–25, the last of its kind locally.[5] Company executives took advantage of the Depression, and of the swelling ranks of the federal work force, to augment further a middle-range clientele concerned with both price and value so that only the venerable Woodward & Lothrop stood as a rival in sales volume on the eve of World War II. The most important figure behind Hecht's ascendancy was Dulcan, who served as the principal buyer, then merchandise manager, before becoming vice president and general manager in 1938. Dulcan enjoyed complete authority in running the firm and soon began to lay the groundwork for a network of branch stores through which regional dominance might be gained.[6]

Like others of the era, Hecht's first branch stores were experiments, ventures made in minimally charted territory that carried potential risks almost as great as the potential rewards. No clear precedent existed for precisely how these outlets were best sited, how large they should be, or the range of goods they should carry. A small flurry of department store branch development occurred in the late 1920s, but within a few years most industry leaders considered the phenomenon a costly mistake. A decade later, conventional wisdom held that the department store branch was an exceptional thing, confined to top-of-the-line emporia purveying a limited range of dry goods to an affluent clientele.[7] Most branches constructed during the interwar decades were smaller than 50,000 square feet; they were for departmentalized clothing and accessory stores such as Best & Company, Franklin Simon, and Lord & Taylor. Only in Los Angeles did the large (150,000 square feet or more) emporia, which stocked a wide range of goods, flourish, and even these were designed to attract a more affluent trade than their parent stores.[8]

Most prewar branches were located on the edge of established suburban shopping districts—in Ardmore on Philadelphia's Main Line, for example, or in White Plains and Garden City, New York, or in Evanston and Oak Park, Illinois—places that were larger and more important than a neighborhood service area, but still subordinate

to downtown. Other branches were sited away from these precincts, which were experiencing traffic problems of their own as early as the 1920s, in places easily accessible to the motorist where congestion and the cost of land were minimal. Known as the lone-wolf store, this alternative type was begun by Sears when it entered the retail sphere and was soon adopted by some downtown-based department stores.[9]

All these precedents had some bearing on postwar trends, but it was not apparent at that time which precedents, or to what degree these precedents, were optimal. Enough study went into both siting and assessment of market demands so that most postwar branches, including Hecht's, proved highly successful operations—the beginning of a tendency that has transformed the department store into a chain where the downtown emporium is one among many, if it exists at all. Yet, the transition from a highly centralized structure to a decentralized one was far from simple. Often historical studies of building types focus on the successes, the pathbreaking examples that had a decisive impact on subsequent practices. Less attention is paid to ventures that, for any number of reasons, were less influential. This latter group merits study nevertheless, for it underscores the complexities, difficulties, and risks entailed in change. With department store branches, the situation generally was not one of absolute success or failure, but a combination of the two. Such circumstances characterized Dulcan's program, which achieved leadership for Hecht's among Washington department stores and which helped set a national standard in its ambitious scale. At the same time, some aspects of the company's expansion proved less than optimal, none of which attracted more attention among retailers across the country than those associated with Hecht's initial branch store, located at Silver Spring, Maryland.

Hecht's was among the first large retail firms in the United States to announce a major postwar expansion program. Plans for a streamlined behemoth, designed by the prominent New York architect William Lescaze, were unveiled in November 1945, soon after the war's end (fig. 18.1).[10] Silver Spring was a middle-class residential community situated just beyond the northern edge of the District of Columbia. For at least two decades, boosters had tried to stimulate the development of an important retail center in their community, but most of Silver Spring's shopping facilities remained small and localized in nature.[11] When construction began on the Hecht store in 1946, the site seemed an unlikely one, lying at the northern edge of the small retail district and surrounded on three sides by residential property (fig. 18.2).

The location was nevertheless strategic. During the 1940s, Silver Spring became one of the fastest-growing areas, not only in greater Washington, but on the East Coast. After the war, the community was touted as being the second largest in the state.[12] Silver Spring lay in the path of what had been the principal axis of residential development in the region since the late nineteenth century, and at a juncture of well-traveled routes to Baltimore and to northwest Maryland. On both sides of the District line, the vast majority of residents were part of the middle-range market, including persons of some means, a target group in Hecht's broadening clientele. From both geographic and demographic standpoints, Silver Spring was an ideal location. There was only one potential Maryland contender, Bethesda, lying five miles to the west along another important corridor of residential development. But Bethesda had several disadvantages. The market was somewhat more upscale, and Woodward & Lothrop, the traditional favorite of that market and Hecht's arch rival for dominance in area retail sales, was simultaneously planning a store in the vicinity.[13]

Fig. 18.1. Hecht Company Store, Silver Spring, Maryland, 1945. William Lescaze, architect; project. Drawing of preliminary design, Evening Star Collection, Courtesy of the D.C. Public Library.

Fig. 18.2. Hecht Company Silver Spring Store, 1946–47. Abbott, Merkt & Company, architects, altered. Photo taken shortly before opening. Courtesy of Lacey Womack, Hecht's.

Perhaps the most important factor in site selection lay with initiatives of the Maryland-National Capital Park and Planning Commission, the powerful county agency with purview over Silver Spring. As early as November 1944, MNCPPC advanced plans to expand Silver Spring's business zone so that it could become a major trading center.[14] Intended to encourage concentrated development and prevent "shoestring" expansion along arteries, the scheme was the brainchild of the commission chairman, E. Brooke Lee, whose family was among the oldest in the area and who held tracts in what he envisioned as the new "downtown" for Montgomery County and northern Washington. Self-gain was not the only motivating factor. Lee simultaneously proposed a similar plan for Bethesda, which was rebuffed by residents who disliked the prospect of commerce encroaching on their enclaves.[15] Aspects of the Silver Spring plan also generated controversy, and while some years elapsed before all its facets were resolved, enough support for key provisions existed from the start to encourage large-scale new development.[16] Hecht's threw its weight behind the proposal, locating on Fenton Street and Ellsworth Drive, one block from the principal thoroughfares, Georgia Avenue and Colesville Road. The new store was oriented toward the area intended as a focus of commercial growth, and it possessed the additional advantage of being removed from the congestion the main arteries were sure to generate.

Soon after the rezoning initiative, Lee launched a complementary plan for a network of county-owned-and-operated parking lots with a total capacity of two thousand cars.[17] Scattered throughout the business district, the lots were intended to prevent what was considered one of the worst problems plaguing city centers. As with rezoning, the scheme took time to implement, but from its inception was used as a means of luring retailers. As with the zoning proposal, Silver Spring boosters promoted this future amenity, while a counterpart which Lee had devised for Bethesda languished.

The parking plan was probably the linchpin that triggered Silver Spring's meteoric rise as a major commercial center. The concept of government-sponsored off-street parking dated from the 1920s; however, such a program had only recently gained widespread acceptance.[18] Lee's proposal was among the most ambitious realized in an outlying metropolitan community prior to the mid-1950s. Little wonder Hecht's picked the location. It was easily reached. The right clientele lived in great numbers all around, and the growth of this population continued to increase. No competing department stores were planned nearby, but the prospects were good for the development of many other retail stores so as to attract the crowds needed to sustain a big emporium. The county was bending over backward to provide adequate space for new construction and for the motorist, so the store could advertise acres of free parking without the responsibilities of ownership or oversight.

Lee and his colleagues envisioned Silver Spring as a new kind of downtown—competitive with the urban core, but without its perceived drawbacks. The form would remain centralized, yet have adequate space for new construction and for automobiles. In its complexion, the precinct would possess all the advantages of newness to which the postwar generation gave so much weight. This downtown was to have none of the dirt or purported tawdriness, none of the underlighted and underventilated buildings, nothing to attract the "wrong" social elements that were increasingly seen as characteristic of the city center. Silver Spring never attracted the elite; however, it was eminently respectable, a haven for the middle class, many of whom had worked their way up the economic ladder and were eager to frequent places not associated with the past.

The Hecht store similarly embraced the middle ground. In size, scale, and character, the design bespoke what were viewed as the best attributes of the city.[19] The form was urban, a massive block that occupied the entire property, its exterior walls rising sheer from the sidewalk without the quasi-domestic trappings cultivated in prewar branches. Containing 160,000 square feet, the store was the largest on the eastern seaboard outside a central shopping district when it opened in November 1947. With 116 departments, the scope of goods and services matched that of the parent store. Hecht's did not create a branch in the way that term was used before the war; this was not a small outlet whose underlying function was to bolster or at least maintain patronage at the parent store. Instead, the Silver Spring emporium was a near equal. County residents viewed the facility as a turning point, when Silver Spring ceased to be an outpost and instead became a destination, a true business center for the metropolitan area.

If the building carried positive big-city overtones, it also departed from convention. On the exterior, Hecht's pushed new limits of simplicity. Early in the design stage, Lescaze was replaced by the

New York architectural and engineering firm of Abbott, Merkt & Company, which specialized in warehouses and other support facilities for department stores. Hecht's was probably the first client to engage the firm for a retail outlet, a realm in which Abbott, Merkt subsequently flourished. The revised scheme was no-nonsense to say the least: no frills, no adornment, no variation—even in the massing—save the rounded corner. This sort of near-utilitarian minimalism was then unusual for a major store, offering a stark contrast to the extravagance of prewar work. Indeed the scheme was much simpler than Hecht's own warehouse (1936–37) also designed by Abbott, Merkt.[20]

Among the most conspicuous departures in the Silver Spring store was the lack of exterior windows, save for street-level display. This change made practical sense, for natural light was now considered a disadvantage in the layout of department stores. Sears had pioneered the move with its 1934 store in the Englewood district on Chicago's south side. Thereafter, windowless walls were a standard aspect of new Sears stores; yet, a strong physical presence was maintained through sculptural manipulation of the mass.[21] Even so, downtown department store executives rejected the concept because of the persistent fear that it would have a negative impact on customer appeal. Not until after the war were these retailers convinced otherwise. Hecht's was among the first to take the plunge, demonstrating in the process that as long as it seemed "modern"—that is, up-to-date—the exterior need not have the slightest pretense. In fact, the exterior treatment was well attuned to its audience. A costlier solution could convey a sense of unnecessary extravagance to a budget-conscious clientele. Furthermore, elite associations no longer held as strong an appeal as they had before the war. Much as Sears had made no frills an asset in its emporia, Hecht's was a leader in demonstrating its efficacy for the traditional department store. In this respect, the build-

ing helped set a standard that was widely followed by others for several decades.

The interior was treated in a more indulgent vein, for the belief was stronger than ever that both the arrangement and ambience of this mercantile landscape was a key means of stimulating purchases. Designed by Sue Williams, a specialist in the field from New York, the interior had an artfully informal arrangement conducive to perambulation. The character was at once relaxed in a way intended to make even moderate-income shoppers feel at ease and polished in a manner suggestive of a great store. Here was a consumers' world far more expansive than anything then found in Washington's outlying areas and bespeaking newness to a greater degree than counterparts in the urban core.

The store was a great success, so much so that two more stories were built in 1950 and a lateral extension made in 1955. The two additions encompassed over one hundred thousand square feet. In its first year of operation the store placed its owners in the forefront of gross sales for the metropolitan area.[22] The results were widely cited as proof that building large, full-fledged department store branches was essential for the future prosperity of the trade.

Hecht's also achieved its aim of fostering retail growth in Silver Spring. Soon after plans for the store were announced, an array of other businesses followed suit. Both the range and caliber of outlets, which included branches of downtown specialty stores, chain store units, and independent enterprises, greatly enlarged the choices available locally, affording consumers the opportunity to comparison shop as well as to purchase goods not carried by Hecht's. By 1955 Silver Spring was the second-largest retail center between downtown Baltimore and downtown Richmond (fig. 18.3).[23]

Yet Dulcan and his associates were far from being elated with the particulars of Silver Spring's

Fig. 18.3. Silver Spring, Aerial View Looking Northwest. Hecht store, with rooftop additions, in foreground; Colesville Road, major artery to right; Georgia Avenue, across center. Photo c. 1953. Courtesy of Lacey Womack, Hecht's.

growth. In a rare public admission of error, problems were enumerated to the business community nationwide: Hecht's had made Silver Spring a major retail center, but had little say in the precinct's development or future.[24] Now there was insufficient room for expansion. Hecht's had no say in who its neighbors would be, what they sold, or when they sold it. Furthermore, the county's parking plan was proving inadequate for the store's own needs.[25] The precinct was becoming overly congested. At the same time, the store remained at the periphery of commercial devel-

opment, most of which was concentrated on Colesville Road. Dulcan vowed not repeat the errors of Silver Spring.

In 1945, Silver Spring seemed ideal ground for retail development, with better long-range planning provisions than most outlying communities. The framing of Hecht's complaint half a decade later suggests that Dulcan had become familiar with a new and potentially more predictable alternative. The still fledgling concept of the regional shopping center entailed greater investment of time and money, but also greater control since the location, buildings, tenants, and operation were orchestrated by a single concern. Very few such integrated business developments existed on a large scale in 1950. The most recent was the huge Crenshaw Center in Los Angeles (1945–47) developed by the Broadway Department Store. The Broadway was much like Hecht's in its trade orientation, and the Crenshaw facility, like Hecht's Silver Spring, was an early experiment in mass merchandising to that market by a major department store outside the city center.[26]

The Broadway-Crenshaw's spectacular financial success was an important catalyst in directing department store executives to the point where they soon embraced the regional shopping center idea. But the Hecht Company's disappointment in Silver Spring no doubt also figured in the equation by underscoring the pitfalls of nonintegrated projects. Just what the optimal form of a fully planned shopping center should be remained an open question, however. In its physical dimension, the Crenshaw Center was not considered a model because the Broadway's store lay at one corner of its sprawling tract, a long distance from where many cars would have to park at peak shopping periods. A wholly new configuration, a pedestrian mall as the spine around which stores were oriented and the complex entirely surrounded by a large parking area, became accepted as the most advantageous form from both merchandising and operational perspectives by the mid-1950s. But prior to that time the mall plan was still viewed with suspicion by many retailers, while no other arrangement emerged as a preferable alternative. Around 1950, the field was never more prone to experimentation.

Hecht's second opportunity to erect a branch emporium occurred at this critical juncture in retail development. The scheme drew from lessons learned at Silver Spring, but also from a failed attempt to create a branch in northern Virginia several years previous. In 1945, Dulcan had planned a store similar to the Maryland behemoth at

Clarendon, the ascendant retail center for Arlington County, which was another prime growth area in the region.[27] The project remained stillborn due to a property owner's refusal to sell part of the required land. Had the store been built, it might have encountered more difficulties than the Silver Spring outlet, for, in contrast to the Montgomery County center, almost no provision was made for off-street parking at Clarendon save by a few individual merchants.[28] Congestion was exacerbated by the fact that most facilities were concentrated along a single artery, Wilson Boulevard, which was narrower and more winding than its Silver Spring counterparts.

If Dulcan could not build a branch in Clarendon, he seemed determined to have one in nearby Arlington. In April 1950, he announced plans for the metropolitan area's first shopping center designed to attract a regional audience, a complex that would usurp Clarendon as a focus of trade.[29] The site lay only one mile to the west, but in a residential area where Wilson Boulevard and the intersecting thoroughfare, Glebe Road, could be widened to accommodate anticipated traffic. Here, too, Hecht's could purchase land across these arteries to preclude any development that might infringe upon its own. As a business venture, the scheme was considered state-of-the-art, with a fully integrated structure, giving Hecht's control of tenant selection and management as well as of the overall design. This latter aspect, however, represented a pronounced deviation from contemporary examples, a solution far more unorthodox than the Silver Spring store had provided half a decade earlier.

Diagrammatically, the Arlington complex was laid out somewhat like a large railroad terminal of the nineteenth century. Rather than a train shed, a multideck parking garage rose as the centerpiece (fig. 18.4). With a capacity of two thousand cars at a time, the structure was touted as being the largest in the world.[30] Without question it was the largest then planned for a single retail facility and the first to be realized as part of a shopping center. All four levels of the garage had direct access to the Hecht store, which was positioned like a headhouse at one end. It, too, was of mammoth proportions. With five floors containing three hundred thousand square feet, the emporium exceeded all others beyond the city center save for one contemporaneous project in Los Angeles County.[31] Flanking the garage on its long sides were one-story buildings designed to contain about thirty stores. Collectively, these supporting units were planned to foster or en-

courage comparison shopping, an essential ingredient in securing the volume of trade needed to sustain the big store and to make the ensemble competitive with Clarendon.[32] The retail mix was intended to function like that at Silver Spring, but here under Hecht's purview.

Dulcan and his associates were aware of at least some of the risks they were taking. The garage was the biggest gamble, for conventional wisdom held that women in particular disliked using such facilities. Pains were taken in laying

Fig. 18.4. Parkington Shopping Center, 1950–53. Abbott, Merkt & Company, architects, Kahn & Jacobs, associated architects; Hecht Company store (lower right) altered, remainder of development demolished, 1984–86. Aerial view looking southeast; stores in unfinished state. Glebe Road is at right; Wilson Boulevard is at lower left. Photo 1951. Courtesy of Lacey Womack, Hecht's.

out the garage to maximize ease of access and egress, with straight ramps to each level on the outside of the deck structure (fig. 18.5). Promotional campaigns emphasized how the garage provided shelter for most shoppers' cars and shortened walking distances to stores. When the complex opened in November 1951, it was christened Parkington, making the garage the focus of identity.[33] Yet, customer convenience was not the generating factor for the garage. It was a necessity because the fifteen-acre site was too small for surface parking alone. Hecht's valued a location central to existing residential development in the county, one that would reinforce the project's role as an alternative to Clarendon, over a more expansive, peripheral tract that might be better positioned in relation to future growth.

The name was only one of the devices used to capitalize on Parkington's novelty. Considerable effort was spent on creating a memorable exterior appearance, in contrast to the approach taken at Silver Spring. The New York firm of Kahn & Jacobs was hired to provide consulting architects who focused on this aspect of the scheme. Buildings were sheathed in glazed, blue-green brick, but the most remarkable feature was the fifteen-thousand-square-foot glass wall extending over most of the department store's west elevation (fig. 18.6). With this giant billboard, where artificial illumination allowed a coordinated display of tenant signs to be changed on a regular basis, ad-

Fig. 18.5. Parkington, View of Garage. Photo c. 1951. From Urban Land Institute Technical Bulletin (May 1957): 107. Courtesy of the Urban Land Institute.

vertising fused with architecture to form a dynamic interplay of a sort long cultivated by the European avant-garde, but seldom realized, and never before on so epic a scale. Robert Allan Jacobs explained his intention "to put the exterior . . . to work," to render it one great display, not of merchandise, but of "color and light."[34]

Like its predecessor, the Parkington store proved a financial boon, one that kept its owner in the forefront regionally for some years. Yet, the great scale of the complex and its comprehensive plan did not ensure complete success. Ultimately, Parkington underscored the pitfalls as well as the rewards of an adventurous expansion program. The development seems to have been instrumental in arresting Clarendon's growth as a retail center, but not in ending its viability as a destination for many shoppers. Had the two commercial precincts been tangent, each might have worked to the other's benefit, the ensemble attracting larger crowds than both could draw separately. On the other hand, the siting was too close for either to function as an independent entity. The situation was further complicated by the simultaneous development of a quasi-integrated shopping center, Virginia Square, with Kann's, a Washington department store of somewhat lesser rank than Hecht's, as the anchor tenant.[35] This complex lay approximately midway between the two others, but on a different arterial, Fairfax Drive, compounding the problems faced by consumers wishing to make the rounds at more than one place. Dulcan may not have known of Kann's plans, unveiled one month after his own, until it was too late to change course.[36] Parkington was the biggest and the most enduring of the three, but never attained the clear dominance its creator envisioned.

Location was not the sole problem. Soon after the Hecht store opened, nearby residents objected to its great illuminated wall. As a compromise, messages were limited to those of community service organizations instead of merchandising.[37] Its purpose lost, the wall seemed a curious anachro-

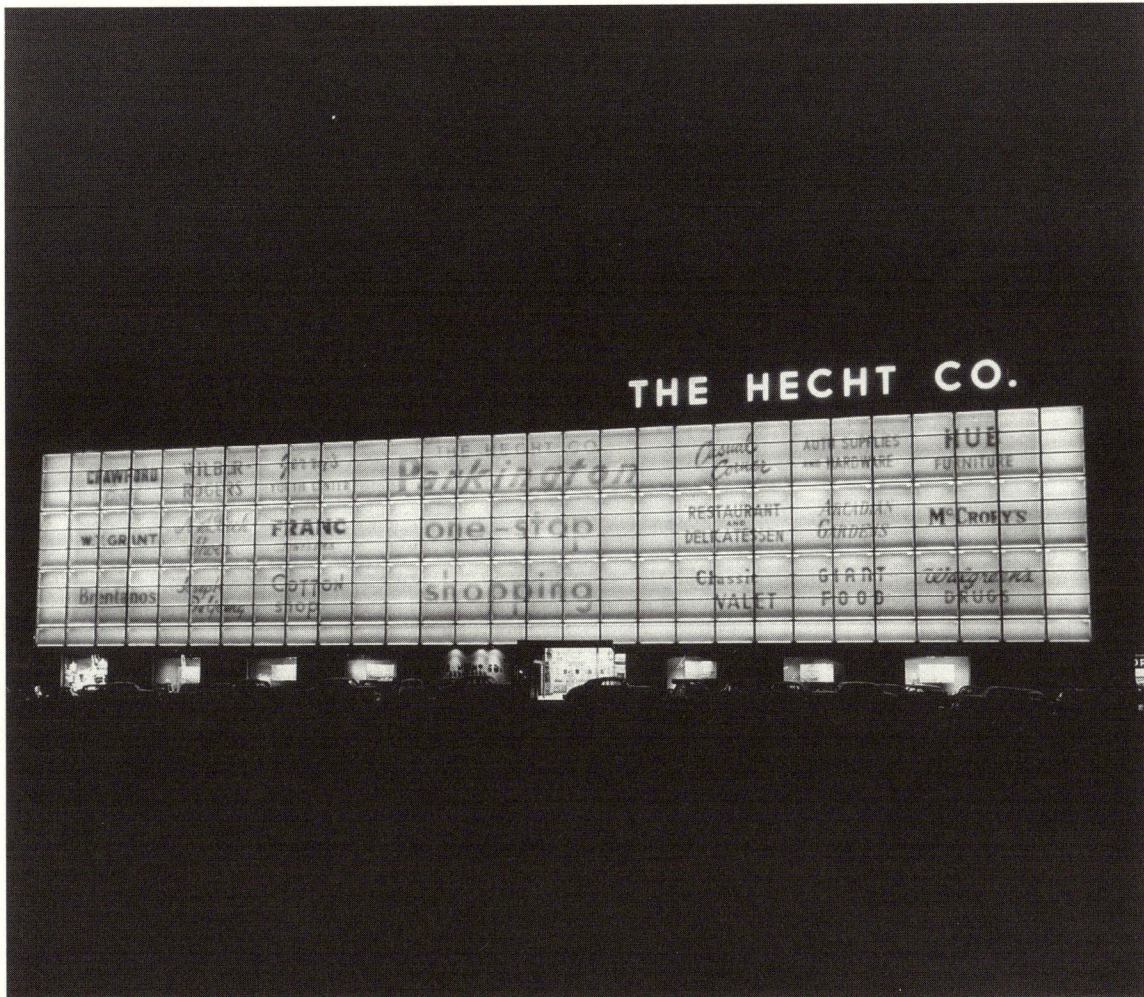

Fig. 18.6. Hecht Company Store, Parkington. Night view showing illuminated glass wall. Photo c. 1951. Courtesy of Lacey Womack, Hecht's.

nism rather than a theatrical source of public engagement. A greater problem in hindsight proved to be the size of the Hecht store relative to its subordinates, which collectively did not equal its square footage. Most of the merchants prospered, but Parkington remained in the public eye foremost as a Hecht store, not a multifaceted retail complex. The orientation of the other stores, to arterials with little curbside parking and almost no pedestrian traffic, did not help matters (fig. 18.7). Most stores also had an entrance facing the garage, but the connection was circuitous, separated by surface parking lots in what resembled residue space. The garage itself lived up to expectations, but remained an anomaly for some three decades. During the interim, site-selection practices favored more peripheral locations, where adequate land for surface parking was readily available. Not until recent years, as such land has become scarcer and as established regional malls have expanded, has the parking deck entered the mainstream of shopping center design.[38]

Fig. 18.7. Parkington, View of Stores from Glebe Road. Photo c. 1957. Courtesy of Lacey Womack, Hecht's.

Circumstances beyond anyone's capacity to predict brought Hecht's go-getting expansion program into abeyance. When Parkington opened, the company's chief rival, Woodward & Lothrop, seemed decisively eclipsed in the struggle for regional leadership. Woodward & Lothrop began the postwar era with an ambitious program of building two sizable lone-wolf stores, one on Wisconsin Avenue near Chevy Chase, Maryland, amid some of the metropolitan area's most fashionable enclaves, the second in Arlington on Glebe Road and U.S. 50, the newest, fastest highway westward to the mushrooming residential tracts of Fairfax County. Neighborhood protests delayed both projects, however. The Chevy Chase store was not realized until 1951, by which time the Arlington store project was abandoned.[39] Ironically, these setbacks enabled the company to allocate capital later for anchor stores at the two most important regional shopping centers in metropolitan area of the next generation: Seven Corners (1955–56), four miles west of Parkington, and

Wheaton Plaza (1958–60), five miles north of downtown Silver Spring.[40]

By contrast, the penchant for experimentation ceased to mark Hecht's building program in later years. Much of the impetus may have gone when Dulcan retired in 1953. His successor, Harry Davidow, took a more conservative course, in part perhaps due to a decline in revenues.[41] Several years elapsed before further expansion in outlying areas was undertaken, missing opportune prospects for growth, at least in the eyes of some executives. The new stores that eventually were built, such as those at Prince George's Plaza (1957–58) and Marlow Heights Shopping Center (1958–59), were of a conventional cast, anchoring some of the less prestigious regional complexes in the metropolitan area. Rather than continue in an upwardly mobile path, the company redirected its focus to its long-standing core constituents, persons of moderate income.[42]

Dulcan's leadership brought Hecht's national prominence as well as an enviable stature locally.

Without an aggressive expansion program, the company might well have gone the way of four Washington competitors—Palais Royal, Kann's, Lansburgh's, and Goldenberg's—which either failed to decentralize or to do so early and extensively enough. Dulcan no doubt hoped that his program would be widely emulated, that his Silver Spring store would stand as a paradigm, and, later, that Parkington would be that model instead. In hindsight, his successors may have viewed his plans as too experimental. But whatever its drawbacks, Dulcan's program gave the store a strong foundation for future growth. After purchase by the Saint Louis–based May Company in the late 1950s, Hecht's resumed its upward path. Today the company enjoys a prominence rivaled by few major retailers in the region, including national chains such as Macy's and Nordstrom's. The Silver Spring store closed in the mid 1980s, reflecting the pronounced decline of that community as a retail center. At the same time, Parkington was completely remade as Ballston Common, a multistory retail mall and

office complex, for which Hecht's continues as the anchor store. In its new form, the facility again functions as a magnet of trade for northern Virginia.

"Success" is not always easy to measure in retail development. Ventures that are pathbreaking in some respects may possess significant drawbacks in others. The size, scope, and character of the Silver Spring store influenced general patterns in the trade, while the locational strategy proved an object lesson in what to avoid. Parkington was even more innovative in its physical characteristics, yet had little direct influence on its successors, and by the late 1950s its siting seemed antiquated. Three decades later, on the other hand, both the location and compact form of the shopping center were well suited to the new, much denser arrangement of Ballston Common. However mixed the blessings, Dulcan's blueprint for Hecht's growth underscores the fluid, somewhat unpredictable nature of retail development, where change is considered imperative if success is to be part of the equation.

## Notes

Generous funding for this project was supplied by grants from the Center for Washington Area Studies at George Washington University. Blair Lee of the Lee Development Corporation, Silver Spring, and Lacey Womack, vice president of the Properties Division at Hecht's kindly granted me access to archival material. I am also grateful to Eileen McGuckian, Phyllis Palmer, C. Ford Peatross, Eric Sandweiss, and Richard Striner for assistance and insights. Many journal and newspaper article titles in the notes section have been foreshortened for brevity's sake.

1. See, for example, William Nelson Taft, "Is the Downtown Shopping District Losing Out?" National Retail Dry Goods Association, *Bulletin* 8 (July 1926): 30–31, 34; Joseph Laronge, "Should We Get Excited About Retail Decentralization?" *National Real Estate Journal* 39 (Dec. 1938): 22–24, 54–55; Earl Burke, "Oakland Keeps Shoppers Coming Downtown," *Women's Wear Daily*, Feb. 21, 1940, 2–3; Earl W. Elhart, "Diagnosing the Dread Decentralization Disease,"

*Women's Wear Daily*, Dec. 26, 1940, II-20, 52; Harry E. Martin, "Chains Still Want Downtown Locations," *Chain Store Age*, Administrative Ed. (Aug. [17], 1941), 10, 38, 40–41; and George J. Eberle, "The Business District," in *Los Angeles: Preface to a Master Plan*, ed. George W. Robbins and L. Deming Tilton (Los Angeles: Pacific Southwest Academy, 1941), 127–44.

2. Contemporary accounts of the subject are numerous. See, for example, "Stores to Expand," *Business Week*, Jan. 6, 1945, 84; "Stores to Expand," *Business Week*, Mar. 23, 1946, 80–81, 83–84; "Department Stores Hurrying to Suburbs," *Business Week*, Oct. 4, 1947, 24–26; "Retail Rush," *Architectural Forum* 85 (Oct. 1946): 10–11; E. B. Weiss, "How to Sell to and through the *New* Department Store," *Printers' Ink* 221 (Nov. 28, 1947): 31–34, 72, 76, 78; Weiss, "Department Stores Are Becoming Chain Stores," *Printers' Ink* 221 (Dec. 5, 1947): 39–40, 62, 66, 68; E. Paul Behles, "Branch Stores," *Retail Management* 43 (Feb. 1948): 21–22, 45; "Big Downtown Stores Are

Threatened," *Changing Times* 3 (Aug. 1949): 19–21;
Faye Henle, "Branches Broaden Department Store
Scope," *Barron's* 30 (Apr. 17, 1950): 19; John Guernsey,
"Suburban Branches," *Department Store Economist* 14
(June 1951): 30–31, 114, 120; (July 1951): 42–43,
78, 111; (Aug. 1951): 32–34, 52, 112; (Sept. 1951):
41–43, 100, 102; Dero A. Saunders, "Department
Stores: Race for the Suburbs," *Fortune* 44 (Dec.
1951): 98–102, 164, 166, 168, 170, 173; Milton P.
Brown, "The Trend in Branch Stores," Retail Trade
Board, Boston Chamber of Commerce, *Twenty-
Fourth Annual Boston Conference on Distribu-
tion 1952*, 77–81; and E. H. Gault, "Suburban
Branches: A New Trend in Retailing," *Michigan
Business Review* 4 (Nov. 1952): 9–13.

3. Trade literature of the period is filled with references to women's concern for efficiency in shopping.
The rise of women in the work force and the general
increase in housework done by women after World
War II offer two reasons why many women would be
less enthusiastic about taking the time and effort to go
on shopping expeditions downtown. For background,
see Eugenia Kaledin, *Mothers and More: American
Women in the 1950s* (Boston: Twayne Publishers,
1984), chap. 4; and Ruth Schwartz Cowan, *More
Work for Mother; The Ironies of Household Technology from the Open Hearth to the Microwave* (New
York: Basic Books, 1983), chap. 7.

4. Three of the major Los Angeles department
stores, the Broadway, Bullock's, and the May Company, were operating at least one large store outside the
city center prior to the war, and all three added equally
large new stores at the war's end. For discussion, see
Richard Longstreth, *City Center to Regional Mall: Architecture, the Automobile, and Retailing in Los Angeles, 1920–1950* (Cambridge, Mass.: MIT Press, forthcoming), chaps. 4, 5, 10.

5. I am grateful to Warren O. Simonds, retired senior vice president of Hecht's, for sharing many insights on the company's growth (interview, Arlington,
Virginia, Mar. 13, 1992). Employed by Hecht's from
1945 to 1986, Simonds emphasized the store's relatively low stature during the early twentieth century.
Woodward & Lothrop was considered the most stylish, then the Palais Royal, which Woodward &
Lothrop purchased in the mid-1940s. Two middle-mar-
ket stores, Kann's and Lansburgh's, also were considered more prestigious than Hecht's prior to the 1930s.

Only Goldenberg's, which made no pretense at being
anything other that a bargain center for working persons, had less prestige. Such a hierarchy existed among
department stores in all cities and was a key determi-
nant of operating policies.

6. For background on Hecht's and its downtown
store, see Donley Lukens, "Beautiful New Hecht
Home," *Washington Post,* Mar. 23, 1924, III-2, 4;
"Romances of Washington Stores," *Washington Post,*
Nov. 8, 1925, Amusements Sect., 11; "Hecht's Will
Open," *Washington Post,* Nov. 12, 1925, 24; "Hecht
Co. Holds," *Women's Wear Daily,* Nov. 17, 1925, 6,
23; "Hecht's Has Spent 30 Years," *Women's Wear Daily,*
Jan. 4, 1950, 69; and "Hecht Company to Mark,"
*(Washington) Evening Star,* Mar. 25, 1956, A-35.

6. Simonds interview; "Dulcan Views Parkington,"
*Washington Post,* Nov. 1, 1951, 10C. According to
Simonds, Dulcan may well have contemplated branch
expansion prior to the war. The company's warehouse
(1936–37) was designed so that its lower floors could be
converted to retail use if market conditions warranted.

7. For background, see John Guernsey, *Retailing
Tomorrow* (New York: Dry Goods Economist, 1929),
136–44; "The Growth of Branch Stores," National Retail Dry Goods Association, *Bulletin* 12 (Oct. 1930):
546–47; "Branch Stores Best for Specialty Types," *New
York Times,* Oct. 19, 1930, II-18; and "Plans for Expansion Studied by Retailers," *New York Times,* Aug.
2, 1936, III-8.

8. See n. 4 above.

9. Longstreth, *City Center to Regional Mall,* chap. 5.

10. *(Washington) Evening Star,* Nov. 5, 1945, B1;
"Silver Spring Hecht Store," *Washington Post,* Nov. 25,
1945, 4R; "Hecht Co. to Build," *(Washington) Evening
Star,* Nov. 1945, A9; "Hecht Co. to Open," *Women's
Wear Daily,* Nov. 26, 1945, 1, 6; "Hecht Co. Will
Build," *(Silver Spring) Maryland News,* Nov. 30, 1945,
1, 9; "The Hecht Company to Open," *Silver Spring
Post,* Nov. 30, 1945, 1, 4; *Silver Spring Post,* Dec. 14,
1945, 1; *Retail Management* 41 (Feb. 1946): 43.

11. For background, see Richard Longstreth, "Sil-
ver Spring: Georgia Avenue, Colesville Road and the
Creation of an Alternative 'Downtown' for Metropoli-
tan Washington," in *Streets: Critical Perspective on
Public Space,* ed. Zeynep Celik, et al. (Berkeley and Los
Angeles: Univ. of California Press, 1994), 237–48;
Longstreth, "The Neighborhood Shopping Center in
Washington, D.C., 1930–1941," *Journal of the Soci-*

*ety of Architectural Historians* 51 (Mar. 1992), 28–31; and Mark Wallston, "The Commercial Rise and Fall of Silver Spring," *Maryland Historical Magazine* 81 (Winter 1986), 330–39.

12. For contemporary accounts, see: "Silver Spring Building," *(Washington) Evening Star*, Apr. 12, 1946, B1; Conrad F. Harness, "Maryland's '2nd' City," *Washington Post*, Aug. 4, 1946, 4R, 7R; "Silver Spring," *Washington Daily News*, Nov. 14, 1946, 28; "Sun Writer Tells," *(Silver Spring) Maryland News*, July 22, 1949, B1, and July 29, 1949, B1; and Conrad F. Harness, "Silver Spring Boasts," *Washington Post*, July 24, 1949, 1R, 3R.

13. "Proposed Woodward & Lothrop," *Record of Bethesda-Chevy Chase*, Aug. 31, 1945, 1; "2 District Stores," *(Washington) Evening Star*, Aug. 31, 1945, B1; "Woodward Store," *(Silver Spring) Maryland News*, Dec. 2, 1945, 1, 5.

14. "Lee Suggests Master Zoning," *(Silver Spring) Maryland News*, Nov. 24, 1944, 1, 7; "County Plan. Committee," *(Silver Spring) Maryland News*, Dec. 15, 1944, 1, 7; *(Silver Spring) Maryland News*, Mar. 2, 1945, 6; "Master Zone Plan," *(Silver Spring) Maryland News*, Mar. 15, 1946, 1, 7.

15. "Bethesda Business District," *(Silver Spring) Maryland News*, Nov. 24, 1944, 1–2; *(Silver Spring) Maryland News*, Apr. 12, 1946, 6; "Collingwood Citizens," *Record of Bethesda-Chevy Chase*, May 3, 1946, 1, 3; "Bethesda Chamber Board," *(Silver Spring) Maryland News*, June 21, 1946, 1, 3; "Hearing Due," *(Silver Spring) Maryland News*, Aug. 30, 1946, 1; "Business and Home Owners," *Record of Bethesda-Chevy Chase*, Oct. 11, 1946, 1, 3; "Master Zone Plan," *(Silver Spring) Maryland News*, Oct. 18, 1946, 1, 9, 12; "Planning Commission Favors," *Record of Bethesda-Chevy Chase*, Nov. 22, 1946, 18.

16. "Allied Civic Unit," *(Silver Spring) Maryland News*, Apr. 26, 1946, 1, 7; "Trade Board Okays," *(Silver Spring) Maryland News*, May 3, 1946, 1, 3; "Citizens Air Views," *Silver Spring Post*, Jan. 17, 1947, 1, 9; "Allied Civic Group," *Silver Spring Post*, Jan. 31, 1947, 1, 13; "County Board Acts," *(Silver Spring) Maryland News*, Feb. 14, 1947, 1, 7.

17. "Lee Suggests," *(Silver Spring) Maryland News*, Dec. 1, 1944, 1, 7; "Public Parking Space," *(Silver Spring) Maryland News*, Jan. 12, 1945, 7; "Highway Committee," *(Silver Spring) Maryland News*, Jan. 26, 1945, 1, 12; "County Planning Committee," *(Silver*

*Spring) Maryland News*, Feb. 2, 1945, 1, 8; "16 Public Parking Spaces," *(Silver Spring) Maryland News*, Mar. 2, 1945, 7; "Silver Spring Board," *(Silver Spring) Maryland News*, Mar. 9, 1945, 1, 8; "Planning Officials Predict," *(Silver Spring) Maryland News*, Jan. 4, 1946, 1, 5; "Board Votes," *(Silver Spring) Maryland News*, Feb. 1, 1946, 1, 6; "Bond Issue," *(Silver Spring) Maryland News*, Apr. 26, 1946, 1, 6; "$800,000 Bond Issue," *Silver Spring Post*, Apr. 26, 1946, 1, 4; "Board Adopts Plan," *(Silver Spring) Maryland News*, May 24, 1946, 1, 2; "Board Authorizes Purchase," *(Silver Spring) Maryland News*, Aug. 16, 1946, 1; "Public Off-Street Parking," *Silver Spring Post*, Oct. 18, 1946, 1, 4; Roger B. Farquhar, "Park Your Car," *Washington Post*, Apr. 4, 1948, 1R; *(Silver Spring) Maryland News*, June 11, 1948, A-8; "Silver Spring's Parking Lots," *(Silver Spring) Maryland News*, Aug. 26, 1949, A-1, A-4; *(Silver Spring) Maryland News*, Nov. 10, 1949, B-1; Stanley Baitz, "Silver Spring Solves Parking," *(Washington) Evening Star*, Sept. 24, 1950, Pictorial Magazine, 3.

The plan received a considerable amount of national publicity. See, for example, *American Society of Planning Officials Newsletter* 11 (Aug. 1945): 67; *Public Management* 29 (Dec. 1947): 365; "Free Parking Lots," *Automobile Facts* 8 (Dec. 1949): 6; *Parking—How It Is Financed* (New York: National Retail Dry Goods Association, 1952), 30–31; and *Parking Programs* (Washington: American Automobile Association, 1954), 169–79.

18. For background, see: Orin F. Nolting and Paul Oppermann, *The Parking Problem* (Chicago: Public Administration Service, 1938), 3–8; Wilbur S. Smith and Charles S. LeCraw, *Parking* (Saugatuck, Conn.: Eno Foundation, 1946), 71–72; Charles S. Rhyne, *Municipally Owned Parking Lots and Garages* (Washington: National Institute of Municipal Law Officials, 1948); Miner B. Phillips and Irving Tenner, *Financing Municipal Off-Street Parking Facilities* (Chicago: Municipal Finance Officers Association, 1948); *Parking—How It Is Financed*, 27–29; and pertinent sections of the *Municipal Year Book* (Chicago: International City Managers Association) from 1937 on.

19. Concerning the facility as realized, see "Hecht Spokesmen Say," *(Silver Spring) Maryland News*, June 6, 1947, 7; "Hecht Co.'s Expansion," *Women's Wear Daily*, July 30, 1947, 49; "The Hecht Co," *Silver Spring Post*, Oct. 24, 1947, 4; "2,500,000 Hecht

Store," *Washington Post,* Oct. 26, 1947, 1R; "Hecht Co., Silver Spring," *Silver Spring Post,* Oct. 31, 1947, 4; "Lane Will Cut Ribbon," *(Silver Spring) Maryland News,* Oct. 31, 1947, 9, 13; "Hecht's Silver Spring," *Washington Post,* Nov. 2, 1947, 6M; "Hecht Sales 'Terrific'," *(Silver Spring) Maryland News,* Nov. 7, 1947, 9; "Hecht's Silver Spring," *Retail Management* 42 (Nov. 1947): 18, 43; and M. O. Waugh, "Hecht's, Silver Spring," *Display World* 51 (Dec. 1947): 30–31, 80–81.

20. Concerning the firm, see Richard Longstreth, *History on the Line: Testimony in the Cause of Preservation,* scheduled to be published by the National Council for Preservation Education and the National Park Service, 1996, chaps. 6–7.

21. "Sears Builds Windowless Store," *Chain Store Age,* General Merchandise Ed., 10 (July 1934): 22–23, 54; "No Windows," *Architect & Engineer* 120 (Feb. 1935): 35–38; "Without Windows," *Architectural Forum* 62 (Mar. 1935): 206–11.

22. Concerning the additions, see "Hecht Co. Will Expand," *Women's Wear Daily,* Nov. 23, 1949, 1, 41; "The Hecht Co. Will Expand," *(Silver Spring) Maryland News,* Nov. 25, 1949, A-1, B-1; "New Downstairs Store," *(Silver Spring) Maryland News,* July 28, 1950, A-1; "Hecht's Silver Spring," *Women's Wear Daily,* Aug. 1, 1950, 3; "Hecht's Opens," *Women's Wear Daily,* Aug. 14, 1950, 39; "Hecht Company Plans," *(Silver Spring) Maryland News,* Feb. 4, 1955, 1–2; and "Hecht Co. Opens," *Washington Post,* Oct. 30, 1955, K2.

Concerning the company's growth, see Annette C. Ward, "Washington—A Problem of Logistics," *Women's Wear Daily,* Apr. 27, 1949, 54, and Apr. 28, 1954, 54; and *Women's Wear Daily,* Oct. 25, 1948, 9.

23. George Kennedy, "Silver Spring . . . Is Real Estate 'El Dorado,'" *(Washington) Evening Star,* Nov. 6, 1950, B1; Wallston, "Rise and Fall," 335–36; Longstreth, "Silver Spring," 241–42. Accounts of key stores include "Murphy's New Modern Store," *Silver Spring Post,* Nov. 22, 1946, 1, 8; *Washington Post,* July 13, 1947, 3R; *(Silver Spring) Maryland News,* Jan. 16, 1948, B-1; "Jeleff's Plans," *Women's Wear Daily,* Mar. 31, 1948, 1, 50; "Sears, Roebuck Plans," *(Silver Spring) Maryland News,* Oct. 22, 1948, 1; "J. C. Penney Co. Plans," *(Silver Spring) Maryland News,* Dec. 3, 1948, A-1; "Jeleff's Opens," *Women's Wear Daily,* Feb. 16, 1949, 5; *(Silver Spring) Maryland*

*News,* Mar. 25, 1949, B-1; *Women's Wear Daily,* Apr. 20, 1949, 62; "9 More Stores," *Women's Wear Daily,* Aug. 1, 1949, 6; "Hahn Shoe Co," *Washington Post,* Aug. 14, 1949, 4R; "New J. C. Penney," *(Silver Spring) Maryland News,* Aug. 11, 1950, A-1; "Penney's Opens," *Women's Wear Daily,* Aug. 18, 1950, 47; "Eig Starts," *(Silver Spring) Maryland News,* Sept. 22, 1950, A-1; "8-Store Building," *(Silver Spring) Maryland News,* Oct. 13, 1950, B-1; *Washington Post,* Nov. 19, 1950, 5R; "New Morton's Store," *Washington Post,* June 24, 1951, 3R; "Mazor Opens," *(Silver Spring) Maryland News,* Oct. 19, 1951, II-3; and Paul Herron, "Silver Spring Hangs," *Washington Post,* Nov. 4, 1951, 1R.

24. See, for example, Guernsey, "Suburban Branches," *Department Store Economist* 15 (July 1951): 43; and Saunders, "Department Stores," 102.

25. Hecht's sought to purchase a lot of its own, a move blocked by the Silver Spring Board of Trade, ostensibly because it would inhibit parking for other stores; see "Move by Hecht's," *Women's Wear Daily,* Nov. 29, 1951, 45.

26. For background, see Longstreth, *City Center to Regional Mall,* chap. 9.

27. "Parkington Homemaker Paradise," *Washington Post,* Nov. 3 1951, C1; "Lots of Planning," *Washington Daily News,* Nov. 5, 1951, 8A-9A. I have yet to find accounts of Clarendon comparable to those of Silver Spring. Some basic information is contained in "Historic Resources in the Clarendon Commercial District," Historic Affairs and Landmark Review Board, Arlington County, Virginia, May 1985. Concerning Arlington County, see: Dorothea Andrews, "Arlington Rides Crest," *Washington Post,* Aug. 4, 1946, 1B, 2B; Conrad P. Harnes, "Building Boom," *Washington Post,* Aug. 25, 1946, 5R, 9R; and Harnes, "Arlington Continues," *Washington Post,* Apr. 11, 1948, 1R.

28. When proposals did surface, they were modest by comparison to Silver Spring. See "Chamber Offers," *(Arlington County) Sun,* Mar. 4, 1949, 1; "Mr. Merchant: Look!" *(Arlington County) Sun,* Dec. 2, 1949, 4; "Writer Says Arlington," *(Arlington County) Sun,* Dec. 9, 1949, 4; "Parking Plan Bill," *(Arlington County) Sun,* Jan. 27, 1950, 1; "Parking Lot Data," *(Arlington County) Sun,* July 7, 1950, II-1; and "50-Space Parking," *(Arlington County) Sun,* Sept. 29, 1950, 1.

29. "Hecht Co. Coming," *(Arlington County) Sun,* Apr. 14, 1950, 1–2; *Women's Wear Daily,* Oct. 19,

1950, 54; "Hecht Company Reveals," *(Arlington County) Sun,* Oct. 20, 1950, 1, 8; *Architectural Forum* 93 (Nov. 1950): 14; "Pick Your Parking Level," *Chain Store Age,* Administrative ed., [26] (Dec. 1950): 40; *Commonwealth* 18 (Jan. 1951): 20. Later accounts include "Shopping Center," *Architectural Record* 109 (Mar. 1951): 137–38; *Stores* 33 (Sept. 1951): 9; Carl Bleiberg, "The Hecht Company's New Shopping Center," *Commonwealth* 18 (Oct. 1951): 12; "New Suburban Hecht's," *Women's Wear Daily,* Nov. 1, 1951, 1, 47; "Hecht's Virginia Branch," *Stores* 33 (Nov. 1951): 52, 54; *Washington Post,* Nov. 3, 1951, Hecht-Parkington Sect.; "Hecht's Opens," *(Washington) Evening Star,* Nov. 11, 1951, A-25; *Washington Daily News,* Nov. 15, 1951, 8A–9A, 118A–19A; and R. H. Tatlow III, "Parkington: Shopping Center Design," *Traffic Quarterly* 6 (Oct. 1952): 440–56. See also nn. 30, 32 below.

30. In addition to references cited in n. 28 above, see Ruth Boyer Scott, "A $3 Million Gamble," *National Real Estate and Building Journal* 54 (June 1953): 42–43; "Garages Grow Up," *Architectural Forum* 98 (Feb. 1953): 132–33; and Dietrich Klose, *Metropolitan Parking Structures* (New York: Praeger, 1965), 34.

31. Namely the May Company store at Lakewood Center, near Long Beach. See Longstreth, *City Center to Regional Mall,* chap. 11.

32. The other stores opened on a gradual basis, the first some three months after Hecht's. See "12 Stores Announced," *(Washington) Evening Star,* Nov. 16, 1951, A-4; "Dulcan Tells," *Washington Post,* Nov. 17, 1951, 13B; *Washington Post,* Feb. 24, 1952, 5R; *Washington Post,* Feb. 26, 1952, 7; *Washington Post,* Mar. 23, 1952, 11M; *Washington Post,* July 27, 1952, 2R; *Washington Post,* Aug. 10, 1952, 2R; *Washington Post,* Sept. 21, 1952, 14M; *Washington Post,* Nov. 22, 1953, 10R; and *Washington Post,* Apr. 8, 1956, G15. Tenants included units of W. T. Grant and McCrory's; three women's, two men's, and a children's wear stores; two shoe stores; two furniture stores; a drug store; jewelry store; bookstore; delicatessen; candy store; supermarket; service station; poultry shop; and several others. For a list, see J. Ross McKeever, "Shopping Centers Re-Studied, Part II—Practical Experiences," *Urban Land Institute Technical Bulletin* 30 (May 1957): 107–8.

33. The name at once became a source of contro-versy among some county residents because it did not refer to the community. Hecht's tried to accommodate concerns by modifying the name to the unwieldy "Parkington at Arlington," but the complex remained known simply as Parkington until it was completely remade as Ballston Common in 1984–86. See "'Parkington' Name Stirs Board," *Washington Post,* Nov. 16, 1951, 17; "Hecht's Advertisements," *(Washington) Evening Star,* Nov. 16, 1951, A-4; and "Now It's 'Parkington in Arlington'," *Washington Post,* Nov. 18, 1951, 19M.

34. "Miracle of Planning," *Washington Post,* Nov. 3, 1951, 1C. Concerning avant-garde precedents, see "Lichtrelame," *Baumeister* 26 (Dec. 1928): B252–58; "Uber Architektur und Schrift," *Baumeister* 27 (Nov. 1929): 349–65; Adolf Schuhmacher, *Ladenbau . . .* (Stuttgart: Julius Hoffman, c. 1934); and Rene Herbst, *Boutiques et Magazins* (Paris: Charles Moreau, n.d.), plates 14, 31, 35, 46.

35. *Women's Wear Daily,* Nov. 29, 1950, 53; "Kann's Building," *(Arlington County) Sun,* Dec. 1, 1950, 3; "Kann's Opens Store," *(Washington) Evening Star,* Nov. 15, 1951, A-29; "New Kann's Store," *Washington Post,* Nov. 16, 1951, 16; *Women's Wear Daily,* Nov. 7, 1951, 69; *Washington Post,* Feb. 26, 1952, 7; *(Washington) Evening Star,* Mar. 1, 1952, B-1; "Arlington's New Shopping," *Washington Post,* Mar. 2, 1952, 10R, 11R; J. Ross McKeever, "Shopping Centers: Principles and Policies," *Urban Land Institute Technical Bulletin* 20 (June 1953): 51–55.

36. On the other hand, he would have known that a local developer had sought to lure a Washington department store to the site nearly a year earlier; see "Rezoning Clears Way," *(Arlington County) Sun,* Dec. 16, 1949, 1–2.

37. Simonds interview.

38. However, the concept was applied to urban-renewal schemes involving retail centers, among the earliest and best known of which was at New Haven, Connecticut.

39. "Montgomery Refuses," *(Washington) Evening Star,* Dec. 29, 1945, B1; "Land Rezoned," *(Silver Spring) Maryland News,* Jan. 4, 1946, 1, 2; "Woodward & Lothrop," *Women's Wear Daily,* Jan. 11, 1946, 39; "Woodward's Buy 7 Acres," *Women's Wear Daily,* Nov. 25, 1946, 1, 6; "Woodward's Plans," *Women's Wear Daily,* Dec. 9, 1946, 1; "Sues to Stop," *Women's Wear Daily,* Dec. 24, 1946, 1, 27; "Court

Upholds," *Women's Wear Daily,* Mar. 14, 1947, 1, 10; "Move to Block," *Women's Wear Daily,* June 26, 1947, 2; "Woodward's Files," *Women's Wear Daily,* July 3, 1947, 8. Concerning the realized store, see "Woody's Breaks," *Record of Bethesda-Chevy Chase,* Oct. 14, 1949, 1, 5; *(Silver Spring) Maryland News,* Oct. 14, 1949, B1; *Women's Wear Daily,* Nov. 16, 1949, 70; and Lucia Brown, "Woodie's Northwest Store," *Washington Post,* Nov. 3, 1950, 10.

40. Concerning Seven Corners, see *Washington Post,* May 24, 1953, 7B; *Washington Post,* Mar. 13, 1955, G4; "Seven Corners Is Giant Boost," *Washington Post,* Apr. 22, 1956, K16; "Seven Corners Shopping Center," *Washington Post,* Oct. 3, 1956, 37–56; and McKeever, "Shopping Centers—Restudied," 70–72. Concerning Wheaton Plaza, see "County Weighs Pros," *(Silver Spring) Maryland News,* Sept. 17, 1954, 1, 3; "Wheaton Plaza Gains Speed," *(Silver Spring) Maryland News,* Jan. 24, 1956, 1; "Woodward & Lothrop," *Suburban Record,* Mar. 27, 1958, 1; "Woodward & Lothrop," *(Silver Spring) Maryland News,* Mar. 28, 1958, 1; and "Woodies Lists," *Washington Post,* Sept. 12, 1958, C22.

41. "Dulcan Made Hecht Stores," *Washington Times-Herald,* Mar. 5, 1952, 4; "C. B. Dulcan Leaving," *Washington Post,* Jan. 30, 1953, 1, 10; "Charles Dulcan Leaves," *(Washington) Evening Star,* Jan. 30, 1953, A-2; "Hecht Co. Net Drops," *Washington Post,* Apr. 25, 1952, 3B; "Hecht Sales Dip," *Washington Post,* Apr. 28, 1954, 29; S. Oliver Goodman, "Dividend Cut," *Washington Post,* Jun. 24, 1954, 30. A rebound came two years later; see Goodman, "Hecht Net Up 22%," *Washington Post,* May 1, 1956, 34.

42. Concerning later stores, see Donald B. Hadley, "Hecht Co, Plans Store," *(Washington) Evening Star,* Aug. 2, 1957, A-20; "4th Suburban Store," *(Washington) Evening Star,* Oct. 7, 1958, A-18; "Hecht's Sets Opening," *(Washington) Evening Star,* Nov. 2, 1958, A-35; and "Sixth Hecht Store," *Washington Post,* Aug. 8, 1963, A17.

# Select Bibliography

Ackerman, James. *The Villa: Form and Ideology of Country Houses.* Princeton: Princeton Univ. Press, 1990.

Adams, Annmarie. "Charterville and the Landscape of Social Reform." In *Perspectives in Vernacular Architecture, IV.* Edited by Thomas Carter and Bernard L. Herman. Columbia: Univ. of Missouri Press, 1991.

———. "The Eichler Home: Intention and Experience in Postwar Suburbia." In *Gender, Class, and Shelter: Perspectives in Vernacular Architecture, V.* Edited by Elizabeth Cromley and Carter Hudgins. Knoxville: Univ. of Tennessee Press, 1995.

Akagi, Roy H. *The Town Proprietors of New England.* Philadelphia: Univ. of Pennsylvania Press, 1924.

Allen, David Grayson. *Diary of John Quincy Adams.* Cambridge, Mass.: Harvard Univ. Press, 1981.

———. *In English Ways: The Movement of Societies and the Transferal of English Local Law and Custom to Massachusetts Bay in the Seventeenth Century.* Chapel Hill: Univ. of North Carolina Press, 1981.

Alvey, Edward, Jr. *The Fredericksburg Fire of 1807.* Fredericksburg, Va.: Historic Fredericksburg Foundation, Inc., 1988.

Amos, Harriet E. *Cotton City: Urban Development in Antebellum Mobile.* Tuscaloosa: Univ. of Alabama Press, 1985.

Axelrod, Alan, ed. *The Colonial Revival in America.* New York: Norton, 1985.

Berlin, Ira. *Slaves Without Masters: The Free Negro in the Antebellum South.* New York: Vintage, 1974.

Berman, Myron. *Richmond's Jewry, 1769–1976: Shabbat in Shockoe.* Charlottesville: Univ. Press of Virginia, 1979.

Billington, Ray Allen. *Westward Expansion: A History of the American Frontier.* New York: Macmillan, 1974.

Bishir, Catherine W. *North Carolina Architecture.* Chapel Hill: Univ. of North Carolina Press, 1990.

———. "Yuppies, Bubbas, and the Politics of Culture." In *Perspectives in Vernacular Architecture, III.* Edited by Thomas Carter and Bernard L. Herman. Columbia: Univ. of Missouri Press, 1989.

Bishir, Catherine W., et al. *Architects and Builders in North Carolina: A History of the Practice of Building*. Chapel Hill and London: Univ. of North Carolina Press, 1990.

Blackman, Margaret B. "Creativity in Acculturation: Art, Architecture and Ceremony from the Northwest Coast." *Ethnohistory* 23 (4) (Fall 1976).

———. *During My Time: Florence Edenshaw Davidson, a Haida Woman*. Seattle: Univ. of Washington Press, 1982; rev. ed., 1992.

Bourdieu, Pierre. *Distinction: A Social Critique of the Judgement of Taste*. Translated by Richard Nice. Cambridge: Harvard Univ. Press, 1984.

Bluestone, Daniel M. "From Promenade to Park: The Gregarious Origins of Brooklyn's Park Movement." *American Quarterly* 39 (Winter 1987): 529–50.

Blumin, Stuart M. *The Emergence of the Middle Class: Social Experience in the American City, 1760–1900*. Cambridge: Cambridge Univ. Press, 1989.

Boles, John B. *Black Southerners, 1619–1869*. Lexington: Univ. Press of Kentucky, 1984.

Bonta, Juan Pablo. *Architecture and Its Interpretation*. New York: Rizzoli, 1979.

Borsay, Peter. *The English Urban Renaissance: Culture and Society in the Provincial Town, 1660–1770*. Oxford: Clarendon Press, 1989.

Bourque, Monique. "Virtue, Industry, and Independence: Inmates and Labor in the Almshouses of the Philadelphia Region, 1791–1860." Ph.D. diss., Univ. of Delaware, 1995.

Brooke, John. *The Heart of the Commonwealth: Society and Political Culture in Worcester County, Mass., 1713–1861*. Cambridge: Cambridge Univ. Press, 1989.

Brownell, Charles E. "Laying the Groundwork: The Classical Tradition and Virginia Architecture, 1770–1870." In *Making of Virginia Architecture*. Richmond: Virginia Museum of Fine Arts, 1992.

Bryan, John M., ed. *Robert Mills, Architect*. Washington, D.C.: American Institute of Architects Press, 1989.

Bunting, Bainbridge. *Houses of Boston's Back Bay: An Architectural History, 1840–1917*. New York: Belknap Press, 1967.

Bushman, Richard. *The Refinement of America: Persons, Houses, Cities*. New York: Knopf, 1992.

Cable, Mary. *Lost New Orleans*. New York: American Legacy Press, 1980.

Campbell, Colin. *The Romantic Ethic and the Rise of Modern Consumerism*. London: Basil Blackwell, 1987.

Campbell, Edward D.C., Jr., and Kym S. Rice, eds. *Before Freedom Came: African-American Life in the Antebellum South*. Richmond: Museum of the Confederacy, 1991.

Campen, Richard N. *Architecture of the Western Reserve, 1800–1900*. Cleveland: Press of Case Western Reserve Univ., 1971.

Carson, Jane. *Colonial Virginians at Play*. Williamsburg: Colonial Williamsburg Foundation, 1989.

Chambers, S. Allen, Jr. *Lynchburg: An Architectural History*. Charlottesville: Univ. Press of Virginia, 1981.

Chappell, Edward. "Acculturation In the Shenandoah Valley: Rhenish Houses of the Massanutten Settlement." In *Common Places: Readings in American Vernacular Architecture*. Edited by Dell Upton and John Michael Vlach. Athens: Univ. of Georgia Press, 1986.

Chesson, Michael. *Richmond After the War, 1865–1890*. Richmond: Virginia State Library, 1981.

Clark, Clifford. *The American Family Home, 1800–1960*. Chapel Hill: Univ. of North Carolina Press, 1986.

Coar, Valerie Hollins. *A Century of Black Photographers, 1840–1940*. Providence: Rhode Island School of Design, 1983.

Cohen, David Steven. *The Dutch-American Farm*. New York: New York Univ. Press, 1992.

Cowan, Ruth Schwartz. *More Work for Mother; The Ironies of Household Technology from the Open Hearth to the Microwave*. New York: Basic Books, 1983.

Cromley, Elizabeth Collins. "Modernizing—Or, 'You Never See a Screen Door on Affluent Homes.'" *Journal of American Culture* 5 (Summer 1982): 71–79.

Cummings, Abbot Lowell. *The Framed Houses of Massachusetts Bay, 1625–1725*. Cambridge: Harvard Univ. Press, 1979.

———. *Rural Household Inventories, Establishing the Name, Uses and Furnishings of Rooms in Colonial New England*. Boston: Society for the Preservation of New England Antiquities, 1964.

Dabney, Virginius. *Richmond: The Story of a City*. Garden City, N.Y.: Doubleday, 1976.

Deetz, James. *In Small Things Forgotten: The Archaeology of Early American Life.* Garden City, N.Y.: Anchor Press/Doubleday, 1977.

de Laguna, Frederica. "Tlingit." In *Handbook of North American Indians. Volume 7: Northwest Coast.* Washington, D.C.: Smithsonian Institution, 1990.

Digby, Anne. *Pauper Palaces.* Boston and London: Routledge and Kegan Paul, 1978.

Donnelly, Marian Card. *New England Meeting Houses of the Seventeenth Century.* Middleton, Conn.: Wesleyan Univ. Press, 1968.

Doucet, Michael, and John Weaver. *Housing the North American City.* Montreal: McGill-Queen's Univ. Press, 1991.

Doucet, Michael, and John Weaver. "Material Culture and the North American House: The Era of the Common Man, 1870–1920." *Journal of American History* 72 (Dec. 1985): 560–87.

Douglas, Mary, and Baron Isherwood. *The World of Goods: Towards an Anthropology of Consumption.* New York: Basic Books, 1979.

Downing, Antoinette F., and Vincent Scully Jr. *The Architectural Heritage of Newport, Rhode Island, 1640–1915.* New York: American Legacy Press, 1967.

Drucker, Philip. *The Native Brotherhoods: Modern Intertribal Organizations on the Northwest Coast.* Washington, D.C.: Smithsonian Institution, Bureau of American Ethnology. Bulletin 168, 1958.

Dwyer, Ellen. *Homes for the Mad: Life Inside Two Nineteenth-Century Asylums.* New Brunswick and London: Rutgers Univ. Press, 1987.

Earle, Carville, and Ronald Hoffman. "Staple Crops and Urban Development in the Eighteenth-Century South." *Perspectives in American History* 10 (1967).

Easterling, Keller, and David Moheny, ed. *Seaside: Making a Town in America.* New York: Princeton Architectural Press, 1991.

Edsforth, Ronald. *Class Conflict and Cultural Consensus: the Making of a Mass Consumer Society in Flint, Michigan.* New Brunswick: Rutgers Univ. Press, 1987.

Edwards, Kathy, Esmé Howard, and Toni Prawl. *Monument Avenue, History and Architecture.* Washington, D.C.: HABS/HAER, U.S. Department of the Interior, 1992.

Ernst, Joseph A., and H. Roy Merrens. "'Camden's turrets pierce the skies!': The Urban Process in the Southern Colonies during the Eighteenth Century." *William and Mary Quarterly,* 3d Series, 30 (Oct. 1973): 549–74.

Evans, Robin. *The Fabrication of Virtue: English Prison Architecture, 1750–1840.* Cambridge: Cambridge Univ. Press, 1982.

Farmer, Charles J. *In the Absence of Towns: Settlement and Trade in Southside Virginia, 1730–1800.* Lanham, Md.: Rowman & Littlefield, 1993.

Favretti, Rudy J. "The Ornamentation of New England Towns: 1750–1850." *Journal of Garden History* 2 (1982): 333.

Felder, Paula. *Forgotten Companions.* Fredericksburg, Va.: Historic Publications of Fredericksburg, 1982.

Finney, Jack. *Time and Again.* New York: Simon & Schuster, 1970.

Fitchen, John. *The New World Dutch Barn.* Syracuse: Syracuse Univ. Press, 1968.

Foucault, Michel. *Discipline and Punish: The Birth of the Prison.* New York: Vintage Books, 1979.

Fox, Richard Wightman, and T. J. Jackson Lears, eds. *The Culture of Consumption: Critical Essays in American History, 1880–1980.* New York: Pantheon, 1983.

Fox-Genovese, Elizabeth. *Within the Plantation Household: Black and White Women of the Old South.* Chapel Hill: Univ. of North Carolina Press, 1988.

Garfield, Viola E., and Linn A. Forrest. *The Wolf and the Raven: Totem Poles of Southeastern Alaska.* Seattle: Univ. of Washington Press, 1948.

Geib, Susan. "Landscape and Faction: Spatial Transformation in William Bentley's Salem." *Essex Institute Historical Collections* 113 (July 1977): 163–80.

Gernsheim, Helmut, and Alison Gernsheim. *The History of Photography from the Camera Obscura to the Beginning of the Modern Era.* New York: McGraw-Hill, 1969.

Gilroy, Paul. *The Black Atlantic.* Cambridge, Mass.: Harvard Univ. Press, 1993.

Glasgow, Ellen. *The Woman Within.* New York: Harcourt, Brace, 1954.

Glassie, Henry. "Eighteenth-Century Cultural Process in Delaware Valley Folk Building." *Winterthur Portfolio* 7 (1972).

———. *Folk Housing in Middle Virginia: A Structural Analysis of Historic Artifacts.* Knoxville: Univ. of Tennessee Press, 1975.

————. *Passing the Time in Ballymenone: Culture and History of an Ulster Community*. Philadelphia: Univ. of Pennsylvania Press, 1982.

Goggin, Elizabeth Howell. "Public Welfare in Delaware, 1638–1930." In *Delaware: A History of the First State*. Vol. 2. Edited by H. Clay Reed. New York: Lewis Historical Publishing Co., 1947.

Goldfield, David R. *Cotton Fields and Skyscrapers: Southern City and Region, 1607–1980*. Baton Rouge: Louisiana State Univ. Press, 1982.

Gould, Elizabeth Barrett. *From Fort to Port: An Architectural History of Mobile, Alabama, 1711–1918*. Tuscaloosa: Univ. of Alabama Press, 1988.

Gowans, Alan. *The Comfortable House: North American Suburban Architecture, 1890–1930*. Cambridge, Mass.: MIT Press, 1986.

————. *Images of American Living, Four Centuries of Architecture and Furniture as Cultural Expression*. Philadelphia: Lippincott, 1964.

Grier, Katherine C. *Culture and Comfort: People, Parlors, and Upholstery 1850–1910*. Amherst and Rochester: Univ. of Massachusetts Press and the Margaret Woodbury Strong Museum, 1989.

Gutman, Robert. *Architectural Practice: A Critical View*. Princeton: Princeton Architectural Press, 1988.

————. *The Design of American Housing: A Reappraisal of the Architect's Role*.

Haber, Carole, and Brian Gratton. "Old Age, Public Welfare and Race: The Case of Charleston, South Carolina, 1800–1949." *Journal of Social History* 21 (2) (1987).

Halttunen, Karen. *Confidence Men and Painted Women: A Study in Middle-Class Culture, 1830–1870*. New Haven: Yale Univ. Press, 1982.

Hamilton, Kenneth Marvin. *Black Towns and Profit*. Urbana and Chicago: Univ. of Illinois Press, 1991.

Hamlin, Talbot. *Benjamin Henry Latrobe*. New York: Oxford Univ. Press, 1955.

Handsman, Russell G. "Historical Archaeology and Capitalism, Subscriptions and Separations: the Production of Individualism." *North American Archaeologist* 4 (1) (1983).

Herman, Bernard L. *Architecture and Rural Life in Central Delaware, 1700–1900*. Knoxville: Univ. of Tennessee Press, 1987.

————. *The Stolen House*. Charlottesville: Univ. Press of Virginia, 1992.

Hirsch, Adam Jay. *The Rise of the Penitentiary: Prisons and Punishment in Early America*. New Haven: Yale Univ. Press, 1992.

Holdsworth, Deryck. "House and Home in Vancouver: Images of West Coast Urbanism, 1886–1929." In *The Canadian City: Essays in Urban and Social History*. Edited by Gilbert A. Stelter and Alan F. J. Artibise. Ottawa: Carleton Univ. Press, 1984.

Hood, Graham. *The Governor's Palace in Williamsburg: A Cultural Study*. Williamsburg: Colonial Williamsburg Foundation, 1991.

Horowitz, Daniel. *The Morality of Spending: Attitudes Toward the Consumer Society in America, 1875–1940*. Baltimore: Johns Hopkins Univ. Press, 1985.

Hubka, Thomas. *Big House, Little House, Back House, Barn: The Connected Farm Buildings of New England*. Hanover: Univ. of New England Press, 1984.

Ignatieff, Michael. *A Just Measure of Pain: The Penitentiary in the Industrial Revolution, 1750–1850*. New York: Columbia Univ. Press, 1978.

James, Marquis. *Biography of a Business, 1792–1942: Insurance Company of North America*. Indianapolis: Bobbs-Merrill, 1942.

Jenkins, Reese. *Images and Enterprise: Technology and the American Photographic Industry 1839 to 1925*. Baltimore: Johns Hopkins Univ. Press, 1975.

Johnson, Donald D. *The City and County of Honolulu: A Governmental Chronicle*. Honolulu: Univ. of Hawai'i Press, 1985.

Johnson, Paul E. *A Shopkeeper's Millennium: Society and Revivals in Rochester, New York, 1815–1837*. New York: Hill and Wang, 1978.

Johnston, Norman. *Eastern State Penitentiary: Crucible of Good Intentions*. Philadelphia: Philadelphia Museum of Art, 1994.

Jones, Douglas Lamar. "The Strolling Poor: Transiency in Eighteenth-Century Massachusetts." *William and Mary Quarterly*, 3d Series, 32 (2).

Judd, Walter F. *Palaces and Forts of the Hawaiian Kingdom: From Thatch to American Florentine*. Palo Alto, Calif.: Pacific Press, 1975.

Kaledin, Eugenia. *Mothers and More: American Women in the 1950s*. Boston: Twayne Publishers, 1984.

Kan, Sergei. "Russian Orthodox Brotherhoods Among the Tlingit: Missionary Goals and Native Response." *Ethnohistory* 32 (3) (1985).

Kasson, John F. *Rudeness and Civility: Manners in Nineteenth-Century America.* New York: Hill and Wang, 1990.

Katz, William Loren. *The Black West.* New York: Doubleday, 1971.

Kelly, J. Frederick. *Early Domestic Architecture of Connecticut.* New York: Dover Publications, 1963.

Kelly, Kevin P. "'In dispers'd Country Plantations': Settlement Patterns in Seventeenth-Century Surry County, Virginia." In *The Chesapeake in the Seventeenth Century: Essays on Anglo-American Society.* Edited by Thad W. Tate and David L. Ammerman. New York: Norton, 1979.

Kelley, Robin, D. G. "The Riddle of the Zoot: Malcolm Little and Black Cultural Politics During World War II." In *Malcolm X: In Our Own Image.* Edited by Joe Wood. New York: St. Martin's Press, 1992.

Kent, Susan, ed. *Domestic Architecture and the Use of Space: an Interdisciplinary Cross-Cultural Study.* Cambridge and New York: Cambridge Univ. Press, 1990.

Kousser, J. Morgan. *The Shaping of Southern Politics: Suffrage Restriction and the Establishment of the One-Party South, 1880–1910.* New Haven: Yale Univ. Press, 1974.

Kurtze, Peter E. "'A School House Well Arranged': Baltimore Public School Buildings on the Lancasterian Plan, 1829–1839." In *Gender, Class, and Shelter: Perspectives in Vernacular Architecture, V.* Edited by Elizabeth Collins Cromley and Carter L. Hudgins. Knoxville: Univ. of Tennessee Press, 1995.

Labaree, Benjamin. *Patriots and Partisans: The Merchants of Newburyport.* Cambridge: Harvard Univ. Press, 1962.

Lancaster, Clay. *Antebellum Architecture of Kentucky.* Lexington: Univ. Press of Kentucky, 1991.

Lanier, Gabrielle. "Samuel Wilson's Working World: Builders and Buildings in Chester County, Pennsylvania, 1780–1827." In *Perspectives in Vernacular Architecture, IV.* Edited by Thomas Carter and Bernard L. Herman. Columbia: Univ. of Missouri Press, 1991.

Lears, T. J. Jackson. *No Place of Grace: Antimodernism and the Transformation of American Culture, 1880–1920.* New York: Pantheon, 1981.

Lebsock, Suzanne. *The Free Women of Petersburg: Status and Culture in a Southern Town, 1784–1860.* New York: Norton, 1984.

Levine, Lawrence W. *Highbrow/Lowbrow: The Emergence of Cultural Hierarchy in America.* Cambridge: Harvard Univ. Press, 1988.

Lindgren, James M. *Preserving the Old Dominion: Historic Preservation and Virginia Traditionalism.* Charlottesville: Univ. Press of Virginia, 1993.

Lipman, Jean, and Tom Armstrong, eds. *American Folk Painters of Three Centuries.* New York: Hudson Hills Press, 1980.

Longmate, Norman. *The Workhouse.* New York: St. Martin's, 1974.

Longstreth, Richard. "Compositional Types in American Commercial Architecture." In *Perspectives in Vernacular Architecture, II.* Edited by Camille Wells. Columbia: Univ. of Missouri Press, 1986.

———. "The Neighborhood Shopping Center in Washington, D.C., 1930–1941." *Journal of the Society of Architectural Historians* 51 (Mar. 1992): 28–31.

———. "Silver Spring: Georgia Avenue, Colesville Road and the Creation of an Alternative 'Downtown' for Metropolitan Washington." In *Streets: Critical Perspective on Public Space.* Edited by Zeynep Celik, et al. Berkeley and Los Angeles: Univ. of California Press, 1994.

Lounsbury, Carl R. "The Structure of Justice: The Courthouses of Colonial Virginia." In *Perspectives in Vernacular Architecture, III.* Edited by Thomas Carter and Bernard L. Herman. Columbia: Univ. of Missouri Press, 1989: 214–26.

Lubin, David S. *Picturing a Nation: Art and Social Change in Nineteenth-Century America.* New Haven: Yale Univ. Press, 1994.

Lukes, Timothy, and Gary Y. Okahiro. *Japanese Legacy: Farming and Community Life in California's Santa Clara Valley.* Cupertino, Calif.: California History Center, 1985.

Marshall, Howard Wight. "A Good Gridiron: The Vernacular Design of a Western Cow Town." In *Perspectives in Vernacular Architecture, II.* Edited by Camille Wells. Columbia: Univ. of Missouri Press, 1986.

Martin, Charles. *Hollybush: Folk Building and Social Change in an Appalachian Community.* Knoxville: Univ. of Tennessee Press, 1984.

Masur, Lois. *Rites of Execution: Capital Punishment and the Transformation of American Culture, 1776–1865.* New York: Oxford Univ. Press, 1989.

McCleary, Ann. "Domesticity and the Farm Woman: A Case Study of Women in Augusta County, Virginia 1850–1940." In *Perspectives in Vernacular Architecture, II*. Edited by Camille Wells. Columbia: Univ. of Missouri Press, 1987.

McCracken, Grant. *Culture and Consumption: New Approaches to the Symbolic Character of Consumer Goods and Activities*. Bloomington and Indianapolis: Indiana Univ. Press, 1989.

McCusker, John J., and Russell R. Menard. *The Economy of British America, 1706–1789*. Chapel Hill: Univ. of North Carolina Press, 1991.

McDaniel, George W. *Hearth and Home: Preserving a People's Culture*. Philadelphia: Temple Univ. Press, 1982.

McManus, Edgar J. *A History of Negro Slavery in New York*. Syracuse: Syracuse Univ. Press, 1966.

McMurry, Sally. *Families and Farmhouses in Nineteenth-Century America: Vernacular Design and Social Change*. New York: Oxford Univ. Press, 1988.

———. "Women in the American Vernacular Landscape." *Material Culture* 20 (1) (Spring 1989): 33–49.

Miller, David C., ed. *American Iconology: New Approaches to Nineteenth-Century Art and Literature*. New Haven: Yale Univ. Press, 1993.

Miller, Lewis. *Sketches and Chronicles: The Reflections of a Nineteenth Century Pennsylvania German Folk Artist*. York, Pa.: Historical Society of York County, 1976.

Morrison, Hugh. *Early American Architecture: From the First Colonial Settlements to the National Period*. New York: 1952.

Nash, Gary B. "Poverty and Poor Relief in Pre-Revolutionary Philadelphia." *William and Mary Quarterly*, 3d Series, 33 (1).

Neiman, Fraser D. "Domestic Architecture at the Clifts Plantation: The Social Context of Early Virginia Building." *Northern Neck of Virginia Historical Magazine* 28 (Dec. 1978): 3096–3128.

Newhall, Beaumont. *The Daguerreotype in America*. New York: Dover, 1976.

———. *The History of Photography from 1839 to the Present Day*, 5th ed. New York: Museum of Modern Art, 1982.

Noble, Allen G. *Wood, Brick, and Stone*. Amherst: Univ. of Massachusetts Press, 1984.

Oberg, Kalervo. *The Social Economy of the Tlingit Indians*. Seattle: Univ. of Washington Press, 1973.

Parrish, Michael E. *Anxious Decades: America in Prosperity and Depression, 1920–1941*. New York: Norton, 1992.

Peck, Amelia, ed. *Andrew Jackson Davis, American Architect 1803–1892*. New York: Rizzoli, 1992.

Peterson, Fred W. *Homes in the Heartland: Balloon Frame Farmhouses of the Upper Midwest, 1850–1920*. Lawrence: Univ. Press of Kansas, 1992.

Pitman, Leon S. "Domestic Tankhouses of Rural California." *Pioneer America* 8 (2) (1976): 84–97.

Pocius, Gerald. *A Place to Belong: Community Order and Everyday Space in Calvert, Newfoundland*. Athens: Univ. of Georgia Press, 1991.

Prudon, Theodore H. M. "The Dutch Barn in America: Survival of a Medieval Structural Frame." In *Common Places: Readings in American Vernacular Architecture*. Edited by Dell Upton and John Michael Vlach. Athens: Univ. of Georgia Press, 1986.

Pulley, Raymond, H. *Old Virginia Restored: An Interpretation of the Progressive Impulse, 1870–1930*. Charlottesville: Univ. Press of Virginia, 1968.

Purser, Margaret. "All Roads Lead to Winnemucca: Local Road Systems and Community Material Culture in Nineteenth-century Nevada." In *Perspectives in Vernacular Architecture, III*. Edited by Thomas Carter and Bernard L. Herman. Columbia: Univ. of Missouri Press, 1986.

Rabinowitz, Howard. *Race Relations in the Urban South, 1865–1890*. New York: Oxford Univ. Press, 1978.

Rachleff, Peter. *Black Labor in Richmond, 1865–1890*. Champaign: Univ. of Illinois Press, 1984.

Rainbolt, John C. "The Absence of Towns in Seventeenth-Century Virginia." *The Journal of Southern History* 35 (Aug. 1969): 343–60.

Redkey, Edwin. *Black Exodus: Black Nationalist and Back-to-Africa Movements, 1890–1910*. New Haven: Yale Univ. Press, 1969.

Reynolds, Helen Wilkinson. *Dutch Houses in the Hudson Valley before 1776*. New York: Dover, 1965.

Ridout, Orlando. *Building the Octagon*. Washington, D.C.: American Institute of Architects Press, 1989.

Rinhart, Floyd, and Marion Rinhart. *American Daguerrian Art*. New York: Clarkson N. Potter, 1967.

Roark, Michael. "Storm Cellars: Imprint of Fear on the Landscape." *Material Culture* 24 (2) (1992): 46–47.

Robertson, Cheryl. "Male and Female Agendas for Domestic Reform: The Middle Class Bungalow in Gendered Perspective." *Winterthur Portfolio* 26 (2/3) (Summer/Autumn 1991).

Rothman, David, ed. *The Almshouse Experience: Collected Reports.* New York: Arno Press, 1971.

Rothman, David J. *The Discovery of the Asylum: Social Order and Disorder in the New Republic.* Boston and Toronto: Little, Brown, and Company, 1971.

Rudisill, Richard. *Mirror Image: The Influence of the Daguerreotype on American Society.* Albuquerque: Univ. of New Mexico Press, 1971.

Ryan, Mary P. *Women in Public: Between Banners and Ballots, 1825–1880.* Baltimore: Johns Hopkins Univ. Press, 1990.

Sanford, Douglas W. "The Enchanted Castle in Context: Archaeological Research at Germanna, Orange County, Virginia." *Quarterly Bulletin of the Archaeological Society of Virginia* 44 (3) (Sept. 1989).

Schmitt, Peter J. *Back to Nature: The Arcadian Myth in Urban America.* New York: Oxford Univ. Press, 1969.

Severini, Lois. *The Architecture of Finance, Early Wall Street.* Ann Arbor: UMI Research Press, 1983.

Siener, William H. "Charles Yates, the Grain Trade, and Economic Development in Fredericksburg, Virginia, 1750–1810." *Virginia Magazine of History and Biography* 93 (4) (Oct. 1985): 409–26.

Sies, Mary Corbin. "Toward a Performance Theory of the Suburban Ideal, 1877–1917." In *Perspectives in Vernacular Architecture, IV.* Edited by Thomas Carter and Bernard L. Herman. Columbia: Univ. of Missouri Press, 1991.

Silver, Christopher. *Twentieth-Century Richmond: Planning, Politics, and Race.* Knoxville: Univ. of Tennessee Press, 1984.

Simons, Albert, and Samuel Lapham. *The Early Architecture of Charleston.* New York: American Institute of Architects, 1927.

Slade, Thomas M. *Historic American Buildings Survey in Indiana.* Bloomington: Indiana Univ. Press, 1983.

Sollors, Werner. *Beyond Ethnicity: Consent and Descent in American Culture.* New York: Oxford Univ. Press, 1986.

———. "Of Mules and Mares in a Land of Difference; or Quadrupeds All?" *American Quarterly* 42 (2) (June 1990).

Stachiw, Myron, and Nora Pat Small. "Tradition and Transformation: Rural Society and Architectural Change in Nineteenth-Century Central Massachusetts." In *Perspectives in Vernacular Architecture, III.* Edited by Tom Carter and Bernard L. Herman. Columbia: Univ. of Missouri Press, 1988.

Stein, Howard F., and Robert F. Hill, eds. *The Culture of Oklahoma.* Norman: Univ. of Oklahoma Press, 1993.

Steinitz, Michael. "Rethinking Geographical Approaches to the Common House: The Evidence from Eighteenth-Century Massachusetts." In *Perspectives in Vernacular Architecture, III.* Edited by Thomas Carter and Bernard L. Herman. Columbia: Univ. of Missouri Press, 1989.

Stevenson, Katherine Cole, and H. Ward Jandl. *A Guide to Houses from Sears, Roebuck and Company.* Washington D.C.: Preservation Press, 1986.

Stilgoe, John R. *Common Landscape of America, 1580 to 1845.* New Haven: Yale Univ. Press, 1982.

Taft, Robert. *Photography and the American Scene: A Social History, 1839–1889.* New York: Dover, 1964.

Tavernor, Robert. *Palladio and Palladianism.* New York: Thames and Hudson, 1991.

Thomas, Alan. *Time in a Frame: Photography and the Nineteenth-Century Mind.* New York: Schocken Books, 1977.

Thornton, Tamara. *Cultivating Gentlemen: The Meaning of Country Life Among the Boston Elite: 1785–1860.* New Haven: Yale Univ. Press, 1989.

Tittler, Robert. *Architecture and Power: The Town Hall and the English Urban Community, c. 1500–1640.* Oxford: Clarendon Press, 1991.

Tomes, Nancy. *The Art of Asylum-Keeping: Thomas Story Kirkbride and the Origins of American Psychiatry,* 2d ed. Philadelphia: Univ. of Pennsylvania Press, 1994.

Trapp, Kenneth R., ed. *The Arts and Crafts Movement in California: Living the Good Life.* New York: Abbeville Press, 1993.

Turner, Paul Venable. *Campus: an American Planning Tradition.* New York: Architectural History Foundation; Cambridge: MIT Press, 1984.

Tyler-McGraw, Marie, and Greg T. Kimball. *In Bondage and Freedom: Antebellum Black Life in Richmond, Virginia.* Richmond: Valentine Museum, 1988.

Upton, Dell. "Anglican Parish Churches in Eighteenth-Century Virginia." In *Perspectives in Vernacular Architecture, II*. Edited by Camille Wells. Columbia: Univ. of Missouri Press, 1986.

———. "The City as Material Culture." In *The Art and Mystery of Historical Archaeology: Essays in Honor of James Deetz*. Edited by Anne Elizabeth Yentsch and Mary C. Beaudry. Boca Raton, Fla.: CRC Press, 1992.

———. *Holy Things and Profane: Anglican Parish Churches in Colonial Virginia*. Cambridge, Mass., and London: MIT Press, 1986.

———. "New Views of the Virginia Landscape." *Virginia Magazine of History and Biography* 96 (4) (Oct. 1988): 403–70.

———. "Pattern Books and Professionalism: Aspects of the Transformation of Domestic Architecture in America, 1800–1860." *Winterthur Portfolio* 19 (Summer/Autumn 1984):107–50.

———. "Vernacular Domestic Architecture in Eighteenth-Century Virginia." *Winterthur Portfolio* 17 (2/3) (Summer–Autumn 1982): 95–119.

Upton, Dell, ed. *America's Architectural Roots: Ethnic Groups that Built America*. Washington, D.C.: Preservation Press, 1986.

Wacker, Peter O. "Relations between Cultural Origins, Relative Wealth, and the Size, Form, and Materials of Construction of Rural Dwellings in New Jersey during the Eighteenth Century." *Geographie historique*. Paris: Centre National de la Recherche Scientifique, 1979.

Wade, Richard C. *Slavery in the Cities: The South 1820–1860*. New York: Oxford Univ. Press, 1964.

Wallace, Anthony F. C. "Revitalization Movements," *American Anthropologist* 58 (1956): 265.

Wallston, Mark. "The Commercial Rise and Fall of Silver Spring." *Maryland Historical Magazine* 81 (Winter 1986): 330–39.

Warner, Michael. *Letters of the Republic: Publication and the Public Sphere in Eighteenth-Century America*. Cambridge: Harvard Univ. Press, 1990.

Waterman, Thomas T. *Mansions of Virginia, 1706–1776*. Chapel Hill: Univ. of North Carolina Press, 1946.

Waterman, T. T. "Observations Among the Ancient Indian Monuments of Southeastern Alaska." In *Explorations and Field-Work of the Smithsonian Institution in 1922*. Washington, D.C.: Smithsonian Institution, 1923.

Weiner, Deborah E. B. *Architecture and Social Reform in Late-Victorian London*. Manchester and New York: Manchester Univ. Press, 1994.

Weiss, Marc A. *The Rise of the Community Builders: The American Real Estate Industry and Urban Land Planning*. New York: Columbia Univ. Press, 1987.

Wenger, Mark R. "The Central Passage in Virginia: Evolution of an Eighteenth-Century Living Space." In *Perspectives in Vernacular Architecture, II*. Edited by Camille Wells. Columbia: Univ. of Missouri Press, 1986.

———. "The Dining Room in Early Virginia." In *Perspectives in Vernacular Architecture, III*. Edited by Thomas Carter and Bernard L. Herman. Columbia: Univ. of Missouri Press, 1989.

Williams, Michael Ann. *Homeplace: The Social Use and Meaning of the Folk Dwelling in Southwestern North Carolina*. Athens: Univ. of Georgia Press, 1991.

Williams, Raymond. *Keywords: A Vocabulary of Culture and Society*. New York: Oxford Univ. Press, 1983.

Willis-Thomas, Deborah. *Black Photographers 1840–1940: A Bio-Bibliography*. New York: Garland Press, 1987.

Wilson, Charles Reagan. *Baptized in Blood: The Religion of the Lost Cause, 1865–1920*. Athens and New York: Univ. of Georgia Press, 1980.

Wojtowicz, Carol. *The Mutual Assurance Company*. Philadelphia: Mutual Assurance Company, 1985.

Wood, Joseph S. "'Build, Therefore, Your Own World': The New England Village as a Settlement Ideal." *Annals of the Association of American Geographers* 81 (1991): 32–50.

Wood, Joseph S., and Michael Steinitz, "A World We have Gained: House, Common and Village in New England." *Journal of Historical Geography* 18 (1992): 105–20.

Woodward, C. Vann. *Origins of the New South, 1877–1913*. Baton Rouge: Louisiana State Univ. Press, 1951.

Woodward, C. Vann, and Elizabeth Muhlenfeld, eds. *The Private Mary Chesnut: The Unpublished Civil War Diaries*. New York: Oxford Univ. Press.

Wright, Gwendolyn. *Building the Dream: A Social History of Housing in America*. New York: Pantheon, 1981.

———. *Moralism and the Model Home: Domestic Architecture and Cultural Conflict in Chicago, 1873–1913*. Chicago: Univ. of Chicago Press, 1980.

# Contributors

*Monique Bourque* received her B.A. from Montana State University and her M.A. and Ph.D. from the University of Delaware, where she was a Hagley Fellow. She is currently assistant director for programs at the Francis C. Wood Institute for the History of Medicine of the College of Physicians of Philadelphia.

*Elizabeth Collins Cromley* is the author of *Alone Together* as well as essays on domestic space, resort architecture, urban parks, and aspects of apartment design. Past president of the Vernacular Architecture Forum, she is currently head of the Department of Architecture at the State University of New York at Buffalo.

*Kathy Edwards* is currently studying vernacular buildings in the swamps, sandhills, and piney woods of North Carolina, where she lives and works.

*Laurel Spencer Forsythe* is the former curator-historian of the Mission Houses Museum in Honolulu. A native of Hawai'i, Forsythe received an A.B. from Smith College in 1990 and has completed graduate work in historic preservation at the University of Hawai'i. Forsythe currently resides in Italy and works as a part-time freelance historian and is a full-time mother of two.

*Bryan Clark Green* received a B.A. from the University of Notre Dame in history and anthropology and an M.A. in architectural history with a certificate in historic preservation from the School of Architecture at the University of Virginia, where he is currently a Ph.D. candidate in architectural history. Green is a research consultant for the Connecticut volume of the Society of Architectural Historians' *Buildings of the United States*.

*M. Jeff Hardwick* is a Ph.D. candidate in American Studies at Yale University. He received his B.A. in anthropology from the University of California at Berkeley and an M.A. from the Winterthur Program in Early American Culture at the University of Delaware. His current research focuses on American urban planning of the 1950s and 1960s.

*Marlene Elizabeth Heck* has conducted architectural survey work in Virginia, Texas, New Hampshire, and Vermont. She holds a Ph.D. in American civilization from the University of Pennsylvania and has taught at the Schools of Architecture at the University of Virginia and Texas A&M University. She currently teaches in the history and art history departments at Dartmouth College.

*Alison K. Hoagland* is the author of *Buildings of Alaska,* published in 1993. Now assistant professor of history and historic preservation at Michigan Technological University, Hoagland was previously senior historian at the Historic American Buildings Survey. Hoagland received her B.A. from Brown University and her M.A. from George Washington University, both in American Studies.

*Esmé Howard* has a B.A. in American Studies and a Master's in Nursing from Yale University. She has taken a turn away from academia and is currently a nurse-midwife working in Newark, New Jersey.

*Carter L. Hudgins* is executive director of Historic Charleston Foundation. He holds a Ph.D. in history from the College of William and Mary and is the author of essays in historical archaeology, material culture, and historic preservation policy.

*Kathleen LaFrank* received a B.A. in English from the State University of New York at Albany and an M.A. in Architecture and Design Criticism from the Parsons School of Design, New School for Social Research. She works for the New York State Office of Parks, Recreation and Historic Preservation (SHPO). Seaside, Florida, was the subject of her master's thesis.

*Richard Longstreth* is professor of architectural history and director of the Graduate Program in Historic Preservation at George Washington University. Former first vice president of the Vernacular Architecture Forum, Longstreth has written extensively on commercial buildings, which is the subject of his latest book, *City Center to Regional Mall: Architecture, the Automobile and Retailing in Los Angeles, 1920–1950.*

*Martha J. McNamara* is an assistant professor of history at the University of Maine, Orono, where she teaches graduate and undergraduate courses in material culture, vernacular architecture, and the history of New England. She holds a Ph.D. in American and New England Studies from Boston University. From 1992 to 1994 she was a Dissertation Fellow at the Buell Center for the Study of American Architecture at Columbia University.

*Alan R. Michelson* received his doctorate in the history of art from Stanford University. He specializes in the architecture of the San Francisco Bay Area and has completed a dissertation entitled "Towards a Regional Synthesis: The Suburban and Country Residences of William Wilson Wurster, 1922–1964." Michelson is currently rare books specialist in the Department of Special Collections, Stanford University Libraries.

*Janet Ore* received her Ph.D. in American social and cultural history with a minor field in architectural history from the University of Utah. She now teaches American architectural history at Colorado State University. Currently, she is working on a book about Seattle's early-twentieth-century neighborhoods.

*Thomas R. Ryan* holds a B.A. from the College of the Holy Cross, an M.Ed. from Boston College, and an M.A. from the Winterthur Program in early American culture at the University of Delaware. He is currently a Ph.D. candidate in the history of American civilization at the University of Delaware and resides in Lancaster, Pennsylvania, with his wife and two sons.

*Nora Pat Small* received an M.A. in architectural history from the School of Architecture of the University of Virginia and her Ph.D. in American and New England Studies from Boston University. She is currently a member of the history faculty at Eastern Illinois University.

*Katherine M. Solomonson* holds a Ph.D. from Stanford University where she completed a dissertation on the Chicago Tribune Tower Competition. While teaching at Stanford University, she co-directed a study of the historic landscape of East Palo Alto, California. Solomonson is currently assistant professor in the College of Architecture and Landscape Architecture at the University of Minnesota.

*Gary Stanton* is a native of California who received his Ph.D. in folklore from Indiana University. He is currently associate professor and chair of the department of historic preservation at Mary Washington College.

*Lisa Tolbert* is an assistant professor in the history department at the University of North Carolina, Greensboro, where she teaches cultural history and museum studies. She received an M.A. in history with a certification in museum studies from the University of Delaware and earned her Ph.D. in history at the University of North Carolina at Chapel Hill, where her dissertation was entitled "Constructing Townscapes: Architecture and Experience in Nineteenth-Century County Seats of Middle Tennessee."

*John Michael Vlach* is professor of American civilization and anthropology at George Washington University where he also directs the Folklife Program. Author or editor of eight books on various aspects of material culture and African-American folklife and curator of several museum exhibitions, his most recent book is *Back of the Big House: The Architecture of Plantation Slavery* (1993).

*Shirley Teresa Wajda* received her B.A. in American history from Boston University and her Ph.D. in American civilization from the University of Pennsylvania, and her revised dissertation, "Social Currency: Portrait Photography and the Fashioning of the American Middle Class," is scheduled to be published soon. She is currently assistant professor of history at Kent State University where she teaches courses in social history, women's history, and material culture.

# Index

Page references to illustrations are in **bold face.**